NEHRU
TIBET
AND
CHINA

engagements of India's first prime minister with this important neighbour features here in rich detail: first visionary and trusting, then ambivalent and ultimately tragic. A must-read!.'

—Vijay Nambiar, former ambassador to China and special adviser
to the UN secretary general on Myanmar

'A.S. Bhasin, a veteran of the Ministry of External Affairs's Historical Division, is an archival document-compiler par excellence with his collections of vital papers covering India's relationship with Bangladesh, Nepal, Pakistan, Sri Lanka and ASEAN. And then came his collection of India–China documents in 2019. *Nehru, Tibet and China* is an outgrowth of the huge work he put into the China collection, offering new insights, all tightly documented. It will generate serious discussion, settling some questions and raising others. It is a splendid capstone on a rich career.'

—Kishan Rana, former ambassador and professor emeritus
at the DiploFoundation, Malta and Geneva,
and Institute of Chinese Studies, New Delhi

NEHRU
TIBET
AND
CHINA

A. S. Bhasin

PENGUIN
VIKING
An imprint of Penguin Random House

VIKING

USA | Canada | UK | Ireland | Australia
New Zealand | India | South Africa | China | Singapore

Viking is an imprint of the Penguin Random House group of companies
whose addresses can be found at global.penguinrandomhouse.com

Published by Penguin Random House India Pvt. Ltd
4th Floor, Capital Tower 1, MG Road,
Gurugram 122 002, Haryana, India

First published in Viking by Penguin Random House India 2021
This edition published in 2024

ISBN 9780670094134

Typeset in Adobe Garamond Pro by Manipal Technologies Limited, Manipal
Printed at Replika Press Pvt. Ltd, India

www.penguin.co.in

To the memory of my wife,
Mandip Kaur (1941–96)

Contents

x   Contents

Cast of Characters

Jawaharlal Nehru	Prime Minister of India
Sardar Vallabhbhai Patel	Home Minister of India
Mao Zedong	President of China
Zhou Enlai	Premier of the People's Republic of China (PRC)
Chen Yi	Foreign Minister of the PRC
Henry McMahon	Former Foreign Secretary and leader of the British delegation to the Simla Conference
Girija Shankar Bajpai	Secretary General, MEA, 1947–52 and Governor of Bombay Presidency, 1952–54
K.P.S. Menon	Ambassador in China until 1948, Foreign Secretary, 1948–52, and thereafter Ambassador in Moscow
V.K. Krishna Menon	Defence Minister, 1957–62

P.N. Menon   Consul General, Lhasa, 1954–56; Chief Liaison Officer to Dalai Lama, 1959

K.M. Panikkar   Ambassador of India in Beijing 1950–52; thereafter Ambassador in Egypt

R.K. Nehru   Foreign Secretary, 1952–55; Ambassador in China, 1955–58; Ambassador in Egypt 1958–60 and Secretary General in MEA

Subimal Dutt   Commonwealth Secretary, 1947–52 and 1954–55; Foreign Secretary, 1955–61; thereafter Ambassador in Moscow

T.N. Kaul   Counsellor in Beijing, 1950–52; Director, North Division, 1952–55; Was member of the Indian delegation which negotiated the 1954 Agreement on Tibet; Foreign Secretary, 1968–72

N. Raghavan   Ambassador in China, 1952–55

G. Parthasarathi   Ambassador in China, 1958–July 1961

H.E. Richardson   Indian Representative in Lhasa, 1946–50

Sumal Sinha   Mission–in–Charge, Lhasa, 1950–52

Hareshwar Dayal   Political Officer in Gangtok, 1948–52

Apa Pant   Political Officer in Sikkim, 1955–61

Loy Henderson   United States Ambassador in India, 1948–51

Dalai Lama	14th Dalai Lama, born 1935, resumed responsibilities in 1950; left Lhasa in March 1959 and presently residing in Dharamshala, Himachal Pradesh, in exile
Chiang Kai Shek	President of China, 1938 until 1949 when he fled to Formosa (Taiwan) and set up a new government there as its President; died in 1975
Swaran Singh	Railway Minister who participated in India–China talks in April 1960 and interacted with Chinese foreign minister, Chen Yi, twice and even travelled with him to Agra
U Nu	Prime Minister of Burma (Myanmar)
P.K. Banerjee	Charge d'affaires in Beijing, 1961–64
Sirimavo Bandaranaike	Prime Minister of Sri Lanka
Sarvepalli Gopal	Official biographer of Nehru
K.L. Mehta	Adviser to the governor of Assam when the Dalai Lama arrived in India
S.L. Chhibber	Consul General in Lhasa, 1956–59
Shakabpa	Tibetan minister who was given the responsibility of negotiating an agreement with China in 1950

Preface

History is often interpreted differently by different historians, thereby giving birth to more than one history of the same event. Each one looks at a particular event differently and interprets it in his/her own way depending on the amount of archival material available and/or his/her ideological predilections in some cases. Historiography, on the other hand, is the science of rereading the past, reinterpreting it and revising the narrative. Historiography is a challenge to history. It keeps the history alive and kicking as more and more new evidence becomes available.

Modern-day governments function under prescribed procedures, where decisions are made on the basis of discussions and debate. There is a legal framework requiring such debates to be archived for posterity, making history somewhat a more precise science, leaving little scope for presumptions. History, like courts of law, demand evidence for or against the validity of any action or decision, and everyone is called to the bar of history to account for his/her acts of omission and commission.

Unfortunately, in India, successive governments, since Independence, have kept the archives under a tight lid of secrecy even after a lapse of more than seven decades, going against archival laws, thus depriving the students of history the opportunity to make a balanced and informed appraisal and analysis of past events. This has resulted in our skewed understanding of our post-Independence history.

The India–China war in 1962 happened more than half a century ago. However, people are largely still ignorant of what brought us so much of ignominy. The lapse of time has dimmed our memory but the incidents along the border that happen now and then keep reminding us of the unfinished agenda of 1962. It is an ongoing story whose historical traces even today cast a long shadow in the region and across the world. It continues to fester and the border incidents cry out for its closure.

A successful foreign policy is one that aims to forge convergences and manage divergences. Such a dynamic process keeps evolving while nations continue to peacefully coexist. To untangle the Gordian knot that India–China relations have become, the people of India need to know what actually went wrong in that short span of a decade and a half of India post-Independence. To continue to be prisoners of the past, stand on a high pedestal and pontificate our presumed righteous stand based on a skewed understanding of the history of those days is the bane of our problem. Such a mindset is unlikely to lead us anywhere. Successive governments have since then chosen to stay with the past narrative and bat on the same old wicket while keeping the nation ignorant of the facts that caused the war in 1962. While the government of India kept the archives tightly shut, a small window to the archives of that period in the body of Nehru Papers, which was in the custody of Nehru Memorial Museum and Library, New Delhi, also remained tightly shut until 2014. It was only then that it passed from private hands to the Department of Culture, Government of India. Though this collection is not complete yet, it lifts the curtain wide enough to throw sufficient light on the main issues that caused the war.

I found myself in a happy situation when the Department of Culture accepted my request for access to those Papers. I found in this collection a treasure trove and selected papers bearing on India's relations with China. Together with documents harvested from other sources on the subject, I published them in a five-volume study: altogether 2523 documents running into 5320 pages, a bulk of them highly classified. As I sifted them for publication, I found that the history of that crucial period is completely asymmetrical to what we know of 1962. Though the events under discussion are now more than half a century away, we still find ourselves stuck with the same old narrative which landed us in the most unenviable situation then. My instinct as a student of history compelled me to undertake the present study and put forward the factual history of those turbulent days before the people of India, as emerging from those documents. It is now for the people to take a call on those events.

For a decade and a half, India's post-Independence story was guided and dominated by Jawaharlal Nehru. He not only determined the broad contours of Indian policies but also executed them. Foreign policy remained his exclusive domain. Even before Independence, as the prominent figure of the Indian National Congress, foreign policy issues remained his exclusive preserve during which period he articulated certain ideas and concepts that became the template for free India's foreign policy. Enough evidence of his interest in foreign relations is to be found in his book he wrote before Independence: *The Discovery of India*. Even in the Interim Government formed in 1946 he headed the Foreign Department.

After Independence, as prime minister, he remained his own foreign minister for all the seventeen years he presided over destines of India and made sure that he implemented his ideas in the form and shape he desired.

Generally, it is believed that the foreign policy of a country is an extension of its domestic policy and is required to serve the national interests of the country. Studying Nehru, one finds he had a different concept of his foreign policy, as he told Parliament on 12 June 1952:

> I beg this house not to consider our foreign policy in terms merely
> of our own petty success or failure, because the success or failure
> of any foreign policy today involves the success or failure of the
> whole world.

He lived with this concept as long as there was no challenge to it but
when the challenge came, he found himself in deep waters.

As I discuss in the Introduction, he was perhaps infatuated with
the Chinese ever since he came into contact with them in 1927 at
Brussels while attending the 'Conference against Imperialism' on
behalf of the Indian National Congress. Since then, he was convinced
that the future of Asia depended on the goodwill and neighbourly
relations among Asiatic countries and, of these, China and India must
obviously play a dominant role. He insisted that it was important for
the two countries to have good relations to forge the concept of Asian
solidarity. When communist China emerged, Nehru welcomed it as
a harbinger of Asian renaissance and looked forward to working with
it towards an Asia that would provide leadership to the post-colonial
world.

The People's Republic of China, however, was not Kuomintang
China. It was a new determined and self-assertive China, as Mao said
at its inauguration:

> We shall emerge in the world as a nation with an advanced culture.
> And one with power.

And that set the agenda for Mao's China. It wanted to be the
dominant power in Asia and the world. Nehru, while willing to share
the glory of Asia with new China, was not willing to abdicate in its
favour and there lies the rub which this book tries to capture.

I would, however, wish to emphasize that this is a book of history
and should be read as such. History has no friends or foes. It traces
the footprints of people who influence the events that make history.
As Arnold Toynbee said:

Historical changes are driven by challenge and response and civilisations are defined not just by the leadership or conditions but by how they responded to difficult problems or crises.

I have used quite a few italics since there are too many important portions which needed to attract attention. These should be seen as author's emphasis, unless specifically pointed out that these were as in the original.

May 2021   New Delhi

Introduction

The Chinese Communist Party, after seizing power, announced the establishment of the People's Republic of China on 1 October 1949. India had achieved its independence a couple of years earlier. The emergence of two new modern states in Asia, large in size and rich in resources, one in East Asia and the other in South Asia, heralded a new era in international politics, particularly in Asia. Throughout history, China considered itself the centre of the universe, the Middle Kingdom, and other peripheral countries its tributaries paying obeisance to the Emperor. Confucianism provided the philosophical base to its thought process and way of life.

The Chinese concept of the Middle Kingdom suffered a jolt when in the nineteenth century it came face to face with the European countries with a different political culture and philosophy of governance, which were more powerful and better organized than its self-centred imperial polity. Its mindset of the past and its tactics to meet the challenges of the new world did not change.

India, too, encountered foreign cultures in its history. Without giving up its civilizational values, it made peace with them. India learnt to assimilate different cultures and all of them coexisted. In the process of assimilating alien values and cultures, India also facilitated foreigners to absorb Indian values and merge them with the mainstream of Indian life. The same, however, did not hold true for most of the British colonizers who came to India. They remained colonialists who imposed their values, lived an isolated life and ruled India in the interest of their motherland. India, assimilating some of the Western values, adopted their institutions of governance, law and justice and education. It innovated them and put them to good use to create a modern polity and society that would empower the people of India like never before. Since most of the British neither assimilated Indian culture nor adopted or adapted to its way of life, they remained alien and finally had to quit.

Communist China made Marxism the base of its polity but did not give up its ancient ethos. It was hardly surprising, therefore, when the new Chinese leaders laid claim to any territory which they perceived had belonged to China at any time in history. In course of time they did not even spare their initial benefactor—the Soviet Union. At the peak of the Sino-Soviet conflict in 1969, China claimed vast areas of the Soviet as well.

For the first time in history, the occupation of Tibet made China a contiguous neighbour of India, Nepal and Bhutan. China also became the neighbour of newly minted Pakistan through the latter's illegally seized parts of the Indian state of Jammu and Kashmir. The British Government of India had dealt with China both in China and in Tibet but mainly through their compatriots. For India it was now a new experience in dealing with them as an independent entity at the political level.

That there had been contacts between the peoples of India and China in the hoary past is accepted by historians, but these interactions were mostly religious and cultural. Jawaharlal Nehru was impressed by these contacts, and was convinced that those relations gave 'an impetus and a kick to the artistic and mental life of China'. He maintained that while India did get influenced by China, India, too, greatly influenced China in art, culture and philosophy, as he wrote to his daughter on 7 May 1932 from prison:

[In the early 7th century] India continued to export not only her fine cloth and other goods but her thought and religion and art. Many Buddhist missionaries went to China from India and they carried with them traditions of Indian art and it is possible that Indian artists and master-crafts men also went there . . . Thus the coming of these thought-currents from India gave an impetus and a kick to the artistic and mental life of China.[1]

The Buddhist connection offered a perfect paradigm for linking India with China. These contacts, however, remained few and far between and were voluntary and not organized institutionally in any concerted way. The people of India and China remained by far strangers to each other. Things, however, started changing in the late nineteenth and early twentieth centuries. With the improvement in communications, some interactions began, and the similarity in the conditions in China and India in the early days of the nineteenth century struck a sympathetic chord between the two nations.

In the political field, it was Jawaharlal Nehru who in 1927 established the early contacts with China at the 'Conference against Imperialism' at Brussels. He compared India's problems of being a colony of the British with China's troubles while it was being exploited by the Europeans, particularly the British. Drawing inspiration from the Chinese struggle, Nehru said. '[T]he noble example of the Chinese nationalists has filled us with hope and we earnestly want as soon as we can to be able to emulate them and follow their footsteps.'[2] At that time in China, there existed an alliance between the Kuomintang government and the Chinese communists, and China was riding on a wave of nationalism, seeking to unite the country. The Chinese delegation was keen on seeking the support and sympathy of public opinion everywhere. The views of the Indian and Chinese delegations reflected the long-term cooperation between the Indian National Congress and the Kuomintang government. This also coincided with the prevalent attitude of cultural nationalism in India and its stress on the ancient civilization of the East. Nehru recalled the close

cultural ties between the peoples of India and China for over three
thousand years and blamed the British for fostering ill-will against
India in China by utilizing Indian mercenary troops 'in support of
British capitalist brigandage'. He was keen that the Indian people
should be educated about China's conditions. 'We must now resume
the ancient personal, cultural, and political relations between the two
peoples,' said Nehru. He blamed British imperialism for keeping
them apart and causing injury to both. The cooperation and oneness
of ideas that emerged between the Indian and Chinese delegations
at Brussels helped them remain in touch with each other later and
develop a common outlook towards the problems of colonialism.[3]

The contacts established in Brussels made Nehru sympathetic
towards China. China, like India, was essentially an agrarian society.
In both the countries, industry was confined to a few cities and was
under foreign control. Millions of farmers and tenants were crushed
under the terrible burden of debt. Rents were also very high in both
the countries. Agriculturalists had long periods of enforced idleness.
Cottage industries had been rendered idle by the consumer goods
manufactured in the industries of Europe flooding their markets.[4]

Rabindranath Tagore's visits to China, in 1924 and again in
1928, and the Cheena Bhavana that he set up in Shantiniketan,
revived old cultural contacts. Nehru's visit to China in 1939 and
the Chinese nationalist leader Chiang Kai-shek's later in 1942
strengthened the bonds of friendship between Nehru and Chiang
Kai-shek personally and between the Congress and the Kuomintang
institutionally.[5]

In 1938 the Congress party sent a medical unit to the communist
areas of China, since they, too, were fighting against Japan. Mao Tse
Tung had thanked Nehru for the same. Nehru in his letter of 11 July
1939 to Mao had expressed India's solidarity with the struggle of the
Chinese against Japan and had described the medical unit as a token
of 'our solidarity . . . and our desire to help you'. He, too, expressed
his desire to visit China 'to convey personally to the Chinese people
the good wishes of the people of India'.[6]

In his speech on 18 November 1938 in Bombay, he said that the geographical frontiers of Indian freedom were no longer confined to its own geographical frontiers but had extended to China where the fight for democracy was being fought.[7] To doubting Thomases, he said, '[W]hat the Congress has achieved by sending the medical team to China could not have accrued by spending lakhs of rupees on foreign propaganda.'[8]

In 1939 when the war broke out, Nehru was in China but before he could go to the communist areas and meet Mao and other communist leaders, he had to cut short his visit and return home hurriedly. He liked the Chinese, who struck him 'as a singularly grown-up people' and he established a personal friendship both with Chiang Kai-shek and his wife. He was excited with the idea of visiting another Asian country and he said that as a result of the visit 'China has grown very near to me, and all my thoughts are mixed up with her'. He was determined that India and China should work together; and this idea did not leave him thereafter.[9]

India was anguished at the Chinese suffering during the war. 'Gandhi assured Chiang Kai-shek', in a letter drafted by Nehru, that 'the plan to secure British withdrawal was intended to enable India to look after herself and to help China, to the best of her ability'. Thanks to Nehru, 'whose love of China is only excelled, if at all, by his love of his country', the Indian people were deeply committed to the Chinese cause.[10]

The communist Chinese leaders, apart from acknowledging the contribution of the medical unit, did not acknowledge any other contacts between India and China in the past, particularly Nehru's personal sympathy with China and his association with the Kuomintang Party. They, however, did remember Tagore and Kotnis. Dwarkanath Kotnis was one of the doctors who were a part of the medical unit sponsored by the Congress party to serve the Red Armies. He stayed on in China until his death in 1942, before he had celebrated his 32nd birthday. The then Chinese premier, Zhou Enlai, while visiting India in 1954, recalled Tagore's support to China's struggle against the imperialists and the Chinese Premier Li Keqiang on his first official visit to India in May 2013, referred to Tagore as a 'sage poet'. In September 2014, President Xi Jinping paid his tribute to Tagore and said that he had read several collections of his poems.

Though Nehru from the beginning was somehow impressed with China for being an ancient land and culture, and Asian above all, one may wonder about the reason behind his extraordinary admiration for China. He found it necessary to justify it every now and then. While in Paris in July 1938 he told Radio Pravo that 'Indian sympathies for China were very understandable, as China was nearest to us and our relations with her were thousands of years old'.[11]

In Chunking on 29 August 1939, he said:

> Before all these considerations, the conviction grew upon me that the Indian problem must be viewed both in historical and world perspective. This necessitated contacts with other countries and an understanding of what was happening there, and this applied both to the countries of the West and the East. The West was important because it dominated the world politics today, and also because it had already gone through various changes, through which we are now in India . . . passing. But the East, particularly China, was equally if not more important for us, as in some respects there was an amazing similarity of problems between India and China. Unfortunately, however, our contacts with China were very limited. It was the intense desire to add to these contacts and to learn from what was happening in China that brought me here.[12]

Looking ahead, Nehru was convinced that the 'future of Asia depends on the goodwill and neighbourly relations among Asiatic countries, and of these China and India must obviously play a dominant role'.[13]

In 1946, as India neared its goal of attaining independence, and as Nehru became a member of the Viceroy's Executive Council, in-charge of the External Affairs department, he was upset at the suggestion of the Intelligence department that the entry of only those Chinese individuals who were visiting India for official work be allowed. He found it odd and rejected the proposal.[14]

As China regained some of its lost glory after the war, unfailing in his trust of China, Nehru lamented that India was yet 'faltering like a sick patient getting up from the sickbed, or a prisoner released from jail'. He predicted it would regain its old glory in the not-too-distant future.

The new Chinese leaders, to Nehru's chagrin, were not willing to recognize India's past contacts with Kuomintang China and looked down upon them. They felt irritated at any reference to any past contacts with the old regime in China. Once the Kuomintang government had been thrown out, new China did not pause and began implementing its agenda of 'uniting' the country and bringing the renegade provinces within its fold, trampling upon any hurdle that came in its way, which a placid India had neither expected nor had time to adjust itself to. India, trying to hold on to its old facilities and privileges in Tibet on the strength of its inheritance and past relations, became an anathema with the new leadership which was bent upon ending, what it regarded, the humiliation of the past. There lies the rub. The old China was dead and it was time for India to adjust to the new China. It was not only India who was caught unawares but also the world.

1

India, Tibet and China—
A Historical Perspective

The Tibet–China relationship has seen many ups and downs in history. Not going too far back, for more than two hundred years, before China finally occupied it in 1950, Tibet enjoyed varied degrees of independence. China maintained a representative in Lhasa, the Amban. His influence and authority varied from time to time, depending on the strength of the imperial court and his own propensity to pecuniary attractions. Sometimes, his authority enhanced to an extent that he became the final arbiter in all matters of the administration, including the Dalai Lama's succession. The Amban was more of a governor than a mere diplomat and had the right to maintain a military escort.

As the Ch'ing dynasty declined towards the end of the nineteenth century, Tibet challenged China's right and authority to approve the Dalai Lama's incarnation. China's defeat at the hands of the Japanese in 1895 had also weakened the Chinese position in Lhasa. Much before Francis Younghusband's expedition to Tibet in 1904, Governor General Warren Hastings had sent George Bogle to Lhasa in 1774 to establish relations with Lhasa and, through Lhasa, with China.

Though he was initially not allowed to enter Tibet, Bogle managed to win over the sixth Panchen Lama, who tried to help him to establish contacts with China. However, the Ch'ing government rebuffed Bogle and he returned to India without having achieved his objective.[1]

The British, having established their protectorate in Sikkim in 1861, became anxious to open Tibet. Finding that China's writ did not run in Lhasa, and given the recalcitrant behaviour of the Tibetans, Viceroy Curzon sent Younghusband on an expedition in 1904. As it reached Gyantse, the Dalai Lama fled Lhasa to Mongolia. Younghusband imposed stiff penalties on Tibet, which were subsequently moderated.

The British Minister in Peking, John Jordan, worried about the larger British commercial interests in China, feared that this would be prejudicial to their interests, and said:

> [N]otwithstanding China's weak position in Lhasa, the Manchu Dynasty attached great importance to the symbols of Tibetan and Mongol sovereignty; and any disregard of Chinese sensitivities over Tibet would probably produce greater damage to British interests in China than could ever be compensated for by an increase in the value of the Indo-Tibetan trade.[2]

Soon the British, who were then seen as anxious to get China's endorsement of their position in Lhasa, entered into a fresh Convention with Peking in 1906 whereby China resolved to not permit any other foreign power to interfere in Tibet. It was clarified unambiguously that while China was not a foreign power in relation to Tibet, Great Britain very definitely was. This in itself gave China a free hand in Tibet and greater control in its affairs.[3]

An equally significant development was the Tsarist Russia's 'Great Game' in the region after consolidating its position in Siberia, as far as the Pacific, and establishing its influence in Mongolia, where there were significant Buddhist minorities (Buryat and Mongols) amenable to Russian influence. They had the potential to provide Russia a toehold in Tibet.

Viceroy Lord Minto informed the Secretary of State on 13 July 1906 that 'in our view, Tibet is a feudatory State under suzerainty of China, but possessed wide autonomous powers, together with power to make treaties in respect of its frontiers, mutual trade and similar matters with coterminous states'. The Dalai Lama, still in exile and seen to be hobnobbing with Russia, remained a persona non-grata with the British.[4]

Since HMG's larger interest in Europe required a modus vivendi with Russia in Asia, and since London was anxious to accommodate its concerns in a larger agreement concerning Asia, London rebuked Calcutta for following unilateral policies and for not keeping the larger British interest in view. It said, 'Britain cannot have two foreign policies . . . be we right or wrong, that is our policy.'[5]

This resulted in the umbrella Anglo-Russian Convention of September 1907, which, among other things, recognized the 'suzerain rights of China in Tibet', and both the British and Russians agreed to respect the territorial integrity of Tibet, to 'abstain from all interference in Tibet's internal administration' and to deal with Tibet only through China, effectively creating a sanitary cordon from Russian advance in Tibet.[6] The 1907 Convention left China in full control of Tibet, free from the worries of any interference from any European power, including the British.

Not reconciled to the conditions imposed by the Anglo-Russian Convention, the British officials posted in Tibet attempted to undermine the Amban's influence in Lhasa by promoting the Panchen Lama in the absence of the Dalai Lama. But the move did not receive enough support either from Calcutta or London and eventually failed even though the Panchen Lama had already been persuaded to play the role. China, too, had made it clear that Panchen had no authority to enter into political negotiations. London, dissatisfied with its officials in Tibet, called their action 'a thoroughly dubious or even obnoxious prospect'.[7]

The new Secretary of State for India, Lord Morley, fortified China's position further in Tibet when he told Viceroy Lord Minto on 3 January 1908 that:

> You will fight them none the less effectively if your hands are scrupulously, austerely and haughtily clean. Take note, however, that we have bound ourselves not to interfere in the internal administration of Tibet; and for my own part I have a suspicion that some of your proposals come perilously near internal administration.[8]

Now China with London's support became more assertive. It insisted on renegotiating the 1893 Tibet Trade Regulations and the British agreed to it. Fresh consultations resulted in the 1908 Tibet Trade Regulations, signed by China, Tibet and the British, but ratified only in Peking and London and not in Lhasa. It left no one in doubt that China had now become the ultimate authority in Tibet.[9]

The Dalai Lama, still in exile, was now anxious to return home and was ready for a compromise. He visited Peking and negotiated his return home. In restoring him, the Empress Dowager conferred on him the title of 'Our Loyal and Submissive Vice-Regent' and instructed him by Decree that:

> [W]hen His Holiness has returned to Tibet, he must be careful to obey the laws of the Sovereign State of China and he must promulgate to all the goodwill of the Court of China. He must exhort the Tibetans to be obedient and to follow the path of rectitude. He must follow the established customs of memorialising us, through the Imperial Amban and respectfully await Our Will.[10]

The Dalai Lama, with his wings sufficiently clipped, got back to Lhasa in December 1909. Calcutta, faced with the rapid expansion of Chinese influence and power in Tibet (and then its disappearance in the wake of Chinese Revolution of 1911), felt the need for a flexible policy regarding Tibet, which the 1907 Convention and London's policies had denied it.

The Dalai Lama on his return discovered that the Chinese had inducted a large expeditionary force in Lhasa under General Er-Feng. He was unnerved and again fled Lhasa in February 1910, this time to India. His flight worried the British that Tibet as a buffer between India and China would cease to exist. The Chinese were now deployed along the Himalayan ranges across the Indian border. Viceroy Minto recommended London for a demarche to be made at Peking. The British minister Jordan did not agree to this and told the British Foreign Secretary on 15 February 1910:

> [N]either the facts as at present known to us, nor the terms of the Convention of 1906 would warrant our making a protest against possible change in the status quo or infringement of the spirit of our agreements with China or Tibet. We have long been aware of the object of the Chinese expedition, and I would therefore deprecate these arguments as being somewhat belated.[11]

The Chinese, encouraged by the attitude of British minister in Beijing, were now undaunted by the murmurs in Calcutta and issued a decree deposing the Dalai Lama. The Secretary of State, John Morley, taking a benign view of China's action, told the viceroy on 23 March 1910:

> China was awakening and beginning to have knowledge and interest in the geography and conditions of her dependencies. So, we have no right to be surprised if China seeks to render more effective that shadowy control that she always possessed in Tibet, and which we vehemently blamed her for not exercising more effectively in practice.[12]

He, therefore, asked the viceroy to tell the Dalai Lama in clear, unambiguous terms that as between him and his suzerain, the British had no interest to intervene.[13]

The political officer in Sikkim, Charles Alfred Bell, and other officers of his ilk were concerned at the weakening effect of the

British policy, which India Office had sought to follow in relation to China in Tibet. As the Dalai Lama was seen to be getting closer to Russia while in exile, a worried Bell feared that Tibet would become a protectorate of foreign powers to the exclusion of the British. He suggested that the trade agent at Gyantse be moved to Lhasa because 'only at Lhasa will his influence deter the Chinese from intriguing with the frontier states, and to convince both the Chinese and the Tibetans that our interests, rights and wishes have to be treated with respect and consideration'.[14] Foreign Secretary Grey dismissed such apprehensions as coming from 'frontier men' and rejected the proposal since it would violate the Anglo-Russian Convention of 1907, specifically the decision that Britain was not to intervene in China/Tibet's internal affairs.[15] In London there was little confidence that 'the frontier officers like Bell (P.O.), if they found the right opportunity, would adhere rigidly to the policy of non-intervention'. [16]

By the middle of 1910 it had increasingly become clear to the Viceroy that the Chinese were there to stay in Tibet and no solution was possible until some way could be found of that 'pestilent animal' (the Dalai Lama) who was still camping in India.[17] The Dalai Lama himself now was getting nowhere and was keen to get back home after working out some understanding with the Chinese. The Chinese, too, were getting nowhere in discovering a new incarnate while the old one was still living and were wondering if he would come back. The Amban sent his emissary to Darjeeling, assuring the Dalai Lama that while he would not be punished on his return, his position as the Dalai Lama would not be restored. The Dalai Lama rejected the offer.[18]

The 1911 revolution in China ended imperial rule and established the Republic of China, which resolved many problems. There were important changes all round. Minto was replaced by Lord Hardinge as the viceroy who, while accepting the Chinese control of Tibet as one of the permanent factors in frontier affairs, soon found himself unable to accept the expansion of Chinese influence towards the Himalayan states and the Assam Himalayas.[19] The Marques of Crewe, the new Secretary of State for India, found himself quite uncomfortable with the earlier policy followed by his predecessors, that is, of leaving Tibet at the mercy of China.[20]

In the wake of 1911 Revolution, the Chinese troops in Lhasa had mutinied, surrendered and were thrown out of Tibet back to China by the Tibetans. The Dalai Lama re-entered Lhasa in January 1913. The Chinese Republican President Yuan Shih-kai, to salvage the Chinese position in Tibet, on 28 October 1912 restored the Dalai Lama his rank, who made use of the opportunity to clarify that 'the existing relationship between Tibet and China had been that one of "patron and priest" and had *not been based on the subordination of one to the other*'. [21]

On 17 August 1912, the British minister in Peking had submitted a memorandum to Weichiaopu (the Chinese Foreign Office) recalling its president's assurance to him that 'there was no intention of incorporating Tibet in China, that the treaties would be scrupulously observed' and that HMG would not tolerate any attempt to reduce Tibet, which had independent treaty relations with Great Britain, to the condition of a province of China. China was warned of grave complications if they crossed the frontiers into Tibet. China could station a representative in Lhasa to advise the Tibetans as to their foreign relations. The most important part of the memorandum which had implications for the future was the need for *a written agreement between them, China and Tibet as a condition precedent to extending recognition to the Chinese Republic.*[22] The aim of British policy at this time was to make Tibet free from Chinese hegemonic control.[23]

On 23 June 1912, China affirmed that there was 'no intention' of incorporating Tibet into China.[24] The Chinese, reacting to the memorandum of 17 August on 23 December, questioned the need for a new agreement, since existing treaties were adequate. It pointed out that HMG had already recognized the Chinese interests in Tibet and pledged not to intervene as long as treaty stipulations were observed, thereby conveying that China had full and uninhibited administrative powers in Tibet.[25]

The British, refusing to respond, later said that the Chinese note was so unsatisfactory that it did not warrant a reply.[26]

Despite the warning from the British, China gathered its wits, and made a fresh bid to integrate Tibet with itself by floating the concept of 'Five Races'—the Chinese, Manchu, Mongols, Tibetans and Tatars—joined in democratic union, and the lands comprised within the confines of Mongolia, Tibet and Turkestan to be part of the territory of the Republic of China, and the races inhabiting these lands would be all equal citizens of the Republic of China.[27]

The Tibetans were not amused and the British government in India perceived in this move a revival of Chinese threat on their north-eastern frontiers. To pre-empt this threat, it moved quickly and in a memorandum to the foreign office in London desired that:

> Tibet, while nominally retaining her position as an Autonomous State under the suzerainty of China, should in reality be placed in a position of absolute dependence on the Indian Government and that there should be set up an effective machinery for keeping out the Chinese on the one hand and the Russians on the other.[28]

By February 1913, the British had finalized the idea of a tripartite conference to promote better relations between China and Tibet to be held in either Darjeeling or Simla.[29] *That the border question between India and Tibet would be discussed and decided was not mentioned.* Secretary of State Lord Morley told the House of Lords on 28 July 1913 that:

> China and Tibet would be, so to call them, the protagonists. Unless something arises we shall be honest brokers, but an honest broker, who will keep his eyes open with regard to those interests which I have described to your lordship. [30]

On 9 March 1914 Henry McMahon, in the background of the campaigns of Chao Erh-feng, said:

> [T]he present conference was called, in order to seek some remedy for a situation which was recognised a menace to the peace and prosperity of the three countries now in negotiations.[31]

The Chinese had not liked the idea of a conference where they would have to sit as equal with the Tibetans. To meet the Chinese sensitivities, the British minister in Peking told Weichiaopu that the declared objective of the conference was 'to decide the position of Tibet *vis-à-vis* China and that this could best be achieved by treating the three delegates on a footing of perfect equality'.[32] Nearer to the date of the opening of the Conference, the Chinese procrastinated. China was warned that if it adopted delaying tactics, 'serious consequences' would ensue. The threat worked.[33]

The three plenipotentiaries with full powers from their respective heads of state—the Dalai Lama, the Chinese president and the King Emperor—formally met in Delhi on 6 October 1913. The Tibetans were happy that the Dalai Lama's position had been accepted as an equal to the British monarch and the Chinese president. The conference concluded on 3 July 1914 in Simla, which gave the Convention its name.

At the conference, the Tibetan representative, Lochen Shatra, insisted that the Anglo-Chinese Convention of 1906 had been negotiated behind its back and was not acceptable.[34] The Chinese representative Ivan Chen, however, traced China's control over Tibet from the seventh century when a Chinese expedition had first entered Lhasa, and recounted the history of Chinese assistance to Tibet at various times and also the Dalai Lama's visits to Peking to pay obeisance to the emperor on various occasions. Chen pledged not to incorporate Tibet in China, while asking Britain to pledge not to annex Tibet or any part thereof to India.[35] After preliminary discussions, the conference adjourned for some time.

McMahon in his statement on 9 March 1914 had pointed out that there were two parts of Tibet, Inner and Outer Tibet. Outer Tibet would be under the Lhasa administration, but under Chinese suzerainty. China would thus not be interfering in its internal administration. Inner Tibet would be under the jurisdiction of the Chinese government.[36]

The Chinese, however, protested throughout the conference, asking for a change in the draft prepared by McMahon. Apart from the question of suzerainty/sovereignty, the Chinese were more worried about the territories comprising Inner Tibet than Outer Tibet. Their objections were concerned with areas in Inner Tibet, which bordered China proper.[37]

It may be relevant to point out that the letters exchanged between the British and Tibetan representatives on 24–25 March 1914 settled the boundary between India and Tibet as marked on the two copies of the map, one copy each was retained by Shatra and McMahon. China was not given a copy of it. The line was probably marked in red by McMahon alone, since there was no mention of the red line in the letters exchanged on 24–25 March nor any mention of the boundary between Outer and Inner Tibet in those letters. In Article 9 of the Convention, two lines, red and blue, were introduced—red for the India–Tibet border, and blue, for Inner and Outer Tibet.[38] Ivan Chen, the Chinese plenipotentiary, dismissed the agreement which worried the Tibetans, who were assured by Political Officer Bell that 'there was no need to be anxious. The Chinese have agreed to all the rest of the Convention except Article 9 regarding the boundaries'.[39] At the end, the Tibetans were happy to sign the Convention even if it was only initialled by China and finally disowned.

The preamble of the Convention referred to the three parties 'being sincerely desirous to settle by mutual agreement various questions concerning the interests of their several States on the Continent of Asia and further to regulate the relations of their several Governments . . .' It did not mention any settlement or demarcation of the boundaries among the three parties. It was only in Article 9 that it said:

> [F]or the purpose of the present Convention the *border of Tibet* (with India) and the *boundary between Outer and Inner Tibet* shall be as shown *in red and blue respectively* on the map attached hereto.[40]

This was indeed a surreptitious manner of fixing international borders, which the British, being the powerful party, tried to force down the throat of China.

London, worried about Russian reaction, wished to consult St Petersburg in view of their 1907 Convention before signing it. On 21 April 1914, London had instructed the viceroy that '[s]ignatures to the Convention must be deferred pending reference to Russia'.[41] The Russians did not make any objection to the Simla Convention. The outbreak of the World War had diverted Russian attention from the Himalayas to Europe.[42] The British minister in Beijing, Jordan, on 1 May in a telegram cautioned Foreign Secretary Crew that he was informed by the Chinese that initialling of the convention by Chen was informal; that instructions had been sent to him to cancel it. He added that China was ready to accept, in principle, all the provisions of the draft Convention, with the exception of Article 9, which demarcated the boundaries between Outer and Inner Tibet.[43] After another meeting, this time with the Chinese foreign minister on 15 June 1914, Jordan once again informed London that China insisted that the boundary question had never been negotiated with it and it would not sign the agreement imposed upon it in 'such an arbitrary way'.[44]

Finally, Weichiaopu in its memorandum of 29 June said that while it did not sign the convention,

> it has absolutely no desire to terminate the present negotiations, and that it is unable to regard the initialling of the Convention

by its special envoy, Mr. Chen which took place without its instructions, as effective. It is earnestly hoped that HMG will still consent to continue in its original intention to act mediator between China and Tibet, in order that the question between the two countries may reach a harmonious conclusion.[45]

Jordan, in his private letter to Assistant Under Secretary of State in the Foreign Office Sir Walter Langley, on 28 June, blamed McMahon for hurriedly closing the conference. Had McMahon not done so, he felt there would have been the possibility of some permanency of the convention. He said:

> [W]hether China signed or did not sign the Convention, the future outlook seemed very unsatisfactory. If it signed, it would do so with a bad grace and with very little intention to observing it. If she refuses to sign, the position will be more acute and perhaps call for more immediate action . . . Apart altogether from the effect such a step would have on our vast commercial and industrial interests in China.[46]

His views in favour of China did influence London. After some correspondence between the viceroy and the Secretary of State on various aspects of the Convention, on 1 July, Secretary of State Crewe instructed Delhi that the final meeting of the Conference be held on 3 July and were the Chinese

> to refuse to sign the Convention, negotiations should definitely be terminated by Sir Henry.[47]

The Chinese remained adamant on not signing it. On 2 July in yet another telegram in response to the viceroy's telegram of 1 July, Crewe said that his orders contained in the telegram of 1 July 'hold good as to the final meeting on 3 July'. He also instructed should China finally refuse to sign, McMahon should 'add in full conference, the statement that the settled views of HMG with regard to the boundaries and status of Tibet are represented by the Convention as initialled'.[48] Crewe also authorized the viceroy to assure Tibet 'that it may depend on diplomatic support of HMG and on any assistance in the way of munitions of war which we can give them, if aggression on the part of China continues'.[49]

On 3 July, the Chinese Minister in London told HMG yet again:

[T]he Chinese Government regret very much that the proposals regarding the boundary question did not meet with their approval and they are unable to sign the agreement as it stands. Nor was his government willing to recognise any deal that the British might enter into with Tibet, without its consent and approval.[50]

In the face of the final Chinese warning, the India Office once again on 3 July reiterated its earlier instructions to Delhi that separate signatures with Tibet could not be authorized.[51]

As it happened the 3 July telegram reached Simla when the convention had already been signed by the British and the Tibetan plenipotentiaries, even when the Chinese plenipotentiary had not done so. The delay was explained on account of the fact that in London 'no one of sufficient seniority to deal with the question was available at the Foreign Office on Friday last (July 3) until 1 PM (approximating to 6.30 PM in Simla) and by the time the telegram landed in Simla, the Convention had already been signed'.[52] Meanwhile, HMG, instead of denouncing the Convention signed against their instructions, accepted it as a fait accompli. China, however, had in a formal statement made it clear both at Simla and in London that it would not recognize any bilateral agreement between the two of them. The world outside remained unaware of these developments and also of the contents of the Convention since it was not published formally until the 1938 edition of the Aitchison's compilation of treaties. It remained a mystery that even on 2 July, almost twenty-four hours before it was signed, HMG's

instructions were clear and unambiguous that the convention was
not to be signed bilaterally with Tibet, and since there were no
further instructions to the contrary, under the earlier instructions the
Convention should not have been signed. On 3 July, the instructions
were simply a reiteration of the earlier instructions in view of China's
reiteration of their stand to London. The convention signed by Great
Britain and Tibet had a notation at the end that said:

> [W]e acknowledge the annexed Convention as initialled to be
> binding on the Governments of Great Britain and Tibet, and
> we regret that so long as the Government of China withholds
> signatures to the aforesaid Convention, she will be debarred from
> the enjoyment of all privileges accruing there from.[53]

Except for the line that McMahon drew on the map, there was no
description of the boundary accompanying the map. The Tawang
Tract became part of the Indian territory. That it was not occupied
is another story. The convention failed to stabilize relations between
Tibet and China that it had set to achieve. It amply served British
India's interests in establishing a secure boundary with Tibet to
their satisfaction and for Tibet a dubious semi-independent status,
which it did not put to use to establish diplomatic relations even
with Buddhist countries. The British virtually replaced the Chinese
as the protecting power in Tibet. China bided its time. The joint
declaration signed between the British and the Tibetans, soon after
the signing of the Convention on 3 July 1914, said:

> We, the plenipotentiaries of Great Britain and Tibet hereby
> record the following Declaration to the effect that we acknowledge
> the annexed Convention as initialled to be binding on the
> Governments of Great Britain and Tibet, and we agree that in
> so long as the Government of China withholds signature to the
> aforesaid Convention, she will be debarred from enjoyment of all
> privileges accruing there-from.[54]

Following the Simla Convention, the British made several attempts to get China on board so that the relations between China and Tibet were put on solid footing but to no avail. In 1921, Britain, once again using the earlier argument to induce China to sign it, repeated that if China failed to sign it, HMG would not feel unjustified 'in withholding any longer their recognition of the status of *Tibet as an autonomous state under the suzerainty of China* and intend dealing with Tibet in future on this basis'.[55] At the end of his tenure in India, McMahon admitted: '[I]t is with great regret that I leave India without having secured the formal adherence of the Chinese Government to a Tripartite Agreement.'[56]

Tibet was not declared an independent state, but still under the Chinese suzerainty. The dichotomy at the very signing of the Convention had a deleterious impact on the relations between the three countries, much against the objectives of the Convention. Later, long after the British had left India, it caused friction between two major Asian countries.

2

The Fall of Kuomintang China

On gaining Independence in August 1947, India inherited Britain's distinctive relationship with Tibet but without its muscles. The British had used Tibet as a buffer against both China and Tsarist Russia. The British achieved for Tibet its new status by manoeuvrings at the Simla Conference and successfully tied it down to their apron strings. It was a dichotomous arrangement in that while Tibet was accepted as an equal party at the Conference, yet in the text of the Convention it was placed under China's suzerainty. That finally China did not sign the convention is discussed in the previous chapter.

India also inherited two trade agencies at Gyantse and Yatung and a seasonal one in Gartok besides right to station a military escort at Gyantse. China, failing to prevent the British hijacking Tibet, bided its time. During the Second World War, China had got rid of extra-territoriality of the foreign powers and had regained at least some semblance of respectability. Taking advantage of its new position, it tried to assert itself in Tibet and took several steps which worried the British Government.[1] While the British government did not consider it prudent to warn China, a war ally, it did remind Lhasa of its treaty rights under Article V of the Simla Convention and assured it as long as it 'safeguarded' its 'autonomous position', HMG would extend Tibet any 'diplomatic support, should it be needed' but no military support.[2] No change, however, took place until the British left India.

Nehru had a particular view of India's role regionally and globally before and after Independence. On 23 December 1945, immediately at the end of the war, in a press interview he said 'when there will be free India, I should very much like the development of closer contacts with China, cultural, and political, besides contacts of every kind of trade and commerce'.[3]

Yet again on 25 December 1945, addressing the Sino-Indian Cultural Society at Shantiniketan, he said, 'We hope that the present state of affairs in India and China will end and both countries will come closer in their friendship not only for mutual advantage but also for the good of world at large'.[4]

In August 1946, he had said that 'India is going to be the centre of a very big federation', which would include China, Southeast Asia and also West Asia.[5] On 15 September 1946, Nehru again emphasized:

> [That] by virtue of its size, resources and historical background during the last 200 years it has been a kind of example for other [nations] ... There has been a tendency for many of the dependent countries in Asia and Africa to look towards India for leadership in their attempt to attain political and economic freedom.[6]

In September 1946, as the head of the foreign department in the Interim Government, he envisioned a leadership role for India at the United Nations and said: '[O]ur natural position in world assemblies is going to be inevitably one of the leadership of all the smaller countries of Asia.' He argued that it was 'obvious' that India by 'virtue of her geographical and strategic position, resources and latent power, should be a member of the UN Security Council'.[7]

In the article that he wrote for the *New York Times* in 1946, he had expressed similar sentiments:

A free India will link together Middle East with China. India is so situated as to form the centre of a group of Asian nations for defence as well as trade and commerce. Her cultural contacts with all these countries date back thousands of years. Already there is a considerable talk about a closer union between the countries in the Indian Ocean region which would include Australia and New Zealand.[8]

Early in 1947 there were clear signs of the British winding up their Raj in India. Reviewing their own policy towards Tibet vis-à-vis China, the foreign department conveyed to the political officer in Gangtok the new policy. This policy was a reversal of their earlier policy and was essentially an advisory for independent India. It suggested:

The conditions in which India's wellbeing may be assured and the full evolution may be achieved for her inherent capacity to emerge as a potent but benevolent force in world affairs—particularly in Asia—demand not merely the development of internal unity and strength but also the maintenance of friendly relations with her neighbours. To prejudice her relations with so important a power as China by aggressive support of unqualified Tibetan independence for which, whatever may have been the situation earlier, there has in the past year or two, been little sign of ardour in Lhasa, is therefore a policy with few attractions . . . The attitude they propose to take may best be described as that of a benevolent spectator, ready at all times—should opportunity occur—to use their good offices to further a mutually satisfactory settlement between China and Tibet.[9]

It was also advised that if in the light of the participation of a Tibetan delegation in the recent session of the Chinese National Assembly, China and Tibet work out some modus vivendi between them, India should neither object nor interfere.[10]

On 23 July 1947 the external department, in a message approved by the HMG, informed Tibet that on the transfer of power to the

Dominion of India, as the only successor, HMG would continue to take a 'friendly interest in the future prosperity of the Tibetan people and in the maintenance of Tibetan autonomy'.[11]

Having said that, it further added:

> HMG trusts that after August 15th the close and cordial relations which had existed for so many years with themselves and the Government of India will continue with the successor Indian Government upon whom alone the rights and obligations arising from the existing treaty provisions will thereafter devolve.[12]

The mission-in-charge in Lhasa, H.E. Richardson, who had been asked to continue to represent the new Government of India (GoI) in Lhasa, was directed to inform the Tibetan government that after 15 August the mission at Lhasa would become the 'Indian Mission representing the Dominion of India only' and he would continue to look after the mission until some other arrangement was made.[13]

Thanking HMG for the assurance of their continued interest, the Tibetan government manipulated the above message to read as 'maintenance of Tibet's independence and common welfare of her people'. It also took the opportunity to rake up the issue of its territories, which it claimed, had in the past been incorporated into India and should be returned and expected the British government's help in that direction.[14]

On the same day, that is, 16 October, in another letter to Prime Minister Nehru, the Tibetan government asked for the return of territories, which it said, had been gradually included in India in the past. The territories claimed were vast and extensive—Sikkim, Bhutan, Darjeeling, Ladakh and others 'on this side of the River Ganges . . . up to the boundary of Yarkhim'.[15]

Nehru told Zhou Enlai later in 1959 that if India were to concede to Tibetan demands, Tibet's frontier would be literally on the river Ganga and as such the GoI could hardly countenance such a fantastic claim.[16]

A confident Tibet had made a similar demand for the return of its territories to the Kuomintang government too. The Chinese National Assembly had responded by suggesting that:

These territories had been under Chinese Government rule for more than a century and at any rate Tibet itself was part of China. It was therefore quite pointless in returning these territories to Tibet.

The reply provocatively added:

However, if Tibet would claim those territories of hers which had been seized by the British and attached to India, such as Sikkim, Bhutan Ladakh, Western Tibet, Towang, and Dzayul, if these territories were returned, China would consider returning some of theirs too.[17]

On 27 March 1948, Tibet yet again repeated its demand for return of territories.[18] Richardson, disputing the Tibetan claim and their fanciful ideas, said that 'there was no encroachment on Tibetan territory as McMahon Line was already agreed to by Tibetan Government and that major portion of Assam tribal area was never under Tibetan administration at any time'.[19] Nothing came out of Tibet's demands on India or China as other developments, such as civil war and communist victory, overtook the narrative.

Meanwhile, on an enquiry from the Chinese embassy in Delhi, the GoI informed it that since the establishment of the Dominion of India, it was the only government which had succeeded to the rights and obligations that 'previously existed between British India and Tibet'. It added 'so far as the GoI are aware, the Government of Pakistan are not assuming any part of those rights and obligations'.[20]

After Independence, a confident prime minister asserted that India held a position in the world that in every way qualified it for a permanent seat in the Security Council of the United Nations. Even if India did not get that seat, it did not prevent him rating India's overall influence within the United Nations as quite high. Nehru subsequently turned down opportunities to gain a permanent seat on the Council at the cost of Communist China, which had been excluded from the United Nations since Kuomintang China was occupying it with the US backing.[21] On 18 January 1947, in a note Nehru again spoke of India's potential and its position being a fairly strong one, whether in the political or the economic fields. He believed that 'the economic prosperity of the UK and the USA depended to some extent on Indian cooperation'. He did not believe that India was in a weak position to be bullied by any power. 'We have something valuable to give in the present and our goodwill is even more valuable in the near future and therefore, we are in a strong bargaining position,' he said.[22]

After the war as China started rubbing shoulders with big countries, Nehru found to his surprise that China was a changed country, more confident of itself than before. Foreign powers had given up their 'Concessions' and after almost a century it could breathe easy. Though the civil war in China was a challenge before the Kuomintang government, it felt confident to meet it. Being an ally of the Allied Powers, China felt like one of them, and its leadership felt elated in the company of other important world leaders. Its dream of returning to the old glorious days of the Empire seemed to have come true. Being a founding member of the UN, it secured for itself a permanent seat on the Security Council with a veto power along with the United States, and three European powers. India, which was still under the colonial rule, did not take long to realize that China, which it had sympathized with and stood by, for almost two decades since 1927, was not the same it had known in the past years. Ambassador K.M. Panikkar found it that way too and described it thus in his book *In Two Chinas*:

> It did not take me long to discover that the Kuomintang attitude towards India, while generally friendly, was inclined to be little patronising. It was the attitude of an elder brother who was

considerably older and well established in the world, prepared to give his advice to a younger brother struggling to make his way. Independence of India was welcome, but of course, it was understood that China as the recognised Great Power in the Far East after the war expected India to know her place. The Foreign Office or the Waichiaopu was the best organised department of the Chinese Government and it was here that the doctrine was most firmly held.

He added, however, 'even in regard to America, the Chinese attitude was one of patronising condescension'.[23]

The Asian Relations Conference was organized by Nehru in March 1947. While it was intended to be the harbinger of Asian unity and its assertion, it turned out to be a disappointment for him. China raised quite a few problems which challenged Nehru's aspiration to be a leader of resurgent Asia. Though before the war both Nehru and Chinese President Chiang Kai Shek enjoyed most cordial relations, there was a perceptible change after the war, as pointed out earlier. The issue of Tibet caused the maximum disagreement. China strongly resented the invitation to Tibet for the conference as an independent country. It sought to attribute motives for Tibet's invitation. China suspected Nehru of wanting to 'promote his personal prestige' and wean away Tibet under Indian influence. China finally agreed to attend only when assured that the Conference was 'half academic, half social' and no political issues or any internal politics of any country would be discussed.[24]

China, however, remained unhappy and, even during the conference, took serious objection to the map displayed that showed Tibet outside of China and its mention as a neighbour of India along with other neighbouring countries. It also took umbrage to Tibet being treated like other participating countries. However, Nehru in his speech at the plenary session of the Conference on 23 March 1947 welcomed China, as 'that great country to which Asia owes so much and from which so much is expected'.

The Tibetan delegation, taking into account the delicacy of the situation, avoided any political reference and just said Tibet was a country

> which administers (her) subjects on the basis of religious aspirations and India being the motherland of Buddhism and specially Tibet have friendly relations with India from ancient times. Therefore our Government have sent us here to attend this great Conference to maintain our relations based on religion.[24a]

The conference, however, did not resolve the issue between China and Tibet nor was it intended to do so, but it created misunderstanding between India and China on Delhi's motives vis-à-vis Tibet. It also highlighted the differences in their relations, and the pan-Asian dream of Nehru did not appear to be within grasp. As it was noted:

> On the verge of decolonisation, however, the contentious issue of Tibet between India and China, which came to the forefront at the Asian Relations Conference . . . made it evident that the idealism of Pan-Asianism could not resolve the problems of territorial sovereignty and border disputes.[24b]

There were also differences of opinion between India and China on other issues, such as the need for a permanent centre for Asian Relations, which India was keen to set up in India. The Chinese were equally keen to host it themselves. The Chinese delegation argued that 'China was and is the centre of Asiatic culture, and that China, by its economic, political and geographical situation could facilitate the economic and political development of the Asiatic countries'. Concluding, it said: *If a centre of inter-Asian relations were to be set up, it should be located in China.*[25] The Chinese suspected that Nehru, in projecting himself a pan-Asian leader, was trying to usurp the leadership of Asia for himself. Although the Conference had decided on a similar conference later in China, the Communist revolution did not allow it to be carried forward and the idea of Asian unity died a natural death since no country took the initiative for it thereafter.

As India attained Independence, the Chinese vice minister for foreign affairs, Dr George Yeh, conveyed to Ambassador K.P.S. Menon his country's desire to abrogate or amend the unequal treaties of the past and enter into a new treaty. He also added that the *Simla Convention had not been ratified by China and therefore China did not recognize it.* Menon told Yeh that while India had no designs on Tibet, it would not forego the advantages accruing to India from its existing agreements with Tibet. Yeh made it clear to him that the commercial treaty under negotiation between them would apply to the whole of China, including Tibet. Menon conceded that while 'we would not ask for specific exclusion of Tibet from the draft of the treaty, nothing in this should be construed to affect the existing trade relations between India and Tibet'. However, the ambassador cautioned Yeh that 'it was unlikely that the GoI would enter into any formal conversation with the Chinese Government to settle the status of Tibet over the head of Lhasa itself. To do so would be to repudiate the autonomy of Tibet which the GoI had recognized'. He, however, added that GoI was not likely to 'object or hamper' any arrangement that China and Tibet might wish to make.[26] Menon, on reconsideration, suggested to Delhi that India should object to specific mention of Tibet in the proposed commercial treaty, as otherwise it would be 'an indication that we are moving away from our policy of recognising and supporting Tibetan autonomy, which it has, in fact enjoyed for nearly forty years'.[27] The proposed treaty, however, did not materialize as the civil war in China intervened.

As the situation grew alarming for Tibet, with the communists gaining ground in the civil war, Tibet decided to send out ostensibly a trade delegation, under a senior Shape (noble), Shakabpa, to visit London, Washington and New Delhi. Its real aim was to get some support from these countries for its independence. The Shakabpa delegation carried Tibetan passports, which were granted visa by both the UK and the US despite Chinese protests. The US Secretary of State,

George Marshall, who met the delegation, reiterated the US recognition of 'China's *de jure* sovereignty over Tibet' and added that '*the fact that it exerts no de facto authority over Tibet is the root cause of the situation*'. Marshall also added that President Truman had 'expressed personal interest in greeting Tibetans'. The Tibetan delegation also met with General Eisenhower, then president of Columbia University. The State Department, however, informed its ambassador in Nanking on 28 July 1948 that the meeting was entirely innocuous in a political sense since only trade matters were discussed. However, the American embassy in New Delhi clarified that:

> The US recognised Chinese sovereignty over Tibet only because of the US policy of supporting the Kuomintang; but a Communist victory would remove the logic from that position.[28]

The visit to the UK was least successful. The British government even tried to refuse the delegation's entry, claiming that the issuance of visa was a 'technical error'. It was finally allowed entry but was treated strictly like a trade mission and 'isolated . . . from notice'.[29]

In India, the Chinese ambassador, Lo Chin-luen, protested the delegation's visit since he said it would 'raise some points affecting the sovereignty and administrative integrity of China'. He wanted the GoI to discourage the visit. India, to assuage the ruffled sentiments of the Chinese, assured Nanking that India 'had no intention to discuss issues which would embarrass China in any way'.[30]

The delegation did meet the prime minister, who could not agree to the delegation's request for a loan of $2 million, since India had shortage of foreign exchange. To Tibet's desire for industrialization, Nehru had suggested development of its mineral wealth and village and cottage industries. At the end, Nehru assured the delegation that 'his Government entertained the most cordial feelings of friendship for Tibet, her Government and people and that it would be his constant endeavour to foster the relations of friendship existing between the two peoples'.[31]

The delegation in its tour, whether it had any success or not, did represent the Tibetan success to engage foreign countries directly and independent of China.

In October 1947, both India and China differed on the question of grant of an Indian visa to the newly appointed Chinese Amban, proceeding to Lhasa *via* India. India insisted that visa would be granted, subject to Lhasa's no-objection, as was the past practice. China, on the contrary, insisted that visa be granted without consultation with Lhasa. It was explained to the Chinese vice foreign minister by Ambassador Menon that since India regarded Tibet an autonomous territory yet under Chinese suzerainty and the Chinese government themselves had in practice recognized the autonomy of Tibet, policies of both were not irreconcilable and as such the procedure that India followed was in order.[32]

While India was trying to protect Tibet's autonomy, the Tibetans themselves committed a faux pas. On being persuaded by Chinese Amban Shen to attend the National Constituent Assembly in Nanking, which was engaged in framing the new constitution for China, Tibet attended the assembly having been promised that that it would enable it to clarify its position vis-à-vis China. To the Tibetans' disappointment, they were given no opportunity to assert their position. On the contrary, no issue of Tibet's interest was discussed. Tibet in the new Chinese Constitution was treated as a 'province' although of a 'special' character. It was a manoeuvre to erode Tibet's autonomy, which was affected by its inclusion in the Chinese Constitution.[33]

Richardson from Lhasa said while he appreciated the need for preservation of the closest relations with China, it was time for India 'to stand firm and to avoid argument about its relations with Tibet'. He added that a firm and courageous stand by the GoI would command respect from the Chinese government, whereas wavering or making even a minor concession would at once open the way for further demands by the Chinese.[34]

The foreign department in Delhi, soon after the transfer of power, informed London that Tibetans had agreed to abide by the

Simla Convention and trade regulations for the present and reserved their position to 'discuss the questions regarding trade and boundaries in the future'.[35]Regarding Tibet abiding by the Simla Convention, Richardson's first impression was that while the Tibetan National Assembly had agreed to honour the Simla Convention, the Tibetan Government's message to the GoI of 17 October 1947 had 'not said anything' about this, as he had reported earlier. He thought it was the Kashag (Tibetan Cabinet) that opposed it.[36]

Richardson in another discussion with the Tibetan foreign bureau assured it that pending discussions on various matters, India was continuing its relations with Tibet on the existing basis and asked 'whether the Tibetan Government were doing the same with India'.[37]

Richardson pointed out to Surkhang Dzasa, a member of the Kashag, that:

It was a senseless attitude for the Tibetan Government simply to complain about the activities of the GOI—sometimes using very questionable language—and yet *to take no advantage of the GOI's offer to negotiate adjustment of the frontier . . . Finally I told them the Government of India's offer of an adjustment of the frontier rested on the acknowledgement by Tibet of the existing basis of relations which the GOI on their part intended to maintain.*

Richardson went to the extent of telling Surkhang that 'almost all the territory which they were arguing about is claimed for China (not for Tibet) and that any difference of opinion between India and Tibet was just the chance the Chinese were always looking for diminishing the GOI's interest in supporting Tibet'.[38]

On 30 July 1948, the GoI asked Hareshwar Dayal, the political officer in Sikkim, and Richardson, to inform Lhasa that:

The GOI who had succeeded to the rights and obligations of the British Government of India would continue to abide by the existing treaties until either party should wish to enter into fresh arrangements. In the meantime Tibet was assured that India would be ready *for an adjustment of the Indo-Tibetan frontier, particularly in the Tawang area.*[39]

Delhi had not taken the Tibetan claim seriously. Richardson later in his book said perhaps this was Tibet's attempt to test the Indian attitude to border regions 'where their British predecessors had, by a series of agreements, established the frontier of India'.[40]

Kuomintang made use of every opportunity to assert its claim on Tibet. As pointed out earlier, they had done so at the Asian Relations Conference. Again in December 1947, China entered into an argument with Delhi over a documentary film on Kashmir, where Tibet was mentioned as one of the neighbours of Kashmir and the map, too, depicted Tibet outside of China. To the repeated Chinese embassy's démarches, the Indian ministry of external affairs did not think it necessary to revise the commentary and the map objected to by them since the film was on Kashmir and it did not affect Tibet in any way. China expressed disappointment at the ministry's attitude.[41]

As the communists made advances in the civil war, the Tibetan Mission in Nanking, where the Dalai Lama's brother was present, sought the Ambassador's advice. They feared that in the event of the communists' victories, their return to Lhasa might become difficult. Apprehensive about communist domination, they insisted that 'Tibet's independence should receive international recognition and that Tibet looked to India's support for claim with Britain and America'.[42]

Delhi advised its ambassador, Panikkar, that if approached again, he was to assure them of Indian sympathy and mention that

(i)   The revision of Tibetan policy was unlikely in the event of change of government in Nanking;

(ii)   support for Tibetan independence or Tibet seeking help from foreign countries would do them more harm than good; and that

(iii) Tibetans' apprehensions were exaggerated.

While conveying the advice mentioned above, Delhi unwittingly added *'we on our part, will adhere steadfastly to our present policy of seeking to uphold Tibetan independence subject to the suzerainty of China'.*[43] Delhi realized later that the use of 'independence' in describing Tibet was inadvertent and advised the embassy that 'Tibetan independence (was) subject to the suzerainty of China' and said:

> *The last sentence in (the above) telegram is not to be taken to mean that GoI have changed their views in regard to the status of Tibet and recognised Chinese suzerainty over Tibet unconditionally. Government of India's willingness to recognise Chinese suzerainty is dependent on Chinese Government's willingness to give formal recognition to Tibetan autonomy and to agree to the frontier between Tibet and China.*[44]

A week before the above clarification was sent to Nanking, Delhi on 13 March advised Panikkar to inform the Nationalist Government in China that India's relations with Tibet were governed by the Convention of 1914. He was also to tell Nanking that GoI 'cannot enter into discussion about (their) relations with Tibet or the status of Tibet without Tibetan participation'.[45] The note went on to add that:

> [I]f the Chinese Government presses for discussions on delineation of frontiers they may be told without reference to McMahon Line areas that in the present disturbed conditions it is not possible to demarcate *undefined frontier between Kashmir and Sinkiang.*[46]

As the communist armies made several gains and the Kuomintang were seen in retreat, the prime minister asked the foreign secretary to keep a close watch on developments in Tibet and 'we shall think of the policy we should pursue there in case anything happens'.[47]

Delhi advised its embassy in Nanking that the consulate in Kashgar was essentially a Pakistani consulate and India had no interest in it.[48]

In the fast-changing scenario, Richardson on 15 June 1949 underlined the importance of Tibet's new status with the communists taking control of China; this was a position with which K.P.S. Menon, now foreign secretary in the ministry of external affairs (MEA), also agreed.[49] He thought that Tibetan officials would resist the communists if they insisted on any major changes and underlined the need for reforms in Tibet. Menon agreed with Richardson on the need to continue the Indian mission in Lhasa and the supply of arms and ammunition to Tibet, as well as strengthening of the Indian north-eastern frontier. However, Secretary General G.S. Bajpai insisted on ensuring that any aid to Tibet should not be taken by communists as provocation and also laid stress on 'social and economic reforms in Tibet' and the necessity of taking precautionary military measures for the defence of the Indian frontier.[50]

Nehru, however, disagreed and said:

> I do not think there is any necessity at present for our Defence Ministry, or any part of it, to consider possible military repercussions on the Indo-Tibetan frontier. The event is remote and may not arise at all. Any present thought being given to it will affect the balance we are trying to create in India. It may also not remain a secret and that would be unfortunate'.[51]

On 4 June 1949, in his fortnightly letter to the premiers of the Provincial governments, Nehru had described the communist revolution as 'one of the biggest changes and upheavals in history and is going to have a far-reaching consequences'. About their Marxist credentials, Nehru had a slightly different perception than usual and said they were certainly Marxists, but that the Chinese interpretation of Marxism fitted realistically with Chinese ethos. He was convinced that their successes were gained on their own strength with little help from the Soviet Union.[52]

The GoI on assuming the responsibilities bequeathed to it by the departing British government continued with the British policies of yesteryears without bringing about any change in its outlook towards Lhasa. Except for the change of flag, nothing changed. Even its representative remained the same, a British national. The consequence of this was that when the Communist Party took over, China's perception of India got distorted and it assumed that India would continue with the British policies. The communist paper *Jen Min JihPao* commenting disparagingly said:

> The retaining of Mr. Richardson's services demonstrated the collaboration of Nehru's reactionary Government with British imperialism.[53]

The final collapse of the Kuomintang regime was sudden and not accompanied by any large-scale regrets on the part of the Chinese people. The regime was so mired in corruption and maladministration that the people welcomed the communists. The Kuomintang elements led by Chiang Kai-shek fled to the island of Formosa (Taiwan) and set up a rival government there with the support of the United States, which rejected the communist government and chose not to recognize it.

The Simla Convention had given Tibet a false sense of equality with both China and the British, since the plenipotentiary powers of the Dalai Lama were equated with those of the British Emperor and Chinese President. It was an agreement in which Tibet participated as an equal party unlike in the past when others decided its fate on its back.

As the nationalist rule ended in Nanking, Tibet was still without any international contacts. During the thirty years between 1914 and 1949, it had failed to achieve even de facto independence from China. Even the British had not allowed it to have a representative based in Delhi or Gangtok. The thirteenth Dalai Lama, who had a modernizing tinge in him, remained fearful of opening up the country to foreign influences, and this was to prove its nemesis. The British, having successfully detached Tibet from China in Simla, were quite happy to make it dependent on themselves. They went on emphasizing Chinese suzerainty over Tibet until they passed it on to Independent India, which, too, insisted on maintaining the status quo, firstly in deference to the friendship with the Nationalists and then out of fear of communist China. If only Tibet had sought membership of the League of Nations at the end of First World War or of the UNO at the end of the Second, it would, perhaps, have escaped the fate it met with at the hands of the communists.

3

India and Communist China
The Beginnings

On 1 October 1949, China emerged from its past to the present under the Communist Party of China and declared the establishment of the People's Republic of China. Mao Zedong gloriously said in his inaugural speech:

> We have stood up. The Chinese have always been a great, courageous and industrious nation. It is only in modern times that they have fallen behind. And it was entirely due to oppression and exploitation by foreign imperialism and domestic reactionary governments. He said that the era when China could be insulted and humiliated, when its people were regarded as uncivilised, was now over. We shall emerge in the world as a nation with an advanced culture. And one with power: No imperialist will ever again be allowed to invade our land.[1]

Not much was known of China's communist leaders. They had worked under challenging conditions in remote areas. The world was mostly wedded to the Kuomintang, and the war, too, did not present the communists with an opportunity to attract much attention.

The leadership of the Indian National Congress, while spearheading India's freedom struggle, maintained relations with the Kuomintang. However, it did sympathize with the sacrifices of the communist leaders when they were engaged in the war against Japanese aggression before and during the Second World War. The Congress had even sent a medical unit to help them. No personal contacts, however, were established between the leaderships of the Chinese Communist Party and the Indian National Congress. Nehru, during his visit to China in 1939, had wanted to visit them but the war intervened and he had to return to India in a hurry.

As the civil war gained momentum and the communists scored many victories, Nehru asked the foreign secretary that while the question of recognition of the communist government awaited formation of their government, our ambassador in Nanking 'might keep up informal contacts' which would be useful for keeping abreast of the latest developments. Even at this early stage Nehru seemed sure that 'new China' was going to play 'an important part in South East Asia and to some extent in the world'.[2]

By June 1949, Nehru had come to the conclusion that:

> The Communist Government is the real government of China (and) it is in our interest to seek early opening to establish whatever relations are possible with that Government . . .[3]

The next day, on 4 June 1949, in his letter to the premiers of the Provincial Governments, he said, 'the Chinese revolution . . . is one of the biggest changes and upheavals in history and it is going to have far reaching consequences'.[4]

He asked the foreign secretary to keep a close watch on the developments and said that they would think of the policy in case anything happened.[5] Ignoring the apprehensions of the Indian representative in Lhasa, Richardson, Nehru opined that while Tibet should introduce social and economic reforms, we should be careful not to take any measure which might be construed as a challenge to the Communists and 'mean an invasion of *Tibetan sovereignty*'. He also rejected 'any chance of any danger to India arising from any possible change in Tibet' and ruled out any danger to India's security from the north or any need 'for our Defence Ministry or part of it to consider any possible military repercussions on the India-Tibet frontier'. He was afraid any such thinking would affect the 'balance we are trying to create in India. It may also not remain a secret and that would be unfortunate'.[6]

He rejected American overtures for joining the Manila Conference for an alliance against communism. He expressed 'considerable surprise' at the Communists' denunciation of India's so-called machinations in Tibet and being a party to the 'alleged Anglo-American plot for the annexation of Tibet'.[7]

As the People's Republic of China was proclaimed, India was anxious to recognize it as early as possible. Nehru wanted to recognize Communist China along with other Commonwealth nations which delayed his decision. He was, however, convinced that the Communists were 'well established, stable and likely to endure' on the mainland of China.[8] However, he had to reckon with the Americans who wanted him to delay the recognition. To pre-empt any early decision by India to recognize Communist China, the United States Secretary of State asked its mission in Delhi, among other things, if Delhi had 'obtained convincing evidence that their recognition will result in marked improvement of GOI ability to protect its interests'.[9] The embassy, after meeting Foreign Secretary Menon, replied, 'GoI feel recognition was something which was inevitable in the light of present trend of events in China.'[10]

A press note issued by the MEA on 13 October 1949 said that a request had been received from the People's Republic of China asking for recognition and it had been informed that their Ambassador in Nanking had been summoned to Delhi for consultations, and that, pending a formal decision, 'informal contacts would continue between the new Chinese Government and India's Consular Representative'.[10a]

On 4 November 1949, Home Minister Sardar Vallabhbhai Patel invited American *Charge d'affaires* Donovan for lunch to discuss the problems of recognition with him. He told Donovan that matters of foreign affairs were usually left to Nehru but he wanted to discuss the question of recognition with him. Donovan found Patel to be alert and the discussions were conducted in his 'usual blunt fashion'. He expressed concern over the situation in Tibet but did not elaborate further. His Secretary who was present remarked that the Chinese in Calcutta had always been a problem and they would serve as a convenient link with communist China for activities in India. Concluding the conversation, Patel said he felt there was no need for hurry in recognizing the communist government and asked Donovan to keep in touch with him regarding the problem of recognition. Other than that, he made no comments on the Indian policy, but Donovan felt assured 'he will weigh very carefully [the] effect recognition would have on Communist problem in India . . .Patel can be powerful factor in opposing the faction which desires prompt recognition of China'. Lest Donovan should misunderstand their meeting, Patel was at pains to assure him that 'there were no differences between the Prime Minister and himself and it was his job to keep order in the country'. Donovan in his comments felt that he had emphasized internal aspects of the problem (of recognition) as they might affect India, should it recognize Communist regime', and at the end cautioned the State Department that 'in view of extreme sensitivity' of his discussions, Patel felt this talk with the American diplomat should not be revealed to the British or the French.[11]

Meanwhile, Kavalam Madhava Panikkar, who was ambassador to the Nationalist Government in Nanking and had come to Delhi, invited Donovan for lunch on 6 November and told him that he thoroughly disliked communism and that he did not intend to press for immediate recognition of China by India. However, facts must be faced, he emphasized, and added that India's position with regard to a thousand-mile frontier with China was more pressing than the economic interests the British and the United States had, and communism was a greatly overrated menace. On Donovan's suggestion that unless there was perceived positive advantage that the new government would live up to its international obligations, Panikkar said he did not expect any particular friendship from the Communist government through the fact of recognition, but 'if diplomatic relations were established, countries so doing would be in a better position to protect their interests and might exert some modifying influence on Communist government whereas without recognition', Panikkar said, 'nothing can be achieved'. He expected relations with China, after recognition, to be on the basis of 'sound unfriendliness such as now exist between Britain and Russia where both recognize each other but both know that there is no danger of war'. Similarly, 'Communist government in China would attack GOI on radio and indulge in pin-pricks but both India and China know there is no danger of war, and nothing could be achieved'.[12] Separately, Bajpai told American Ambassador Henderson, who had returned to Delhi, that in recognizing China, the GoI was not undertaking to 'flirt' with Chinese communists or, for that matter, with Soviet or any other communists. The GoI fully recognized communist danger and had no illusions regarding existing tie-ups between Communist China and Communist Russia. The GoI, however, would be in an embarrassing position if Burma (present-day Myanmar) and other Asian powers should recognize Communist China while India held back. Furthermore, if the GoI should wait for the UK to recognize Communist China, 'it would be charged internally with following in UK's footsteps rather than having a foreign policy of its own'.[13] Finally, on 30 December 1949, India informed China of its decision to recognize it.[14]

Before doing so, Foreign Secretary Menon told Ambassador Henderson on 19 December that Nehru had requested him to express the hope that the US Government would not take it amiss such an early recognition on the part of the GoI. In view of its geographical position, he said, 'GOI felt it could not wait longer to establish relations with the regime controlling so close a neighbour.' The GoI hoped to use its relations to prevent Chinese communists from passing completely under Moscow's domination.[15]

China's response to India's decision to recognize it was quick and positive. Significantly, China's representative who delivered its message to the Indian *Charge d' affaires* A.K. Sen in Nanking made a reference to the 'Sino-Indian cultural relations from the long past and expressed the hope that China and India would work together for world peace'.[16] At China's request, Delhi asked Sen to conduct preliminary negotiations for the establishment of diplomatic relations.[17]

India accepted the pre-conditions for recognition prescribed by Beijing, which were:

The properties and assets of China in India would pass on to the new Chinese government;

GoI would not recognize the remnants of the Kuomintang reactionaries in India;

Expulsion of Nationalist China from the United Nations and support for Communist China's entry in the UN.[18]

India became the first non-communist Asian country to recognize the new regime.

On 20 May 1950, K.M. Panikkar presented his credentials to Mao Zedong in Beijing. Accepting the credentials, Mao said, 'India and China cannot afford to have war. We have too many important problems to think about,' and added, 'China had no aggressive intentions towards any body and least of all towards India.'[19] While some other countries also extended recognition, the endorsement of Washington, which was crucial, continued to be denied.

The Communist Government was radically different from all the previous governments. Panikkar described it thus:

With the establishment of the communist regime, there came into existence in China for the first time in history a strong unified central government having authority over the area of the Celestial Empire, from the borders of Siberia to Indo-China and from the Pacific to the Pamirs. In the old imperial times under the Hans, the Tangs, the Yuans, the Mings and the Manchus, no doubt the Empire had been united under a central authority, but the character of that authority, dependent on the mystique of a Son of Heaven with a divine mandate exercising his control through great viceroys, was different from the all-pervasiveness of the Central People's Government with the whole paraphernalia of rail and air communications, telegraphs and wireless and above all a powerful national army and an indoctrinated and disciplined party spread all over the country. This centralisation may or may not be a good thing, but it is a fact of supreme importance as it has converted what was an inchoate mass into a united nation, capable of organising and bringing into use the immense resources of China. By this process China had become in fact, what it had always claimed to be—a Great Power. It also insisted that it be recognised as such.[20]

The Indian National Congress (INC) and the Chinese Communist Party (CCP) had in their struggles followed different paths. The CCP's struggle was an armed one, while the INC had followed the path of peaceful satyagraha and had remained non-violent throughout the freedom movement. The Communists were pitted against a domestic entity, the Kuomintang, while the INC faced a powerful colonial power. The experiences of their struggling years had a great impact on their future strategy in facing both domestic and non-domestic issues. The new Chinese leaders were seasoned soldiers, Marshals and Generals. They were an impatient and a determined lot, anxious to get over the past and restore the glory of old China. The Indian leaders had no such pretensions. Their basic differences created misunderstandings when approaching issues that confronted them at the very beginning of their new careers in the government.

These differences apart, the leadership of India and China had come to power in their respective countries almost with equal advantages and disadvantages and practically at the same time. Both the countries were heirs to ancient civilizations. Both Mao and Nehru were unquestioned leaders of their respective parties. Both inherited underdeveloped economies and large populations. Their ideological predilections were nationalistic. Both sought to modernize their countries and revive the past glory and splendour of their countries. The task of nation-building was as difficult for one as for the other. They not only needed to modernize the administration and economies of their countries but also the mindset of their people, from feudal to modern and from congenital to scientific.

They differed from each other in many respects too. Mao was a Marxist, Nehru was a Fabian socialist. Nehru was urbane, Mao was not. Mao was self-educated, bred in Chinese classical literature, and had learnt his history and economics from Marxist and Leninist texts. He had no use for liberal ideas of individual liberty and democracy. Nehru, on the other hand, had a public school education in England, attended the University of Cambridge and had enriched himself with liberal and democratic ideas of his time. Nehru had widely travelled abroad, Mao had not. Nehru had the advantage of inheritance, Mao did not. While China's was a revolution and Mao came to power by winning a civil war against a regime established by law—a war that had lasted for more than two decades—India evolved from colonial suppression to independence which came by an act of British Parliament through transfer of power. Both wanted change: Nehru by consensus and democratic process, Mao by breaking from the past completely, anchoring his new administration and politics on the ideology of Communist Party, where the Party was supreme. Nehru did not attempt any such thing and continued to work with the same old system and the cranky and creaky machinery of governance and administration which had neither served the nation in the past nor in the years ahead. Even the new Constitution of India framed by the Constituent Assembly was modelled by and large on the Westminster model and the Government of India Act, 1935, with some provisions of the American Constitution added. In China, the Constitution followed the communist philosophy where Party had the supreme position, which Congress Party did not have in India. Every functionary of the Chinese government owed allegiance to the Communist Party. The Indian Constitution did not give any such position to the INC. Every citizen of India owes allegiance to the Constitution of India. While China is 'ruled by law', India is governed by 'rule of law'. Unlike the revolutionary outlook of the Chinese leadership, the INC leadership remained conservative in its thinking. Mao believed in the inevitability of war, Nehru abhorred it and sought to avoid it at any cost. Mao was the strategist who left the execution of his policies to his deputy Zhou Enlai; Nehru was not only a strategist but executed his policies too. As it happened, the two diametrically diverse personalities were left to engage themselves in the war of wits, which diplomacy is all about.

In the wake of Independence, India was split and a new country was created with the consent of contending parties. In the case of China, Formosa (Taiwan) broke away to set up a new country and became a rebel. The communist Chinese Government is sworn to bring it back to the 'motherland', while India is sworn to respect Pakistan's territorial integrity and sovereignty. In China, the PLA remained intact and became an important instrument to unite the country and carry forward the agenda of the PRC. It was on the shoulders of this army that communist China first captured power, then used it to 'liberate' Tibet and finally pushed back the mighty American army in Korea. The Communist leaders had little faith in the slow process of negotiations which necessarily meant compromise, which they detested. In India, the army like other assets and liabilities of undivided India was split between the two successor States. A part of the Indian Army was also demobilized since India did not expect to use it for settlement of any of its disputes with any country.

As pointed out earlier, India had welcomed communist victories as the harbinger of a new political, social and economic order in Asia. The Communist revolution was peasantry-led and had rural bias, which Nehru understood as part of the centuries-old dissatisfaction in Asia. His panacea was land reforms.[21]

During the civil war, not knowing which way the wind would finally blow, Nehru maintained Kuomintang's friendship while looking at the communist victories benignly. His instructions to the Indian delegation proceeding to take part in the United Nations General Assembly session in 1948 reflected his caution, which were contained in his note of 12 September 1948:

> In regard to China and the Far East, nothing much can be done except to maintain friendly relations. China is in a state of utmost turmoil. We should not attach ourselves too closely to any party in China so as to make the other party hostile to us. Naturally as a Government we incline towards the present Government of China . . . .[22]

Nehru, even when approached by Kuomintang leaders for mediation, did not feel inclined to involve himself since he felt time was not ripe for it. In declining to intervene, he was conscious that it would not yield results since the Communists were apparently not well-disposed to him and appealing to them would be 'discourteous'.[23] He felt it prudent to wait and watch the developments before taking any concrete steps towards the communists. He advised the ambassador to stay in informal contact with the communists without recognition or commitment.[24]

As an aside there was, at this stage, an interesting conversation between Ambassador Henderson, Prime Minister Nehru and Governor General Mountbatten. Henderson observed:

> During the last few days (both) were less concerned at Chinese developments. Both appeared confident of Communist victory in China but expressed the view that a Communist China would not necessarily be dominated by the Soviet Union. [The] Governor General went so far as to say that China under Communist control would probably be more Asiatic and anti-Western and might therefore be more cooperative with India than Kuomintang China, which had contrived 'to survive so long only because of its support from without.

Henderson, giving his impression of the conversation, told Washington:

> In general I find a certain smugness in Indian government circles regarding China. There is apparently feeling that China is destined to disappear for some time as a world force leaving India as the foremost Asiatic power, courted on one side by capitalistic powers of the West and on the other by Communist powers of Eastern Europe and Asia.[25]

India, however, remained cautious on some specific issues of concern to Asia. Cautiously, Nehru told the United Press of America that while Communist China's victory would have a 'considerable psychological effect in Southeast Asia, it was too early to predict any other impact of their victories generally'. He, however, maintained that it would be 'a very heavy factor in future Asian problems'.[26] As the communists scored more successes, he gave up his earlier view of mainland China splitting between the communists and the Kuomintang.[27] While generally blaming the communist movements, including the one in India, for subversive propaganda, Nehru told Sir Stafford Cripps in his letter of 18 December 1948 that for almost a year or so 'what was likely to happen' to the Kuomintang government had been evident'. He had a word of praise for the communists who, he said, had administered their areas better than the Kuomintang had done theirs. He felt in the communist hierarchy there were 'able men at the top and they had with some success adapted the communist theory to Chinese circumstances'.[28]

He observed that 'the Chinese never lose their essential characteristics and pattern of living and thought'. In the long run, he hoped, this Chinese pattern might maintain itself and a special Chinese type of communism might be evolved. His analysis of the situation convinced him that since China was in a state of acute 'disintegration' there was no danger of any aggression on its part in any neighbouring country for a considerable time to come. He, however, believed communist parties in other countries would be greatly encouraged by their success.[29]

In his letter on 1 April 1949 to the premiers, Nehru said that while 'the success of the Communist armies' would affect Asia and the world 'more and more', their success was of 'utmost importance' to India.[30]

Apprehensive of its impact on Indo-China and Siam (Thailand), he was particularly worried about Tibet where not only the society but the monastic order was also feudal and the people serfs, creating an explosive situation. He instructed the foreign secretary to keep in touch with their actions in Tibet. He, too, expressed his worry about Sinkiang, which bordered Kashmir and Afghanistan.[31] Responding to the Indian embassy in Nanking, Nehru denied the American ambassador's claim that 'Indian Government had promised to cooperate with the USA in China'.[31a]

The history of the Chinese Communist Party did not offer much comfort with regard to Tibet since even in 1922 at their second National Congress the communists had declared the liberation of Tibet, along with Mongolia and Sinkiang as their goal. Later, in 1949, Mao had said, 'Although Tibet's population is small its international position is extremely important and we must occupy it.'[32]

As communist China appeared entrenched in Beijing, it became imperative to understand the communist leadership better. Nehru himself admitted that he had never met them though had known them. Even his correspondence with them was limited. He groped in the dark about their leadership and their policies, and he kept guessing about their behaviour once they settled in Beijing. Yet he welcomed their victories. In his speech on India's third Independence Day, 15 August 1949, he said, 'In eastern Asia a great and ancient country is experiencing revolutionary changes of tremendous significance.'[32a]

His view of new China essentially evolved during the 1950s. He was appreciative of the fact that they did not rely on the Soviet Union and stood their own ground.[33]

Welcoming communist victories, he did not hide his worries about Tibet and impact on India's north-eastern borders. Expressing the need to improve and develop communication in the border areas,[34] he drew some policy guidelines:

> Our mission must continue in Lhasa;
> Maintain friendly relations with Tibet and give them such aid we have been giving them in the past;
> We should recommend to Tibet social and economic reforms;
> Avoid any action which may be considered challenge to Communists;
> No occupation of any part of Tibetan territory, which would itself be provocation to China.[35]

However, he remained confident that whatever be the final shape of China's policy in Tibet, there was 'no chance of any military danger to India arising from any possible change in Tibet'. He did not think it necessary 'at this stage for Defence Ministry to consider possible military repercussions on the India-Tibet frontier'. He feared any thought given to it 'will affect the balance we are trying to create in India. It may also not remain a secret and that would be unfortunate'.[36] He prudently tried to fasten India's linkages with the cis-Himalayan states of Nepal, Bhutan and Sikkim by renegotiating their earlier treaties signed with the British, since they constituted India's inner buffer where India could zealously defend its interests. These were mere declarations of intent, without the necessary muscles to back them.

On 7 September 1949, Panikkar had described the communists' attitude to India and the Asian countries as 'one of cautious watchfulness'. He said India's only interest in China was the development of sound neighbourly relations based on a policy of mutual toleration and non-interference in each other's affairs'. He advocated a policy of 'patience and caution'.[37] Where Tibet would fit in such a restricted brief the ambassador did not appear to worry about.

Americans had found Tibet's value strategically limited yet they found it useful as part of their Cold War diplomacy to embarrass the communists. It was apparent that the Americans found it was worthwhile to provide limited assistance to Tibetan freedom fighters, not because they cared about Tibetan independence but as part of their worldwide efforts to destabilize all communist governments.

On 24 September 1949, the commander-in-chief of the PLA, Zhu De, in a speech to the Chinese Peoples' Political Consultative Conference said:

> The Common Programme demanded waging of the revolutionary war to the very end and the liberation of all the territories of China including Formosa, the Pescadores, Hainan Island and Tibet.[38]

A day before the founding of the People's Republic of China, the Communist Party in its Common Minimum Programme had already announced the new task for the PLA—the liberation of Tibet.

The Tibetans, too, invited the communists' wrath by their reckless and suicidal step of expelling the Chinese Amban, even when he was an appointee of the Kuomintang Government, with his entourage and escort, from Lhasa just before the communists had settled down in Beijing. The Chinese condemned Tibetan action and held India complicit in their expulsion. It perhaps hastened the communists' determination to end the Tibetan anomaly. An editorial in the *Hsin Hwa Pao* on 2 September 1949 described it a plot 'undertaken by the local Tibetans, instigated by the British imperialists and their lackey, the Nehru's administration of India'. India denied any involvement and described the Chinese charge 'fantastic'.[39] A Peking Radio's statement insisted that India was part of the plot 'for the removal of Chinese mission in Lhasa'.[40] The *People's Daily* through an article by a Chinese Jurist rejected the Indian denial, challenged India's relationship with Bhutan and angrily commented:

> Suzerainty stands for the dark vassal system, the protective system and that is another name of foreign oppression, enslavement . . .The Nehru Government has no legal right to announce its protectorate over Bhutan. The United Nations should examine the matter . . .Nehru and Company are openly

engineering a cleavage between the different peoples in China undermining their unity, and interfering in their internal affairs by declaring in the name of foreign country that Tibet has now recognised Chinese suzerainty.[41]

In the article carried by the *People's Daily* under the title 'Hands off Tibet and Truth about Incident', the foreign secretary saw irredentist tendencies which *'the Chinese Government had always shown and which the new Chinese Government may be expected to prosecute, whenever they get an opportunity'.*[42]

The incident of the eviction of the Amban convinced the Communists that the foreign influences had penetrated Lhasa and unless Tibet was cleansed of them, China would continue to face similar humiliations. In the background of the anti-India propaganda that China had unleashed, it suspected none other than India as responsible for the unfortunate incident. India had to suffer the collateral damage. Mao was distressed at the continued Chinese weakness, which enabled the British in the past and now India under Nehru to humiliate China. He was determined to end this saga of humiliation. Foreign concessions had been put an end to during the war. It was now time to end the unequal treaties and to bring the outlying areas which, in the name of autonomy and under foreign influences had drifted apart, back within Chinese fold.

As the civil war progressed and complete victory of the Communist Party seemed almost certain, Nehru welcomed the communists and the revolution. He disregarded Panikkar's apprehensions that it could revive China's 'immediate claims against Nepal, Bhutan and Sikkim and also the denunciation of the McMahon Line'.[43] The political officer, too, apprehended it. Panikkar had pointed out that the 'idea prevalent among certain people (Nehru was one of them) that Tibet was a difficult country to invade was a myth since in the recent past; it had been crossed and invaded four times—by the Dogras, the Gurkhas, the British and the Chinese. He described as disastrous any idea of intervention in Tibet to save a monastic regime. Panikkar in conclusion recommended:

a solution of the Tibetan issue must therefore be sought through diplomatic negotiations and sooner we abandon such ideas as maintaining Tibet as a buffer state or political or military intervention or of thinking wishfully about effective resistance by the Tibetans, the better we shall be to deal with the issue on diplomatic level.[44]

The Foreign Secretary, commenting on Panikkar's observation, said that apart from various other problems, the most vital concern was to safeguard the borders with Tibet, which was not going to be easy since they rest on the 'Simla' which apart from China, the Tibetans, too, were hesitant to accept, particularly when they were asking for the return of Tawang. Foreign Secretary Menon noted:

> It is true that we are *not* now in a position to uphold, by force or by diplomacy Tibetan independence or even Tibetan autonomy, but it is no use blinking the fact that if we proceed to treat a Chinese invasion of Tibet 'as an internal affair' of China, we shall be executing a *volte face* and lending ourselves to the reproach that we have backed out of solemn engagements. Tibet will accuse us of a breach of faith and the unkind critics in the U.K. itself will not hesitate to say that we have let Tibet down.[45]

Secretary General Bajpai, commenting on the FS's note, said:

> We cannot and therefore should not expect to help the Tibetan Government militarily in order to pick a quarrel with and wage a war against the Communists. We cannot however, without the most careful consideration, give up the special relationship that we have with Tibet. My provisional view is that *this is one of the matters to be taken into account when we take up with the Communist regime the question of recognition.*[46]

Nehru saw these notes but made no comments. By doing so, he ignored the views of his Secretary General linking China's recognition with Tibetan status in some way. For Nehru, the recognition of communist China was independent of any other consideration. Since communists controlled the mainland of China, the recognition was inevitable and was not related to China's policies in any manner.[46a]

Even the British, long before they quit India, had started doubting the success of their policy in Tibet after the war and had been sure that China would assert its control on Tibet sometime. In their review it was said:

> Neither Britain nor India had any power to prevent a unilateral
> re-imposition of Chinese control over Tibet by force, and that
> their intervention in any form might provoke China to take action
> in Tibet, while in the absence of any foreign threat to China's
> authority in Tibet, Chinese might be content to allow Tibet its
> traditional autonomy.[47]

In the next two years that the British were in India, they allowed the status quo to prevail. They did not even strengthen their control in the area to the south of the McMahon Line, and the Tibetan administration was allowed to continue in Tawang. In this background of vacillation on the question of Tibetan independence versus autonomy, it was remembered that even the Kuomintang had not forsaken its claim over Tibet altogether and even at their Sixth Congress, held on 5 May 1945 at Chungking, it had called for Tibet's return to China.[48] Be as it may, it was clear that the British were convinced that China at some stage would try to bring back Tibet under its control.

Nehru publicly continued to welcome the communist revolution while harbouring reservations on its impact on Tibet and India's north-eastern frontier and other areas in the region where Tibetan culture, language and religion prevailed. Unlike many Westerners, Nehru, despite his apprehensions, viewed the establishment of the communist regime as a culminating act in a century-old process of revolution and a manifestation of Asia's political renaissance. The fact that it was led by the communists he did not mind. He believed, given its civilizational ethos, China was unlikely to succumb to Marxist dogma.[49]

After the establishment of the People's Republic of China, Zhou Enlai had emphasized to Panikkar the need for friendly relations among Asian countries in general and India, Nepal and Burma and Indonesia in particular, which would lead to a better understanding of the Chinese position in South East Asia. China was particularly keen to involve Nepal at the earliest in its policy calculations since, apart from India, Nepal was an important contiguous neighbour of Tibet.[49a] Nehru, however, thought it better that:

> In the first instance, conversation should take place between China and us regarding our interests in Tibet and common boundary between India and Tibet. If, as we hope, they progress smoothly and satisfactorily, Nepal can be brought in at the later stage . . . we are not aware of any boundary dispute, at least in recent times between Tibet and Nepal. [The] real purpose of suggestion to include Nepal in conversations is to prepare ground for early establishment of diplomatic relations between China and that country.[50]

Zhou while showing his anxiety to safeguard Indian interests in Tibet expressed the view that stabilization of the Tibetan frontier was a matter of common interest to India, Nepal and China, and it could best be achieved by discussions among the three countries. Given the unsettled political conditions in Nepal, Nehru feared various disgruntled elements there could try to 'play India and China against each other'.[51]

Whatever Delhi's perceptions about its relations with Beijing, Political Officer Hareshwar Dayal continued to be worried about the developments around Tibet. The fall of Chinghai on the borders of Tibet to the communists and the occupation of Sinkiang prompted the Political Officer to suggest an urgent consideration of the Indian policy both from the military and political angles. He, of course, ruled out use of force for Tibet's defence but in view of it being in imminent danger, he warned:

Occupation or the domination of Tibet by a potentially hostile and possibly aggressive Communist power should be a threat to the security of India. Apart from the opportunity that such proximity would afford communist infiltration into India it would encourage the Chinese Communists to press their country's long-standing claim to a large parts of the Assam Tribal areas and also perhaps to revive pretensions to suzerainty over Ladakh, Sikkim, Bhutan and Nepal.[52]

He pleaded that unless some military supplies were made to Tibet, it would be unable to defend itself and while this 'might not save Tibet, but it might gain time for India and would be proof of India's respect for her obligations'. He said the recognition of Communist regime was inevitable, therefore:

It would . . . be prudent to seek an early opportunity of explaining the GOI's views and commitments in regard to Tibet to the new Government of China . . .[53]

It was a very long letter from the Political Officer to bring home to Delhi the implications of China's occupation of Tibet even before India had recognized the new regime. He warned since the Indian mission in Lhasa had an informal existence, China could ask for its closure, besides one had to consider the risk it entailed to the life and property of the trade agencies and their personnel. Dayal had doubts that Tibet would be able to withstand the Chinese pressure, if China wanted to occupy it.[54] The suggestion to leverage recognition with the future of Tibet was unacceptable to Nehru, as he had already ignored a similar suggestion from Bajpai.

Dayal said while the Indian Mission in Lhasa existed by default, the Indian Trade Agencies had been set up with the consent of China and therefore:

In my view it would be justified to meet any military threat to these posts with force. Military operation in Tibet would necessarily be attended with great difficulties, but *there seems a reasonable chance that a foothold could be retained—at any rate in Chumbi Valley— even against a direct Communist attack.* The lack of such foothold would greatly complicate the task of guarding India's north-east frontier.[55]

Dayal's warning made little impression on Nehru. The suggestion to hold Chumbi Valley and leverage it for Tibet held some merit but was against his fundamental thinking and, therefore, unacceptable to him. He had already on 9 July 1949 said, 'I do not think that any question arises at present at least, of our occupying any part of Tibetan territory.'[56] He continued to believe India had nothing to worry from Chinese occupation of Tibet and said:

All the border countries are affected by these developments. India *is not directly affected in the sense of any military danger.*

He continued to repose faith in the inhospitable terrain and climate of Tibet, as well as the mountains that separate Tibet from India:

Our policy has been vague about Tibet. It has been inherited from the British days. We have recognised the autonomy of Tibet under some kind of vague suzerainty of China. Strictly speaking, in law, we cannot deny that suzerainty.[57]

The British policy, even if it was vague, was backed by their military strength and they had the ability and the will to enforce their writ and look after their interests. Admitting his inability to enforce the old policy, yet staying with it, he said:

We would like Tibet to be autonomous and to have direct dealings with us and we shall press for this. But it is clear that we cannot bring any effective pressure to change the course of events in Tibet.

He remained cautious about the steps that might be necessary and avoided those that might entangle India in enterprises which were beyond India's strength. 'One thing is clear,' he insisted,

> We shall not permit the slightest intervention, aggression or invasion of any Indian territory wherever it might be.[58]

These views contradicted the facts on the ground but continued to influence him. He had laid down his policy in a vacuum, ignoring China's determination and relying on factors which were no longer valid. As earlier stated, he would not consider it desirable to leverage China's recognition with Indian concerns in Tibet even if these had become necessary. On this, too, he dithered for lack of will to oppose China.

In the midst of these uncertainties, he decided to recognize the Communist Government in Beijing since as he said it had now come to stay and would endure.[58a]

On 17 December 1949, he told the Standing Committee of the Indian Legislature on Foreign Affairs that 'if the Chinese wished to enter Tibet there was no one to hold them back except perhaps the climate'. Climatic factor was an erroneous assumption, though he invoked it time and again to justify his inaction. Be as it may, his repeated assertions that the geography could hold the Chinese back was as wide off the mark as his assurance to the members that there was no danger 'to India of any sweeping down over the Himalayas'.[59] His assurance to the Tibetans that he intended to deal with them on the basis of the 1914 Simla Convention, too, lacked conviction.

In a policy review with the ministry's senior officials on 30 December 1949, the day India had decided to extend recognition to Communist China, Nehru, contrary to his earlier assumptions, suddenly discovered some weaknesses, and said:

1. Tibet, particularly in the military sphere, but also in diplomatic is weak;

2.   There was no international general recognition of Tibet's autonomy;

3.   China never accepted provisions of 1914 Convention;

4.   The GoI would let China know that they propose to abide by the 1914 Convention in their dealings with Tibet, which would depend on the state of relations between China and India;

5.   Tibet's request for arms be considered in accordance with the existing understanding with Tibet and perhaps give it a little more than had been customary, not giving the impression that the GoI was actively encouraging Tibet against China; and finally he said

6.   It should be made clear 'to all concerned that any threat to Nepal, Sikkim, Bhutan or the McMahon Line areas will be resisted with all our force.[60]

A strong policy statement of such a magnitude needed to be backed up by steps on the ground to make it credible, which were not considered then or later. It was true that the Indian Army had just disengaged from Kashmir campaigns after more than a year of fighting, and its limited military resources had not yet been replenished, and it was perhaps not considered prudent to take on the battle-hardened revolutionary army of China. But brave statements nevertheless continued to be made.

The Americans, on the other hand, were quite serious to help Tibet if China were to completely fall in the hands of the Communists. But Washington grasped the limitations of its policy in Tibet. In a memorandum of 12 April 1949, the State Department had little doubt that given Tibet's remoteness, and being only contiguous to India for the outside world, no help could be rendered to it without Indian cooperation, and India was certainly not ready for such a role. The Department argued that:

> By recognising Tibet as independent while we are not in a position to give Tibet necessary practical support, because of its remoteness,

we may, in fact, be pointing the way for Communist absorption of the area . . . (in view of this limitation) we should accordingly maintain friendly attitude towards Tibet in ways short of giving China cause for offence.[61]

Nehru had strong reservations to allow the use of Indian territory for an 'imperialist'-type action against China. He was a great proponent of Asian solidarity and to spearhead an imperialist plan of action from Indian soil, that too against an Asian country at the behest of the 'imperialists', was abomination to him. The attitude of India disappointed the Tibetans.

Despite Indian reluctance, the Americans, pestered by the Tibetans, went on giving hope to them but in view of Indian reluctance, the Americans had little choice. Days before India decided to recognize China, American Ambassador Henderson met Secretary General Bajpai in the MEA to sound him if India would be prepared to help out the Tibetans even at the United Nations. Bajpai stressed that the GoI position had remained unchanged and held on to the view that:

> If the GOI should press the Tibetan case just now in the UN, Communist China would be alienated to such an extent (that) GOI would lose all ameliorating influence in Peiping, re: Korea, and related problems. Therefore the Tibetan case would remain temporarily in abeyance.[62]

The Americans' anxiety to help Tibet was part of their hostile agenda against the communists and it took the form of imparting training in camps organized for Tibetan resistance against China in Colorado, USA. These trained people were air-dropped in Tibet from bases in East Pakistan. Later in 1959 when Nehru was disenchanted with China, he, too, joined in and Tibetans were provided training in the hill-forests of Uttar Pradesh (now Uttarakhand). Bruce Riedel, a Brookings scholar, in his book claimed that

Behind the scene Nehru was already thinking about a new strategy for dealing with China—providing aggressive support for the Tibetan resistance. (Krishna) Menon and (B.M.) Kaul . . . now urgently suggested the arming of Tibetan guerrillas to strike at the PLA's supply lines and depots in Tibet. A recently retired army officer Brig. Sujan Singh Uban was appointed for organising the campaign.[63]

However, in 1950, Nehru was in a different frame of mind. He remained against any kind of military action in favour of Tibet for safeguarding its autonomy or to defend its own rights in Tibet or for the security of its north-eastern frontiers.

There were too many contradictions in the policy that Nehru had enunciated. While apprehending no danger to the north-east from China, he still remained concerned for Sikkim and Bhutan which, he said, should be considered part of India 'from this point of view' but not Nepal. Nevertheless, he was concerned about what happened in Nepal internally or externally since 'any threat to Nepal ultimately becomes a threat to us'.[63a]

He was not against communism *per se* despite agreeing that they generally follow an agenda of violence. In India the communist activities in Telangana, in south India, were violent. West Bengal wanted to control communist activities by banning the Communist Party but he advised Dr B.C. Roy, the then Chief Minister, against the ban and said:

In the world today we have to face the dominance of the communist party or its associates over a vast area. The communist victories in China have made a tremendous difference to Asia and the world.[64]

However, in the Madras Presidency, the communist party was banned on 26 September 1949.[65]

Towards the end of 1949, as the Communists declared the People's Republic of China, the United States wanted to move a resolution in the UN on China in favour of Kuomintang. Delhi was of the opinion that it would not help the regime in any way except that it would add to ill-will and tension between the Soviet Union and the Western Powers. On 21 November 1949, India instructed its mission at the UN that it should 'avoid any speech or action that may be inconsistent with unavoidable recognition of new Chinese regime', when the Chinese Communist army was rapidly advancing towards Chungking.[66]

On 28 November 1949, HMG had informed the GoI that they had no ambitions in Tibet other than maintenance of friendly relations with the Tibetan government. Since China had already declared Tibet to be a part of China they would sooner or later assert suzerainty over Tibet and that the Tashi Lama (Panchen Lama), then living in exile in China, was likely to facilitate the Chinese in this task and he did.[67] Britain, however, offered help in the form of small arms to India in exchange for their supply to Tibet to enable it to offer some resistance to China, otherwise they were doomed.[68] This suggestion was welcomed by India.

In an audacious move, the Dalai Lama addressed a letter to Mao asking for an assurance that 'no Chinese troops would cross the Tibetan frontier', and added that Tibet would like to get into a discussion with the Chinese Government for the return of its territories annexed by China in the past, once the civil war ended.[69] Before the letter was sent out, Tibetans were advised against this adventitious attempt by Political Officer Dayal, since his advice had been sought. The Tibetans, too, had asked India to recognize its independence, which, they thought, would enable them to get similar declaration of its independence from the UK and the USA. Dayal, however, disabused them of this idea. The Tibetans were not happy and insisted on getting a direct answer to their request for recognition of Tibetan independence.[70]

As the above narrative would bear out, India viewed new China with apprehensions, yet it remained positive, notwithstanding Chinese Communist propaganda which, to start with, was hardly anything but friendly towards India. The Chinese Communist Party regularly portrayed Nehru as a British stooge and Mao personally encouraged the Communist Party of India (CPI) to throw off the yoke of imperialism. On 10 August 1949, the Indian embassy in Nanking reported that 'during April and May there was much propaganda in Chinese papers against Indian policy generally and against Prime Minister personally for alleged complicity in American policy in Asia'.[71] Yet the Prime Minister in his Independence Day (15 August 1949) speech, clearing the air, described the developments in China as 'revolutionary changes of tremendous significance', and said 'whatever our individual reaction, each country and each people should have the freedom to go the way they choose'.[72] These positive remarks of Nehru did not propitiate the Chinese and they continued with their rant against India. On 4 September, Delhi brought to the notice of the political officer in Sikkim the denouncement of the GoI by Peiping Radio for its alleged machinations in Tibet.[73] Interestingly and ironically, the Chinese perception of Indian interference in Tibet was based on an article in the Bombay-based weekly *Blitz* which was circulated by the Soviet news agency, TASS.[74] Nehru worried about the future of Tibet, where, he said, the government was 'feeble' and 'a lama hierarchy controls the whole country'; any Chinese attempt to occupy it could hardly be resisted and India may have 'the Chinese or Tibetan communists right up on our Assam, Bhutan, and Sikkim borders'. However, he added, 'that fact by itself does not frighten me'. He was worried more about its impact on the tribal areas along the border and, therefore, suggested to his Finance Minister John Matthai to rethink and restore the financial cuts made on the proposal of the Assam Government for improvement of communications in that area.[75] The *People's Daily* in an article under the heading 'Nehru Government cannot explain away the plot to annex Tibet' quoted a spokesman of 'the Nehru Government' that the 'Chinese Communist Party had no ground for accusing the British and American imperialists for plotting with their lackeys, the Indian Government to encroach on Tibet', and justified its criticism of India's announcement that 'Tibet had never recognized Chinese suzerainty'. Referring to another statement of the Indian spokesman that 'Bhutan had become a protectorate of India', it asked 'since Nehru Government has announced its suzerainty over Bhutan and declared that Tibet had never recognized Chinese suzerainty, will it now declare suzerainty over Tibet?' It further said, 'Suzerainty stands for the dark vassal state system, the protectorate system is another name of foreign oppression, enslavement . . .the Nehru Government has no legal right to announce its protectorate over Bhutan.' It stated that 'the United Nations should examine this matter'.[76]

On Nehru's return from the United States, the *New China Daily* described the hospitality extended to him in Washington as 'unusual' and said it was out of American desire to make him a 'thoroughly loyal servant of the United States imperialists' and a 'leader of anti-Communist and anti-national liberation movements of Asia'.[77]

Another daily, the *Ta Kung Pao*, on 26 October in an article titled 'The American Running Dog-Nehru' mentioned that Nehru was not only 'engaged in an attack on his own people but also in countering world anti-imperialists and democratic camp' and that he had fallen into the embrace of the United States imperialists and was willing to be the enemy of the people of the world'. On 3 November, the *New China Daily* said, 'Prime Minister Nehru who cherishes the hope of 'begging for huge U.S. aid . . . of being given the leadership of Asia' has been discussing with his 'U.S. masters' about the South East Asian situation arising out of the victory of the Chinese people. In the speeches, Nehru has expressed his loyalty to the US and has assumed that 'he must NOT and will NOT remain neutral in international affairs'.[78] There was no dearth of such uncharitable platitudes that the Chinese paid to him in this period.

India had only a year earlier taken a bold stand against the Dutch in relation to Indonesia and had organized a conference in New Delhi in favour of Indonesian independence. Organizing a similar international conference and or even marshalling international opinion in favour of Tibetan autonomy in the press would have possibly helped but it was neither considered nor tried.

In retrospect, one could say it would have little impact on new China, but that is a different matter. It would have at least been seen as an earnest step by India to help Tibet. It involved risk of antagonizing China at the very beginning. It was a risk worth taking. China's reaction would have helped Delhi to know where it stood in relation to Communist China and would have also helped to chisel its own policies accordingly and not be disappointed later.

The contrast between the Indian approach to new China and new China's to India was devastatingly clear. India, however, ignored and continued to plod along while single-mindedly pursuing a meek and docile approach to Communist China until it was too late.

4

The Tibet Conundrum

In the previous chapters we saw that historically Tibet was under China's sovereignty/suzerainty for almost two hundred years. The degree of China's hold depended on the equation between China and Tibet during various periods of history. Its representative in Lhasa, the Amban, was the agent of China's control. In the wake of the communist revolution he had been expelled from Lhasa by the Tibetan and the Chinese had not taken it kindly. Besides Tibet, they blamed India for his expulsion.

Burmese Prime Minister U Nu's letter dated 5 January 1950 stated that 'there was no immediate danger of any open war-like activities from China directed either towards Burma or any other adjacent territories'. This strengthened Nehru's own conviction that new China had no aggressive intentions towards its neighbours.[1] U Nu's remarks had no relevance to Tibet, which was far from his mind. That China had already on 1 January 1950 announced Tibet's liberation was ignored in Delhi.

Nehru had welcomed the emergence of New China as the harbinger of a new political, social, and economic order in Asia. Like Nehru, the foreign secretary and secretary general were not in favour of initiating a quarrel with China and waging 'a war against the Communists'. Notwithstanding China's declared objective of liberating Tibet, Nehru continued to insist that India could not sacrifice its special relations with Tibet without most careful consideration.[2] Tibet, however, as a buffer was ruled out, since it was not an independent country.

These remarks were not based on any in-depth study of the new Chinese leadership or how serious the Chinese were in their pronouncements. Nehru remained somehow convinced about the greatness of China and always referred to it as a great country.[2a]

When the Chinese threatened to liberate Tibet, India was in a dilemma regarding how it would react to it, particularly when the security of its north-eastern frontier was tied to it.

It may be recalled that in 1944, the British, while agreeing to make adjustments in the border involving Tawang, had assured Lhasa that India would maintain direct contacts with Tibet and would not agree to any arrangement that did not preserve the status quo between India and Tibet and also that the British would not enter into negotiations with China if Tibet was not in the loop.[3] Just a year before this, the Eden memorandum of 5 August 1943 addressed to the Chinese ambassador in London had established that British recognition of Chinese suzerainty was *conditional* on Chinese acceptance of Tibetan autonomy.[4]

But 1950 was neither 1943 nor 1944, and China was now under a revolutionary leadership which was neither weak nor meek. Independent India, too, had its compulsions with its own multitude of problems. Being committed to peace and harmony with its neighbours, newly independent India was neither willing nor able to take up the cudgels on Tibet's behalf as the British had done in the past.

In order to provide some help to Tibet so that it could face the Chinese on their own, the chief of general staff of the Indian Army decided to send a team of senior army officers to Gyantse to assess Tibet's requirements pertaining to military supplies and also draw up a scheme for the training of the Tibetan army at Gyantse by attaching Indian Army officers to the military escort there. It was also recommended that Lhasa be requested to prepare an airstrip at Gyantse besides making the road 'jeep-able' from Gangtok to Gyantse.[5]

On 28 November 1949 HMG had circulated a note to all Commonwealth Governments about its past and current thinking on Tibet. Principally, it laid stress on Tibetan autonomy under Chinese suzerainty and the fact that Britain now had only a friendly interest in Tibet and China was likely to use the Panchen Lama, living in exile in Beijing, as an excuse for Tibetan liberation.[6]

The Panchen Lama, as anticipated, in his congratulatory messages to Mao and Chu Teh wished an early liberation of Tibet. In their reply both assured him that 'the People's Government and the liberation army will satisfy the wish of the Tibetan people'.[7]

Delhi was not unaware of China's suspicions that India was acting as a 'Trojan Horse' for the UK and the USA.[8] Nehru's discussions with Foreign Secretary Menon, Ambassador Panikkar, and Political Officer Hareshwar Dayal resulted in acknowledgement of the fact that Tibet's autonomy lacked acceptance internationally and China's refusal to recognize the 1914 Convention was an impediment to India to bat on Tibet's behalf. He asked his officers to ensure that nothing was done to foster the Chinese accusation that India was acting as an instrument of the UK or the USA in Tibet. He repeated that the 'threat to Nepal, Sikkim, Bhutan, Ladakh and McMahon Line areas will be resisted with all our force'.[9] That there was a lack of military capability to actualize this determination was glossed over.

There was some scepticism when on 1 January 1950 China announced its plan to 'liberate' Tibet, since it was felt that China still had too many challenges to face. The Kuomintang in Formosa under US protection was one of them. Even on the mainland there were still some pockets of resistance, which were yet to be subdued and integrated. The internal administration was in complete disarray. The economic situation was not healthy either. Externally it was yet to be recognized by a large number of countries. America, while refusing

to recognize it, was actively hostile. There were indeed security
concerns among its smaller neighbours, despite what Burmese Prime
Minister Nu had said. China needed to establish its credentials as
a peace-loving nation to be beholden to its neighbours. Due to the
existence of these constraints, it was expected that they would leave
Tibet alone for some time or take over Tibet slowly by infiltration,
rather than by military means, unless Tibet asserted its independence,
in which case China would feel justified using military force. Tibet
was advised to avoid bellicose statement(s) or provocative action(s).[10]

Unfortunately for Tibet, these sympathetic forecasts proved
elusive. People making such forecasts had not bargained for the
communists' ingenuity and determination to meet formidable
challenges in pursuit of their agenda. The communist leaders were
hardcore soldiers and revolutionaries and the 'China' in them exuded
the old glory of the empire. They wanted to redeem the past glory
and were appalled at the miserable situation into which China had
fallen due to the shenanigans of the Europeans and the ineptness of
the Kuomintang who, after the revolution of 1911, had made peace
with the situation instead of fighting it out.

Nehru's hallucinations about India-China-Tibet relations were
unfathomable. On the one hand he was impressed with China's
greatness and on the other he was worried about its long-term
intentions both towards India and Tibet. He was reconciled to
China's takeover of Tibet but wanted it to be done peacefully by
negotiating with Lhasa. He knew China had never recognized the
Simla Convention yet he insisted that China recognized Tibetan
autonomy flowing from it. He knew China had never recognized the
McMahon Line yet he insisted that it was India's border and non-
negotiable. Dichotomously, Nehru saw in the Chinese revolution
the rise of Asia from the ashes of colonialism. He had welcomed the
new Chinese leadership as a messiah who would make China a great
country once again and help foster his dream of Asian solidarity.
He looked forward to working with them. Even before Indian
independence, as a member of the Viceroy's Executive Council

in-Charge of Foreign Department, he dreamt of closer relations between India and China and said:

> China that mighty country with a mighty past, our neighbour has been our friend through the ages and that friendship will endure and grow. We earnestly hope that her present troubles will end soon and a united and democratic China will emerge, playing a great part in the furtherance of world peace and progress.[11]

Whether it was ruled by Kuomintang or the communists did not make much difference to him.

To get communist China recognized internationally and to help restore to it, its rightful place in the United Nations, replacing the Kuomintang China, became Nehru's unsolicited priority concerns. In a letter addressed to the British Foreign Secretary Bevin, Nehru wrote that 'every effort should be made to ensure early entry of new China in the Security Council' replacing the Kuomintang.[12] Opposition from the United States not only to China's entry in the UN but its recognition was a formidable challenge. This was a dampener to Nehru's efforts since he found too many countries under US influence denying recognition to communist China. One of the weighty considerations against its entry in the Security Council was that China enjoying the right to veto, along with the Soviet Union, could paralyse the Council. Nehru did not give up. He was convinced that India was also well-qualified for a permanent seat in the UN Security Council, but also believed that even if India did not get it, India's overall influence within the United Nations would still be quite high. Nehru subsequently turned down opportunities to gain a permanent seat on the Security Council at the cost of communist China.[13] There were vague hints that the Americans would support India's candidature for the Security Council if it did not canvass for communist China, but Nehru had spurned such offers. Until recently there was little credible evidence to support this view. Recently in an article in the *Times of India* of 15 May 2019, a retired Foreign Service officer D.P. Srivastava, has drawn attention to a file in the MEA which confirmed the possibility of such a move in 1950. Even the Indian Ambassador in Washington, Vijayalakshmi Pandit, Nehru's sister, advised the State Department 'to go slow in the matter [of India replacing China in the admission to the Security Council] as it would not be received with any warmth in India'. Nehru agreed with her and said it would otherwise 'mean some kind of break between us and China'. The above article also drew attention to yet another proposal floated in 1955 that India be admitted to the Security Council and China be admitted just as a member in the UN. Nehru did not accept this proposal either. He said, 'India is not anxious to enter the Security Council at this stage, even though as a great country she ought to be there.' He therefore suggested that the first priority was for China 'to take her rightful place and then the question of India might be considered separately'.[14] It was perhaps his sense of morality that prevented him from accepting such offers.

Mao had underlined the importance of Tibet to China when he said 'although Tibet's population is small, its international position is extremely important and we must occupy it'.[14a] Mao described it as a strategic gateway leading to China's south-west with vast valuable natural resources. He was not unaware of its potential to fuel British and Americans ambitions. Its value as a strategic location abutting Xinjiang as well as the Qinghai, Sichuan, and Yunnan provinces was overwhelming. Mao was apprehensive that should it fall into the hands of foreign powers these regions of China proper would be put at risk. Hence the 'liberation' of Tibet had become necessary. Since China considered India as a proxy for the West, it could not be trusted either. Besides, India's position, with all its appurtenant facilities and privileges had become anachronistic for China. Tibet's attempt to send missions to the UK and the USA to seek their recognition, elicited a strong warning from China:

The fact that Tibet is Chinese territory is known to all the world and
has never been denied by anybody. Lhasa authorities have no right
to send any mission and to express its so-called 'independence'. . .
This has been stipulated in the Common Minimum Program of
the People's Political Consultative Council.

The statement concluded with a warning that 'any country receiving
such illegal mission will be regarded as cherishing enmity towards
the Chinese People's Republic'.[15] China too separately warned
Lhasa: 'If Tibetan authorities violate the will of the Tibetan people
and if they obey the orders of the imperialist aggressors and send
out illegal missions to engage in splitting and traitorous activities,
then the Central People's Government of China will not tolerate
such traitorous actions of the Lhasa authorities.' It also warned
'any country receiving any such illegal mission will be regarded as
harbouring hostile intentions towards the PRC'.[16]

This was the first such policy statement on Tibet coming
from China and this remained the Chinese position throughout
without any deviation. In the face of this warning and considering
the logistical problems, Delhi asked Mission Lhasa to advise
Tibet not to send out any such mission as they 'would be liable
to misunderstanding in other countries with possible adverse
repercussions on Tibetan interests'.[17]

Tibet had become the bugbear for India seeking friendly relations
with China. India remained anxious to protect its inherited facilities
and privileges in Tibet, even if these were gains of the imperialist
policies of the British, but was shy of any action which could be
a challenge to China. While welcoming new China, Nehru said
China had never accepted the provisions of the 1914 Convention
and added so far as the GoI was concerned they would make China
aware that India proposed to abide by the 1914 Convention in
their dealings with Tibet.[18] This was what the Chinese detested the
most and regarded as an imperialist desire of India to hold on to
the privileges which had grown out of unequal treaties imposed on

a weak China by foreign powers. Nehru remained worried about the reaction of the communists, since he remembered even the Kuomintang had not accepted the 1914 Convention and neither did it abide by the Convention in the past. Therefore, communist China's determination to bring back Tibet into its fold was only a continuation of the Kuomintang's policies.

When the new leadership of China emerged in the wake of the communist revolution, the Indian establishment made little effort to understand its ethos. Nehru expected them to be cognizant of his past sympathies for China and be reverential. On the contrary the new leaders felt indebted to none for their victories. For them India claiming its privileges in Tibet was no different from the British who had detached Tibet from China and had passed on their illegal gains to India while leaving India.

Foreign Secretary K.P.S. Menon had conveyed to the minister in the US embassy, Donovan, in Delhi on 9 January 1950, that the GoI had no intention of raising the question of the political status of Tibet with China nor did it desire to make an issue out of this question. The same was conveyed to the State Department by Ambassador Henderson. India would recognize Chinese suzerainty *provided* the Chinese recognized Tibetan autonomy. Menon indicated that should China refuse to recognize Tibetan autonomy, 'India would raise the question of Tibet's political status'.[19] Menon separately clarified to Henderson that India would not allow Delhi to be the venue for talks between the Tibetans and the foreign powers as the 'communist government would probably charge Delhi with becoming the centre of conspiracy to effect separation of Tibet from China and might speed up plans for conquest (of) Tibet'.[20] Peking Radio, perceiving that something was cooking between the Governments of US and India, accused them of conspiring an imperialist expansion into the territory that was under the authority of the Chinese Government.[21] It was proof of China's belief in India's malevolence against it, which Delhi ignored.

As Nehru saw trouble brewing in Tibet, he consulted the British Government. HMG, refusing to be drawn in an issue which had ceased to be their business, made it clear to Delhi that Tibet was now India's baby and it was for India to hold and nurse it. Nevertheless, it promised to support any action that India might take to assist Tibet in maintaining its autonomy but wished to discourage direct military intervention or the acceptance of Tibetan independence.[22]

The advice of HMG was in line with their assessment made in 1943 when they could see that their rule in India would not last too long. It felt desirable for Britain to slowly disengage with Tibet and leave it to the future GoI to take a stand on its relations with China.[23]

It may be recalled, a few months before demitting power, Britain had advised an independent India that while recognizing Tibetan autonomy, it should avoid 'any initiative which might bring India into conflict with China on this issue'.[24]

India was worried that its single-minded pursuit of getting China an entry in the UN and recognition was failing to find traction because of China's caustic policies towards Tibet. China did not even acknowledge India's unsolicited efforts made on its behalf on both counts. It also remained unconcerned about Indian sensitivities on issues of its concern. American hostility to the regime, though challenging and daunting, did not trouble China. They continued to challenge Formosa (now Taiwan which had come under American protection) periodically while never taking any particular action to support their threats. But Tibet was geographically not another Formosa. It was isolated from all sides except its southern flank. It found itself capable enough to brush aside Indian advocacy of Tibet. As the communists occupied Sinkiang and Inner Tibet by November 1949, it was believed that the next target would be Outer Tibet (Dalai Lama's Tibet).[25]

Tibet with no international recognition, not even among the Buddhist countries, found itself vulnerable to Chinese threats. For this situation of Tibet, the British must hold themselves fully responsible. Worried about their commercial interests in China, they remained apprehensive of China's adverse reaction and did not encourage Tibet to build even rudimentary relations outside the country.[26] In 1944 a proposal was mooted to have a Tibetan representative with the British GoI. The secretary of state for India recalled to the British Foreign Office in London that in 1943 a similar proposal had been considered and it was suggested that the proposed representative office need not be a diplomatic office, and could be located in Gangtok instead of Delhi.[27] London turned down the suggestion, since it was felt 'a forward move of this nature at present juncture would inevitably breed suspicion of HMG's motives and would call for explanations' from China. Since then no change took place in the British policy to keep Tibet isolated.[28]

Tibet in the past occasionally did resist China's influence, but never looked beyond its frontiers. The British with their limited interest in Tibet at Simla only monopolized its relations and used it as a buffer. Russia, sufficiently chastened after its defeat at the hands of Japan in 1905, and mired in its internal problems did not protest against Britain monopolising Tibet's foreign relations and arrogating to itself the right to conduct relations directly with Tibet to the exclusion of even China in violation of the 1907 Anglo-Russian Convention.

Even before the People's Republic was formally declared, Nehru was careful not to take any action which China might take amiss. Tibet became particularly worried and vulnerable after the communists occupied the neighbouring Changhai and Sinkiang provinces. As a pre-cautionary measure, a Tibetan representative met the US Charge d' affaires, Donovan, in Delhi and requested him for 'extensive aid of civil and military nature' to defend Tibetan independence. While conveying the Tibetan request to the State Department, Donovan added that after consulting the British High Commission in Delhi, the prevailing opinion in the GoI was that 'Tibet must be written off'. It was also stated that Panikkar on return from Nanking had told the GoI that 'Tibet was wide open from east and any effort to help it would merely involve India in conflict with Chinese Communists'.[29]

On 21 November 1949 Nehru told the Indian Mission at the UN, where the Tibetan appeal to the UN was likely to come up, 'that our primary aim is to avoid speech or action that may be inconsistent with unavoidable recognition of New Chinese regime, which, considering rapid advance of Communist armies on Chunking may become necessary soon'. It was further mentioned that 'we respect China's sovereignty and integrity' and 'it is for the Chinese people to decide what Government they shall have'.[30] These constraints of the Indian policy towards China were conveyed by the American embassy to the State Department on the same day.[31]

While the US was willing to do its bit, its hands were tied by the attitude of both the U.K. and India.[32] The US, however, was keen to render some concrete help to Tibet and hinted at this in its conversations with Delhi. On 1 March 1950 Secretary of State Dean Acheson had asked his Ambassador in Delhi that since Chinese occupation of Tibet would be a threat to the security of India and Nepal, 'it was desirable (that) India continue to bear primary responsibility for doing so within its capabilities, but should it be unable to do so (State) Department would appreciate being so informed'.[33] Implied in Acheson's message was that should it (India) need any help in this task, the United States would be prepared to provide it. Ambassador Henderson informed the State Department that India would be reluctant to collaborate with the US because '(1) GoI itself was providing what Tibetans wanted and could use; (2) political undesirability from GoI viewpoint in collaborating with U.S. in apparent joint program directed against Chinese Communists, and (3) U.S. has been unable to meet GoI's own requests for military assistance such as tank spare parts'.[34]

The British had strong doubts regarding Tibet's capacity to resist an organized communist invasion as the Tibetan army knew little or nothing of modern warfare. The British regarded military assistance more in the nature of a measure to raise Tibetan morale and assistance in combating infiltration and subversion than to engage China in a combat.[35]

For India's security, Nehru continued to put his faith in geography, climate, and mountains as possible hurdles in China's path to India. Expressing doubts regarding Tibet's future, he threw up his hands and said, 'none knows what will happen in Tibet'. He, however, ruled out any danger to Assam or Nepal.[36]

China, while threatening to liberate Tibet, offered it autonomy as available to other national minorities under its Common Minimum Programme. It was, however, not the same as understood in Tibet or in India as was available under the Simla Convention of 1914. Unilaterally committed to China's friendship, Nehru continued to be cautious. He was not in favour of doing anything which would give China any offence. He told the political officer on 9 January 1950:

> Nothing should be done which creates complications and which cannot be followed up later. Insistence on recognition to Tibetan independence is likely to affect Tibetan interests adversely and bring Tibet into direct collision with Communist Government of China. GoI do not propose to act as instrument of any anti-communist bloc in Tibet or elsewhere.[37]

Torn between China and Tibet, Nehru perhaps did not realize the contradictions in his policies, which neither helped Tibet nor made Delhi beholden to Beijing. Nehru's assurances to Tibet, which were never discussed with Beijing, did not carry much conviction in Lhasa either. When the political officer was asked to assure Lhasa that

> the GoI intend to continue their relations with Tibet as an autonomous State on the basis of 1914 Convention. It is clear that new Chinese Government will raise Tibetan question sooner or later and when they do, GoI will help Tibet diplomatically . . . But the effectiveness of their help will largely depend on maintenance of friendly relations between India and China. The GoI therefore consider that every effort should be made to avoid bellicose statements and actions. They would impress upon Tibetan Government need for extreme discretion and avoidance of provocation.[38]

The Tibetans were not assured and remained sceptical. They had a longer experience of interactions with China and were perhaps amused but certainly not convinced by Indian assurance since it sounded to them more like a *sermon*. They also found it neither unexpected nor surprising as it was characteristic of the 'non-violent spirit of India'.[39] The ministry of defence was asked to follow the above-stated policy in relation to Tibet.[40]

Tibet felt vulnerable and helpless. China, having warned other countries against interference in Tibet, felt free to integrate it. It kept a watch on the movements of the Tibetan representative Shakabpa who was camping in Delhi and waiting to head to Beijing to negotiate the terms of the new relationship between Lhasa and Beijing. They had found him lobbying for help, particularly from the US, and were suspicious of his intentions.

Delhi was reluctant to allow the Tibetan issue to derail its policy of friendship with China. It even advised Nepal to be extremely cautious in its desire to extend help to Tibet. The US embassy in Delhi reported to the State Department on 30 March 1950 that:

> It was evidently the view of the GoI that obvious and direct assistance by Nepal to Tibet whether under the Nepalese-Tibetan Treaty of 1856 or not, might provoke earlier Chinese Communist reactions. However, the Nepalese Government has received a couple of Tibetan officers in Kathmandu where they are understood to be serving in a liaison capacity with the Nepalese army.[41]

On 18 January 1950 China had convened a Forum on Tibetan Issue in Peking at which it reiterated its intention to 'liberate' Tibet.[42] Before taking any coercive action, China in the first instance sought to build pressure on Tibet. It asked Lhasa to send a mission to Beijing with full powers to negotiate the terms for its 'peaceful liberation'. As stated earlier, Shakabpa had arrived in Delhi in February on his way to Beijing. China, however, warned that Tibet was 'certain to be liberated in any event' despite 'geographical factors or British or American assistance'.[43] Simultaneously China moved its troops to Chinghai, Sinkiang and Yunnan, which were the areas bordering Tibet. By August the PLA had moved into positions all along the River Yangtze in Kham and into Nangchen and Jyekundo in Chinghai. They were thus spread all along the de facto political border of Tibet. The Chinese, to calm Tibet's nerves, assured it that when the job was completed they would leave Tibet for the Tibetans to manage their own affairs.[44]

It was clear to Tibet that its days as a separate entity from China were numbered. Lhasa conveyed its apprehension of a possible conflict with China to Delhi and requested supplies of arms and ammunition 'to keep them to a certain extent militarily . . . prepared'. India had already made some military supplies to Tibet for its small army. This request was for additional supplies.[45]

Political Officer Hareshwar Dayal, while endorsing Tibet's request, assured Delhi that there was no risk in doing so, since earlier supplies had attracted little attention from China and additional supplies could be explained as being necessary to meet Tibet's needs to maintain internal security and not for any aggressive purpose. Regarding training the Tibetan army, it had already been decided that it could be imparted in Gyantse by Indian military officers being attached to the military escort stationed there.[46] However, the events moved so rapidly that this possibility never materialized.

On May Day, 1950, Peking Radio once again reiterated that one of the tasks of the PLA was to liberate Tibet besides Taiwan. On 9 May, Sherab Gyatso, the vice chairman of the Chinghai People's Government in a message from Radio Sian addressed to the Dalai Lama warned that the PLA would soon set out to liberate Tibet. He invited Dalai Lama to send a delegation to Peking for the peaceful liberation of Tibet.[47] Four days later on 13 May, a week before Panikkar presented his credentials to Mao, China accused the Indian Government of being part of a 'reactionary clique' along with the American Government and 'conspiring an imperialist expansion into a territory under the authority of the Chinese Government—namely Province of Tibet'. Quoting a despatch from New Delhi, Peking Radio said according to an agreement between them 'the U.S. Government would send weapons such as rifles, machine guns and so forth to Calcutta and from there these weapons would be carried into Tibet over the mountain roads'.[48] These remarks were lost on Nehru when Mao Zedong made effusive remarks a week later, on 20 May when Panikkar presented his credentials.[49]

Shakabpa, who was camping in Delhi, was in a dilemma. The brief given to him regarding his dialogue with China was an impossible one—an assurance of Tibet's territorial integrity, non-interference in the succession arrangement of the Dalai Lama, an acknowledgement of Tibet's desire to remain independent, and no deployment of Chinese army in Tibet.[50]

Shakabpa's departure had been delayed because the British High Commission in India had denied him the visa for Hong Kong. It became a handy excuse for him since, expecting duress in Beijing, he was already reluctant to go ahead. He had requested Beijing for a change in venue to either Delhi or Hong Kong, but China remained adamant on Beijing.[51]

While being held up in India, Shakabpa kept himself busy meeting officials from the British and the American missions both in Delhi and Calcutta, hoping against hope for their support. He saw a ray of hope from the Americans. America was following its strategic policy of containing communism anywhere and everywhere in the world. It had become guardian of the so-called free world. In Europe it had created the Atlantic Alliance for the defence of Western Europe. In Asia it had started working to forge similar alliances, the South East Asia Treaty Organisation (SEATO) for the eastern region and for West Asia, the Central Treaty Organisation (CENTO). As pointed out earlier, the US was overanxious to get involved in Tibet and assist India if India decided to help Tibet. But India had refused to play ball. Not giving up, Washington told its embassy in Delhi on 22 July 1950 that military assistance to Tibet had been approved and was contingent upon Indian cooperation.[52] But Indian reluctance was not unknown to the US since Delhi was not keen to make India a base of American ideological and strategic interests against communism.

Already disappointed at India's 'unhelpful' attitude, Shakabpa told the American embassy officials ruefully that India 'seemed prepared to hand Tibet over to the Chinese'. He was consoled when told by the Americans that 'the recognition of Chinese "suzerainty" over Tibet by India or anyone else did not mean agreement to loss by Tibet of its autonomy and of Tibet being incorporated into a centralised Communist Chinese state'. But he insisted that without outside help Tibet could not be sure of its freedom.[53] In his next meeting on 14 August with Steere, of the American embassy, he was happy with the response which was quite encouraging. This time he was told:

> US had given aid to certain countries which were resisting Communist subversion and aggression. He said that Shakabpa's inquiry had been reported to Washington and that reply had now been received. *He was authorized to state that if Tibet intended to resist Communist aggression and needed help, US Government was prepared to assist in procuring material and would finance such aid. He added that US considered it important that prompt steps be taken now as it would be extremely difficult to make aid available in time if Tibet were to wait until invasion had started.*[54]

Shakabpa, worried about India's stance, told Steere that India might come to some understanding with the Chinese communists at Tibet's expense. But Steere told him that India did not want Chinese in Tibet right on the borders of India and would not go towards the communist camp. He reminded Shakabpa that India had recently given Tibet considerable military aid and that it would be difficult for the GoI to refuse Tibet additional aid or cooperation in securing foreign aid in the event of GoI not having additional (military) supplies to spare.

In promising American aid to Shakabpa, Steere laid down the procedural requirements that Tibet must follow. He said Tibetans should first ask India for additional aid and, if refused, they must ask the GoI to cooperate with them by permitting passage of such aid from abroad. This approach towards the GoI should be without any reference to the aid promised by the US. Shakabpa, unsure of Indian cooperation, offered to prepare landing fields at Lhasa, Gartok, or Chamdo if military supplies could be airlifted. But he got no encouragement from the Americans in this, since Americans were keen on Indian involvement, tacit or otherwise. Shakabpa also told the Americans that the Tibet National Assembly had decided that 'Tibet in no circumstances would agree to Chinese suzerainty'. He admitted that Tibet's tactics 'all along had been to play for time'. That was why he had wanted to go to Hong Kong. He said he had rather welcomed the British refusal of visa. He was now waiting for the Chinese communist ambassador to arrive in India, and he would endeavour to contact him. Shakabpa promised to get back to the Americans within fifteen days after consulting Lhasa.[55]

Shakabpa's admission was an indication of his tactics to stall his visit to Beijing where he was sure to meet tough demands that would be unacceptable to Lhasa. When Shakabpa returned to the embassy on 10 September, expressing his government's deep appreciation to the US Government for their offer of help with military supplies, he conveyed his Government's decision to approach the GoI only for their help 'to meet any Communist incursion with force'. He also said that another delegation was on its way to Delhi under the garb of a trade mission to conduct negotiations with Delhi for this purpose.[56]

When the American embassy received no further information from the Tibetans, an officer from the US embassy called on Foreign Secretary Menon, who categorically told him that Tibetans had never raised this question with the ministry. The Americans were disbelieving. The impression that the embassy got from the conversations with Menon, the British High Commissioner, and the Nepalese Ambassador was that:

The Tibetans have completely lost heart from attitude of Government of India encountered in New Delhi and that this attitude was largely responsible for fact that they failed to pursue the matter further either with Government of India or the United States. Nepalese Ambassador yesterday informed us that Government of India seemed to be 'washing its hands off Tibet' and said that Shakabpa had informed him that position of Tibet was hopeless unless aid could be obtained from Nepal or India. Nepalese Ambassador said that since India was doing nothing Nepal was also helpless.

Embassy can only assume in circumstances that question of military aid for Tibet is therefore dead, although Calcutta has been requested to endeavour to contact Tibetan delegation there, where they might feel freer talking about what happened in New Delhi.[57]

The Chinese, who had kept their antenna up, later were right in claiming that they had proof of the Tibetans trying to garner foreign military support.[58] Delhi was not aware of Shakabpa's activities in this regard, until Ambassador Henderson told Secretary General Bajpai of Shakabpa's contacts with the Americans. The ambassador told him that he (Shakabpa) had been promised military assistance if attacked by China, after clearance from Washington and subject to Tibetans' arranging transit through India of the aid material. Bajpai confessed that Delhi had no such information. Thanking Henderson for the information, he said he contemplated no action immediately unless the Tibetan government approached the GoI.[59] On 25 August Bajpai informed Ambassador Henderson that China had told Ambassador Panikkar:

It must maintain its sovereignty over Tibet; that it did not however wish to have armed conflict; that it therefore had instructed its Ambassador to India to enter into tentative conversation with Tibetan representative after his arrival in

Delhi with the understanding final conversation would take place in Peking".

Bajpai added, 'he was convinced from tenor of Panikkar's telegram that Peking did not contemplate at least in the immediate future dispatch of armed forces into Tibet'.[60]

Panikkar however was not too optimistic regarding the future of Tibet. He thought China would insist on a communist regime in Tibet and 'working with Peking would gradually make Tibet integral part of China'. Bajpai told Henderson that 'there was little India could do [to] assist Tibet'. He was of course worried that with this Chinese attitude the Tibetans might decide not to go to Beijing at all and 'then fat would be in fire'.[60a]

Shakabpa's mission, apprehending coercion and intimidation in Beijing, was still stuck in Delhi since February. He continued to lobby for a neutral venue, but China insisted on Beijing only. A meeting with the new Chinese Ambassador in New Delhi did not help. The ambassador however gave him an idea of what was in store there. Shakabpa was informed about the minimum which Tibetans must accept:

(i)   Tibet must be regarded as part of China;
(ii) China will be responsible for Tibet's defence; and
(iii) All trade and international relations with foreign countries will be handled by the PRC.[61]

Shakabpa now found it all the more difficult to pursue his mission in Beijing since there appeared to be no middle ground between the two positions. The Chinese had told Shakabpa that their embassy in Delhi would help in making arrangements for the mission's journey to Beijing, but after contacting the embassy once, he avoided it completely, fully aware that his mission would not be able to carry its brief in Beijing and might face coercion and duress. Shakabpa's contacts with the Americans were not unknown to the Chinese and they smelt Indian complicity.

With little help coming from any source, it had become clear to the Tibetans that the Chinese were out to grab its territory. Shakabpa went on dragging his feet in Delhi instead of making any earnest attempt to go to Beijing. Fearing intimidation, he continued making pleas for a neutral venue. The GoI had almost given up on Tibet but went on assuring Lhasa that it would stand by its claim to autonomy. Lhasa had lost all faith in the GoI's protestations. The US, too, had come to a dead end with India, and Britain, in any case, had little faith in the ability of the Tibetan army to put up a credible fight against the mighty PLA. The inevitable appeared inevitable.

5

The Chinese Occupation of Tibet

China was determined to 'liberate' Tibet. The question was whether it would occupy it by peaceful means or by use of force. The first approach was strongly urged by Nehru. China was indeed seen to be anxious to negotiate a suitable agreement with Tibet for which it had asked an empowered mission to be sent to Beijing. As seen in the previous chapter, Shakabpa, a senior official, had stopped in Delhi on his way to Beijing but he procrastinated and remained in Delhi, giving China enough reason to use force.

Ambassador Panikkar's assessment was not wide of the mark when he told Delhi that he was inclined to think that the 'Chinese were working in the first instance for peaceful liberation with show of military force, if this policy fails, they will certainly attack'.[1]

The Ministry of Defence on 12 June warned the MEA of the early possibility of Chinese invasion with 300,000 PLA men poised in Khotan under Chu Teh, the Chinese commander-in-chief. It predicted that the invasion would happen from Chamdo or Jyekundo since it was a shorter and less difficult route from these places and also because they were adjacent to Chinese-occupied eastern Tibet, with Lhasa being easily accessible from there.[2] And finally the Chinese did use this route.

Political Officer Hareshwar Dayal remained worried about the venue of the talks for negotiations between Tibet and China. He feared if these were held in Beijing then the Tibetans would be prisoners there and India a spectator, and the negotiations most unequal.[3] These were the fears harboured by Shakabpa too. India felt helpless. To India's disappointment, China mounted further pressure on Tibet by moving its troops, already in Tibet's vicinity, still closer to its borders and at the same time dangling the carrot of negotiations, which did not carry much conviction in Lhasa. Ambassador Panikkar once again reiterated that the Peking Government would first opt for peaceful methods to assert its authority and 'only if Lhasa authorities are recalcitrant will take military action'. He also warned that in the meantime the 'Governor of Sinning in Inner Tibet has now made definite offer of autonomy to Tibet with warning of military action in case Tibet does not agree, indicates completion of military preparations'.[4] This message sent by Panikkar and the one he wrote on 26 May gave sufficient warning to Delhi of the possibility of China using force should Lhasa fail to negotiate a settlement.

Delhi continued to be indulgent towards Shakabpa's dilatory tactics. There was an urgent need to mount pressure on him. He was camping in Delhi and did not seem to be in any hurry to proceed to Beijing. If he was being difficult, which he was, then one way to proceed would have been to warn Lhasa of the consequences of his failure to appear in Beijing. However, Delhi did not use either its mission in Lhasa or its political officer in Gangtok to warn Lhasa directly. Shakabpa kept Nehru in the dark about his contacts with the American embassy and of the help they promised him. He knew Nehru would not approve of it and, on the contrary, would be upset with him for talking to the Americans behind his back.

Delhi adamantly stuck to its position that 'an amicable solution of the Tibetan problem lies in firmly establishing friendship and understanding between Delhi and Beijing'. It believed that friendly relations would enable it to 'discuss the status of Tibet (with China), free from rancour and past encumbrances'. Delhi also rejected

Richardson's (its representative in Lhasa) suggestion for some publicity to the Chinese threat to Tibet.[5] Delhi discounted Chinese accusations that Tibet had been stalling negotiations 'on one excuse or another'. It asked the embassy in Beijing to inform the Chinese that the Tibetan mission's departure was delayed on account of a visa problem and insufficiency of travel documents and barring these issues it was ready to leave Delhi for Beijing.[6] In the same telegram, the MEA asked the embassy that since Richardson had discounted stories of Chinese military action in Tibet,

> it is not therefore necessary now to make any suggestion to the Chinese Government regarding desirability of settling Sino-Tibetan affairs by negotiations. If China had embarked on military action, such representation would have been desirable whatever the Chinese reaction.[7]

It was an erroneous reading of the situation that led Delhi to give greater credence to Richardson's assessment from Lhasa over that of the Ambassador sitting in Beijing or that of the Ministry of Defence which, too, had warned of a possible attack by the Chinese.

In the meantime, to propitiate Delhi, Zhou Enlai appreciated Nehru's efforts 'for limiting conflict in Korea and assured that China was 'determined to keep out of conflict giving only indirect support to North Korea and nothing short of direct threat to her territory will force China into action. Zhou had even suggested a joint declaration by four independent states—India, Burma, Indonesia and Pakistan—affirming the 'desirability of settling Korean issue by negotiations'.[8]

On 2 August, Panikkar had assured Delhi of China's desire to maintain 'friendliest relations with India'.[9] A week later, the ambassador still remained optimistic of China's friendly attitude towards Delhi.[10] As long as reports from Beijing remained optimistic about China's friendship, Delhi seemed to be happy despite China being silent on Delhi's concerns in Tibet.

China was pursuing a two-pronged policy—that of keeping the ambassador, and through him Delhi, assured of its friendship, while remaining indifferent to India's concerns in Tibet. Panikkar was, of course, unaware of what was happening in Tibet since the mission in Lhasa was not answerable to him but to the political officer in Gangtok, Dayal, both for administrative and political matters. The latter reported to Delhi, and had little contact with Beijing. The ambassador would remain oblivious of what was happening in Lhasa unless informed by Delhi.

Delhi came under intense pressure from Dayal since he could sense trouble in Tibet. He warned Delhi that Tibet losing its autonomy would hurt India's interests. He sardonically cautioned Delhi:

> Communist domination of Tibet would cause nervousness and unrest among border peoples along whole of India's northern frontier from Ladakh to Assam and policing of that frontier which has hitherto required negligible military effort and expenditure would assume immediate practical importance.[11]

Political Officer Dayal further mentioned that China's claim that it would free Tibet from the Anglo-American influence and leave the Tibetan autonomy undisturbed was clearly insincere. He added that 'the example of Eastern Europe makes it quite clear that establishment of communist autonomy meaningless'. Pointing to the reports of the Chinese troops concentrating on the Tibetan border, Dayal pleaded with Delhi to acknowledge that *India's interest in Tibetan autonomy was, essentially for its own security*.[12]

Gangtok's warning bells did ring in Delhi but mutely. It caused Nehru some concern as he cautioned Panikkar that the invasion of Tibet might well upset the present unstable equilibrium affecting some of India's border states, and added there was no foreign influence in Tibet. Moreover, Tibet was anxious to negotiate and, therefore, China should desist from invading Tibet.[13] The Chinese could not have been unaware that there was no physical presence of either the US or the UK in Lhasa, but in China's perception India still represented their (US and UK's) influence, much to the embarrassment of Nehru.[14] Nehru remained immune to any such understanding of India by China.

China was expecting Shakabpa's mission in Beijing. However, he had been camping in Delhi since February and was seen to be dragging his feet. It irked the Chinese who then blamed India for his failure to leave Delhi for Beijing. Their patience was running thin. The Chinese had other problems too, particularly security concerns in the wake of the Korean War and the American bombing in Manchuria. It was anxious to end the Tibetan obstinacy. Shakabpa had already met with the Chinese Ambassador, and Beijing continued to expect him there. Having failed to get any succour from the Chinese Ambassador, Shakabpa was torn between two extremes—Lhasa's insistence on independence and China insistence on controlling Tibet's foreign and defence policies, including its military forces.[15] Poor Shakabpa was in a quandary. He was aware that once in Beijing, his space for manoeuvring would shrink.

China had its own reasons for deciding to end the Tibetan uncertainty. Having repeatedly assured Delhi of its friendship, it had convinced itself that Delhi would acquiesce in its takeover of Tibet without much fuss. India's statement that 'they never had nor have now any political or territorial ambitions in Tibet' and its desire to stabilize the Chinese–India border were welcome to Beijing. China, too, made it clear that it would not discuss Tibet with any other country because it regarded Tibet as its internal problem. By the same token, China's insistence on negotiations with the Tibetan mission being held in Beijing and not in any foreign country left little space for Delhi to intervene.[16]

The conflict in Korea further complicated matters for Tibet. American involvement in Korea, for instance, moving its Seventh Fleet in the Taiwan Strait, inducting its army in South Korea to help push the advancing North Koreans out and then pursuing them beyond the borders of South and North Korea, the 38th parallel endangered China's security. China joined the Korean conundrum, and the subsequent American bombing of Manchuria created an explosive situation. Caught on more than one front simultaneously, China was getting impatient with Delhi. It felt India was not pushing Shakabpa enough to leave for Beijing and resented India's repeated advice to have a peaceful approach to Tibet. China's use of force under the circumstances appeared inevitable. To immobilize India, Zhou once again, for Delhi's benefit, told Panikkar that Tibet was its internal problem and it did not even have a semi-independent status.[17]

Panikkar saw a parallel in China's action in Tibet and India's police action in Hyderabad in 1948.[18] It may be recalled that India had used force against the recalcitrant Nizam to integrate Hyderabad with itself.

Nehru feared China's threats to Formosa could result 'in a major war, possibly a world war'. In his telegram to Panikkar, he said while India was working towards a friendly settlement, which would 'aim at autonomy of Tibet being recognized together with Chinese suzerainty', any invasion of Tibet would 'upset the present unstable equilibrium', affecting some of Indian border states. Worried about the larger question of 'preserving peace generally', it seemed to him that the 'path of wisdom for [the] Chinese Government is not to precipitate conflict' when the Tibetan Government was eager for a settlement. He felt if China delayed action it would lead to a 'much more enduring settlement with goodwill and redound to China's credit'. He left it to Panikkar to put forward these views, in whatever way he could, to the Chinese government.[19] Panikkar, after discussing Nehru's concerns with Zhou, received a blunt reply that Tibet was 'wholly its internal problem' and China did not recognize that 'Tibet enjoys anything like [a] semi-autonomous status'. Panikkar, to Nehru's annoyance, again reminded him that the Chinese approach to Tibet was 'very similar to our own attitude towards Hyderabad'. Nehru paid no heed to this. Panikkar, however, to propitiate Nehru, expressed his satisfaction that as a result of his efforts:

> They [the Chinese] will not now proceed to attack Tibet unless all efforts at peaceful settlement have been exhausted; and secondly they realise that India will not tolerate any kind of interference with her established boundaries.[20]

This assurance was more Panikkar's perception than an actual assurance from China. In fact, this perception appeared to be wide of the mark, considering Zhou's blunt rejection of any Indian *locus standi* in Tibet. Interestingly, Panikkar also said 'it will strengthen our influence greatly if even at this stage Americans withdrew their opposition to seating this (Chinese) Government in [the] Security Council'.[21] The reference to China's admission to the UN at this critical moment was quite irrelevant and one may question whether Panikkar mentioned this only to humour Nehru.

To Delhi, China's intentions remained ambiguous. China was anxious to end the uncertainty in Tibet and was in no mood to wait for Shakabpa indefinitely. China was well aware of Shakabpa's contacts with the Americans.[22] Had Shakabpa kept in touch with the Chinese Ambassador, his delay in departing for Beijing would have devolved on the latter. Later, when he returned to Tibet, Shakabpa blamed India for the delay in going to Beijing.[23] India felt it necessary to assure China that its intervention on behalf of Tibet was not motivated by its own interests and that it had 'no material or territorial ambitions in Tibet'. India also insisted that it did not wish to seek 'any novel privileged position for itself or its nationals in Tibet' but only looked for the continuance of India's rights, which had grown out of usage, and agreements, which were natural between neighbours with close cultural and commercial relations. It also asked China to 'recognise [the] boundary between India and Tibet which should remain inviolate'.[24] While communicating this message, Delhi sincerely hoped that:

> The forthcoming negotiations (between Lhasa and Beijing) will
> result in a harmonious adjustment of legitimate Tibetan claim to
> *autonomy* within the framework of *Chinese Sovereignty*.[25]

The use of phrase 'Chinese Sovereignty' was most unfortunate at this
juncture. It negated the very basis of Indian assurances to Tibet that
it intended to respect its autonomy under Chinese suzerainty. China
believed that India had finally recognized Tibet as part of China. The
Chinese in their note of 16 November reminded Delhi now that it
had recognized Chinese sovereignty over Tibet and

> when the Chinese Government actually exercised its sovereign
> rights and began to liberate the Tibetan people and drive out
> foreign forces and influences to ensure that the Tibetan people
> will be free from aggression and will realise regional autonomy
> and religious freedom, the Indian Government attempted to
> influence and obstruct the exercise of its sovereign rights in Tibet
> by the Chinese Government. This cannot but make the Chinese
> Government greatly surprised.[26]

It took two months and twenty-four days for Delhi to realize its
faux pas *and that too on receipt of the Chinese note.* It now asked
the ambassador to advise China that the use of '*sovereignty*' in
the 24 August note had been an 'oversight'.[27] On 20 November,
in a telegram to Panikkar Nehru mentioned that the question of
'sovereignty' or 'suzerainty' was rather academic.[28] Panikkar said that
his own discussions with the Chinese authorities based on the same
phraseology had helped China to justify its military action in Tibet.
Later, the Indian clarification on 'sovereignty' led China to attribute
the modification to outside influences. Panikkar now wondered
whether subsequent explanation would serve any purpose.[29] On 7
December 1950, Nehru in his speech in Parliament said that there
was a 'slight difference though not much' between 'sovereignty' and
'suzerainty'. He once again described the difference as 'academic' in

nature. Applying a strange logic, he said 'autonomy plus sovereignty leads to suzerainty'.[30] A few years later, at the time of the Tibetan revolt in 1959, Nehru agreed at a press conference that 'suzerainty is obviously less than sovereignty'.[31]

It has sometimes been said that in the note mentioned earlier Panikkar had changed 'suzerainty' to 'sovereignty'. This was not likely. In the telegram of 24 August,[32] sent from Delhi, the ambassador was asked to 'handover following *aide memoire* with appropriate oral explanation to [the] (Chinese) Foreign Minister'. This aide memoire received from Delhi indeed contained the word 'sovereignty'. In any communication coming from headquarters for delivery to the host government, ambassadors are not allowed to make any change. If an ambassador held a contrary opinion, he could write back to Delhi and seek instructions. In this case, one may assume that he had used his discretion to alter the telegram before presenting to the Chinese, then Delhi, when it realized its mistake, simply asked him to clarify to Beijing that the use of 'sovereignty' was a mistake, instead of reprimanding him since it was a big embarrassment. Either Delhi suffered from contradictions or it was a case of the ministry using loose language or it did not know what it was doing. It was an exhibition of India's casual approach to important issues.

This was not for the first time something like this had happened. It was a repeat performance of January 1949. It may be recalled on that occasion the Ministry of External Affairs had in its telegram to its embassy in Nanking said that 'we on our part will adhere steadfastly to our present policy of seeking to uphold Tibetan *independence* subject to the suzerainty of China'.[33] In this case, too, India took its own time to realize its use of loose language. It was only on 21 March 1949 that the ministry clarified that it was 'not to be taken to mean that GoI have changed their views in regard to status of Tibet and recognized Chinese suzerainty over Tibet unconditionally'. GoI's willingness to recognize Chinese suzerainty is dependent on Chinese government's willingness to give formal recognition to Tibetan autonomy and to agree on the frontier between Tibet and China.[34]

In diplomacy, where nuances and semantics matter so much, exercise of care in choosing words becomes critical. India continued to excel in making vague pronouncements. Yet again on 9 July 1949, the prime minister in his note on 'policy Towards Tibet', while cautioning that we should be very careful in taking any measure which might be considered a challenge to Chinese Communist Government, added 'or which might mean an invasion of Tibetan *"sovereignty"*, made the same mistake of using vague language.[35]

On 3 September, Panikkar had Zhou Enlai as his guest for dinner. The main subjects for discussion were China's apprehensions regarding Formosa and the Manchurian border incidents. On Tibet, Panikkar told Delhi that the Chinese were worried about the unruly tribes of Sinkiang and they had no intention of 'taking immediate military action against Tibet itself'.[36]

On 6 September, Shakabpa met Nehru. The latter advised him to settle for autonomy under Chinese suzerainty. Shakabpa hesitated. Nehru warned a crestfallen Shakabpa:

> Indian diplomatic support was available only for autonomy. [The] alternative was Chinese invasion. Tibetan[s] must make a choice between war and peaceful settlement.[37]

While advising Shakabpa to accept autonomy, Nehru could not assure him that Chinese autonomy was the same as it enjoyed hitherto. In his meeting, Shakabpa did not tell Nehru of his contacts with the American embassy, nor did he mention that he had been promised help by the Americans in resisting Chinese occupation.

While these developments were taking place, Nehru continued with his efforts to have China admitted to the UN. He was, however, disappointed because yet another attempt had failed. He described the American opposition to China's entry as 'misconceived and wrong', and told Zhou that 'India's firm attitude and [the] fact that in this matter other countries of Asia fully agreed with India, has had powerful effect on the USA, the UK, and other European countries'.

Trying to strike a sympathetic chord with Zhou, Nehru added that the restraint and patience China had shown in this matter 'had added greatly to your Government's prestige in the world'.[38] One wondered if Zhou felt obliged at all! He did not even acknowledge Nehru's message. Meanwhile, in making his report to the National Committee, Zhou re-emphasized China's

> willingness to undertake peace negotiations to bring about this— liberation of the Tibetan people. The patriots in Tibet have expressly welcomed this idea. We hope that the local authorities in Tibet will NOT hesitate in bringing about a peaceful solution to the question.

The most important part of his report was about Korea. He said:

> [The] Chinese people absolutely will not tolerate foreign aggressor nor will they SUPINELY [emphasis as in original] tolerate seeing their neighbour being SAVAGELY [emphasis as in original] invaded by imperialists . . .There is no doubt that China views international situation as menacing her security and independence and will fight if American forces try to occupy Korean territory.[39]

It was a clear enunciation of the Chinese policy on the country's security, faced with the presence of American forces camping on the banks of the Yalu River. China was determined to face the situation squarely.

In the meantime, Nehru's disappointment with China had turned into remorse, which he shared with Panikkar:

> Zhou Enlai and his colleagues should be aware of our friendly feelings towards China and our continued efforts as regards her entry into United Nations . . . we have done this not for any political or economic advantage to ourselves, but out of genuine friendship for a *great neighbour whose cooperation in the cause of world peace and enhancement of Asian weight and dignity in international councils, we*

value and consider necessary. In adopting this attitude we have often displeased many of the western powers but we have followed our own independent line because we considered it right.

Even as regards Tibet, we have sought no special or economic advantages for ourselves; we have merely asked for continuation of such relations that have been built up between Tibet and us owing to geographical contiguity and cultural and economic links. All that we have suggested for Tibet is autonomy within the framework of Chinese *sovereignty*, to be attained by peaceful negotiations.[40]

This was sheer self-delusion because China never explicitly requested India to undertake this mission on its behalf. Once again, the use of *sovereignty* indicated a confusion that prevailed in Nehru's mind. It was a different matter that this time the note was meant for Panikkar only. However, it is important to note that once a term is used by the prime minister, others follow it routinely. This is how bureaucracy works. Hence the need to focus on the correct and appropriate use of language at all levels.

The political officer, unaware of Nehru's disenchantment with China, suggested that if China used force against Tibet and the matter came to the UN, India would have no option but to join in condemnation of the new China. Therefore, he mentioned, that India should:

Not only advise [the] Chinese to proceed peacefully but should let them know in most friendly terms that we are interested both in the manner in which their negotiations with the Tibetans are being conducted and their outcome. If the Chinese value our friendship it is reasonable to expect them to heed our representations.[41]

Meanwhile, a day earlier, the Indian Mission in Lhasa in a panic-stricken message had already reported that the Tibetan government had received reports from the border of a clash with the Chinese at Chamdo. The Chinese were upset that Shakabpa had not reached Beijing for negotiations. After arresting the governor of the Kham province, Ngabo Ngawang Jigme, had asked Lhasa for another mission to be sent to Eastern Tibet for conducting peaceful negotiations at the border failing which Tibetans were asked 'to prepare for the worst'.[42]

The next day China decided to send a direct and stern message to Delhi to keep its hands off Tibet. The Chinese ambassador called on the foreign secretary K.P.S. Menon and said:

> Tibet was a part of Chinese territory and the problem of Tibet was . . . [China's] internal problem. It was the intention of the PLA to enter Tibet and to defend China's clearly defined boundaries . . .The Chinese Government has ordered the PLA to move towards Chengtu in the western part of Sinkiang province because of Tibetan failure [to send a negotiating mission]. In view of the friendly relations between China and India, the Minister for Foreign Affairs said, the Central People's Government desired to see the Tibetan problem settled in a peaceful way . . .[43]

He added that the Chinese government had ordered the PLA to move in Tibet since the Tibetan mission had deliberately delayed its departure from India. The foreign secretary reminded the ambassador of India's efforts for China's admission to the UN and its feelings of friendship towards China but it cut little ice. The ambassador insisted that if the Tibetan mission reached Beijing forthwith, there was still scope for negotiations since the Chinese army was 'at some distance from the borders of Tibet'. The statement lacked even a modicum of courtesy.[44] Panikkar had already warned Delhi of China's fear of an imminent 'aggression in Taiwan' by the US and the prospect of a war between the United States and China, with the latter possibly invoking the Sino-Soviet Treaty to claim Soviet's help. Girija Shankar Bajpai, the secretary general in the MEA, spoke to the American ambassador Henderson briefing him of Panikkar's assessment and asked him 'to issue some statement to cool the atmosphere between the Chinese and the Americans'.[45]

As the reports of Chinese invasion of Tibet gained currency, the US ambassador met Bajpai to seek confirmation, and was told that a strong message had been sent to Panikkar asking for confirmation. But if the reports were true, Bajpai told Henderson in great confidence that he had sent a note to the prime minister in which he had suggested with considerable heat that:

> If it were true that China should now invade Tibet, it should be regarded as sign of indifference of Indian sensibilities and lack of appreciation of India's efforts on China's behalf. After India had aroused irritation in U.S. and other countries by supporting China with regard to Formosa, Korea and entrance into [the] UN, and after it had conveyed to world China's insistence that China would intervene in Korea in case US forces should enter North Korea it would be ironical if China instead of intervening in Korea should now invade Tibet.

Henderson in his telegram to the secretary of state, while conveying the above, cautioned the State Department against any leak since that would cause grave embarrassment.[46]

The press reports were replete with news about Chinese invasion of Tibet. The Soviet paper *Pravda* had quoted Zhou on 1 October saying that 'China was fully determined to liberate the people of Tibet'. When the *Times of India* on 2 October and the *New China News Agency* on 7 October reported that the PLA had 'liberated Xinjiang and Tibet', the GoI was still awaiting confirmation from the ambassador in Beijing.

Paripassu with developments in Tibet, Lhasa had reported to Delhi that Chinese troops had crossed the Yangtze at a ferry near Changra within China; and there was a strong concentration of Chinese troops in Jyekundo in Chinghai province in eastern Tibet which is Chinese territory, aiming at Chamdo in Tibet, which, according to the ambassador, was already occupied by the Chinese.[46a] In Korea, on 20 October, the Chinese had already crossed the Yalu River to meet the American forces. Disappointed by the Chinese action, the foreign secretary informed Panikkar of his discussions with the Chinese ambassador in Delhi on 17 October (referred to earlier) and asked him to urgently convey to the Chinese government that if their invasion of Tibet continued, *'in these circumstances it would be difficult for us to continue with [the] efforts that we have been making for the past many months to secure recognition of China by other nations'.*[47] Since India's actions in this regard were unsolicited, the Chinese were not even bothered. China never acknowledged India's efforts in this direction.

Two days later, on 19 October, the prime minister once again flogged the failed argument that 'any invasion of Tibet would have serious consequences in regard to their position in the UN and strengthen the hands of [the] enemies of China and weaken those who were supporting China's cause.[48] China remained smug—'Tibet's Liberation' was a priority, while the admission to the UN could wait. Delhi refused to understand this clear message from Beijing.

In Beijing, Panikkar's perception of the dangers being faced by China from various directions, for instance, in Korea and/or Taiwan Straits, were not shared by Delhi. Bajpai believed China's apprehensions were 'utterly devoid of foundation and cannot in our view be justified for military action there (against Tibet)'.[49] Under pressure from Delhi, Panikkar on 25 October once again told Weichiaopu (the Chinese foreign office) that while the Tibetan mission was expected shortly in Beijing, it should halt further advance of its troops. It appeared by now Delhi had lost confidence in its ambassador. Commenting on this, *de'marche* Foreign Secretary Menon expressed his displeasure and noted that:

While we have been expressing our grave concern on Chinese invasion, the *Ambassador did not appear to have conveyed our sentiments with anything like the force with which we expected him to do so. He* does not appear to have realised that not merely India's honour but her interests are involved in the satisfactory settlement of the Tibetan problem. The McMahon Line, our trade marts in Gyantse and Yatung and our

representation in Lhasa all these will now be in jeopardy and more
than these, the interests of world peace will be retarded.[50]

Bajpai, not to be left behind, in his note dated 27 October 1950
took a swipe as well and described the Ambassador's note as being
'lamentably weak' and not conforming to the spirit of the PM's
telegram. Bajpai noted:

> The ambassador for some inexplicable reason, seems to persist in
> his erroneous conceptacle of Chinese claim and Chinese maps.
> Even in his note, he expresses the 'earnest hope that further military
> action will not be necessary', conceding by implication that such
> military action as may have been taken already was necessary.[51]

An upset prime minister told Panikkar that he was at a loss to
understand how China's security could be threatened along the
Tibetan borders. He thought that whatever the situation and reason
for attack, they were 'devoid of foundation'.[52]

On 25 October, Panikkar informed Delhi that he had told
Weichiaopu that the Tibetan delegation had received instructions to
proceed to Beijing' and would arrive soon. Nehru, disagreeing with
Panikkar on China's justification for its attack on Tibet, discounted
China's fear of being attacked by the Americans, and was convinced
that if China thought India was intriguing against them, then they
(Chinese) were 'less intelligent than I (had) thought them to be'.[53]
Despite these unsavoury developments, Nehru was worried for the
future of India's relations with China and said: 'There can be no doubt
that the future of Asia and to some extent some other parts of the world
also depends upon this relationship.'[53a] However, when all reports
pointed to China's invasion of Tibet, he said, 'China's attitude to Tibet
again becomes more and more incomprehensible to me.' One lost the
number of times Nehru recounted his efforts to get China admitted
to the UN. Yet again he expressed his worry that China's actions were
creating a 'good deal of prejudice against China', thus 'putting an end
to our efforts' at the UN. Talking about India's interest in Tibet, he

insisted that the McMahon Line must stay as it was and that India recognized Tibetan autonomy under Chinese suzerainty, and there was no Chinese interference with the Indian representative and trade agencies in Tibet.[54] These observations were directed at the ambassador and at no time were meant to be conveyed to China formally. China's repeated warnings to India that Tibet was its internal problem and asking India to have its hands off Tibet were perhaps lost on Delhi.

It was clear that the MEA and its ambassador were not walking in tandem. While the ambassador was apprehensive of China's perception of dangers from various directions, Delhi remained focused on Tibet alone. On 26 October, Nehru was perturbed about the Chinese attacking Tibet and asked Panikkar yet again to remind the Chinese foreign minister of his promises to resolve the problem with Tibet peacefully. However, with the Chinese invasion, Tibet would be right to conclude 'that negotiations will be under duress'.[55] Panikkar still rightly persisted with his earlier stand that the Chinese feared attack from the US in Manchuria and, moreover, the Korean developments had worried China and it decided to get Tibet out of the way at the earliest.[56] Obviously Panikkar's word had ceased to have currency in Delhi.

Meanwhile, Shakabpa told the US embassy on 25 October that he had received instructions from Lhasa to proceed to Beijing immediately and he was preparing to leave. Press reports indicated that the problem of the Hong Kong visa had been sorted out.[57] However, soon after China launched its attack on Tibet, Delhi advised Lhasa to stop Shakabpa from proceeding to Beijing since the discussions would not be free from pressure.[58] Lhasa agreed with Delhi's advice and asked Shakabpa not to proceed.[59]

On 30 October, Secretary General Bajpai told US ambassador Henderson that he had drafted a strongly worded note for delivery to the Chinese Foreign Office, which he subsequently read out to Henderson. The note accused China of 'acting with certain amount of deceit'. The note further dismissed Chinese fears that 'an un-liberated Tibet presented danger to Communist Chinese security in view of ambitions of great powers in that region'. When Henderson asked how could the US help India, Bajpai said:

For the time being it would be preferable for U.S. to take no action which might give Communist China excuse to renew its charges that great powers were unduly interested in Tibet or which might make it appear to Indian leaders that U.S. was endeavouring to use Peiping [Peking] offensive in Tibet in order create rift between Communist China and India. If rift should come, he pointed out, it should clearly come through force of events and not with help of outside powers.[60]

In the Chinese invasion of Tibet, the US sensed an opportunity, and yet again offered India help in combating China. On 27 October, Secretary of State Acheson in a top-secret telegram to Henderson pointed to the threat to India's security posed by China. Considering the fact that Tibetans looked up to India for help and support in maintaining traditional autonomy, which India was only capable of rendering, Acheson advised Henderson to speak to Nehru and convey that in view of these developments and also in Korea and Indo-China, Delhi, at a bare minimum, needed to 'reassess its views regarding character of Peiping regime'. While Acheson advised it was for Delhi to take its decision but 'if it decided to act, we shall do what we can to help'.[61]

Henderson discussed Acheson's message both with Bajpai and Nehru. Bajpai told Henderson 'in utmost confidence [that] he personally had almost arrived at the opinion that Peiping was [a] mere puppet of Moscow and represented grave danger (to) Asian peace'. He also told Henderson that he was preparing instructions for Panikkar to convey that India had decided to stay put in Tibet and should China ask India out of Tibet, he was sure 'it would eventually be [a] breach which could not so easily be closed'.[62] On the same day, Henderson had sent another telegram to Washington conveying what Bajpai had said in a strongly worded note to Beijing, pointing out that China had acted 'with certain amount of deceit' ignoring the Indian feelings and friendly suggestions and at a time the Tibetan Mission was about to start for Beijing.

It described Chinese action as one that was against world peace, dismissing Chinese justification that its action was to thwart dangers to Chinese security emanating from 'ambitions of great powers in the region'.[62a] When Henderson called on Nehru on 2 November, the prime minister admitted he had been disappointed with Beijing, but insisted that *friendly relations with China were in the interest of peace in Asia and world.* He, of course, added that if the present friction with Beijing persisted, it 'might result in considerable friction in future'. He did not consider it wise to say anything 'which might be construed as an attempt to drive any deeper wedge between India and China'. When Henderson asked Nehru how the United States could help in the present situation, Nehru replied '*US can be most helpful by doing nothing*'. Acheson's efforts to take advantage of India's problems with China over Tibet, and involve it in a confrontation with China did not bear fruit.[63] The Americans were once again disappointed with India. Nehru could see the American desperation to open a front against China in Tibet to relieve the pressure in Korea.

On 26 October, in the absence of the Chinese ambassador from Delhi, the foreign secretary called in the Chinese counsellor Shen Chien, and referred to him the reports of China's invasion of Tibet. The foreign secretary said that India had expected the Chinese embassy to show the courtesy of informing the GoI of its decision. It flogged the same old argument that China's actions had caused a setback to India's efforts for China's entry in the UN, and so on. This had no impact on Shen, who only responded to say that since the Chinese Government regarded Tibet to be a part of China, the foreign secretary's description of it being an invasion was erroneous.[64]

Panikkar persisted that China's decision to launch its attack on Tibet was prompted by a 'firm conviction that war will be forced on China'. Bombing in Manchuria by the US, the war in Korea and the extension of war towards the north-eastern part of China were factors responsible for China's decision. 'PERCIPITANCY [emphasis as in original] of action in Tibet is linked . . . with the possibility they foresee of a general war in which they fear that unfriendly countries may stir up trouble in that area'.[65]

Addressing a press conference on 27 October, Nehru still maintained that China's real intentions were not clear. He explained it on account of the US hostility towards Beijing, America's continued support of Formosa (Taiwan) and their crossing the 38 parallel in Korea. He added that while Moscow might not have dictated Chinese policy, it certainly influenced it. He discounted that there would be *any impact of Chinese action on Ladakh*.[66] Informing some of the Indian missions abroad, Delhi tried to tone down the impact of the Chinese invasion, suggesting that 'Chinese *incursions* occurred mostly in the disputed territories on the eastern border of Tibet'.[67]

On 27 October, Lhasa reported the situation was grim in the face of Chinese advance at several places. To give publicity to the Chinese invasion, Tibet decided to appeal to the UN, but India conveyed to Lhasa its 'hesitation' to sponsor its appeal'. Tibetans were shocked to hear All India Radio (AIR) denying reports of a Chinese invasion even when Beijing Radio was loudly blaring forth that their armies had been ordered into Tibet. Another AIR broadcast on 25 October quoted the spokesman of the MEA as saying that the Chinese would find it 'INSUPERABLE [emphasis as in the original] to negotiate mountains of Eastern Tibet in mid-winter' because of the extreme climate.[68] From Lhasa, Sumal Sinha, the mission-in-charge, in his message of 27 October was critical of the recent policies of Delhi towards China and said:

> Chinese action against Tibet when negotiations were in progress and when the Chinese had assured GoI of their desire to seek amicable settlement,[is] extremely reprehensible and hardly distinguishable from imperialism. The present crisis in Tibet is largely the outcome of un-thwarted Chinese ambitions to bring weaker nations on her PERIPHERY within her active domination. I am reminded of PROPHETIC warning of Chinese friends in

1948 that within three years there will be no Himalayas. I do not see that in the present circumstances the Mission can serve any useful purpose by remaining in Lhasa.[69]

Sinha, approached by the Tibetans for Dalai Lama's asylum, informed Delhi of the tense situation in Lhasa and the Tibetan request for asylum and also their request to intercede on their behalf to stop Mao's military action.[70] The very next day India assured Lhasa asylum for the Dalai Lama. However, India also expressed its inability to support Tibet's request to sponsor its appeal to the UN.[71] The political officer told Delhi that deferring to India's advice, Tibet had decided not to appeal to the UN which, he said, placed a heavy responsibility on India.[72]

China, on 28 October, in a hard-hitting note once again asked India to keep its hands off Tibet. On 30 October, China followed it up with the vice foreign minister personally telling the Indian ambassador the following:

> The PRC would like to make it clear that Tibet is an integral part of Chinese territory and the problem of Tibet is entirely a domestic problem of China. The Chinese PLA must enter Tibet, liberate the Tibetan people and defend the frontiers of China. This is the resolved policy of the Central People's Government.[73]

To make sure that the message reached its destination, on 2 November the Chinese ambassador in Delhi called on Foreign Secretary Menon and repeated to him what had been told to Panikkar in Beijing. The foreign secretary disputed the contentions of the ambassador and said that India's advice was friendly in nature and the Indian facilities in Tibet were essentially established to ensure better intercourse between the two *neighbouring countries* by agreements between them. Menon argued that the Indian establishments in Tibet were not 'symbols of any political or military domination' and they did not violate *Chinese sovereignty* and 'no modification in the present arrangement could be effected except by mutual consent'.[74] Now it was the Indian foreign secretary's turn to use the term 'sovereignty'.

An upset Nehru blamed all this on Panikkar's soft-pedalling the Indian point of view. Perhaps influenced by the earlier remarks of Menon[75] and Bajpai[76] about Panikkar's supposed failure to convey the Indian concerns forcefully, Nehru, too, joined them in taking out his frustration on the ambassador for his failure to make China fall in line with his wishes. As bad luck would have it for Panikkar, on the same day, he had once again attributed the Chinese action in Tibet to its fear of war developing in the north-eastern part of China and had said that China's action in Tibet was governed by their fear of unfriendly countries stirring up trouble in Tibet.[77]

Frustrated and infuriated, the prime minister reprimanded Panikkar:

> [W]e cannot help thinking that your representation to the Chinese Government was weak and apologetic. In fairness to the Chinese Government as well as to ourselves, our views regarding the threatened invasion of Tibet and its probable repercussions should have been communicated to them clearly and unequivocally. This has evidently not been done . . . the Chinese Government's action has jeopardised our interests in Tibet and our commitments to Tibet and our persistent efforts to secure the recognition of China (and) the interests of world peace have suffered a serious setback.[78]

After Nehru's reprimand, Bajpai took another swipe at Panikkar and compared his protests to China on Tibet to Chamberlain's protests to Hitler on Czechoslovakia and told Nehru on 31 October:

> What interest the Ambassador thinks he may be serving by showing so much solicitude for the Chinese Government's policy of false excuses and wanton high handedness towards Tibet, passes my understanding . . . .I feel it my duty to observe that, in handling the Tibetan issue with the Chinese Government, our

Ambassador has allowed himself to be influenced more by the Chinese point of view, by Chinese claims, by Chinese maps and by regard for Chinese susceptibilities than by his instructions or by India's interests.[79]

The circumstances influencing the Chinese decision to quicken the pace of developments in Tibet, as reported by Panikkar, were important and relevant. From the Chinese strategic point of view, their decision was obvious and derived from circumstances then prevailing. As stated earlier, the Chinese had on 31 October conveyed to India that '[i]t could not afford in context of [the] world situation to wait for long (for) Tibetan to make up their mind'.[79a]

This covered both the points. First, that Chinese action was in the context of the world situation and that they had waited long enough for Tibetans to make up their mind. On 1 November, in his letter to the chief ministers of the states, Nehru, while saying that the Chinese action had 'hurt us considerably' and it was an 'act of discourtesy to us', conceded what Panikkar had said:

It seems clear that owing to the development of the war situation in the Far East, and the accounts of repeated bombing of Manchurian towns, the Chinese Government believed that they were threatened with war by their enemies. As temper arose there, full of fear and apprehensions and resentment against those real or fancied enemies and this led possibly to a change in policy or to a speeding up of what might have taken much longer to develop'[80]

Nehru failed to see that Shakabpa was stonewalling the negotiations with China as a deliberate strategy, as he had told the Americans earlier, while canvassing their support. Shakabpa, too, had been given an impossible brief by Lhasa—to defend the independence of Tibet, but it had little chance of acceptance by the Chinese. China had formally announced the liberation plan in January 1950 and had launched its attack in October after waiting for almost ten months. The Tibetans had taxed Chinese patience far beyond endurance. Nehru himself had admitted that there were external factors such as the Korean War and the American bombing of Manchuria, which had hastened China's action. Other factors did indeed contribute in forcing Chinese hands. Having said that, Nehru, at the end, remained wedded to his pet theory of all these developments causing India 'no particular danger', since the great Himalayas were impenetrable.[81]

There were clearly differences in the perceptions of Delhi and the ambassador in Beijing regarding the reasons behind these developments. There was a tinge of superciliousness in Nehru's reprimand to Panikkar. There was little doubt that generally Panikkar was seen leaning on the Chinese side, but it was an erroneous understanding of Nehru and the MEA that had his representations been more forceful, which, in any case, were sufficiently strong, China would have been amenable to Indian entreaties. The notes were prepared in Delhi and sent to Beijing for delivery to the Chinese foreign office by the embassy. As pointed out earlier, ambassadors generally have little authority to amend them. In presenting the notes to the foreign office of a host country, the ambassador can be forceful to an extent but cannot behave arrogantly or adopt a threatening tone unless the two countries are at war. If the notes were not forceful enough, Delhi, which had drafted them, had to blame itself.

In an interview with I.F. Scot, Nehru mentioned his feelings of disappointment at being 'ill-repaid for India's diplomatic friendliness towards Beijing'.[82] Nehru's policy in Tibet was stumbling. He had perhaps erroneously convinced himself that since he was struggling to secure for China its rightful place in the UN and in the world generally, China should have been grateful. This seemed to indicate his lack of understanding of the Communist Chinese leadership, whom he had neither met nor known personally. He did not seem to understand their psychology either. The liberation of Tibet to them meant the end of a 'century of humiliation' and they were bent on achieving it 'at any cost'. It appeared that Delhi had conveniently forgotten that China had repeatedly warned that Tibet was its internal problem in which Delhi must not interfere.

Nehru's reprimand was all the more unfortunate in view of the fact that the Chinese vice foreign minister had personally conveyed to Panikkar on 30 October that China had repeatedly told India that the problem of Tibet was 'a domestic one for China to solve' and it 'cannot tolerate foreign intervention in regard to domestic problems'. In addition, the Chinese had made the following points:

(i) Just as [an] internal question relating to India should be decided solely by India, China cannot tolerate foreign intervention in regard to domestic problems. The Central People's Government were surprised that the Indian Government and non-officials opinion should talk of 'invasion or aggression' against Tibet;

(ii) the negotiations and their results were wholly domestic matters with which no foreign power was concerned;

(iii) [the] Peking Govt. had proofs that outside influences hostile to China were exercising influences in Tibet and many delays of the Shakabpa mission were due to these foreign influences;

(iv) In view of friendly relations with India they informed the Indian Government themselves but they strenuously denied the right of any foreign government to be interested in the future of Tibet or in the negotiations'; and finally

(v) such foreign elements which wish to invade China and carry out aggression on China would disregard Chinese sovereignty over Tibet and they do not constitute world opinion.[83]

The Chinese were certainly not wrong when they blamed foreign influences for Shakabpa's delay in his departure for Beijing. He was certainly talking to the Americans who were keen to involve themselves in Tibet as is evident from what has been stated earlier.

Hurt by Nehru's reprimand, in a lengthy letter to Nehru on 1 November, without appearing to contradict him, Panikkar tried to provide oblique justification for the Chinese actions. He said that China was itching for war with the United States and all their efforts were directed at creating a war-psychosis at all levels in the country. Regarding Tibet, he added that the Chinese attitude from the beginning had been that it was a purely domestic problem and no other country had any right to interfere. Despite India having made more than seven representations to the Chinese, they had insisted that their urgency to clinch the issue was for the 'security of their frontiers' and their apprehensions that 'in case of a general war, the Americans will create trouble in Tibet by flying supplies to them (Tibetans), which they can do from Bangkok'.[84] This was China's unimpeachable defence, but Nehru was not impressed.

The irony was Nehru himself writing to the former governor general of India C. Rajagopalachari on 1 November admitting that 'morally' he found 'it difficult to say that the Chinese deliberately deceived us at any stage'.[85] On the same day, in his fortnightly letter to the chief ministers of the states, Nehru spoke of the Chinese actions as 'acts of discourtesy'. Yet justifying the Chinese action the prime minister said it was due to the American bombing of Manchurian towns, which made China believe that they were under threat and they responded to these 'real or fancied enemies . . .' and that led to China speeding up their action in Tibet. Nehru still felt that 'China acted not only wrongly but foolishly and done injury to itself, to some extent to us'. At the end he remained confident that it involved 'no particular danger to India'.[86]

Within a week of this observation he suddenly realized that China's occupation of Tibet had created new problems for India and said:

> China's aggression in Tibet immediately raises new frontier problems for us. We cannot be happy to have a strong centralised and communist government in control of [the] Tibetan border with India and yet there were no obvious means of stopping this and even legally Indian position was not strong one . . . If China demands, and she is certain to do so, we shall have to withdraw

our Representative at Lhasa and our military escort at Gyantse. We cannot keep them there against the wishes of the occupying power and we cannot go to war on this issue.[87]

In his policy note of 8 November, he absolved China of any 'studied deception' because they did not hide their intentions, except that they showed 'extreme discourtesy' to India by using force against its advice for peaceful negotiations.[88] What Nehru perhaps expected was that the Chinese were duty bound to accept his advice. He forgot that India, too, had used force in Hyderabad under similar circumstances. What is good for the goose is good for the gander!

The leadership in Delhi suffered from a hubristic interpretation of their standing with the Chinese leaders. It seemed as though the entire ministry of external affairs, led by the prime minister himself, was taking out its frustration on the ambassador for the failure of their policy in Tibet. It was a collateral damage that Panikkar had to suffer.

After a while, Nehru said, 'I am convinced of the importance of India-Chinese friendship from the short and long-term point of view.' Even now he was anxious to continue friendly relations with China. He once again insisted that India was going to stand by McMahon Line. Stating the logic of his policy, Nehru said, 'Our present policy is primarily based on avoidance of world war, and secondly the maintenance of honourable and peaceful relations with China.'[89] If the second point was also the criteria, then certainly the Chinese at no time had shown any reciprocal friendship or respect for India. Their notes on Tibet and démarches were invariably couched in unfriendly and curt language.

In another note on 18 November Nehru conceded that:

[China] will take possession, in a political sense, at least, of the whole of Tibet (and) there is no likelihood whatever of Tibet being able to resist this or stop it. It is equally unlikely that any power can prevent it. We cannot do so. If so, what can we do to help in the maintenance of Tibetan autonomy and at the same time avoiding continuous tension and apprehension on our frontiers.[90]

Despite all the Chinese rebuffs, Nehru remained optimistic that India could help Tibet in the maintenance of its autonomy.

Despite his disappointments with China, he advised the Indian delegation at the UN that while supporting the Tibetan appeal generally because of prior assurance to Tibet, it should avoid recrimination or strong language since the UN could not do much except 'appeal to the two parties to come to a peaceful settlement. Condemnation of China will not help Tibet and neither the Security Council nor (General) Assembly is in any position to render physical help to Tibet'.[91]

If failure to sponsor the appeal was disappointing to the Tibetans, the subsequent Indian action was more so. India's stand that it was certain that the Tibetan question could still be decided by peaceful means led to the postponement of Tibet's case indefinitely at the UN.[92] Tibet once again felt betrayed by India.

While India could not ensure Tibet's autonomy, Nehru satisfied himself with the belief that the remoteness of Tibet, combined with factors of 'geography, terrain and climate', would make the exercise of autonomy by Tibet inevitable.[93]

His attitude towards China seemed inconsistent. Speaking in Parliament on 7 December, he said:

> They gave us to understand that a peaceful solution would be found, though I must say they gave us no assurance or guarantee to that effect. On the one hand they said they were prepared for a peaceful solution; on the other, they talked persistently of liberation . . .

He concluded his speech with the remarks:

> But it is right and proper thing to say and I see no difficulty in saying to the Chinese Government that whether they have

suzerainty over Tibet or sovereignty over Tibet, surely, according to any principles, they proclaim and the principles I uphold, the last voice in regard to Tibet should be the voice of the people of Tibet and of nobody else.[94]

As Tibet had come under attack, an upset Political Officer Hareshwar Dayal acerbically asked if the GoI contemplated any other action in the matter. Considering the danger to the personnel of the Indian trade agencies, he asked Delhi to assert its right to warn Beijing against interference with them and their properties.[95] Delhi simply directed the mission-in-charge in Lhasa that the 'withdrawal of [the] mission from Lhasa, in the present circumstances will be a great blow to Tibetans. Whatever the developments or the hazards the mission must continue in Lhasa. Government of India are confident that you will stay at your post, whatever might happen'.[96]

On 17 November, in yet another fortnightly letter to the chief ministers, he once again dwelt on the larger issue of security of the region, since he felt that the recent developments had 'made a great difference to the balance of power in the world' and wondered if China were to align with the Soviet Union, it could pose danger not only to India but also to other Asian countries as well and said:

The fact of its (China's) emergence was patent enough and no one could doubt that the old balance had thus been completely upset . . . If China came out as a Great Power, and a power allied to the Soviets, all previous calculations had to be reconsidered. To us in India and many other countries in Asia, this had a particular significance . . .[96a]

Recent events had perhaps given him a better understanding of the Communist Chinese leadership than before, and remembering old days, Nehru said: 'The previous China, under Marshal Chiang Kai-shek's government was important in many ways . . .it did not raise these new problems!'[97]

It was a late but new realization for Nehru. All of a sudden, he seemed to have frightening thoughts:

[W]hat would happen when China, with its new born strength and dynamism and certain aggressiveness, came right up to the borders of India? Would there be peace between the two or tension and conflict?

He no longer looked benignly at communism since he felt it had added 'gravity' to the situation and 'the people feared infiltration of communist ideas even more than the attack of armed men'. Perceiving China as being aligned with the Soviet countries, he wondered 'whether this new and Communist China would function as some kind of a satellite or as an independent entity having a will and objective of its own'.[98] After all this bickering, he still held on to the question of Tibetan autonomy. He told Panikkar that 'our present policy is primarily based on avoidance of world war and secondly on maintenance of honourable and peaceful relations with China. These relations inevitably will depend, to some extent, on Chinese policy in Tibet. If peaceful settlement is arrived at there and Tibet's autonomy recognised, this should meet Chinese demands and satisfy more or less both Tibet and India'.[99]

To silence a lot of loose talk in political circles in India that China could attack and overrun India, an upset Nehru said that China, though internally big, was in a way amorphous and easily capable of being attacked on its sea coasts and by air and that it would be fighting 'for its very existence' and that it was therefore inconceivable that it should divert its forces and its strength across the insurmountable terrain of Tibet and undertake a wild adventure across the Himalayas. Any such attempt would greatly weaken its capacity to meet the real enemies on other fronts. 'Thus I rule out any major attack on India by China.'[100]

It did not take him too much time to put Tibet behind and concentrate on world peace. After he had returned from his

European tour in January 1951, he sent Zhou Enlai a personal message suggesting the great desire for peace in Europe and the recognition of the emergence of China 'as a great power' and the fact that China was in a position to give a lead for peace 'which can result in an immediate removal of tension and fear from the world'. In the end he called upon China to call for a ceasefire in Korea, leading to negotiations which would change the whole world. His letter concentrated on the Korean question alone and asked China to work for ceasefire. Any reference to India–China relations was restricted to their having 'close and friendly relations' who should 'cooperate for peace and progress in Asia and the world'. All his resentment over Tibet of the previous year had evaporated, since there was not even a remote reference to those events in his lengthy letter of more than 1200 words, in which reference to India was confined to only forty words but no reference to Tibet.[101]

Apparently, Nehru had been pursuing his policies towards China independent of his important Cabinet colleagues, particularly his deputy prime minister Sardar Vallabhbhai Patel, as was evident from the latter's letter of 7 November to Nehru and his earlier letter of 4 November to Bajpai on the same subject. Both letters were indictments of Nehru's policies in which he regretted that India had been humiliated. He told Nehru that while India regarded China its friend, China did not regard India its friend. Expressing his misgivings for the future of India's north-eastern frontier, the tribes living there and the Himalayan states, Patel described them as weak spots with unlimited scope for infiltration with all the elements of potential trouble between China and India. He dismissed communism as a shield against imperialism and described the communists as good or as bad imperialists as any other. He stressed the need to deal with the Chinese with 'the greatest suspicion' and that *we cannot be friendly with China and must think in terms of defence against a determined and prejudiced combination of powers which the Chinese will spearhead*. Speaking of China's hideous designs, he expressed his worries about Pakistan's shenanigans and the possibility of India facing a security threat at both its fronts: east and west. Finally, he suggested measures needed to shore up Indian defence of the area.[102]

In his letter to Secretary General Bajpai on 4 November, Patel described China as a 'thoroughly unscrupulous, unreliable, and determined power practically at our doors'.[103]

The long note penned by Nehru on 18 November was part introspection and part justification of what had happened. About China's claim to 'sovereignty' over Tibet and, therefore, it being its domestic problem, he acknowledged that India had indeed used the word 'sovereignty' in one of its notes, but had informed the ambassador that it was a mistake. He now agreed that the autonomy Chinese had offered to Tibet was not the same as it had enjoyed during the last forty years. He did envisage a situation in which China and India would be hostile to each other, like France and Germany. Should that happen 'then there would be repeated wars bringing destruction to both. The advantage will go to other countries.'[104]

Having ruled out any attack on India by China, Nehru did not rule out infiltration and taking possession of 'disputed territory' by China if there was no obstruction to this happening. He advised taking all 'necessary precautions to prevent this'. His note of 18 November was full of many security scenarios, one of which was China and Pakistan joining together against India. He insisted Pakistan remained 'India's major possible enemy'. He expressed his worry if India was to think of another enemy in China and prepare for both, India would weaken itself against Pakistan. He noticed Pakistan taking interest in Tibetan developments, even though it had 'absolutely nothing in common with China', its media suggesting India's problems in Tibet as a possible solution of the Kashmir dispute. Then he added:

> But if we fall out completely with China, Pakistan will undoubtedly try to take advantage of this, politically or otherwise. The position of India thus will be bad from a defence point of view. *We cannot*

have all the time two possible enemies on either side of India. This danger will not be got over, even if we increase our defence forces or even if other foreign countries help in arming.[105]

In his long-term view, he termed India and China as two of the biggest countries of Asia, bordering each other, having certain expansive tendencies, because of their vitality and if they developed bad relations that would affect their future for a long time to come.[106]

The irony was what he feared happened in his lifetime and India found itself unprepared. The immediate aftermath of his policies did not enhance his stature as a far-sighted statesman, which he had tried to build for himself.

6

The 17-Point Agreement

China's attack on the border town of Chamdo in Kham in November 1950 and the arrest of its governor, Ngabo Ngawang Jigme, was enough to scurry the Tibetan government to appeal to India to 'intercede in their behalf with Mao to stop present military action' and also to request the GoI for asylum for the Dalai Lama, which was granted and conveyed to Lhasa.[1] Contrary to Tibetan fears, the Chinese stopped at Chamdo and accused the Tibetans of 'insincerity' since Shakabpa had failed to show up in Beijing after keeping the Chinese waiting indefinitely. They now demanded the despatch of an accredited representative to negotiate the agreement at Chamdo, failing which the Tibetans were warned to prepare for the worst.[2] The Chinese assured the Tibetans that their traditional social and religious practices and their social structures, including the monastic order and their privileges, would not be disturbed. However, the Tibetan army would be a part of the national army, the National Defence Force of China.[3] The Chinese also launched a propaganda blitz assuring the general public of their good intentions.

Nehru had no objection to China's occupation of Tibet as long as it was done by peaceful means. Now that the Chinese invasion had halted, and their peaceful intentions started unfolding, Delhi's attitude became passive. That the future relations of India with Tibet would be subordinated to China's overweening interests was not a worrying prospect immediately. But soon enough, as the fact of China taking control of Tibet dawned on Delhi, contrary to earlier perceptions, Nehru became seriously apprehensive of Indian security and perceived grave dangers lurking behind these developments.

As early as 1949, when the tide of civil war was turning in favour of the communists, Nehru, while welcoming communist victories, perceived their adverse impact on Nepal. He had shared his concerns with the Indian ambassador in Kathmandu:

> Owing to development in China and very probably a little later in Tibet, Nepal will have to face a very serious problem on the border before very long. Those problems will not be of a military character so much as an invasion of ideas and dangerous ideas at that.[4]

Later, India's role in Nepal's political developments became a source of worry to the communist regime in China. They wondered if Delhi would intervene in Lhasa in the same way as it was doing in Nepal! China was determined not to allow India to play any role in the Tibet conundrum. As we have seen in the previous chapter, China repeatedly warned India that Tibet was its internal problem and no foreign country must intervene.

Be that as it may, Nehru perceived that with these developments the old balance of power was being disrupted in the vicinity of India. Nehru could see in communist China a country very different from the old Kuomintang China, which, according to him, had not created problems of security in the past.[5] The shield which he thought the Himalayas provided suddenly appeared to him to be brittle.[6] He saw new frontier problems emerge in the wake of 'Chinese aggression' in Tibet and remarked, 'We cannot be happy to have a strong centralised and communist Government in control of the Tibetan border with

India . . .'[7] He suddenly seemed to discover that 'the Himalayan border was not quite so effective as it used to be. He feared that 'the addition of communism (had) added to its gravity because many people feared infiltration of communist ideas even more than the attack of armed men'.[8]

Nehru, at the same time, had no qualms in calling those people who expressed concern about these developments as 'amateur strategists'.[9]

The foreign secretary had anticipated that China which had not signed the Simla Convention might not recognize it later.[10] As stated in the previous chapter, the Chinese ambassador had warned the foreign secretary of China's intentions to repudiate all past engagements.[11] It was apparent that India's right to establish direct relations with Tibet was under the Chinese scanner.[12]

The Chinese press accused the imperialists for trying to maintain their control on Tibet which 'obliged (China) to intervene to restore China's sovereignty rights in Tibet'.[13] That in China's perception India was still an imperialist country was not to be doubted. Nehru conceded that should China demand that India withdraws its representative at Lhasa and the military escort at Gyantse, India would have to toe the line. On the frontier question, Nehru remained convinced that India was in a favourable position since it considered the *McMahon Line as its frontier and India 'was not prepared on any account to reconsider this question'*.[14] This revealed that his thoughts were dichotomous. On the one hand, there were doubts about China standing by the Simla Convention and, on the other, Nehru insisted that the McMahon Line, which was the product of the Simla Convention, was its firm border with Tibet.

Nehru's policies towards China had come under critical observations of his deputy prime minister Sardar Patel who said that a border which 'seldom' caused us any worry in the past, now with 'the undefined state of the frontier and the existence on our side of a population with its affinities to the Tibetan or Chinese have all the elements of the potential trouble between China and ourselves'.

He, too, warned that China's interpretation of suzerainty was different and 'we can safely assume that very soon they will disown all the stipulations which Tibet had entered into with us in the past'. That his assessment turned out to be true was not fortuitous.[15]

Nehru, however, continued to grapple with the wider and theoretical question of China's emergence and its place vis-à-vis the Soviet Union. In his fortnightly letter to the chief ministers of the Indian states, he wondered 'whether this new and communist China would function as some kind of a satellite, however big, to the Soviets or as an independent entity having a will and objective of its own'.[16] To overcome his worries, he tried to comfort himself by placing China in a scenario which was too fanciful but audacious. He said that if a war came:

China would have its main front in the south and east and it will be fighting for its very existence against powerful enemies. It is inconceivable that it should divert its forces and its strength across the inhospitable terrain of Tibet and undertake a wild adventure across the Himalayas . . . Thus I rule out any major attack on India by China.[17]

These were self-delusional ideas. His worry was mainly about 'infiltration and intrusion of small groups'. Having worked out various scenarios, he was more or less convinced that Indian security was not threatened by these developments. If the Chinese wanted to negotiate with Tibet for a peaceful settlement, so be it.

He remained convinced that China meant no harm to India. He described the people who believed that communism inevitably means expansion as 'naïve'.[18]

As the Chinese entered Chamdo, Lhasa had appealed to the UN with the hope of getting some succour. The developments in Korea, however, crowded out Tibet's complaint at the UN. India was unwilling to say anything that would risk its relations with the People's Republic of China in any way. On 18 December

1950, American Ambassador Henderson, after meeting Secretary General Bajpai, reported to Washington that the attitude of the Indian Government was 'negative' and that of the British high commissioner even 'more negative'. London, however, authorized the High Commission to issue a visa for Hong Kong to the Tibetan delegation. Bajpai had also reportedly told Henderson that the 'GOI had decided that criticism by it of Communist China might adversely affect India's ability to exert influence on China in the direction of Ceasefire' [in Korea].[19]

Despite earlier rebuffs from India, the United States' eagerness to help Tibet did not diminish. Secretary of State Acheson told Ambassador Henderson that the Tibetan question should not be allowed to 'go by default'.[20] The US State Department tested London directly and found its response least encouraging. The feeling in the British circles was that 'the American policy in regard to Tibet is part of the general pattern of their policy towards China: *resist Chinese pressure even if only by propaganda* and embarrass China'. Foreign Secretary Menon had told an official of the American embassy that 'the Indian Government had definitely decided to take no action over Tibet in the UN which might have the effect of lessening their influence with the Chinese People's Government'.[21] Abandoned by India, Tibet found itself forsaken by the UN as well. Unable to match China's military strength, Lhasa had no alternative but to talk to the Chinese to secure a favourable modus vivendi and redeem whatever little was possible. Kham governor Ngabo's report of the benign behaviour of the Chinese had been encouraging to Lhasa; however, the brief finalized by Lhasa asking China to accept Tibet's independence was like asking for the moon.

The Tibetans' feelings towards China, however, remained hostile, and China could smell it too. The Chinese apparently thought it prudent to neutralize India's role in Tibet. It had consequently become necessary to propitiate Nehru. As a first step, Mao Zedong decided to attend the Indian Republic Day Reception on 26 January 1951 at the Indian embassy. Making use of the opportunity, he described the Indian nation, a great nation and the Indian people an excellent people. For thousands of years excellent friendship existed between them and hoped that both would continue to 'unite together to strive for peace'.[22]

India was happy and appreciated Mao's gesture of attending the reception and also his remarks.

The other move was friendly yet full of forebodings. Zhou Enlai, the premier of the PRC, while welcoming Nehru's possible visit to China, gave details of the assurances that the Chinese had given to the Tibetans, namely the 'recognition of Dalai Lama as the temporal and spiritual leader, protection of lama church and autonomy for Tibet subject to Central Government control of frontiers and foreign policy etc'.[23] He also added that Tibet had agreed to send a delegation to China to negotiate a peaceful settlement. Ambassador Panikkar assured Zhou that India's interest in the matter was peaceful and she had no desire 'to carry on political intrigues'. Zhou, appreciating his assurance, said that China 'recognised India's friendly interest in Tibet and that their decision not to advance on Lhasa or undertake military operations within Tibet but to carry on peaceful negotiations was in conformity with India's views' and expected India to 'recognise the moderation of Chinese policy'.[24] While referring to the assurances China gave to the Tibetans, Zhou minced no words. He warned Panikkar that should the Dalai Lama be persuaded by some groups in Tibet to seek asylum in India, it *would bring a dark cloud between our good relations of friendship*', and to the Tibetans he warned, 'even if he went away an agreement will now be reached but it may lead to minor unpleasant incidents in Tibet and troops will have to enter by force'.[25]

To make sure that his warning was driven home, Zhou gave another strong cautionary message to India:

As India's interests were that peace of her frontier should not be disturbed leading to unsettled conditions, he hoped that *Indian Government will not encourage Dalai Lama to leave the country.*[26]

It was now clear to Delhi that China's friendly gesture was not as friendly as it appeared. Panikkar told Zhou that since India had already promised asylum to Dalai Lama, if he decided to come it would not be possible to refuse him entry into the country. He, however, assured Zhou that it would be only spiritual and not political. Zhou left it at that with the remarks: 'In the interest of peace in Tibet we (India) would not encourage the Regent Group's plan to get him out of the country', leaving little doubt of what he meant.[27] It may be clarified that since the Dalai Lama was yet a minor there was the Regent who wielded authority on his behalf.

The Americans, however, did not expect the Dalai Lama to seek asylum in India since they had doubts whether India would allow him to provide the required leadership to his people from Indian soil.[28]

The Chinese warning did reach Delhi. Giving a gist of the conversation mentioned above to Hareshwar Dayal, Delhi advised him to convey the following to Lhasa 'informally and tactfully':

> We feel that the flight of the Dalai Lama to India will leave Tibet leaderless and will serve no useful purpose.

Regarding the frontiers, the political officer was told:

> We have expressed hope (to the Chinese) that this will not mean appreciation of incursions of Chinese troops into Tibet and that such incursions would be regarded with alarm by Tibetans. We have pointed out that the Himalayas and a friendly India (were) best protection for Tibet's southern frontier.[29]

The next day the political officer confirmed that he had already advised Lhasa along these lines and would reiterate this advice to the Tibetan foreign secretary who was expected in Gangtok. Lhasa also told Delhi that 'the Chinese were prepared to assure [the] Tibetan Government that they would place troops on [the] Indo-Tibetan border only as long as there was an "unfriendly" Government of India'.[30] As these events unfolded, the Dalai Lama, taking Delhi's hint, returned to Lhasa from Yatung where he was camping.

Before deciding to negotiate with China, the Dalai Lama had consulted all his high officials, both temporal and spiritual, on the desirability of negotiations. Shakabpa, the most experienced of all his advisers in international affairs, informed him that there was 'general lack of support' for Tibet's independence, particularly in India. The high priests of the three major monasteries—Gera, Derpung and Gading—and other senior abbots advised talks with the Chinese since they found the terms offered by them were not inimical to the continuation of the institution of Dalai Lama, and the Buddhist religion. That settled the issue and it was decided that they would go ahead with the negotiations.[31]

Shakabpa confirmed to the US ambassador in Delhi that the delegation for the negotiations in Beijing had not been given the plenipotentiary powers even though Dalai's brother-in-law was a member of the mission since it was feared that it might yield to pressure.[31a]

The negotiators selected for the job, apart from Ngabo who was named the leader, were Lhawutara Thupten Tender and Phuntsog Tashi Takla. Later, two more were added. The brief given to the mission was practically the same that had been given to Shakabpa—independence for Tibet, no deployment of Chinese army in Tibet and so on. Secretary General Bajpai thought that while Tibet might have to agree to China controlling its foreign affairs, instead of defence, he felt 'they should break on neither' since the alternative would be Chinese invasion of Tibet.[31b]

When the Tibetan delegation, which had stopped in Delhi on their way to Beijing, met the prime minister, his advice regarding the deployment of Chinese army in Tibet was:

Tibet's southern frontier marches with India, which is at once friendly to Tibet and China. We hope [the] Chinese will not insist on moving troops into Tibet on [the] pretext that this frontier needs protection. Tibet will view any incursion of Chinese troops with alarm and there will naturally be unfavourable reaction in India. The most Tibet can be expected to concede is that in case of threat of invasion from any quarter she (Tibet) will seek assistance from China.

Nehru finally assured the Tibetans of India's diplomatic support. After all that had come to pass the previous year, he still conveyed to the Tibetans that 'we would naturally like to continue direct relations between India and Tibet'.[32]

Nehru's advice on the deployment of the Chinese army in Tibet came close to the Tibetans' claim that Nehru had advised that 'Tibetans *must not* agree to the stationing of Chinese troops in Tibet since this would have serious repercussions on India'.[33] Melvyn Goldstein in her book *History of Modern Tibet* quoting Lhautara (who was one of the members of the Tibetan delegation, claimed that 'he [Nehru] strongly urged them not to permit Chinese troops to be stationed in Tibet'.[34] All the versions seemed to reinforce the same thing: that Nehru was against Tibet allowing Chinese troops on its soil.

Foreign Secretary Menon told the American ambassador that the talks with the Tibetan delegation were in generalities. Since Tibet had relations only with India and Nepal, with its frontier running along theirs, and both countries were being friendly towards Tibet and China, there was nothing to be worried about.[35]

The delegation upon its arrival in Beijing on 23 April 1951 was surprised to find itself being received by Premier Zhou Enlai himself.[35a] However, they were in for a bigger surprise and embarrassment when they were told about the arrival of the Panchen Lama the next day in Beijing and were asked to receive him on his arrival. Since the Panchen Lama, the tenth in the line of succession, had not been officially recognized by Lhasa, it was embarrassing for an official delegation of the Dalai Lama to give him the honour of being received. Nevertheless, they complied but only some of the delegation members were present when he arrived.[35b] It must be noted that the then Panchen Lama was the successor of the ninth pontiff, who had died while in exile in China. The new Panchen Lama was selected by the Chinese and approved by Mao as the tenth Panchen and was still living there in exile. The Chinese were very particular that he should not only feel honoured by the delegation's presence at the Railway Station but also that his official status be acknowledged by the Dalai Lama's representatives. It was after several discussions that he was finally recognized as the tenth incarnate by Lhasa and his status confirmed to enable the negotiations to begin on a serious note.

The Chinese negotiating team was headed by Li Wei-han, the chairman of the National Minorities Commission. This was done to convey to the Tibetans that this was not an inter-governmental discussion, but between two non-governmental bodies of the same country. [35c]

The Kashag's (Tibetan cabinet's) brief for the leader of the delegation, Ngabo, had called for independence in the first instance, arguing that the past relationship between Tibet and China was that of 'priest and patron'. However, if that was unacceptable to China, it could agree to Tibet being a part of China on the following conditions:

(1) Tibet must have full internal independence;
(2) No Chinese troops would be stationed in Tibet;
(3) The Tibetan army would be responsible for its defence;
(4) The Chinese representative to Lhasa, his personal staff and guards must not exceed 100 men;
(5) The Chinese representative must be a Buddhist.[36]

The delegation was aware that refusal to agree to the deployment of Chinese troops would not be countenanced by the Chinese, and it sought fresh instructions from Lhasa, which not only insisted that no Chinese troops would be deployed but also suggested a compromise which would incorporate Tibetan troops in the Chinese army and their deployment alone in Tibet as part of the Chinese army. [36a]

With this flexibility, Ngabo was confident that he could bat during the negotiations. He also made his other colleagues agree to use their discretion and take decisions on the spot as the situation demanded, instead of referring each issue to Yatung (where the Dalai Lama was then camping) and wait for instructions, thereby delaying negotiations indefinitely. [36b]

The new terms for settlement offered by the Chinese were not different from the terms they had offered the Tibetans at Chamdo when they had captured it: 'The Tibetans should return to the big motherland, guaranteeing their religious freedom, etc.'. Ngabo's insistence on relationship of 'priest and patron' was dismissed by the Chinese who made it clear that the status of Tibet was not under discussion, since historically it was an accepted part of China and China's claim to Tibet was internationally recognized. The main problem arose with the Chinese being insistent on setting up a Military Administrative Commission to oversee the implementation of the agreement. The Tibetans pointed out that this would contradict the assumption that the Dalai Lama would continue to be the head of the Tibetan government. It was the Dalai Lama who should have been responsible for the implementation of the Agreement and not the Commission. The Chinese would not accept any deviation from their decision. Since the Chinese held all the aces, the Tibetans had to relent on every point. There were no detailed discussions on any particular issue and the Tibetans had little option but to sign on the dotted lines. Finally, the details of the agreement were captured in a 17-Point Agreement, which was signed on 23 May 1951. [37]

Though the leader of the Tibetan delegation, Ngabo, had his seal of office with him, he had not disclosed it. The Chinese got another seal made locally for him to sign and authenticate the agreement. Even if Lhasa had not given him plenipotentiary powers, he claimed to have them. [37a]

The Dalai Lama and his ministers and high officials heard details of the agreement from Radio Peking. They were appalled, as they said it was full of 'communist clichés, vainglorious assertions, which were partly true and the terms were far worse and more oppressive than anything they had imagined'.[37b] They were shocked that the agreement had not only compromised Tibet's independent status but had also accepted the deployment of Chinese troops in Tibet. The Tibetan government insisted that Ngabo had no authority to sign such an agreement. The similarity in the agreement that had been signed now and the terms offered after Chamdo had fallen last year stared them in the face. Giving the benefit of doubt to Ngabo, Lhasa even suspected that he might have been made to sign it under duress.[37c] While no particular pressure was applied, Ngabo knew he had little choice but to sign it. At one stage when there was disagreement on the question of Dalai Lama's power to administer the agreement, the Tibetans were told: 'If you disagree then you can leave whenever you like. It is up to you to choose whether Tibet would be liberated peacefully or by force. It is only a matter of sending a telegram to PLA group to recommence their march into Tibet.'[37d]

When Lhasa contacted Nagabo on the agreement, to silence Kashag, he arrogantly told Lhasa that 'the agreement had been signed and if Kashag was not satisfied, they should send a new team to Beijing'.[38] Given the poor reception the agreement received from the Tibetan government, the Chinese suspected that if Ngabo returned via India, he might not reach Lhasa at all and the agreement would be disowned by the Tibetans. They made him return by the arduous land route to Tibet. The other members returned via India.

Along with the signing of the 17-Point Agreement, a seven-point 'secret' document was also signed. It had in it a provision on Dalai Lama's exile, which said that 'should he go into exile, he could remain out for up to five years; during the exile he would be allowed to maintain his existing status and power'. Another important item on the secret agreement was that one or two members of the Kashag would be part of the Tibet Military Commission. The other points related to the phasing out of the Tibetan currency, the right of Tibetans to maintain a small police force and so on.

In the preamble to the 17-Point Agreement, Tibet agreed to be a part of China by accepting the phrase 'Tibetan nationality was one of the nationalities of China' and in the last 'hundred years or more, imperialist forces had penetrated into China and in consequence also penetrated into Tibet region and carried out an all-out policy of deceptions and provocations'. This implied Tibet's acceptance as part of China until a hundred years ago.

The Agreement was a disappointment for India as well. India was indirectly described as an 'imperialist aggressive force.' It was also a signal to India that it would have to leave Tibet soon. All Chinese actions hereafter were aimed to squeeze India out of Tibet.

Interestingly, no proof was sought by the Chinese at the beginning of the negotiations to confirm if the Tibetan delegation actually had 'full powers'. Ngabo's verbal claim, made at the end, that he had the powers to negotiate and sign the agreement was accepted at face value. The preamble stated that 'a delegation *with full powers* of the local Government of Tibet arrived in Peking'. Similarly, the preamble spoke about the appointment of a Chinese delegation '*with full powers* to conduct talks on a friendly basis with the delegates *with full powers* of the local government of Tibet'. Since for the Chinese it was an agreement between two parties of the same country, their obsession with 'Full Powers' has to be understood in the context of its importance for external use. The agreement compromised the autonomy that Tibet was enjoying for almost four decades. Whatever autonomy Tibet might enjoy after the signing of the agreement was to be exercised under the unified leadership of the Central People's Government. The agreement provided a legal basis for the PRC's takeover of Tibet.[39]

The members of the Tibetan delegation at the end met Mao who welcomed them as 'part of the big family' and said 'now Peking is yours and Shanghai is yours. Now the PLA will go to Tibet'.

When Mao asked Tibetans if they had any doubts, Ngabo expressed full confidence in China. Mao promised best behaviour of the PLA, which would win their hearts. The delegation felt confident if the Chinese sincerely implemented the agreement, Tibet would have the freedom to preserve its religion and culture and the Dalai Lama's institution would continue as before. The agreement legalized Chinese sovereignty over Tibet and 'provided China with mechanism for the gradual transformation of the social and economic system in Tibet in the communist mould'.[40] On 28 May, Mao, speaking at a reception held in honour of the Tibetan delegation, said that 'the forces led by Dalai Lama and Panchen have united together with Central People's Government. This has been achieved only after the Chinese people overthrew imperialists and domestic reactionary rule'.[41] The Commander-in-Chief of the PLA, Chu Teh, praised Panchen who was the first to declare his support to the Central People's Government a year ago and then only praised the Dalai Lama who, he said, had 'assumed temporal powers and began to correct the former erroneous policy of local Government of Tibet'.[42] The Agreement laid excessive stress on the importance of Panchen Lama vis-à-vis Dalai Lama, since the former had turned out to be their protégé, thereby sowing the seeds of future conflict between the two.

The Indian embassy, while providing the full text of the agreement to Delhi, found that the agreement placed 'Tibet in a better position than Inner Mongolia which only is an autonomous region', besides guaranteeing the position of the Dalai Lama, the Buddhist church and the continuance of the present system of government without direct intervention from Peking. The embassy also underlined the undue importance given to the Panchen and pointed out that in case of any conflict between them in the future, it would provide China an excuse to intervene. In the embassy's assessment:

On the whole the Agreement would appear to be a reasonable one reconciling China's claim to sovereignty with Tibet's right for autonomy and desire for non-interference with existing political and social structure.[43]

An editorial in the *People's Daily* described Tibet and Taiwan as 'invisible parts of Chinese territory'. It promised the continuation of the present temporal and spiritual institutions of Tibet. Stressing on the 'unavoidable necessity for reforms to be carried out step by step', it left to the people themselves without interference from the Central Government. The editorial recognized that certain doubts could crop up in the minds of the people, but these would be removed after 'considerable time by means of factual proof'.[44]

On 31 May, the Indian mission in Lhasa informed Delhi that the Chinese troops were already on their way to Lhasa.[45] Nehru, replying to the debate on foreign affairs in the Council of States (Rajya Sabha), said, 'Tibet is part of the Chinese State and the Chinese State can send its troops anywhere it likes within its boundaries.'[46]

The agreement which brought fundamental changes in the status of Tibet, affecting India's relations with it in more ways than one, received little attention in India both among the people and the officials. India had enough of its own problems. In any case, it had burnt its fingers in the previous year and it was not worth its while to be commenting on the agreement between Tibet and China or interfere in it in any way. India perhaps thought that if China and Tibet had sorted out their problems without involving it, so be it. However, the *Statesman* of Calcutta observed on 29 May 1951:

Indian statesmen would be neither human nor politic if they failed to consider the latent dangers, were Tibet subsequently absorbed in a more drastic manner. Even, as things are, a Communist power might prove an uneasy neighbour.[47]

The agreement received attention in England, too, where the editorial in the *Manchester Guardian* said:

The immediate danger to India is that Chinese may build air bases near the Himalayas from which it might threaten the Ganges valley, and second that, by political infiltration the Communists may work revolutionary havoc all along the frontier.[48]

India stood aloof or, rather, was made to stand aloof when the agreement was negotiated. In any case, as Nehru said later, 'India had no political interest in Tibet.'[49]

After the 17-Point Agreement had been signed, an official of the American embassy, Steere, met the secretary general in the MEA, Bajpai, and was told that the Indian embassy had failed to obtain any authentic information about the Agreement and that the Tibetan delegation had not kept in touch with the Indian embassy. Steere, the US *Charge d' affaires* formed the impression that Bajpai was unhappy at India's helplessness in the whole affair. According to Steere, Bajpai confirmed that India had promised support to Lhasa during the negotiations, but the Tibetan delegation, as far as he knew, had never ventured near the Indian embassy in Beijing. He felt that 'it was inevitable that [the] present Chinese government should gain control of Tibet, and there was nothing that the GoI could do about it'.[50] On 3 June, US Ambassador Henderson informed Washington that India was somewhat shocked at the stiff conditions China had imposed and was inclined 'to adopt an attitude of philosophical acquiescence'. He quoted the officials of the UK High Commission who had discussed the agreement with the Indian officials that 'the latter were inclined [towards] rationalising that in view of historic and present friendship between India and China, Communist Chinese political and military control was not likely to have [an] adverse effect on [the] security of India'.[51]

On 2 June 1951, the Indian Mission in Lhasa had reported utter dissatisfaction of the Tibetan prime minister Lukhangwa Tsewang Rapten with the agreement. He blamed this tragedy on the failure of Shakabpa's mission to reach Beijing the previous year. Lukhangwa lamented that it could have been possible to resist China at Chamdo but for the Dalai Lama's insistence on a negotiated settlement. China's refusal to negotiate at Chamdo and insisting on talks at Beijing made any communication with the delegation impossible, which proved disastrous and the Dalai Lama, too, found it unacceptable.[52] The Indian embassy, however, reported satisfaction that in all the Chinese propaganda while there was criticism of the British and American 'imperialist activities', there had been no criticism of India. It expected the Chinese to go slow, at least for the time being, to be able to consolidate their position in Lhasa and they would perhaps also go slow in inducting Chinese troops in Tibet for the same reason. Any reference to the Dalai Lama was accompanied by a reference to the Panchen Lama to stress the latter's importance. It called upon the local government to take 'earnest steps to assist the PLA's peaceful march into Tibet'.[53]

At his press conference on 2 June, Nehru suggested that India was aware of the agreement but that the details were not complete and hence he would not comment on them. But he suggested the existence of Chinese suzerainty and Tibetan autonomy in the past and he mentioned the existence of India's cultural and trade interests and desired their 'preservation . . . in a friendly way with the people concerned'. When asked whether the presence of the Chinese army would hinder Indian interests in Tibet, Nehru said the facts being 'vague' it was not clear.[54] Perhaps it was for a tactical reason that Nehru said that the details of the agreement as known to him were incomplete. The text of the agreement was available with the ministry since 28 May, and had been found to be a 'reasonable one' as quoted earlier.[55] Perhaps India was diffident and felt wary of accepting China's overlordship of Tibet in public.

Since the Tibetan delegation, either by design or under compulsion, had kept India out of the negotiating exercise, India felt peeved. Later when the Tibetans asked for India's diplomatic support, Delhi told Lhasa 'the time for diplomatic support was during negotiations' and now that Tibet had signed the agreement any representation by India would be misunderstood and rejected as interference in its internal affairs. India, however, hoped that the India–Tibet border would remain demilitarized.[56]

The American embassy in Delhi and their consulate in Calcutta under instructions from Secretary of State Acheson made every effort to get Dalai Lama to denounce the agreement. The consulate played a major role since it was easier and convenient for it to keep in touch with Shakabpa, who was then based in Kalimpong, and through him exert maximum pressure on the Dalai Lama to denounce the agreement. At one point, a senior officer of the consulate camped in Kalimpong for long, ostensibly on holiday with the family, to be readily available for consultation.[56a] The Americans would have preferred that the Dalai Lama sought asylum in Ceylon or Siam where he would have little or no constraint on his activities.[56b] To pressurize the Dalai Lama to denounce the agreement, the Americans even offered him asylum in the United States and were willing to consider what assistance to provide, making sure that while it would 'be advisable that they live in modest and dignified fashion. The U.S. will do (its) utmost (to) help Tibetans solve(their) financial problem.'[56c] When nothing worked out, they sought support from India and the American *Charges* Steere called on the Additional Secretary in the MEA, S. Dutt, on 27 June 1951 and informed him of their contacts with the Tibetans, and their wish to get the agreement denounced by Dalai Lama. Steere added that US policy was in consonance with their recognition of Tibetan autonomy.[57] Delhi checked with its mission in Lhasa if it had any additional information,[57a] it found that it had none. New Delhi, too, told its political officer that while India would discourage the Dalai Lama from leaving Tibet, should he seek asylum, India would provide it on the clear understanding that he would not indulge in any political activity.[58] Not much notice of it was apparently taken by the GoI and no official displeasure of any kind was conveyed to the American mission or to the Tibetans for carrying on such negotiations behind its back. American efforts met with little success and, to its embarrassment, the Dalai Lama, under pressure from the high priests of the three big monasteries and other senior lamas, opted to accept the agreement and gave his approval to it in a telegram to Mao Zedong on 24 October 1951, a full five months after it had been signed in Beijing by Ngabo. Mao acknowledged his message on 26 October, conveying his thanks and 'heartfelt greetings'.[59]

The Dalai Lama after accepting the agreement returned to Lhasa from Yatung. He and other senior Tibetan officials were disappointed with India for its failure to stand up for Tibet. 'Tibetan officials were unhappy and felt insulted that the political officer Hareshwar Dayal, although residing a short distance away in Gangtok (Sikkim), made no attempt to pay even a courtesy call to the Dalai Lama while he was camping at Yatung, despite the fact that Dayal had been warmly welcomed in Lhasa a year before.' The Tibetans were disappointed with the US, too, since they failed to help as they had done in Korea by despatch of their troops.[60]

The story of loss of even autonomy for Tibet ended on a melancholy note, and Tibet became a part of the People's Republic of China. At the end it gained 'national autonomy' instead of 'autonomy' under the Chinese Constitution, whatever it meant. India lost all its clout in Lhasa. The 17-Point Agreement prepared the ground for the final ousting of India from Lhasa.

7

India–China Agreement on Tibet

Taking control of Tibet, China looked into Tibet's contacts with other countries, which had become incongruous with its new status as a part of China. Tibet, by virtue of its 1856 treaty with Nepal, was paying an annual tribute of rupees ten thousand to that country. This was being paid until 1952. In 1953 when the tribute did not arrive, Kathmandu reminded Lhasa about it. Lhasa told Kathmandu to refer the matter to Beijing and that was the end of it.[1]

India's involvement was far too deep to be dismissed so easily. It had two permanent trade agencies at Gyantse and Yatung, and a seasonal one at Gartok. There was the mission at Lhasa, but its status was undetermined. India also had a military escort stationed at Gyantse for the security of the trade agencies. It operated post and telegraph services to ensure smooth communication with India. To facilitate movement of touring officers and couriers, it also maintained guest houses en route to India.

On 24 April 1952, the Chinese had informed the Tibetan government that Beijing would shortly take up the question of relations between Tibet and its neighbouring counties such as India, Nepal and Bhutan, without further delay. Regarding 'Tibetan areas' in India, including Ladakh, Bhutan and Tawang (present-day

Arunachal Pradesh), the Chinese said they were waiting for a favourable opportunity to regain these areas and until then the issue would remain alive.[2] On 14 June 1952, speaking to Ambassador Panikkar, Zhou presumed that India did not wish to claim the 'special rights' arising from the unequal treaties of the past that Lhasa had signed with India earlier, and would be prepared to negotiate fresh arrangements 'safeguarding its legitimate interests'. Having said that, he added that he did not wish to bring the old arrangement that had existed between Tibet and the British before 1947 abruptly to a close, as otherwise it would leave a vacuum. Panikkar showed willingness 'to negotiate a settlement on all points' and Zhou, in turn, suggested pending settlement of other points, conversion of the Indian mission in Lhasa into a consulate general and, reciprocally, China setting up a consulate general in Bombay.[3]

Panikkar requested Delhi's approval to Zhou's proposal for converting the Indian mission in Lhasa into a consulate and China reciprocally setting up of a consulate in Bombay. Panikkar also added that Zhou had not touched the boundary question.[4]

Nehru conveyed his no objection to the proposal within twenty-four hours without due diligence. He, however, added a caveat that this proposal should be part of a comprehensive agreement.[5] The embassy, without waiting for formal orders, conveyed it to the Chinese, making no mention of the caveat.[6] Losing no time, China suggested that the new incumbent to replace the existing one should be a consul general.[7] India agreed to this as well.

As soon as the mission converted itself into a consulate general (CG), India's old relationship with Tibet became anachronistic. The CG now automatically came under the jurisdiction of the Indian embassy in Beijing and *ipso facto* India accepted Chinese sovereignty over Tibet. Every Chinese action in Tibet hereafter became China's internal affair.

It also eliminated the role of the political officer in Sikkim, who was strategically placed to look after Indian interests in Tibet. The political officer lost his long-standing status in Tibet and with that his right to visit Lhasa as and when he considered it necessary. Soon the Chinese instructed Kashag (Tibetan Cabinet) to inform Yatung (a town close to the Sikkim–Tibet border, where regional offices of the Tibetan government were located) not to observe any protocol for the political officer when he visited the place.[8] Meanwhile, the mission in Lhasa understood that another set of orders had been issued to all Tibetan government departments, monastic establishments and individual officials forbidding direct contact with the consulate.[9]

Girija Shankar Bajpai, former secretary general in the MEA and the then governor of the Bombay State, expressed his worries regarding the impact that the proposed Chinese consulate in Bombay would have on 'the large population of industrial workers, and the militant proletariat of communist persuasion'.[10] Regarding Tibet's status, especially after the signing of the 17-Point Agreement, Nehru declared at a press conference, 'You cannot treat Tibet as an independent country with an independent representative from us . . . it has to be negotiated with China and Tibet both.' Answering another question, he said, 'There is no doubt that we will withdraw (military escort) if necessary.'[11]

China, after expressing its desire for a change, began nibbling at Indian facilities, making the functioning of the mission and the trade agencies difficult. Often mail bags would be snatched from couriers, and returned only after protests. There were occasions when the mail bags would be released only after their contents had been examined. At the time of the turnaround of the personnel of the military escort at Gyantse, there was an impasse. The matter had to be brought to the notice of the prime minister in a comprehensive note, drawing his attention to the intolerable situation which had developed in Tibet not only on any particular matter but also generally speaking.[12] He decided to take action. In his message to the Chinese premier Zhou, Nehru pointed out the various problems which had obstructed the functioning of the Indian establishments in Tibet.[12a] He said:

The GoI have been anxious to come to a final settlement about pending matters so as to avoid any misunderstanding and friction at any time. On the 2nd August, 1952 a note was sent to Your Excellency's Government about all pending matters expressing willingness to discuss them and modify certain practices and even to remove some of them, if they are considered as affecting the dignity of China.[13]

A significant point in the PM's message was the mention of note of 2 August 1952 that listed the pending matters that had to be addressed. The matters listed were the following:

(i) Status of [the] mission in Lhasa; (ii) trade agencies at Gyantse and Yatung; (iii) seasonal trade agency at Gartok; (iv) [the] right of Indians to trade in Tibet; (v) post and telegraph offices; (vi) military escort at Gyantse; and (vii) pilgrimage.[14]

The question of frontiers was not among them. The PM in his message to Zhou said since 'piecemeal consideration of each problem did not lead to satisfactory solution', the need for discussion on all pending matters had become necessary.[15]

Another note drafted by Nehru himself, along the lines of the previous one, was handed over to the Chinese ambassador in New Delhi. This note informed the Chinese ambassador:

All such pending matters affecting relations between the two countries in Tibet were specified in a note handed to the Ministry of Foreign Affairs, Peking on the 2nd August, 1952.

The note went on to furnish details of some of the serious incidents that had taken place, which had led to the functioning of the Indian agencies being obstructed.[16]

This note, too, referred to the Indian note of 2 August 1952, which had excluded frontier question among the pending issues.

This was in spite of the fact that the Chinese had told Ambassador Panikkar already on 18 July 1952 that 'we want to make it clear that we do not recognise old British unequal treaties and wanted to set up relations between New Delhi and new China in Tibet on a new basis'.[17]

Delhi recognized that 'the question of frontier with Tibet' was 'obviously important'. However, since the prime minister had maintained in Parliament and in public that 'there is no frontier question to be discussed and the frontier had been finally demarcated along the McMahon Line', the discussion of the frontier question with China was not proposed.[18] Bajpai, then governor of the Bombay state, said since China had never accepted the McMahon Line, the frontier question could hardly be regarded as settled.[19]

Soon, thereafter, the Chinese embassy requested the withdrawal of the military escort from Gyantse as an immediate step before discussions on any other matter could be initiated. Delhi, as a gesture of goodwill, agreed to this but emphasized that, in the meantime, there should be no interference with the existing practices in Tibet.[20] However, there was no further development on this question until after the agreement had been signed.

Finally, Zhou agreed to Nehru's proposal for negotiations and suggested that they begin in Beijing in December 1953. Nehru, acknowledging his message, said 'since discussions are to take place soon, I do not wish, at this stage, to go into the details of all pending matters which were mentioned in a note presented to your Excellency's Government on the 2nd August, 1952 at Peking', and expressed the hope that this would be an opportunity to settle 'all *outstanding* issues' between the two countries.[21] Repeated emphasis on the note of 2 August 1952 highlighted the seven issues listed in that note which had excluded the frontiers that needed settlement.

It was now time to chalk out a strategy for the discussions ahead. Former ambassador in Beijing, Panikkar, who was now the ambassador in Cairo, volunteered a suggestion based on a policy that Nehru had accepted in the past and which he himself had followed meticulously while in Beijing. He suggested that not only should no discussions on the frontiers be allowed, but if the Chinese insisted on discussions, India should break the negotiations. Regarding Bhutan, he suggested that India should convey to the Chinese that 'any attempt on their part to open diplomatic relations with Bhutan would be considered by us an unfriendly act'.[22] In another letter on the same date, Panikkar told the foreign secretary, R.K. Nehru, that, according to his judgement, 'in the next three or four years China will not take any decisive step which can alienate us, nor do I think in the present circumstances she will want to challenge us on a matter which is not very important to her but is vital to us'. About the frontier question, Panikkar told the foreign secretary, 'We should not allow the matter to be opened at all.'[23] Girija Shankar Bajpai from Bombay, while repeating his earlier advice, added that China should be formally told in a note that India regarded the McMahon Line as its frontier, without asking the Chinese for confirmation, and he added that if the Chinese did not react now but raised objections later, India could legitimately quote their silence as acquiescence. If, however, they did not accept India's position, 'that may possibly leave us sadder men but also wiser'. Panikkar dismissed Bajpai's apprehensions and remarked: 'The Chinese have not asked that any other point (other than the seven issues mentioned by us) should be discussed or settled.' Panikkar also told Bajpai that Nehru, too, had decided to exclude the frontiers in the discussions.[24]

Bajpai's suggestion was cautious but prudent. Panikkar's suggestion, based on presumptions, was hardly the way to settle an important matter such as borders. Be that as it may, his views, as in the past and now, once again conditioned the thinking of Delhi. Before the ministry sat down to discuss the brief for the forthcoming negotiations, a top-secret telegram from Lhasa alerted Delhi that China had held detailed talks with Tibetan officials and that one of the main issues discussed was the frontier question for which all the relevant documents and maps were studied.[25]

This led the MEA to go into some details while chalking out the strategy on frontiers. At the strategy meeting in Delhi, all the questions anticipated were discussed, including the seven issues which had already been conveyed to China. Bhutan was also added to the list. The consensus that emerged was India should not raise the border question at all and, as Panikkar had suggested, if the Chinese insisted on discussing the borders, India must break off the negotiations. Taking cognizance of the legal advice, it was also concluded in the meeting that since China had not ratified the Simla Convention, 'the Chinese could very well make this contention' of not recognizing the McMahon Line. Aksai Chin in the western sector and Tawang and Walong in the eastern sector, along with some other areas, were listed as 'disputed' areas.

The approach decided at the meeting, in the end, echoed what Nehru had advocated initially—that our borders were 'well recognized by long custom and usage' and they must stay. As to the attitude that India should adopt about these disputed areas, it was suggested in the brief that: '*prima facie* . . . we should not be prepared to give up these places except in return for an overall acceptance of our frontier by the Chinese. In that case also, we should examine and then give up each area on its merits taking into strategic importance into consideration'.

It is relevant to note that in all these discussions only the McMahon Line or the eastern border was considered in detail but not much attention was given specifically to the Aksai Chin. There were concerns that if India refused to discuss the border question, it might lead to incidents along the borders. Responding to these fears, a modification was made in the decided approach. If China wished to discuss the borders, India was to ask the Chinese to proceed with the other items on the agenda first and discuss the frontier at the end. Should the Chinese still insist on discussing the borders first, then the brief suggested breaking off the negotiations.

On Bhutan, the brief suggested that it should be conveyed to the Chinese that the external relations of Bhutan were directly guided by

India. This was the position stated in the treaty that India had with Bhutan, and was well known.

Other issues did not take much time and were also not too contentious in nature. Nehru had already said that India would be ready to modify or give up altogether anything that was against the dignity of China. The trade activities were not of much significance, and it was the Tibetans who were importing most of the essential consumer items for their use. In comparison, India's imports were confined to wool, yak tails and borax. Indian trade agencies were already functioning there, and the Chinese, too, had one in Kalimpong and another recently established in Bombay. It was also considered that if, reciprocally, the Chinese were to demand an additional trade agency, India should not agree to one in Gangtok or Leh, since both the places were sensitive from the point of view of security.[26] The brief finalized at the meeting on 3 December 1953 was sent to the prime minister for his approval. He approved it, except the matter regarding the frontiers, about which he said:

> I agree about the attitude we should take up in regard to the frontier. We should not raise this question. If the Chinese raise it, we should express our surprise and point out that this is a settled issue. Further that during the last two years or so, when reference was frequently made about Indo-Tibetan problems, there has never been any reference to the frontier issue and it is surprising that this should be brought up now. Our delegation cannot discuss it. *We should avoid walking out unless Chinese insist on taking up this question. If such an eventuality occurs, the matter will no doubt be referred to us.*

He had no comments on Aksai Chin and Tawang and Walong listed as 'disputed areas'. Regarding Bhutan, he said:

> We should make it perfectly clear that external affairs of Bhutan are under our direct guidance and not raise this question. But inferentially this should be bought out and that the Chinese will have to deal with us in regard to external affairs of Bhutan.[27]

A few days later, the head of the eastern division in the ministry, T.N. Kaul impressed on the Chinese embassy the 'desirability of settling issues promptly in [a] friendly spirit to show to the rest of the world that two friendly Asian countries can solve their problems successfully (within a week or two) unlike the interminable and inconclusive talks at Panmunjom'. [The reference was to the talks on armistice in Korea between the North and South Koreas.][28] The same expectation and sentiments were expressed by the new Ambassador Nedyam Raghavan to Zhou Enlai in Beijing on 23 December 1953. Zhou reciprocated 'warmly', and said:

> We would show to the world that India and China had no differences and in mutual interest and with regard to each other sovereignty and territorial integrity we could settle matters amicably. Incidentally it would also show what Asians left to themselves could do.[29]

Ambassador Raghavan was asked to head the Indian delegation. The other two members, T.N. Kaul and Dr Gopalachari, deputy director in the historical division of the MEA, were sent from Delhi. Kaul had served in Beijing until recently. On the Chinese side, the vice minister of foreign affairs, Chang Han Fu, led the discussions, assisted by Asia Director Chen Chia Kang, Vice Director Ho Ying and Assistant-in-Charge Foreign Affairs Bureau, Yang Kung-su.

Zhou Enlai received both the delegations at his residence at 1300 hours on 31 December 1953. While welcoming them, he said that the Chinese Government had already laid down its principles in 1949 for any settlement. Referring to them as the Common Program he said:

> All outstanding problems between China and other countries could be solved on the basis of mutual respect for territorial integrity, non-aggression and non-interference in internal affairs so as to enable peaceful co-existence. I know Prime Minister Nehru's

Government and people of India also feel the same way. On basis
of this principle, *all outstanding questions between* us *which are ripe
for settlement* can be resolved smoothly.[30]

Ambassador Raghavan in his remarks conceded that under
the Premier's guidance '*all outstanding issues*' would be settled
smoothly.[31] It is to be noted that in his inaugural remarks Zhou
used three significant phrases: (i) the principles for settlement of
disputes; (ii) the outstanding questions *which were ripe for settlement*
and (iii) problems between neighbours with *long common frontier*.
He, however, did not spell out which were the problems that were
ripe and which were not. The Indian ambassador, too, stated that
'all outstanding issues' would be settled without any elaboration.
Presumably, *both understood the difference but chose to remain smug*.

As it happened, both continued to make the same point about
the scope of the talks at the beginning, during the discussion and at
the end.

It was agreed on the very first day that during the course of
the negotiations no communiqué would be issued by either side.[32]
India, in its presentation, covered practically all the points except the
frontiers and Bhutan, as per its approved brief. The ambassador also
remarked, 'We both would continue to live as ideal neighbours with
mutual respect for each other's sovereign independence, territorial
integrity and that our frontiers will always be symbol of peace and
cooperation.'[33]

The uphill road began when the Chinese sought all sorts of
clarifications on the points made by India, for most of which the Indian
delegation needed to confer with Delhi. China, using the principle
of reciprocity, divested India of all the privileges and facilities it had
historically but unilaterally enjoyed in Tibet. Whatever facilities were
allowed to be retained by India were reciprocally conceded by India
to China.

The Chinese laid down the five principles to facilitate discussions
and, at request of the Indian delegation, spelt them out as:

1. mutual respect for each other's territorial integrity and sovereignty;
2. mutual non-aggression;
3. mutual non-interference in each other's internal affairs;
4. equality and mutual benefit;
5. peaceful coexistence.

These were the same principles that had been mentioned by Premier Zhou in his opening speech on 31 December. They emphasized that if these principles were adhered to, '*all pending questions that were "ripe for settlement"* would be discussed and settled'.[34]

China, too, added that either side could bring any issue which was ripe for settlement.[35]

The five principles were unexceptional and were accepted without much debate or reservations. They finally became the template of India–China relations, which were included in the agreement following these negotiations, and thereafter repeated *ad nauseam* in various statements. The Chinese can legitimately claim their authorship.[36]

Following the principle of reciprocity, India granted China the same number of trade agencies in India as it had in China—three. India retained the old ones at Gyantse and Yatung and the third which earlier was a seasonal one at Gartok was now made permanent, while China got its trade agencies at Kalimpong, Siliguri and Calcutta.

The Indian hospitals attached to the trade agencies which offered free treatment to even the local population were allowed to continue on the condition that they would *not serve the local population*.[37] Indian officials' access to Tibetan officials was further restricted when they were told that they could not contact Tibetan officials directly any more, except on specific trade matters, and that too after getting appointments through the Chinese Foreign Bureau in Lhasa.[38]

By the time the Chinese had finished their presentation, all aspects of the India–Tibet relationship had come under attack in one form or another. Finally, on 12 January, Ambassador

Raghavan told Chen Chia-Kang that since the scope of the talks had widened and their viewpoints appeared to be divergent, these were all outside delegation's brief and he needed to go back to India. Chen said:

> Neither we nor you can show face to the world unless we have agreement on principles of equality and mutual benefit (and) that does not mean our agency etc., will be immediately established or non-Tibetans would enter India as traders. We could have separate understanding, protocol or exchange of letters about it, apart from formal agreement.

The ambassador replied:

> Your principles of equality should not be applied mathematically just as thoughts of Mao are not Marxism in abstraction, abstract sketch application to concrete conditions in China. We have come here to stabilise existing conditions with your agreement and without infringing China's sovereignty but you have raised new issues not based on existing facts. (He) cited as unreal their demand for trade agency at Almora on existing facts and trade marts at places like Shillong, Dehradun, Simla etc., and permission for all Chinese nationals (including Han Chinese living in Tibet) to enter India as traders (without passport or visa).[39]

India had accepted the facility of passport- and visa-free travel for trade for ethnic Tibetans only but not for the Han Chinese even if they were born in Tibet.[40] The Chinese said that this would amount to discrimination between two classes of citizens of the same country and was not acceptable to them. After much discussion, the relevant article was so worded as to not show any discrimination and yet accommodating the Han Chinese as well. It referred to '[t]raders of both the countries known to be customarily and specifically engaged in trade between [the] Tibet Region of China and India'. The use of the phrase 'traders known to be customarily and specifically engaged' accommodated the Chinese perspective on apparent discrimination.[41]

For India, the real test of Chinese friendship arose when Tibet's trade with Ladakh came up for discussion. It may be pointed out that on the day of the inaugural session in Beijing, Kushak Bakula, the venerable Lama of Ladakh, had in his meeting with the prime minister in New Delhi suggested that the traditional biennial trade missions from Ladakh to Lhasa should be revived. Bakula was also anxious and requested the prime minister for continuance of facilities for education of Ladakhi Lamas in Tibet. Nehru told Ambassador Raghavan that though these facilities had not yet been interfered with, the desirability of their continuance should be kept in mind. He instructed the ambassador, 'You may in your discussions include a general reference to Ladakh-Tibet trade without going into the details of exchange of missions.'[42]

At the very mention of Ladakh, and the associated trade and pilgrimage, the Chinese perked up and resisted any attempt to discuss this question. India felt it was imperative to open the two passes, Rudok and Rawang, which directly linked Ladakh to Tibet, in order to facilitate Ladakh's links with Tibet.[43] As India pressed for this, the Chinese shocked the Indians, suggesting:

[I]f we were to discuss now [the] question relating to Ladakh we cannot but get involved in Kashmir and the question of Kashmir is pending settlement through negotiations between India and Pakistan. Therefore we are not prepared now to discuss questions relating to Kashmir.

Kaul had pointed out that India could not accept that position since it involved the principle of territorial integrity. It was speculated that China might be thinking of a separate agreement on Ladakh later depending on future developments.[44]

Since there was no agreement, India presenting a draft of the agreement to the Chinese included the two passes. China once again refused to consider Ladakh's links with Tibet, suggesting it to be 'impossible even if there is a deadlock'.[45] India was stunned. The Chinese were prepared to concede an alternative indirect link to Tashigong for Ladakh's trade with Tibet via Demchok but not the direct route even if there was a possibility of a 'deadlock'. This was a new situation that India was facing. Delhi, changing its track, on 21 March said, 'If the Chinese continue to insist on their (Rudok and Rawang) exclusion, we shall have to agree. We must however ensure that Ladakh's trade does not suffer by diversion to Tashigong route.' The ministry asked the ambassador to consider this 'carefully' and inform Delhi what he thought of this.[46] The ambassador, in his reply, said, if 'we agree to [the] exclusion of Rudok and Rawang, the only route will be Leh-Tashigong via Demchok' and quoted the Asia director, Chen, to suggest that Ladakh's trade would not suffer. The ambassador, too, appeared anxious to accept the exclusion of the two passes. He added that the Chinese reluctance was *perhaps* due to there being military installations in that area.[47]

On the same day, Delhi replied that since 'the Chinese were unwilling' these (the two passes) may be excluded.[48] The ambassador's 'discovery' of military installation in those areas and Delhi's instant acceptance appeared to cover the surrender on an issue which involved India's territorial integrity. It is relevant to point out that the Chinese at no time had referred to the military installations as the reason for their not agreeing to the Indian suggestion. They had no qualms in referring to the Kashmir factor for their reluctance. The ambassador's presumption was self-delusional. It was indeed surprising that China should have been worried about Pakistan's sensitivities even in 1954 when their contacts with Pakistan were still minimal compared to India's. It was a notice to India that China was not sold to India and had its own independent views on sensitive issues that concerned India.

When the general question of inclusion of passes was under consideration, Delhi suggested that three passes in the western sector—QaraTagh La, Lanak La and Domjor La—be considered for inclusion.[49] Ambassador Raghavan pointed out that the three suggested passes adjoined the disputed territory of Aksai Chin and that raising the question of their inclusion would involve territorial questions.[50] Delhi agreed to withdraw its suggestion.[51] That Aksai Chin was a disputed area stared India in the face once again but was ignored. It was thought prudent to avoid the problem than face it squarely.

Regarding the other passes, Delhi clarified to the ambassador that the passes—LipuLeh, Darma, Niti, Mana, Shipki, Unta and Dhura—were border passes where entry was on the Indian side and exit on the Tibetan side. It was also confirmed that the Kungri Bingri pass was not on the border. Similarly, Demchok was not on the border, it was on the right bank of Indus. The village of Demchok was wholly within Indian territory.[52]

Finally on 23 March, after almost three months of leisurely negotiations, a draft of the preamble along with draft letters of exchange, as written by the ministry of external affairs, reflecting the five principles which had been proposed by the Chinese, was presented to the Chinese.[53]

The letters of exchange clarified the facilities that the trade agents and the traders on both sides would enjoy equally on the basis of reciprocity. In the letters, India also agreed to withdraw completely its military escort from Tibet within three months. They had the provision for handing over of all the telegraph lines and guest houses maintained by India in Tibet to the Chinese Government on reasonable payment. In the end, India gifted the telegraph lines free of cost, as a gesture of goodwill, while the depreciated cost for the guest houses was paid by the Chinese. It also outlined the details of the facilities to be provided to the pilgrims of both the countries.[54] But the negotiations were not over yet even after they had dragged on for three long months. They were only at the draft stage.

Delhi was getting impatient. On 2 April, the MEA told Raghavan that the prime minister had 'some days ago' said in Parliament that the negotiations would be completed 'within a fortnight or so'.

The ministry now asked the ambassador to finalize things as quickly as possible.[55]

The ambassador justified the delay and said that it was not 'entirely due to the Chinese'. He also hinted at further delay since the Chinese were not satisfied with the draft presented to them and also because of the possibility of their senior officials being involved in the discussions in Geneva on the question of Indo-China. The ambassador thought the delay that had been caused in the negotiations was not specific to India and generally 'Chinese negotiations, as with other delegations, always drag on like this'.[56] One was left wondering if that was reason enough to be satisfied. It was the Indians who were cooling their heels in Beijing and were absent from their headquarters for months. The Chinese were sitting pretty, giving the Indians a taste of negotiations with the communist government. Further objections were raised about the facilities and immunities that the trade agents were to enjoy and some other mundane matters. The ambassador told Delhi that since the residual matters were 'petty' problems, Delhi delegate him the powers to take a view on those issues in Beijing, ensuring that India's fundamental interests were not compromised.[57] Delhi agreed.[58]

There was also some discussion on the life of the agreement and its further renewal after its expiry. The Chinese insisted on eight years' life of the agreement and did not agree to the Indian suggestion for automatic renewal. Both delegations, however, were agreed on ratification of the agreement after signatures. The ambassador also suggested to Delhi that 'we need not ask that English text should prevail (a normal practice) in [the] event of [a] disagreement but may agree that all texts have equal validity'.[59]

But still there was no finality and there appeared to be no end in sight to the negotiations. The prime minister was getting increasingly exasperated at the delay. He appeared worried about the policies of the American secretary of state, John Foster Dulles, at the Geneva Conference, where the future of Indo-China was under discussion, and wanted to make his own statement but, before that, he was anxious that the agreement on Tibet be concluded and out of the way, which he was convinced would have a 'salutary effect'. He was worried that if Zhou left for Geneva, the talks would be inevitably postponed. Concerned, he telegraphed Raghavan and said:

> We cannot have our men sitting in Beijing hoping for something to happen. They have stayed there much too long already. We shall then have to fix some distant date probably in Delhi for future resumption of talks. This will create impression of failure which will not be good.[60]

The PM asked him to convey to the Chinese that 'our men who have gone from Delhi will have to return even before Geneva conference begins'.

In yet another climbdown, Foreign Secretary R.K. Nehru agreed to the Chinese insistence that there would be no restrictions on areas where 'Tibetan may trade'. They would be free to trade in Kalimpong, Calcutta and Siliguri in addition to other places. The foreign secretary wanted it to be explained to the Chinese that *we will be giving greater facilities to their traders on our side than will be available to Indian traders on Tibetan side*.[61] Before the agreement containing six articles was finalized on 26 April, there were some more hitches which were stitched. The Chinese insisted that before the agreement was finalized India had announced that it would hand over 'post and telegraph installations and services without compensation'. The ambassador asked Delhi to authorize him to announce that India would offer this gift 'in the spirit of friendship'. He referred to some file where the prime minister had 'agreed to this provided agreement went through without difficulty'. That the difficulties that were encountered were too many was forgotten, and it was agreed to make a gift of them.[62]

The finalized agreement was signed on 29 April 1954 by Vice Foreign Minister Chang Han Fu on the Chinese side and Ambassador Nedyam Raghavan on the Indian side.[63] It contained the five principles of peaceful coexistence, which the Chinese had stated at the outset, and had said that if these were adhered to '*all pending questions that were ripe for settlement* could be discussed and settled'. It remained a matter of perception whether only issues that were 'ripe for settlement' were resolved or 'all outstanding issues', since neither side made any explicit statement. India erroneously continued to believe even if the borders were not discussed they stood settled. The Chinese strategy appeared to be to see India out of Tibet first and then rake up the question of borders, and they succeeded admirably in this.

Prime Minister Jawaharlal Nehru, making an announcement in Parliament about the conclusion of the agreement, described it 'as a very important event', glossing over the various hurdles the Chinese created that delayed the finalization of the agreement, and the surrenders India had to make. He justified the delay because, as he said, the delay was 'not because of any major conflict or difficulty but because the number of small points were so many and had to be discussed in detail'. Sticking to friendly vibes, he drew the attention to the five principles in the preamble, which he said 'indicate the policy that we pursue in regard to these matters not only with China but with any neighbouring country and for that matter any other country'. He described them as 'wholesome principles'. Though he did not refer to the frontier question, in an indirect reference, he said:

> It is a matter of importance to us, as well as, I am sure to China that these countries, which have now almost about 1,800 miles of frontier, should live on terms of peace and friendliness, respect each other's sovereignty and integrity and agree not to interfere with each other in any way and not to commit aggression on each other.[64]

Notwithstanding any other consideration, he was so elated with the five principles that he asked his ambassador in Burma (Myanmar), K.K. Chettur, to commend these principles to Burma in its relations with China.[65]

There was some muted criticism of the agreement in Parliament, which upset Nehru and he said that some members had referred to these developments as 'the melancholy chapter of Tibet'. He disabused them of their notions by referring to the past history of Tibet, and said:

> Many things happen in the world which we do not like and which we would wish were rather different but we do not go like Don Quixote with lance in hand against everything that we dislike; we put up with these things because we would be, without making any difference, merely getting into trouble.[66]

Since the full details of the negotiations and the climbdowns that India had to make remained hidden from the people, they welcomed it. The press, with its limited reach then, had to depend on what was dished out to it by the government. The *Amrita Bazar Patrika*, welcoming it erroneously, said:

> From the very beginning (Nehru) had ruled any discussion of the India China frontier, and in the resulting agreement he succeeded in getting approval of the McMahon Line.[67]

The *Times of India* in its editorial on 1 May 1954 said that the silence on the border question was 'welcome, in as much as it is an acknowledgement of the existing boundary line . . . In any case the Indian Government will stand by the McMahon Line and will not allow anyone to cross that boundary'. This, too, was a mistaken analysis in the face of lack of any real time information.[68]

The *Pioneer,* however, was nearest to the truth when it said in its editorial:

> Nothing had been secured to shut out further penetration of Chinese communists into regions bordering on China. India has yet to wake to the reality on her north-eastern frontiers and to events which are likely to follow.[69]

It appeared to be a minority view that India had given up all its facilities in Tibet as a price for the agreement. Considered in the context of Nehru's views of 8 November 1950,[70] it was evident that he had made up his mind to surrender the unilateral facilities and privileges India enjoyed in Tibet, and, to that extent, he did not mind their loss. The Chinese reservations on Ladakh remained under a tight lid then and thereafter.

The agreement was India's attempt to disinherit its inconvenient legacy of the British. China ensured that everything was negotiated on a reciprocal basis. The agreement was so crafted as to appear that it was for the first time that the two countries had entered into such an arrangement or a relationship, and no contacts ever existed between India and Tibet prior to this. Old practices which were to be abolished were excluded from the main agreement and put in the Letters of Exchange to ensure the dignity and sensitivity of China.

A deeper analysis would convince one that the agreement was nothing short of surrender by India. It not only failed to protect India's core interest in Tibet but also accepted Chinese challenge to the territorial integrity of India when it insisted that Ladakh, as a part of Kashmir, was a disputed area. China showed greater sensitivity to Pakistan vis-à-vis India, and that was reason enough to break the negotiations. The interests of Ladakh, nay of India's territorial integrity, were sacrificed at the altar of an elusive Chinese friendship.

Even Intelligence Chief B.N. Mullik in his book *Chinese Betrayal*, while explaining the developments leading to the military confrontation between India and China, wrote that the Intelligence Bureau was 'disturbed' by the signing of the 1954 agreement and felt that it 'had gone entirely in favour of China and against the interests of India'.[71] At the same time, it was generally believed that Nehru depended a lot on the assessment of Mullik in structuring his policies on Tibet and in relation to Tibet on China. However, since the book was published after Nehru's death, one has to take the book's credibility with a pinch of salt.

Nevertheless, it was an erroneous understanding on the part of India that all *outstanding issues,* including frontiers, which were not even discussed or rather were intentionally excluded by India itself from discussions, were settled. Delhi could not have been unaware that in any agreement there are two parts, the preamble which defines the scope of issues being discussed, and the main part which spells out in the subsequent articles the methodology to resolve them. In the present agreement, the preamble read:

> Being desirous of *promoting trade and cultural intercourse between Tibet Region of China and India and for facilitating pilgrimage and travel by the peoples of China and India*

As the agreement stood, only the issues relevant to trade and travel and pilgrimage were negotiated in the agreement, as had also been hinted at by Nehru in his own note of 1 September 1953 to Zhou,[72] which perhaps acted as a trigger for the present agreement. These were also the issues on which the brief for the Indian delegation was finalized in the ministry on 3 December 1953 and approved by Nehru.[73] These were precisely the subjects that were discussed at Beijing. Nehru's perception that by not raising the question of frontiers, China had accepted the Indian frontiers as understood by India was erroneous and he made this claim too often hereafter.

To harbour the illusion that everything had been settled and to live with it was a recipe for disaster. As pointed out earlier, the border in the western sector, which caused the maximum trouble later, remained completely forgotten and was never discussed even remotely despite the fact that India was aware that the area of Aksai Chin in this sector was disputed and 'UNDEFINED'.

Should the expiry of agreement later be taken as the expiry of the agreement on borders too? Border agreements are considered permanent documents internationally, unless amended or modified by mutual agreement.

Incidentally, even when the agreement referred to issues relevant to Tibet alone, not a single Tibetan official was involved on the Chinese side in the discussions. One was not even sure if the Chinese had taken the Dalai Lama into confidence about the negotiations. It was on 27 January 1954 that Nehru asked the Consulate at Lhasa to discreetly inform the Dalai Lama 'orally and very confidentially' that these negotiations were being conducted and that 'we hope that with agreement of the Chinese we shall be able to continue our existing close relations with Tibet'.[74]

T.N. Kaul on his return to Delhi in his report on negotiations in Beijing[75] described it as the *quickest international agreement signed by any Chinese Government past or present*. Kaul was perhaps right from his point of view. He had served in the Chinese capital earlier and now he had returned as member of the delegation. He was having an affair with a Chinese woman while being engaged in political and important sensitive discussions, in breach of all norms of behaviour expected of an officer of his rank. He was audacious enough to seek permission to marry her, when already married, and even asked for two months' ex-India leave for his honeymoon, at the end of the negotiations. An upset prime minister in a top-secret telegram asked him 'to return to India as soon as possible without waiting for the end of Tibetan talks'. It is a different matter in the face of opposition from the PM and the ministry with the prospects of resigning from the service, he decided not to go ahead with his plan of marrying the Chinese woman.[76] Later he rose to be the foreign secretary of India and was rated as one of the most celebrated officers of the foreign service.

From his point of view, Beijing was perhaps a party, a holiday which he enjoyed thoroughly, and did not mind the delay and absence from Delhi for four months. Nehru did not seem to agree with Kaul's assessment that it was a 'quickest negotiated agreement' when he remarked 'any future negotiations with the Peking Government (should be) in Delhi and not in Peking'.[77]

Kaul's claim that the talks were cordial except for one or two points and the advantage of the prolonged negotiations was that China realized that 'we meant business and would not be cowed down or exhausted into submission' was again questionable. Regrettably, despite the tall claims of Kaul, it was India which compromised all the way to clinch the agreement. The sensitive points on which India had to compromise were never revealed to public then or later.

Nehru agreed with Kaul that at 'all disputed points, wherever they might be, our administration should be right up to these borders'. He laid great stress on the development of communications in the border areas. Nehru did not accept Kaul's suggestion for a non-aggression pact with China. However, he accepted his suggestion to invite Zhou Enlai to India on his way back home from Geneva.[78]

Nehru perhaps found Gopalachari's report on the negotiations substantive, which was a trigger for Nehru's order to mark the 'undefined, western border with a definite line and make it non-negotiable like the McMahon Line in the east'.[79] It was a different matter that his orders to unilaterally demarcate an international border were to create trouble later. The need for checkposts all along the borders was recognized in the PM's remarks on the report, but these were not set up on the ground. The bureaucratic lethargy, lack of continuous supervision, cranky machinery for implementation and lack of single-point responsibility remained the curse of India's political and administrative set-up. After signing this agreement, India lost its contact with Tibet and Tibetans, and the ability to speak for them. What initiated the agreement were the problems that the Indian establishments were facing, and yet these problems after the agreement was signed multiplied instead. The Indian establishments struggled for their survival in the face of hostile local Chinese administration. In the next few years, the avalanche of Tibetan unrest and non-cooperation of the local

Chinese administration washed away the entire Indian set-up in Tibet. Nehru, in trying to chase the mirage of Chinese friendship and Asian solidarity, achieved neither, nor could the security of India be ensured.

8

Revolt in Tibet and the Dalai Lama's Flight to India

China had occupied Tibet in 1950 and tied it down to a servile relationship. It deployed the People's Liberation Army (PLA) all over Tibet. Its presence in every nook and corner, particularly of Lhasa, was not only daunting for an average Tibetan but perhaps also a sight that they could hardly live with. The autonomy Tibet enjoyed under the Simla Convention vanished altogether. Contrary to the assurances they had been given while signing the 17-Point Agreement, the Tibetans saw their religion and practices as well as monasteries and monastic order coming under attack. The Tibetan bureaucracy, too, was alienated because of the overbearing attitude of the Chinese, which left no space for them to serve their people. There was a studied attempt to undermine even the Dalai Lama's authority in favour of the Panchen Lama. In short, the understandings and the promises Chinese made under the 17-Point Agreement were observed more in breach than in their observance.

Political Officer Apa Pant, after spending more than three months extensively touring Tibet (November 1956–February 1957), and meeting important personalities both in Tibetan and Chinese hierarchies, made a lengthy report, running into twenty-seven pages, and 11,676 words to the ministry of external affairs in which he concluded:

> If Tibet turns into a communist country and has a government guided and inspired by the Chinese, there is no doubt that she will certainly exert pressure on our frontiers—or as a matter of fact China will. Whatever the assurances given from time to time to us, it is evident that the Chinese would also not be able to resist the temptation of "calling back to their motherland" all those who belong to the Chinese family. Bhutan, Sikkim districts of Darjeeling and Kalimpong as well as parts of NEFA, Ladakh would be areas to which such a call will be sent. This may not happen within the next twenty years, but the possibility of it happening under certain circumstances does exist and we just cannot close our eyes to it. It is therefore to our interest to see that Tibet remains Tibetan and the people of Tibet remain friendly and attracted towards us.[1]

He noted that despite the presence of about 15,000 Chinese soldiers in and around Lhasa, the Tibetans were not subdued and even when the Chinese had 'literally spent millions on constructing roads, schools, hospitals etc., and though they had taken innumerable Tibetans to China for indoctrination and education as well as for sightseeing'. According to Pant's report, a modest estimate was that at least 5000 persons had been taken for a sightseeing tour into China and nearly 6000 students had been educated and returned to Tibet. In his estimate, there were still two to three thousand Tibetan students in China who were being indoctrinated. Despite all this, the Chinese had failed to win their affection or even friendship.[1a]

Pant held out the possibility of nationalist forces in Tibet rising against China. He believed that some of these forces were in touch with the outside powers such as Nepal, the United States and the United Kingdom for procuring small arms and ammunition and thousands of hand grenades smuggled across Nepal into Tibet. The Dalai Lama, too, remained apprehensive of being whisked away to Peking. He met the Dalai Lama thrice, once over a lunch hosted for him by the Pontiff, but he felt that his talks with him 'could not deal with what he had to say to me'.[2]

The prime minister was not impressed with Pant's report. He was against its wider circulation, since 'it involved the risk of wrong persons seeing it and if that happens, it might well involve us in difficulties'. He was even against the ambassador in Beijing getting a copy of it, and directed that he should only get a summary of it. While he conceded the report was 'important and interesting and factually a correct representation of the present situation in Tibet', he also felt that the note went further and gave one 'the impression of the writer being so much impressed by certain facts as to lose perspective. The note thus ceases to be completely objective'.[3]

According to Nehru, it was natural for China to adopt policies which would in the long run 'absorb Tibet in China more and more and make it accept the major pattern in political and economic matters'. Reacting to Pant's fears that India might have to feel the pressure on its frontiers in the future, Nehru felt it was rather 'a static and even out of date view of the forces that are at work in the world. If these pressures come, other new forces will also arise in India or in the rest of the world'. Regarding smuggling of arms into Tibet, the prime minister felt that this needed to be checked further.[4]

Even earlier, in his letter of 3 January 1957, from Lhasa, Pant had raised some points which were important in the perspective of his lengthier report. He had said that the entire monastic system was based on privileges and was 'corrupt and there is no point calling it a Buddhist land . . .' He believed that Tibet had now 'joined the stream of modern life and can never go back to its isolation'. He noted some 'important and valuable contributions from communism in this process of social, scientific and economic advancement of man in society which cannot be overlooked'.[5]

A year later, Nehru again emphasized:

> Change has become imperative in Tibet and if the Tibetans
> themselves did not promote such a change, it would come from
> outside. They should not challenge Chinese sovereignty but keep
> united and seek full autonomy.[6]

Several steps taken by China in the religious, social and economic
domains alienated the Tibetans. One noticeable factor was that the
reformist activities in the Tibetan Administrative Area (TAR) or the
Dalai Lama's Tibet were relatively benign as compared to those in
eastern Tibet (Kham and Amdo), which was populated with the
warrior tribe of the Khampas. They were the first to be impacted.
By 1956, the local population comprised mainly of Khampas had
resorted to violence against the Chinese because the Chinese had
started seizing their arms, which was part of the normal attire of the
Khampas. This invited retaliation by the PLA. Though the Khampas
were not of Tibetan stock, they owed spiritual allegiance to the
Dalia Lama. It was a different matter that the Khampas despised
the Tibetan bureaucracy, particularly the regents, who were ruthless,
unscrupulous and 'who over the past two hundred years had more
than once murdered the young Dalai Lamas, before they came of age.
Such had been the fate of (so some claim) the ninth, tenth, eleventh
and twelfth Dalai Lamas who all 'died mysteriously before attaining
their majority'.[7]

By June 1958, the disparate armed Khampas managed to form
the National Volunteer Defence Army, which then mounted raids
against the PLA outposts and convoys around Lhasa and in southern
Tibet.[8] The Khampa revolt gave the Americans the opportunity that
they were looking for since 1950. The CIA became involved in the
Khampas' activities. As pointed out earlier in the book, the CIA
was already training Tibetans in Colorado, USA. Now they started
training the Khampas, too, in small groups in insurgency tactics and
clandestine operations in Mustang, north Nepal, bordering Tibet.
They were using East Pakistan bases for flying those trained in the
United States and air dropping them in Tibet.[9] Often China, unable

to identify the intruding aircraft, blamed India for air violations and lodged protests, which were rejected by India.

The United States was looking at the struggle between India and China from the social and economic angle. In his speech, Senator Kennedy in May 1959 said:

> No struggle in the world today deserves more of our time and attention than that which now grips the attention of all Asia. That is the struggle between India and China for the leadership of all Asia, for the opportunity to demonstrate which way of life is the better.[10]

The central theme of the speech was a battle between a democratic India that supported 'human dignity and individual freedom' against China which represented 'ruthless denial of human rights'.[10a]

On 10 July 1958, Weichiaopu (the Chinese Foreign Office) in a note to the Indian embassy in Beijing protested about the so-called disruptive activities of the US and the clique headed by Taiwanese President Chiang Kai Shek in collusion with the fugitive reactionaries from Tibet (read the Khampas) who, the Chinese believed, were using the Indian city Kalimpong as a base for their activities against the Chinese. The note conveyed that Premier Zhou had during his visit to India in 1956–57 brought their activities to the notice of Prime Minister Nehru and later to the attention of Ambassador R.K. Nehru since they caused a threat to China's territorial integrity.[11] It may be recalled that Zhou during his second visit to India had specially taken up the issue of Kalimpong being used as the nerve centre by the Khampas and other Tibetans for promoting revolt within Tibet, and wanted Nehru to look into it. Nehru had then lightly dismissed this, suggesting that 'Kalimpong was a nest of spies and the spies are probably more than the population'.[11a]

It was obvious that the activities of the Khampas had unnerved the Chinese, which made them even discourage Nehru from visiting Tibet after having invited him.[12] India on 2 August denied the

Chinese allegations, recalling its traditional friendship towards China, and added that India had no definite evidence of such subversive activities by the elements mentioned by Beijing.[12a]

A few days earlier on 19 July the consul general in Lhasa, S.L. Chhibber, had reported that a large number of monks had left the monasteries and joined the Khampas in their struggle to fight against the Chinese.[13] On 2 August, London's *Telegraph* reported a clash between the Khampas and the Chinese in east Tibet.[13a] It appeared that the Chinese were so nervous that the very next day, on 3 August, their ambassador in Delhi made a personal statement to the foreign secretary, Subimal Dutt, pointing out the activities of various Tibetan individuals and organizations in Kalimpong and charged that they were planning to send out an appeal to 'various countries in the world' for 'assistance and their support to the independence of Tibet' while slandering China and the PLA.[14] The Ministry of External Affairs learnt that the Chinese had started imposing restrictions on pilgrimage traffic and trade contacts between Tibet and India, and also asked for confirmation of the report that the Chinese checkposts were not recognizing Indian certificates issued to the Ladakhi traders and they were told that they were free to travel to Tibet without any travel document.[15] The political officer, Apa Pant, reported on 1 November 1958 that Tibetan guerrilla rebels had captured 'large quantities of arms and ammunition' from the Chinese, and according to the Bhutanese prime minister, Jigme Dorji, the Chinese had been driven to the area 'south of Brahmputra and north of the frontiers of Sikkim, Bhutan and NEFA areas' and 'the rebels seem to be temporarily in complete control'.[16]

The reports of the Chinese wanting to take the Dalai Lama to Beijing and then prevent him from returning to Lhasa worried Delhi. When Lhasa approached for advice, Delhi said that the best excuse for the Dalai Lama would be that in the existing condition of turmoil his presence in Lhasa would be useful, as he could play the role of a mediator.[17] This worked for the time being.

Perhaps overawed by China, Nehru did not approve of the proposal to post Indian police at the checkposts on the Sikkim–Tibet border, which was being manned by the Sikkim police (readers would recall Sikkim at that time was a separate entity as a protectorate of India) for two reasons:

> (i) If only small numbers were posted they would be 'quite helpless' and (ii) a larger number would be 'a major development of international consequences. Obviously this would bring us into trouble with China and create new situations which will be very troublesome for us'.[18]

Similarly, Nehru was reluctant to post Indian personnel on the Bhutan–China border and, instead, suggested that Bhutan guard the border, and India could extend financial assistance for this purpose.[19]

The Dalai Lama was in a quandary with regard to the attitude he should adopt towards the rebellion in Tibet. He was indeed sympathetic to the rebels but could not extend open support and he did resist pressure from China to use the Tibetan army against the rebels. To wriggle out of difficult situations, he would always tell the Chinese that the Tibetan soldiers were not well equipped to fight the insurgents and there was always the fear of them joining their rebel brethren in sympathy. Until the final crisis in March 1959, the Dalai Lama attempted to prevent a complete break, even asking the rebels to lay down their arms. But he was not happy with the manner in which the Chinese were handling the revolt. The desperate Chinese, unable to control the revolt, accused him and his government for sympathizing with the insurgents and even supplying them with arms. They did not care to analyse the reasons for the revolt. They blamed the Dalai Lama for everything. As upset Dalai Lama later recalled in his biography:

> The revolt had broken out in the district they themselves had controlled for seven years; yet now they furiously blamed our government for it. Their complaints and accusations were endless, day after day, the cabinet was not trying to suppress the

'reactionaries', it was leaving Tibetan armouries unguarded, so that 'reactionaries' could steal arms and ammunition. Consequently, hundreds of Chinese were losing their lives and the Chinese would take vengeance in blood for them. Like all invaders, they had totally lost sight of the sole cause of the revolt against them: that our people did not want them in our country, and were ready to give up their lives to be rid of them.[20]

The Tibetans had come to realize that the Chinese were surreptitiously enforcing reforms that sought to upset the social and religious fabric of their society and even violated the 17-Point Agreement of May 1951. The deployment of the Chinese army had only further contributed to their alienation. The sporadic disturbances in pockets were the smokescreen which warned of bigger conflagration that the Chinese refused to see. They had a lot of faith in their military power. This situation had to inflame the sky one day and it did. A trigger was needed and that, too, came most unexpectedly. An innocuous invitation from the commandant of the Chinese military headquarters in Lhasa to the Dalai Lama for a lunch-cum-cultural performance provided the spark which lit the fire. The Tibetans saw in the invitation an attempt to whisk away the Dalai Lama to Beijing. They would not allow him to leave his residence, Narbulka, and came out on the streets, raising the standard of revolt.[20a]

To pre-empt further deterioration of the situation, the Chinese made a public announcement that the invitation to the Dalai Lama was not a secret one and senior officials were aware of it.[21] This was confirmed by the Indian Consul General too.[22] Whatever the truth, it triggered the final break between the Chinese and the Tibetans and sparked off a major revolt against the Chinese. Earlier, it was mostly the warrior Khampas who were involved. Now it was a mass revolt. The Dalai Lama felt insecure and decided to shift to Lokha in southern Tibet and, if necessary, he intended to seek asylum in India or Nepal to avoid either being captured by the Chinese or being made to take unpalatable decisions against his own people.[22a]

Since a group of ladies had approached the Indian consul general, S.L. Chhibber, and asked him to accompany them as a witness to lodge a protest with the Chinese, he was advised by Delhi to remain detached and neutral and not encourage them to look upon (him) as their adviser. He was told that it was important not to give the Chinese the impression that he was in any way advising the Tibetans.[23]

Unable to see that the key to their woes was within their own establishment and their high-handed and arrogant behaviour, the Chinese blamed India for continued attempt to foment trouble in Tibet. On 25 March 1959, the general secretary of the Chinese Communist Party, Deng Xiaoping, pointing towards Nehru, blamed India for their troubles in Tibet. Nehru's speeches were particularly seen as stoking the fires of revolt.[24] Deng blamed Nehru personally for the rebellion and warned, 'When the time comes, we certainly will settle accounts with them.'[25] Reacting to the concerns of President Rajendra Prasad, Prime Minister Nehru informed him that India was not very clear about the facts of what was happening in Tibet and was thus not 'suppressing or doing anything patently wrong for fear of consequences', but he added, 'we cannot take military measures. At the most we can express our opinion, in more or less forcible language'.[26]

The Dalai Lama's sister had already conveyed to the Indian consul general privately that she, along with her mother, intended to go to India to seek help.[27] The troubles in Tibet did attract the attention of the people in India and questions were raised even in Parliament. Prime Minister Nehru, while replying to the debate on the budget of the MEA in the Lok Sabha on 17 March 1959, referred to Tibet and said that it was 'rather embarrassing to discuss events happening in a neighbouring country about which we know something, of course, naturally, what we know is limited . . .It is not easy to get full picture'. Referring to the 17-Point Agreement, of May 1951 between China and Tibet, he said that it was 'under stress of circumstances'. He again stressed, as he had done in the past, that 'no country had ever recognized the independence of Tibet'. Giving an indication that something serious was happening, Nehru said:

> I do not mean to say that at present there is no large scale violence there—here and there, there has been—but it is a difficult situation. It is therefore clash of wills than, at present, a clash of arms or clash of physical bodies.[28]

It was indeed a sensitive issue but Nehru's speech was diplomatically worded.

On 22 March, the Chinese had described their actions in Tibet as security precautions and they were certain of crushing the revolt. They blamed the revolt on the 'imperialists and foreign reactionary elements', which was a euphemism they often used for India, and described the Tibetan action as 'treason' and warned that 'it was an entirely internal affair of China and [it] shall never permit interference from outside' and 'the intrigue aimed at splitting Tibet from China is doomed to total failure'.[29]

China took exception to the discussion of Tibetan affairs in the Indian Parliament and described this as interference in China's internal affairs and mentioned that such discussions were 'impolite and improper', and also went on to describe Kalimpong as 'the commanding centre of rebels'. Dalai Lama was described held under duress.[30]

The Chinese vice foreign Minister, Lo Kwei Po, assured Ambassador Parthasarathi that Chinese troops would 'not infringe' on the Indian consul general (in Lhasa). The ambassador, however, expressed his 'deep concern for the safety of our personnel and property' in Lhasa.[31] The consul general from Lhasa reported on 22 March 1959 that the 'situation has been quiet except for occasional cannon and automatic firing'.[32]

The Chinese vice minister for foreign affairs on 22 March in his statement to Ambassador Parthasarathi blamed the Tibetan government for tearing up the 17–Point Agreement of May 1951 under instigation of the 'imperialist and foreign reactionary elements' and had risen in armed revolt.[33] Delhi asked the ambassador to convey to the Weichiaopu (the Chinese Foreign Office) that while India recognized that Tibet was a part of China and had scrupulously observed it, nevertheless, the people of India were concerned with the happenings in Tibet since it was a place of pilgrimage for the people of India, both Hindus and Buddhists, and also because the 'Dalai Lama is looked upon with veneration' in India.[34]

Nehru, speaking on an adjournment motion in the Lok Sabha, on 23 March said the situation in Lhasa had somewhat quietened down, and asked the members to appreciate that this was a difficult situation and they should avoid doing anything which will worsen it and added 'we have no intention of interfering in the internal affairs of China with whom we have friendly relations'. About the Dalai Lama, he hoped he was safe.[35]

The Tibetan revolt was indeed a national uprising against the Chinese rule, which was finally put down by the Chinese use of force. Nevertheless, it caused a huge embarrassment to the Chinese. The Dalai Lama's unscathed escape to India at the same time caused additional embarrassment to Beijing since he attracted worldwide attention and sympathy. Later even the secretary general of the Soviet Communist Party, Nikita Khrushchev, blamed the Chinese for the failure of their intelligence and their ineptness in handling the events in Tibet.[35a]

A proclamation issued on 20 March 1959 by the Chinese Government after charging the Tibetan local government of 'heinous crimes and non-compliance with orders' called upon the PLA to take punitive action against the rebels and crush the rebellion. Simultaneously, Premier Zhou Enlai issued orders dissolving the Tibetan local government and delegating Tibetan government's authority to the 16-member preparatory committee with the Panchen Lama as its chairman. The Dalai Lama was described 'held under duress' but was not denounced. Eighteen 'high ranking' Tibetan officials were declared traitors.[36] The failure of the revolt settled once and for all the political future of Tibet as a colony of China.

As stated earlier, the fourteenth Dalai Lama, fearing for his safety and also afraid that he might be used against his own people, had already moved to Lokha in southern Tibet so that he would be able to escape to India easily, should it become necessary. On 15 March, responding to Dalai Lama's request, India had already assured asylum for him.[36a]

On 21 March, the vice director of the Chinese foreign bureau in Lhasa, Lo Shih Sen, called on the consul general, S.L. Chhibber, at the consulate, and informed him about the revolt of the 'reactionary elements in the foreign countries [read Tibetans based in Kalimpong] with the support of the imperialists [read Indians]' had torn the (17-Point) agreement and launched armed attacks on the 'Central Government troops and civilians'. What he actually intended to convey was couched in a language that had often been used in 1950, at the time of Tibet's occupation:

> Our Central Government can by no means allow the criminal acts of high treason committed by the local Government of Tibet and can surely suppress them. This is absolutely internal affair of China and no interference from outside is allowed. Tibet is integral part of our country and an intrigued attempt to separate Tibet from the territory of China will meet with thorough defection.[37]

The same was repeated to the Indian ambassador in Beijing personally by the Chinese vice foreign minister on 22 March.[38] It was clear that they wanted to warn India to keep its hands off Tibet. However, Lo Shih Sen feigned concern about the safety of the personnel of the consulate, offered protection to them and their families in the foreign bureau, which Chhibber did not accept, considering the large number, about a hundred, involved and asked the protection to be arranged at the consulate itself. Thereupon Lo told Chhibber that in offering him the facility of foreign bureau he was following the instructions of his government. Since he did not accept it, he would 'be responsible in case of any incident'. Regarding Indian nationals residing in Tibet, Lo asked Chhibber to advise them to strictly follow the orders of the Chinese government and stay indoors.[39] Meanwhile, Weichiaopu assured Ambassador Gopalaswami Parthasarathi that the Chinese troops would not violate the Indian consulate in Lhasa.[40]

In Gangtok, the Tibetan-origin Lepchas and Sherpas were concerned about the situation in Tibet and desirous of going to Delhi to meet the prime minister for seeking his help; however, Political Officer Pant succeeded in persuading them to drop their plan.[41]

On 25 March, the Chinese announced that the Dalai Lama had fled with some senior officials. While the Dalai Lama was described as a 'good person', his officers were blamed for the problems in Lhasa and warned that they would be dealt with severely.[42] The Indian ambassador in Moscow, Vishnu Ahuja, informed Delhi of an article in *Pravda* about the failure of the 'reactionary insurrection in Tibet'. It completely supported the Chinese stand.[43] A report prepared by the 'Head, Department of Ties with Communist and Worker Parties' and presented to the Communist Party of the Soviet Union (CPSU) supported the Chinese version of the events and, quoting the 'Chinese friends', said:

On 19 March 1959 about 30,000 rebels blocked the Chinese garrisons in Lhasa and other places and began to fire on them. The Internal centre of the uprising was Lhasa and the foreign one was the Indian city of Kalimpong. The revolt took place under the battle slogan: 'For the Independence of Tibet and for her separation from China'.[44]

It was obvious that the Chinese were firing at India keeping the gun on the CPSU's shoulders. But, in hindsight, this was incongruous in view of the strong indictment of Mao by Khrushchev for the revolt in Tibet and for the worsening of relations with India, only a few months later on 2 October 1959.[45]

An editorial in the *People's Daily* on 31 March, recalling Panchshila, or the five principles for peaceful coexistence which were first initiated in the 1954 agreement on Tibet, said, 'No foreign country should interfere in Tibetan rebellion which is an internal matter [of China].' It also welcomed the prime minister's statement of 23 March (referred to earlier) and concluded:

> We believe that the Chinese and Indian Governments will continue to observe Panchshila faithfully and will not permit the friendly relations between our two countries to be damaged.[46]

The revolt in Tibet and Chinese repression made a large number of Tibetans leave Tibet and seek refuge in India. The prime minister, responding to questions in the Lok Sabha on the influx of refugees from Tibet, stated that the number was not large and there were instructions to the checkposts to stop anyone entering without valid travel documents. There were several other questions which the prime minister avoided answering, perhaps because he did not wish to get involved in discussing China's internal matters.[47] However, answering a query from the Indian High Commissioner in London, the foreign secretary referred to the prime minister's statement in Parliament on 30 March 1959 and said, 'There is no question of our sealing the border nor have we been asked to do so.' He also said, 'While we cannot open our borders to everyone who wants to come across, we shall exercise our sovereign right in giving asylum on the merit of individual cases.'[48] In the course of time, under the stress of circumstances several thousand refugees from Tibet entered India following Dalai Lama's arrival in India.

On 26 March, the Dalai Lama had sent a personal message to the prime minister, narrating the circumstances in which he had to leave Lhasa. He recalled the religious ties between India and Tibet for thousands of years and said he intended to 'enter India *via* Tsona' and hoped that the GoI would 'make necessary arrangements for us (for him, his family and entourage) in the Indian territory'.[49]

Before proceeding further, it may be clarified that as per the existing administrative arrangement for the northeast frontier, it was the governor of Assam who was in charge and he had an adviser in the person of K.L. Mehta attached to him in Shillong, the then capital of Assam. As such, all instructions from the MEA went to him for any further action. Accordingly, on receipt of the Dalai Lama's message, Mehta was informed by Delhi that it had been decided that India would offer asylum to the Dalai Lama and he was asked to make all arrangements to receive him and make sure that any information about his movements was shared strictly on a 'need-to-know' basis.[50] On the same day, replying to Political Officer Pant's message, Delhi assured him that all arrangements for his reception etc., were in hand.[51]

Beijing Radio on 31 March broadcast the text of six letters exchanged between the Dalai Lama and the head of Chinese administration in Tibet, General Tan Kwan San. These letters were exchanged between 10 and 16 March, in which the pontiff blamed his own people for preventing him from responding to the general's invitation for lunch-cum-cultural performance.[51a] Later the Dalai Lama confided in Nehru, saying that he did write those letters as a tactical move.[52] Interestingly, his last letter was dated 16 March and the very next day he left Lhasa incognito for Lokha where arrangements had already been made for his stay and security. It shows that the Dalai Lama while writing those letters had already decided to leave Lhasa.

On 1 April, Mehta from Shillong informed Delhi that the Dalai Lama with an immediate entourage of eight had 'crossed CHUTANGMU border in our territory evening 31 March'. The border was sealed thereafter since it was apprehended that some danger may be brought upon him by some agents who were following him.[53] Delhi instructed Mehta not to release the information 'without specific instructions from us [Delhi]'.[54]

Prime Minister Nehru, while announcing in Parliament on 3 April that the Dalai Lama had arrived in India, said that he had arrived 'at our border check-post at CHUTANGMU' in NEFA on 29 March and since such a development had been expected, the checkpost had been forewarned and he was received by the assistant political officer of the Tawang sub-division, which was part of the Kameng frontier division of the North East Frontier Agency (NEFA).[55] While the Chinese press blacked out the statement, Peking Radio broadcast it without the mention of asylum.[56] Delhi, while doing everything it could for the Dalai Lama's convenience, did not agree to his request to allow his brother Gyalo Dhondup, based in Kalimpong, to visit Tawang to meet him, since his name was 'connected by Chinese authorities with foreign espionage activities'.[57] The prime minister conveyed to the governor of Assam, Fazal Ali, that there existed tremendous public feelings of sympathy not only about Dalai Lama but also about events in Tibet which no government could ignore yet he had to express himself 'with restraint'.[58]

Prime Minister Nehru, replying to the Dalai Lama's message of 26 March seeking asylum, greeted him and assured every facility for him and his family and entourage and also assured him that the people of India 'would accord their traditional respect to (his) person'.[59]

P.N. Menon, former consul general in Lhasa, was appointed senior liaison officer who, on arrival in Bomdila, was expected to orally advise the Dalai Lama to not issue any long statement to the press after reaching Tezpur and not say anything 'which could cause embarrassment to him and to us'. The people in his entourage were also to be advised similarly. While his final place of residence was undecided, places such as Shillong, Kalimpong or Darjeeling were ruled out.[60] The MEA kept the political officer fully informed.[61] To ensure all of this, a worried Nehru advised the Dalai Lama in a personal letter to be brief in his initial statement to the press and consider a longer statement later after he had reflected on the events. He conveyed that arrangements were being made for his and his family's stay at Mussoorie. Nehru advised the Dalai Lama not to come to Delhi to meet him since Delhi was getting hot. He would himself meet him in Mussoorie.[62] Prime Minister Nehru faced a barrage of questions on Tibet and the Dalai Lama, when he addressed a press conference in Delhi on 5 April. He clarified that the asylum was spiritual and cultural with no political activity involved. Answering questions, he also confirmed that the Dalai Lama did write those six letters to the Chinese General for tactical reasons. He attributed the happenings in Tibet to the breakdown of the 17-Point Agreement of May 1951. Regarding the functioning of autonomy in a communist regime, Nehru said that the people were gradually and wrongly conditioned by the Cold War attitude. He conceded that India was affected and concerned with the developments in Tibet and could not ignore what had happened there. He clarified that China did not seek India's good offices to handle the situation in Tibet, but he dwelt on the importance of good relations with China and not interfering in its internal affairs. He also confirmed that in the last few years there had been no correspondence with China on any matter relating to Tibet. He dismissed a proposal of suggesting to China to restore the autonomy of Tibet.[63]

On the same day in his message to the British prime minister, Nehru traced the developments in Tibet since China's occupation, and said that the situation in Tibet could not be compared to the one in Hungary, where there was a similar people's uprising against the Soviet Union since, unlike Tibet, Hungary in international law was an independent country. He doubted if the Chinese took 'the initiative in bringing about this crisis but their broad policies and the gradual deterioration in the situation made the conflict inevitable'.[64]

The political officer of the Kameng Division, Har Mander Singh, in his two reports made on successive days to the adviser to Assam Governor K.L. Mehta gave an account of the situation in Tibet, as given to him by the Dalai Lama, before leaving Lhasa that made him leave Tibet. Singh formed the impression that the pontiff had initially no plans to leave Tibet but he could not remain inactive while his people suffered. His ministers, too, had come to realize that they had no future in Chinese-dominated Tibet. He said it appeared to him that he (Dalai Lama) wanted the GoI to promote activities which would restore Tibet's independence. Singh was given a copy of the draft communiqué, which the Tibetans intended to release to the press on behalf of the Dalai Lama.[65] On 6 April, the prime minister's letter acknowledging Dalai Lama's message of 26 March giving the circumstances in which he had to leave Lhasa, informing him of his plan to enter India and requesting reception, etc., was read out in the presence of all principal advisers of His Holiness.[66]

The draft communiqué claimed Tibetan independence and highlighted the differences between them and the Chinese and the latter's attempts to destroy Tibetan culture and religion. The draft also declared that the seat of the Tibetan government had been shifted to Yu-Gyal-Lhuntse (Ugyal Lhunpotse or Lhuntse Dzong) with effect from 26 March. Finally, the communiqué requested the GoI and 'all other countries of the world to recognize the new government' at its new headquarters. It hoped that the assistance would be forthcoming to them in their struggle. The statement was said to be from 'the Cabinet of Government of Independent Tibet'.[67] Har Mander Singh, in his forwarding letter, which was also his report on the entry of Dalai Lama in India, to K.L. Mehta said that the Dalai Lama wanted to maintain contacts with the Tibetan forces fighting the Chinese in Tibet through special messengers and wanted the GoI to issue them special permits. The Dalai Lama, however, realized that this course of action would not be desirable from the perspective of the Indian government.[68]

The foreign secretary in his comments on Singh's reports conceded that while the draft communiqué was not suitable, the statement could not be too bald either, and that the Dalai Lama would have to say something to the press, which should include the circumstances which made him leave Lhasa, otherwise it would give 'the impression that the GoI were putting pressure on him not to say anything'.[69] Prime Minister Nehru only commented about the arrangements for his stay in Mussoorie and advised the Dalai Lama's family and his senior ministers only need to stay with him in Mussoorie.[70] Delhi continued to remain worried about the statement that the Dalai Lama might make, since a large number of journalists from national and international press were assembling at Tezpur, where he was to emerge from the NEFA. The senior liaison officer, P.N. Menon, on reaching Bomdila was informed that the prime minister would be meeting the Dalai Lama on 24 April in Mussoorie.[71] A worried Delhi asked Menon to advise the Dalai Lama yet again not to make any controversial statement when he met the press in Tezpur. He could make an elaborate statement later once he had settled down and had met the prime minister.[72] The same day, Menon was advised in another message to arrange the Dalai Lama's programme in a way that he reached Mussoorie before 20 April for his meeting with the PM on 24 April.[73] In his first report from Bomdila, Menon assured Subimal Dutt, the foreign secretary, that all arrangements had been made and, as suggested, the Dalai Lama would only make a brief statement to the press.[74] With all precautions, the prime minister remained worried. In a personal letter to the Dalai Lama on 13 April, he informed him of the various arrangements made for him, and advised him yet another time on the need to be brief since there would be a big crowd of journalists waiting to meet him. The Dalai Lama was also asked to advise the members of his entourage to shun the media to avoid any embarrassment to him or to India.[75]

Menon, in his first detailed report to Delhi, gave a resumé of what he had been told by the Dalai Lama and his cabinet ministers of their struggle in Tibet and thanked India for giving them asylum. Menon had to use all his persuasive power to make them agree to his suggestion that they would not speak of the various developments that took place in Tibet during their journey or about their future plans for Tibet, which they should speak about only after meeting the prime minister in Mussoorie. Menon sent the foreign secretary a draft of a statement which the Dalai Lama had with great difficulty agreed to make.[76]

Before Menon's draft could reach Delhi, the foreign secretary had sent his own draft for the Dalai Lama's press statement with instructions that Menon should personally take it to the Dalai Lama and allow him to make any change if he so desired. It was found necessary that the Dalai Lama should clarify whether or not he left Tibet under duress, since the Chinese were making a big issue of it.[77] The Dalai Lama with some changes accepted the draft sent from Delhi. It was made clear in the draft statement that the Dalai Lama came to India 'of his own free will and not under duress'.[78]

In the midst of these developments, the Chinese foreign minister, Chen Yi, during a meeting with a visiting Indian steel delegation already in Beijing, stressed the importance of maintaining Sino-Indian friendship, and added that 'certain sections of the Indian opinion seemed to be very agitated about Tibet'. He further mentioned that he would ignore such reactions and take no retaliatory action. He appreciated the prime minister's attitude of non-interference in the internal affairs of China and his stress on maintaining age-old ties between their countries. He accepted the difficult state of India–China relations but hoped it would get normal soon. He confided that out of three million Tibetans only twenty thousand had rebelled.[79]

However, Chen Yi's friendly remarks did not prevent the *People's Daily* a week later to carry an Observer commentary which did not sound very friendly. It warned India that Tibet was part of China, its political system was the concern of China alone as 'the policy of Indian Government in relation to one of India's states or one of India's national minorities was the concern of India alone'. It persisted with the accusation that India had allowed Kalimpong to be used as a base for anti-Chinese activities by the Tibetan reactionaries.[80] A circular telegram to select Indian missions abroad spelt out the Indian thinking on Tibet, which it said was determined by three elements—providing asylum to Dalai Lama, maintenance of friendly relations with China and a wish to see genuine autonomy restored in Tibet. It also reiterated that 'we cannot recognise any Tibetan

Government in India nor would we permit them to carry on hostile propaganda against any friendly country' while in India.[81]

The ambassador in Beijing expressed his concern that the Dalai Lama's speeches were straining India's relations with China and had made 'the situation even more intricate'. The Chinese believed that the theocratic rule in Tibet and the Lamaseries were, according to communist hypothesis, perpetuating feudalism and serfdom and needed to be eliminated. Ambassador Parthasarathi observed that since China appreciated firmness, 'we should not in the present situation weaken in any way in sympathy we have extended to Tibetans'. His assessment was the Chinese did not question the bona fides of India's policy, which was based on the following:

(i)   The nature of the Tibetan revolt; and
(ii) India will not play into the hands of those who wish to disrupt Indo-Chinese friendship.[82]

As regards the frontier question, Parthasarathi wrote to the prime minister, saying that 'our position has been stated firmly. I consider however that a courteous retort to the implications in Premier Zhou's statement that we are holding or claiming territories occupied by the British imperialism is overdue'.[83]

Replying, the prime minister said:

Recent developments in Tibet have raised difficult problems not only for India, but for China also and of course, for Tibet itself. I can appreciate to some extent Chinese attitude, constituted as Chinese are at present . . . Nevertheless the regimented and virulent attacks on India in China and their insistence on patent falsehood have surprised and distressed me. It seems to me that Chinese authorities have developed a habit of trying to bully and imagine (that) offensive language will produce results they desire. It produces exactly opposite results in any self respecting country . . . our general policy will remain firm though not unfriendly to China. We realise the importance of these friendly relations, but friendship cannot be obtained by threats and coerce attitude.

It seems to me that the Chinese would like to get Dalai Lama back and his remaining in India is a continuing affront and irritation to them.[84]

Political Officer Pant met the Dalai Lama in Siliguri, when he was on his way to Mussoorie. He was forthright in his conversation and told him:

(i) It would be wrong for the Tibetans to expect India to take any side in this struggle though . . .[her] sympathies were with them;

(ii) It is impossible to imagine India going to war with China over Tibet;

(iii) The happenings in Tibet have made [a] deep impression throughout the world and that the people of India were deeply moved; and

(iv) It was mainly due to his spiritual position and his learning that in the outside world he would find many admirers.[85]

Prime Minister Nehru met the Dalai Lama in Mussoorie on 24 April. The Dalai Lama gave Nehru a detailed account of the happenings in Tibet and his efforts to work out a compromise with the Chinese for a smooth running of the government, but his efforts had been thwarted by the Chinese. He admitted to the three letters he had written to the Chinese but mentioned that they were part of a 'tactical move' to keep the doors open for a compromise if one was possible. When the Dalai Lama hinted that he may seek help from India in preserving the religion and the way of life of the Tibetans, and in the long run for its independence, the Prime Minister was quite categorical in stating that India 'cannot go to war with China or Tibet and even that would not help Tibet'. He assured him of a 'good deal of sympathy' for Tibet in India. To the Dalai Lama's expectation of achieving independence in the long run, the prime minister said:

> [T]he whole world cannot bring freedom to Tibet unless the whole fabric of the Chinese State is destroyed . . .To defeat China is not easy. Only a world war, an atomic war can perhaps be the precursor of such a possibility.

He advised him not to be under any illusion and 'to fashion his policy with reference to actuality'. Concluding, the prime minister said that in the present situation, India could not even 'privately' advise China. 'The so-called help being given to you would close all the doors to such help.'[86]

Ambassador Parthasarathi again reported on 26 April that there had been no let up in the Chinese press and radio campaign against 'Indian expansionist' designs and India's alleged collusion with Tibetan rebels or of interference in internal affairs of China, as seen in the attitude of the Indian officials. He said lately the 'Indian expansionists' had been brought to the centre stage along with the imperialists as the main targets of criticism.[87]

Regarding the attitude of Indian officials, even the Communist Party of India organ *New Age* had accused them and had named the political officer in Sikkim, Apa Pant, as one who had been colluding with the spies. An upset prime minister said that this showed:

> [A] certain lack of balance of mind and total absence of feeling of decency, and nationality. What they are I do not know. They cease to be Indians if they talk in this way.[88]

On 26 April, the foreign secretary, Subimal Dutt, made a statement to the Chinese ambassador about the Dalai Lama's arrival in India and the arrangements made for him. He took the opportunity to express his regrets for the statements made in the Chinese National

People's Congress recently calling India 'expansionist'. India was also accused of 'stepping up (its) interference in internal affairs of China and trying to split Tibet from China through Tibetan upper strata reactionaries and turn it into their colony or protectorate'. Dutt said the Chinese attack was 'unbecoming and unjustified attack on the GoI' and described the allegations 'as patently untrue'. He rejected the Chinese accusation that the Dalai Lama was being held under duress. It was pointed out that the Indian prime minister had already clarified that the Dalai Lama would be accorded respectful treatment in India and was not expected to carry on any political activity.[89]

The prime minister, speaking in the Lok Sabha, on 27 April made it clear that the Dalai Lama was entirely responsible for his statements. Referring to Chinese propaganda, Nehru said that he had been 'greatly distressed at the tone of the comments and the charges made against India by responsible people in China'. He expressed his 'deepest regret' that China had levied charges which were both 'unbecoming and entirely devoid of substance'.[90]

The protest meeting in Bombay where the portrait of Mao, as alleged by the Chinese, was insulted by the demonstrators was treated as an excuse to up the ante against India. The Chinese were not mollified even when the prime minister conveyed his regrets about the incident.[91] The foreign secretary who spoke to the Chinese ambassador told him that India would investigate the reported insult to Mao's portrait and if it was true, it was deplorable.[92] Meanwhile, the prime minister of Bhutan, Jigme Dorji, told the political officer in Gangtok that the Chinese had sent an emissary to Bhutan to speak to the Tibetan refugees who had come to Bhutan persuading them to return to Tibet. Jigme, however, said that Bhutan would fight the Chinese if they entered Bhutan and he wanted Prime Minister Nehru to lodge a protest with China.[93]

The Dalai Lama persisted in making such suggestions to the prime minister which put him off. On 7 May, he suggested a four-point plan to rescue the Tibetans in Tibet. He demanded:

(i)   China should stop its atrocities and free all detained people;

(ii) the Chinese military force to be withdrawn from Tibet;

(iii) a Committee representing neighbours of Tibet and some
      Buddhist countries along with some Tibetans be sent to Tibet
      to find out the damage done to Tibetan icons, monasteries
      and Tibetan manuscript; and

(iv) to give medical assistance to the wounded Tibetans and to
      prevent outbreak of epidemics Red Cross should be permitted
      to open a branch in Tibet.[94]

Reacting to this, an exasperated Nehru regretted that the Dalai Lama
had not fully appreciated the situation and asked P.N. Menon to
convey to the Dalai Lama orally that for China to agree to these
suggestions would mean that it had been defeated in a war, had
surrendered and terms could be dictated to it. He added that no
government, least of all the Chinese Government, 'can accept such
terms or conditions'. The Dalai Lama was asked to understand
that while there was sympathy for the Tibetans in many countries,
including Buddhist countries, none of them would be willing to take
any action against China. He, therefore, advised him to 'await the
events and not take any further steps'. Nehru was afraid any further
step against China would intensify China's hostility. He also added
that even the Soviet Union had not come out in support of China.
Of course, while it would not support it, it would not openly criticize
China. Similarly, European countries had remained silent on Tibet.[95]

Earlier on 4 May, the prime minister, speaking in the Rajya
Sabha (the Upper House of the Indian Parliament) had insisted that
whatever the Chinese might have said, India would, on its part, not
follow the policy that 'endangers the friendly relations of the two
countries, and which are so important from the wider point of view
of the peace of Asia and the world'. He warned these relations would
be 'gravely impaired if unfounded charges are made and the language
of the cold war was used'. Sounding hopeful, he said the present
difficulties would gradually pass but regretted that 'something

we have laboured for, for all these years which may be said to be enshrined, if you like it, in the Panchsheel or in Bandung has suffered very considerably in the people's minds . . .'[96]

Despite the prime minister's conciliatory speech, there was no let up in Chinese propaganda and use of undignified language against India. On 6 May 1959, the Chinese official paper *Renmin Ribao* published an editorial titled 'The Revolution in Tibet and Nehru's Philosophy', in which Nehru was accused of not understanding the Tibetan society which was an 'unchanging static society' held by the 'upper strata reactionaries'.[97] Ambassador Parthasarathi regarded the article 'as the culmination of the campaign' against India, arguing it with dialectical skill of a particular variety and prepared at the highest level. The Indian sincerity and goodwill towards China had little impact and it was clear to the ambassador that there was 'no meeting ground in their respective approaches to problems of nationalities, autonomy, social reforms and progress'. He believed further efforts 'on our part will only earn us more ill-will'. He agreed with Nehru that the presence of the Dalai Lama and the thousands of Tibetan refugees in India 'was an affront to the Chinese', thereby making reconciliation difficult, and if the Chinese wanted Indian help to defuse the situation in Tibet it was up to them to approach India but there appeared to be little chance of that.[98] The ambassador noted that somehow there was some toning down of Indian criticism in the Chinese media after the above article. He also noted a spurt in reports of Tibetans welcoming the Chinese in Tibet for ushering social reforms.[99]

Nehru agreed with the ambassador and said that 'we do not intend to carry on a controversy', but some criticism from individuals could not be stopped. He felt relieved that since Parliament had adjourned for three months, there would be no opportunity to discuss this issue there. He would allow the matter to rest and it would be for the Chinese to take the next step. He said that the Chinese often act as a bully and added 'India for all her moderation and restraint, has also a good deal of pride and self-respect'. Noting that the Soviet

Union and other communist countries had been quiet on Tibet, not necessarily out of love for Tibet, but they might think that 'China has gone too far' and 'to some extent, their (Soviet) friendly reaction with us lead to some restraint' on the part of the Chinese.[100]

On 8 May, the prime minister had told the Lok Sabha that India had placed no restrictions on the Dalai Lama except the 'limitation of good sense and propriety of which he himself is the judge'. He rejected the suggestions of some members that 'India should be the headquarters of some kind of a campaign' for Tibet. Not agreeing with members who said India should not have signed the 1954 agreement on Tibet, he insisted that 'there is no doubt in my mind that the agreement made with [the] Chinese with regard to Tibet was the right agreement . . .and we shall stand by it' and not break it. He did not think being hostile to each other was good for either country. He conceded that 'China may be very strong country as it is and is growing stronger, but even from the Chinese point of view it is not a good thing to have a hostile India'. Giving the number of Tibetan refugees at 10,000, he said they were going to be 'a bit of a problem'.[101]

As Nehru's biographer Sarvepalli Gopal noted, 'Despite provocations, Nehru continued to maintain a moderate and courteous tone in his rejoinders and while not concealing the full sympathy for Tibet, which was not an empty sentiment, asserted that he would not allow posterity to blame him for leaving behind a trail of bitterness towards China.'[102]

On 20 June, the Dalai Lama made an elaborate statement in Mussoorie and spoke of the sufferings of the Tibetans and traced the history of Chinese behaviour in Tibet and their various promises of respecting Tibetan religion and culture. Throwing a challenge to the Chinese, he said that if they doubted his statement, investigation could be done through an international commission. His statement claimed Tibet to be an independent sovereign country. While appealing for peace, he insisted on certain conditions precedent on negotiations for a peaceful settlement. He thanked the press for its help in keeping the 'struggle alive for survival and freedom'.[103] There was some confusion regarding the Dalai Lama's status in India since the statements made by him were found to be acrimonious and liable to be misconstrued. The MEA clarifying his status said:

> The Government of India don't take responsibility for any of these various statements. So far as Dalai Lama is concerned the Prime Minister has made it clear on more than one occasion that while the Government of India are glad to have given asylum to Dalai Lama and shown him the respect due to his high position, they have no reason to believe he will do anything which is contrary to international usage and embarrassing to the host country. The Government of India want to make it clear they do not recognise any separate government of Tibet and there is, therefore no question of a Tibetan Government under the Dalai Lama functioning in India.[104]

As the Nehru–Zhou talks in April 1960 failed (which is discussed in chapter 10) the Dalai Lama perhaps felt that the prime minister might be in a better frame of mind to listen to some suggestion from him regarding Tibet's future. He suggested UN mediation and, if the GoI were unable to do so themselves, to extend help in securing the support of other countries.[105] Replying to the Dalai Lama, Prime Minister Nehru once again reiterated the difficulties that prevented such an action. He said, 'Unfortunately it is not always possible to give effect to our wishes and desires and circumstances beyond our control prove limiting factors.'[106]

There were many occasions when New Delhi had to reiterate this policy which has not changed since then and has stood the test of time. India recognized the Dalai Lama as the religious and spiritual leader who had been given asylum on those grounds only and it continues to maintain the same position.

Meanwhile, a few thousand Tibetans who followed him in 1959 have over the years multiplied into roughly a hundred thousand and have rehabilitated in different settlements across India. To enable them to preserve their culture, separate schools are functioning in various Tibetan settlements with grants from the Government of India. The Dalai Lama continues to be recognized as a religious and spiritual leader of the Tibetans, and has been accepted as such by most countries of the world, though not officially.

If the Chinese were upset about Indian low-key support to the Dalai Lama, the Indian public was equally furious in the manner the Chinese had treated the Dalai Lama who was a venerable religious figure in India and held in great esteem by the people.

Nehru was man of high intellect, well read and passionately devoted to world peace. Unfortunately, in his devotion to peace he did not see that in the Chinese perception it was a sign of weakness!

9

India–Tibet Frontier

The Sikkim–Tibet boundary delimited in 1896 was 'the only boundary along the entire frontier which was properly delimited'.

—Foreign Secretary Subimal Dutt at the Governors' Conference,
28 October 1959

We have discussed in chapters 1 and 7 the position of India's borders with Tibet both in the eastern and western sectors. While on Independence the western border was undefined in the Survey of India maps and also in those printed until 1953, in the eastern sector there was the McMahon Line set up in 1914 between the British and Tibet which separated India from Tibet. Nehru had predicated the security of Indian borders on geographic factors. Foreign Secretary Subimal Dutt addressing the governors of the Indian states in 1959, had said that except for the Sikkim–Tibet boundary no other part of the frontier with Tibet was delimited. As discussed in chapter 1, the Chinese had not signed the Simla Convention. Subsequently, too, the British made several attempts to get China sign it but were not successful. There were doubts in Prime Minister Nehru's mind whether Communist China would stand by it.

Strong Borders Secure Nations is the title of a book written by an American scholar, M. Taylor Fravel, published in 1971. If this axiom holds good, should the nations which are militarily not too strong suffer from 'insecure' borders? Not necessarily. How might they then ensure the security of their borders? A key proposition: through agreed borders with their neighbours, strong or otherwise, arrived at after surveys and delineation and their demarcation with markers on the ground.

Borders by their very nature are shared between two nations and hence it is of vital importance that they are mutually acceptable by both the stakeholders. Unilateralism in deciding or altering an international border is a sure recipe for conflict. Frontier agreements are fundamental to friendship between two countries with common borders. They are governed by adjustments of rival claims, interests and ambitions at points where the borders of any two countries adjoin. Many countries as they emerged from colonial rule to independence found their frontiers un-demarcated. As Shyam Saran, a former foreign secretary, wrote in his article 'A Line Runs Through It' for the *Indian Express*:

> The notion of boundaries as lines drawn on a map is a recent concept—as is the nation state. This is particularly true in the subcontinent where empires and kingdoms shaded into one another across ambiguous frontiers rather than be separated by boundaries making sovereign jurisdictions.[1]

The borders that the colonialists established by their conquests were generally bequeathed by them to their successor states when withdrawing their power. The British, too, during their rule had established Indian borders by conquests, and independent India inherited them in 1947.

When India was partitioned, the frontiers of India and Pakistan were fixed by Cyril Radcliffe in a hurried manner on a map by drawing a line on the basis of his restricted brief that left many gaps.

This later gave rise to border problems between the two nations. In one case, even a dispute on the East Pakistan–India border had to be referred to international arbitration by a Swedish judge, Justice Algot Bagge.[2] Finally, it was only after the borders between India Pakistan/Bangladesh were scientifically surveyed, delineated on the maps and demarcated on the ground that there has been peace on their international borders.

China's main objection in not signing the Simla Convention was Article 9, which laid down the borders between India and Tibet and Tibet and China. This was discussed in detail in the first chapter. Henry McMahon, the then foreign secretary, in promoting the Convention was motivated by a sense of history. Back in 1893, as junior to the then foreign secretary Mortimer Durand, McMahon had assisted in fixing the frontier between India and Afghanistan. He had thus witnessed Durand being immortalized. McMahon perhaps saw this as his opportunity to preserve his memory in history; he seized this moment to immortalize himself. Interestingly, McMahon had resigned from the position of foreign secretary to take up the new assignment. For over a century now both Durand and McMahon have become household names and the subject matter of many books.

The British, after declaring the McMahon Line as the border with Tibet, left a vacuum by not occupying the areas between the then existing north-eastern border of India and the new McMahon Line and allowed the Tibetans to stay in its occupation, who also collected the civil revenues. This area is known as Tawang to the Tibetans.

Tawang is a town that got its name from the famous Tawang monastery, attached to one of the three main Tibetan monasteries, Drepung, the other two being Sera and Gaden. In Chinese perception, it is south Tibet which comprised much of the erstwhile NEFA, which is now the state of Arunachal Pradesh in India.

The cartographic liberties that China took in its maps since the 1930s continued even after the British withdrawal from the subcontinent. However, given the Tibetan sensitivities, the British Government of India, after due consultations with India Office and the Foreign Office in London, had conveyed the following to Lhasa through the political officer, Sir Basil Gould:

> The British Government of India would be willing to alter the frontier '*to run from the Se La* not *to north of Tawang but to the south of Tawang.*'[3]

This sought to put Tawang back into Tibetan territory. However, the adjustment of the borders had not been formally carried out by August 1947 and Tibet remained in occupation of Tawang, though by the Simla Convention still part of India.

Soon after the British withdrawal, Tibet declaring itself to be an 'independent' country told Prime Minister Jawaharlal Nehru that it had in the past discussed with the British the return of the '*indisputable Tibetan territories that had been gradually included into India*'. It was also claimed that the Tibetan representatives to the Asian Relations Conference in March 1947 had also discussed this question with the Indian leaders. Their claims included Bhutan, Sikkim, Darjeeling, Ladakh and many more territories in India.[4] India ignored the Tibetan demand but, in responding to their request for an assurance of Article 2 of the Simla Convention, which had sought to assure Tibet of its territorial integrity, said that it would not annex any Tibetan territory and would be prepared to the 'adjustment on the Indo-Tibetan frontier particularly in the Tawang area'.[5] Earlier, the Tibetan foreign bureau had told the Indian representative, H.E. Richardson (who had been retained as India's representative, after the British withdrawal from India), that 'the frontier question was the only point in dispute between Tibet and India, which it ought to try to settle it'.[5a] Richardson, reporting to Delhi, said:

> It was a senseless attitude for the Tibetan Government simply to complain about the activities of the Government of India—sometimes using very questionable language—and yet to take no advantage of the Government of India's offer to negotiate adjustment of the frontier.[6]

India found Tibet a difficult customer. India thanked Lhasa for its assurance to continue their relations with India 'without change' and mentioned that it would continue to abide by the existing treaties 'until either party should wish to enter into fresh arrangements'.[7]

Subsequently, the political office in Gangtok asked the Ministry of External Affairs on 28 October 1948:

> We must also be prepared to make an early gesture to the Tibetans in the matter of implementing our undertaking to consider an adjustment of the boundary in the Tawang area.[8]

The prime minister welcomed quick communist victories in the civil war against the Kuomintang. However, India's expression of sympathy for Tibet at a time when China was threatening to occupy Tibet invited strong reaction from the Chinese. Declaring Tibet its internal affair, China said Indian establishments in Tibet were unacceptable.[9] These have been discussed in detail in the fourth and fifth chapters. As the China–Tibet negotiations for their new relationship commenced in Beijing in April 1951, the question of Tawang started bothering Delhi, particularly in view of its commitment to adjust the border in the Tawang area in favour of Tibet. China, in the meantime, had already given Delhi a taste of its aggressiveness while occupying Tibet and on the question of providing asylum to Dalai Lama in 1951. Delhi feared that if Tawang was restored to Tibet with China threatening to occupy it, Tibet's (read China's) borders would come down to the plains of Assam, and the geographic and climatic factors which Nehru believed would ensure India's security from the north, would vanish forever. Tawang had become important both for India's and Bhutan's security.[10]

As an Indian officer with a sixty-man escort occupied Tawang in March 1951, the Tibetan officials protested and asked for its withdrawal. They refused to acknowledge Indian occupation unless instructed by Lhasa.[11]

In deciding to take control of Tawang, Delhi felt it was not necessary to justify its action to Lhasa since it was only assertion of its right under the 1914 Simla Convention. If Tawang had been left alone in the past, it was because of Tibet's special interest in that area and of its association with the Tawang Monastery. The Tibetans were informed that 'if the position was left fluid, the area would be lost to the Chinese, and therefore it had become necessary to vindicate what is rightly ours'.[12]

The political officer reporting to Delhi on the mentioned developments said that the Tibetans were informed that recent changes had made it necessary to forestall any possible encroachment on the frontier by a more aggressive neighbour and also to guard approaches to Bhutan.[13]

Given the sensitivity of the matter, Delhi instructed the political officer that 'nothing should be said to create impression in Chinese or Tibetan minds that our action is directed against China'.[14]

Dissatisfied and unhappy, the Tibetans accused India of taking 'undue advantage of the situation to establish their claim over Tibetan territory', which the Tibetan government regretted and they also claimed that they would 'definitely [be] unable to accept the occupation'.[15]

Sumal Sinha, the mission-in-charge in Lhasa, reading the ground situation and in his wisdom, cautioned Delhi that while the Tibetans had made no further representation, they would 'neither forget nor condone our armed occupation of territory under their established control for so long'. He added:

Tawang will in future cause uneasiness on our frontier (Tibetans) not only refused to reconcile themselves to loss of this territory which they seem to have absentmindedly ceded and never surrendered possession of but also regard present Indian action as both improper and unfair.[16]

The peeved Tibetans asked Sinha 'whether GoI would be generous enough to act on previous assurances to amend the frontier in favour of Tibet?' An embarrassed Sinha, unable to answer, asked them to discuss that with the political officer in Gangtok.[17]

In view of the Chinese occupation of Tibet, this move had indeed become necessary for strategic considerations. Later developments did cause problems, but they also established the prudence of this decision. India allowed its moral compunctions to be sacrificed at the altar of strategic necessity. All this happened in March–April 1951, just before the 17-Point Agreement between China and Tibet was signed on 23 May 1951.

Once the 17-Point Agreement was signed, Lhasa informed Delhi that the Chinese were pressing Kashag (Tibetan cabinet) to take up the question of Tawang with India and if they failed, China would take action against Indian interests in Tibet. They requested Sinha not to suspect them 'to be willing partners if any trouble the Chinese might create'.[18] Faced with this information, Delhi instructed Sinha on 17 November 1951 that should the Tibetan or the Chinese approach him for discussion on the 'boundary disputes', he would hear them out and tell them he had no authority to discuss these matters.[19]

In the face of these unsettling reports, Nehru thought it prudent to declare India's borders. In his speech in Parliament on 20 November 1951, he said:

> Tibet is contiguous to India from the region of Ladakh to the boundary of Nepal and from Bhutan to the Irrawaddy/Salween divide in Assam . . . the frontier from Bhutan eastwards has been clearly defined by McMahon Line which was fixed by the Simla Convention of 1914. The frontier from Ladakh to Nepal is defined chiefly by long usage and custom . . . Our maps show that the *McMahon Line is our boundary and that is our boundary—map or no map.* That fact remains and we stand by that boundary and we will not allow anybody to come across that boundary.[20]

Nehru's statement conceded that the western frontier was defined *chiefly by long usage and custom.* The maps produced by the Survey of India until 1954 had shown the western sector of the frontier as 'UNDEFINED'. In 1949, the Kuomintang government, in its last days, had even suggested delineation of this part of the frontier but Delhi had advised the ambassador that should Nanking press for it, he should convey:

> *In the present disturbed conditions, it is not possible to demarcate undefined frontier between Kashmir and Sinkiang.*[21]

Delhi in this statement admitted that it was indeed an undefined border that needed delineation and demarcation, for which stable conditions were necessary.

India, however, was happy at Mao Zedong's assurance, when Ambassador Panikkar presented his credentials on 28 May 1950 that China had no aggressive designs towards India.[22]

India's northern border with Tibet is divided into three sectors—the north-east which has the McMahon Line (except for the Sikkim–Tibet border); the central sector (bordering Uttar Pradesh and Punjab/Himachal Pradesh), which though neither delineated nor demarcated was more or less well understood; and, finally the western sector where the frontier, as indicated earlier , was 'UNDEFINED'. All three sectors had different backgrounds and each had problems peculiar to it. The prime minister had taken a simplistic view of the frontiers, as can be deduced from his words, and had made them sacrosanct and non-negotiable. The importance of agreed, well-defined, delineated and demarcated borders stood ignored. Those who spoke up in favour of adopting a clear and direct approach towards China at the frontiers, that is, Sardar Patel and G.S. Bajpai, were not heeded. Paradoxically, this did not mean that the principal protagonists were confident of their standpoint. Nehru, while declaring Indian borders non-negotiable, continued to have doubts about their acceptance by China, particularly that of the McMahon Line. On 8 November 1950, Nehru had said that the following was possible:

Our frontier line itself may be challenged as it had been challenged by the previous Chinese Government. In regard to this we have to be perfectly clear and we are in fact on strong ground. We consider the McMahon Line as our frontier and we are not prepared, on any account to reconsider this question.[23]

Nehru remained unsure of the reaction of the newly emerged strong, centralized communist government, which had come right up to India's frontiers and had upset the old balance of power. In his letter to the chief ministers of the Indian states dated 17 November 1950, he said, 'The developments in Tibet rather suddenly made people realise that China might have a long common frontier with India and this new China was probably very different for the old. Also, the Himalayan border was not so quite effective as it used to be.'[24] Within a day of expressing these fear, he did not, on 18 November, rule out the possibility of China entering and taking possession of the disputed territory if there were no obstructions. He suggested all precautions be taken to prevent this possibility and said, 'We must differentiate between these precautions and those that might be necessary to meet a real attack.'[25] Nehru, however, from the beginning had different ideas regarding the security of borders. He had put his faith in the climate, the terrain and the Himalayas which separate India from Tibet.[26]

Commenting on Sinha's note on the 'Situation on the North East Frontier', Nehru on 5 March 1953 took cognizance of the changes taking place in Asia, and said:

In the ultimate analysis we have to build our strength. That strength means not so much frontier outposts and the like, but internal strength—political and economic . . . We have, of course, to be alert and vigilant on our borders. This is not so much from the point of view of resisting any major incursion but rather to make it clear to China and the world that we are going to stick to our frontiers. Any challenge to our frontiers will have to be met.

In fact, it means a challenge to the whole of India and not merely
to the frontiers.[27]

Having said that, in the same note, he was satisfied to align Indian
strength with 'certain geographical factors which cannot easily be
changed or overcome . . .'[28]

In another note, while pledging Chinese friendship, he defined
India's basic rights as:

> The preservation of the frontiers . . . It is important today and
> even more so in the long future that India and China should have
> friendly relations and not have a dangerous frontier.[29]

Paradoxically, Nehru's worries were only for the McMahon Line,
which was the outcome of the Simla Convention. Other parts of
India's borders did not receive any attention. There was no hint
of any worry about the western frontier where the border was
'UNDEFINED'. The fact of this frontier being undefined was not
even mentioned while discussing frontiers.

Having advocated caution, Nehru conceded that there was no
general international recognition of the autonomy of Tibet, and
China never accepted the provisions of the 1914 Convention.[30]

He had told the Burmese prime minister that while there was 'not
much danger of any Chinese aggression across the Indian border',
he wanted to make it clear that 'if occasion arises . . . the slightest
attempt at such aggression, whether in India or Nepal, would be
stoutly resisted by us'.[31] These were his self-ignited doubts and self-
satisfying assurances. The intolerable burden, financial or otherwise,
that it would cast on India's resources perturbed him. He did not
think it necessary to deploy the army at the distant frontiers.[32] He felt
it was imperative for India to have friendly relations with China in
view of Pakistan's hostility. Refusing to either increase in the armed
forces or the defence budget, he said that India could not afford these
at this stage in its development, and even if other countries helped

India, it would be difficult to meet the combined challenge of China and Pakistan.[33]

Pakistan had made sure to develop friendly relations with China and it, too, had reciprocated. Pakistan was the first Muslim country to recognize China in 1951. Illegal occupation of a portion of the state of Jammu and Kashmir gave it contiguity with China. It apparently did not trouble India that China was more sensitive to Pakistan's concerns regarding Kashmir (as discussed in Chapter 7) than India's. On the question of Pakistan's anti-communist military alliances, China readily accepted Pakistan's alibi that they were not against China but India. In 1953, a trade delegation from China had received a friendly welcome in Karachi and a trade agreement was signed between Pakistan and China. In March 1956, Pakistan welcomed a Chinese official delegation at the inauguration of its constitution. Basically, China never slammed its doors on Pakistan. Nehru's strategy of wooing China to neutralize Pakistan never found traction.

Initially, Zhou was keen on tripartite discussions among China, India and Nepal to stabilize Tibet's frontier, while clarifying that there was no territorial dispute or any controversy between them in this matter.[34]

Nehru, however, suggested that at the first instance, conversations pertaining to India's interest in Tibet and their common boundary be held between China and India, and later Nepal could be involved as their talks progressed. Nehru's lukewarm response did not encourage Zhou any further and the proposal made little progress. Since there was also a border problem between China and Burma, Nehru felt Burma was more vulnerable from the north. Burmese Prime Minister U Nu was expected in India on a visit and Nehru planned to talk to him and mentioned that he would welcome discussions between China and Burma '*and would be ready to lend our good offices by direct participation in conversations if both parties desired this*'.[35] Nehru remained committed to China's friendship, ignoring the fact that China's attitude towards India was intimidating since it had occupied Tibet. Nehru did not measure the success or failure of his foreign policy, whether it served India's interests or not, as long as world peace was ensured.[36]

With this perspective, China's pin-pricks were ignored in the larger interest of peace. In 1950, China had remained unmindful of India's concerns for a peaceful settlement of Tibet's future. In the notes that were exchanged between them during October and November 1950, China showed little concern for India's pleas for Tibetan autonomy and peaceful resolution of its relations with Tibet. Neither did it appreciate India's efforts to secure for China its rightful place in the UNSC.[37] Early in November 1951, at a press conference, Nehru had acknowledged differences on borders with China, but had ignored them as minor ones.[38] The very next year, China's reaction to the Indian resolution in the UN General Assembly on the repatriation of Korean prisoners of war was extremely hostile and insulting.[39] China had described Nehru's resolution as the 'parent of all evils'. He had even challenged India's claim to Chinese friendship. Nehru, however, remained overawed and docile while feeling embarrassed.[40] He asked the secretary general to speak to the Chinese ambassador and convey that India deeply regretted the criticism from the Chinese and that India had 'refrained in saying a word in answer to these repeated criticisms because we are anxious to maintain our friendly relations with that great country'.[41]

The induction of a large Chinese army in Tibet had caused food shortages there. To overcome it, Nehru readily agreed to China's request for transit facilities for rice from China through India despite the opposition both from the political officer in Sikkim and the mission-in-charge in Lhasa. Both of them felt it would facilitate large-scale deployment of the Chinese army in Tibet, which the Tibetans would construe as facilitating the consolidation of China's control in Tibet.[42] Snubbing both, Nehru said:

Our policy towards China is of greater importance to us than our policy towards almost any other country. History, geography and recent developments have forced this upon us. In future this will continue to be important.

He feared that the denial of facilities might weaken India's capacity to influence events in Tibet.[43] Disparaging comments on the way in which India's first general elections in 1952 had been conducted were ignored.[44]

In the wake of the 17-Point Agreement, Panikkar had discussions in the Chinese foreign office (Weichiaopu) about outstanding problems in Tibet and had handed over a note to Weichiaopu.[45] When Panikkar discussed the note with Premier Zhou, the latter said he was studying it but assured him that 'he saw *no difficulty in safeguarding economic and cultural interests of India in Tibet*'.[46] Panikkar in his report to Delhi said, 'I did not allude to the position of frontiers or of our relations with Bhutan, nor did he raise it.'[47] Both presumed things which were not said explicitly. China's game plan was to first end India's special rights in Tibet and only then rake up the issue of borders, and it followed this strategy meticulously and successfully.

Panikkar again missed the opportunity to mention frontiers while expressing readiness to give up the Indian facilities in Tibet.[48] Nehru felt it 'odd that in discussing Tibet, Zhou did not refer at all to our frontier'. He told Panikkar that India was not only interested in its own frontier but 'also frontiers of Nepal, Bhutan and Sikkim and that it had been made clear in Parliament that these frontiers must remain'.[49] Panikkar cleverly pinned down Nehru in his telegram of 17 June 1952 reminding him of his own instructions at the time of his taking up the assignment as the ambassador in Beijing. Reminding Nehru, Panikkar said that he (Nehru) had told him that since he had emphatically and publicly declared the borders of India, raising the question now would give China 'an opening and might indicate our doubts' about our own frontiers. Since Zhou had not alluded to the borders, it should be taken to '*mean (his) acquiescence in if not acceptance of our position*', insisted Panikkar, and Nehru too *acquiesced.*[50]

G.S. Bajpai, the governor of Bombay State, when consulted on the note sent by the Chinese on 11 July 1952[51] in which Zhou had referred to the 'scar' left by the British, advised a comprehensive approach to the borders.[52] Ignoring his sane advice, as discussed in Chapter 7, a note was sent to Beijing listing seven outstanding issues which needed settlement. The border question was not one of them.[53] Panikkar justified the exclusion of the question of frontiers to Bajpai, saying that the PM had finally decided that it was not necessary to raise this issue since India had declared its borders, and it was for China to bring it up. He was apprehensive that if India initiated a discussion:

> We would have forced them to one of the two attitudes, either the acceptance of the treaty signed by us with Tibet (Simla Convention) or a refusal of it with an offer to negotiate. The first is not altogether easy to imagine considering that every previous Chinese Government had refused in terms to accept an Indo-Tibetan treaty as binding on them. The second would not have been advantageous to us . . . If, on the other hand, the Chinese raise the issue we can plainly refuse to reopen the question and take the stand the Prime Minister took that the territory this side of the McMahon Line is ours and there is nothing to discuss about it.[54]

There was still no mention of the western border. As far as the eastern sector was concerned, the hesitation was apparent on account of well-known reservations of the Chinese regarding the Simla Convention. An unhappy Bajpai later repeated his advice, elaborating on his point of view. He advised that a note be formally presented to Beijing detailing Indian frontiers, and added:

> If they are friendly and accept the present position, they need not say anything about it. If they should do so now but a dispute arises sometime in the future, we can quote their silence as acquiescence in support of our case. If, they are not friendly to us as we are to them, and do not wish silence to be construed as acquiescence, they will have to come out into the open now and we shall know where we really stand: that may leave us sadder men but also wiser.[55]

Panikkar, commenting on this, said that since the Chinese did not add any other subject for discussion apart from the seven issues raised by India, there was no need to mention frontiers. Panikkar also said that technically Bajpai might be correct but the Chinese 'surely cannot plead ignorance of the fact that our troops are in occupation of the line and that we treat the territory without protest from them as our own'.[56]

As the Chinese hold on Lhasa tightened and the deployment of the Chinese army on the borders swelled, the Indian establishments in Tibet came under pressure. China explained away their deployment in Tibet as a development that was not due to any hostility towards India but to 'consolidate the frontiers of China' and to maintain friendly relations with Nepal, Sikkim, Bhutan and India.[57] This was a sign that China would have separate relations with each of the three Himalayan States. Panikkar, having relinquished his post in Beijing in September 1952, had moved to Cairo, but he continued to be consulted by Nehru on issues related to China. Panikkar, while commenting on Sumal Sinha's note on 'dangers to north-east frontier', had opined:

> No one is in a position to be dogmatic about it one way or the other, we have of course, to be prepared in every sense and take every action necessary to safeguard our frontiers and further to make it clear to the Chinese that we have no intention of discussing our frontiers with any one and we shall resist by every means any attempt to encroach on them.[58]

Nehru being fully aware and conscious of China's stand on old treaties insisted that in international relations previous agreements could not be forsaken unilaterally.[59] India knew that all revolutionary governments tend to denounce the past and China was no exception. Besides, no Chinese government had, since 1914, accepted the Simla Convention and had denounced it as illegal and Nehru was not unaware of it.

Henry McMahon, who drew the line between India and Tibet in 1914, in his lecture at the Royal Society for the Encouragement of Art in London on 15 November 1935 on international frontiers, had said:

> I need only refer here to the boundary portion of our treaty work which on this occasion was a matter purely of delimitation *i.e.*, the determination and *verbal definition of the boundaries between Tibet and India* and Tibet and China. Including the boundary with China and Tibet the line we had to deal with was of very formidable length—over 1,500 miles—but want of accurate local knowledge and absence of detailed surveys rendered it impossible to define large portion of it, except in somewhat general terms.[60]

This proved that the line was drawn without any proper survey, apart from other infirmities of the Convention.

Nehru, reluctant to raise the frontier question 'for the present', said that at some stage it 'will have to be brought [up] in a larger settlement'.[61] In 1954, when the opportunity presented itself for doing this, he allowed it to slip away. His message of 1 September 1953 to Zhou[62] suggesting negotiations on Tibet had referred to the earlier note of the MEA that had listed the seven outstanding issues which needed to be resolved. The question of the frontier was not among them.[63] Later Nehru, while acknowledging Zhou's reply for Tibet negotiations, had repeated the note, that is, seven issues which needed settlement.[64]

As discussed earlier in Chapter 7, Panikkar's advice had been accepted, that is, the frontiers were not to be discussed and should the Chinese insist on discussions the negotiations were to be broken.[65]

The brief that the MEA finalized for discussions on Tibet had four elements:

(1) Aksai Chin was listed as a disputed territory along with other disputed areas;
(2) the legal opinion was that the McMahon Line could be repudiated by China;

(3) it recommended Nehru's stance: our frontiers were well
defined and well recognized by long custom and usage . . .
etc., map or no map, and were not open for discussion; and

(4) should China insist on discussing borders, to break the
negotiations, as Panikkar had suggested.

Nehru, while approving the brief, had only added a caveat saying
that before breaking the negotiations, Delhi should be consulted.[66]
That Aksai Chin was a disputed territory was ignored. It was this
brief on the basis of which the Indian delegation batted in Beijing.

Later, Nehru explained his hesitation in discussing borders. He
said that since we were sure of our borders, the question was 'why
invite discussion about a thing on which we had no doubt?' But with
the advantage of hindsight, he conceded 'that [it] was not a very wise
policy'. Yet, he said that 'a lingering doubt remained in my mind and
in my Ministry's mind as to what might happen in the future'. But
still it was felt:

> We should hold our position and the lapse of time and events
> would confirm it, and by the time challenge came, we would be in
> a much stronger position to face it. It is not as if it was not thought
> about. After the longest and the clearest thinking and consultations
> with those who were concerned, between our Ambassadors, our
> Foreign Affairs Committee and others we came to this decision.[67]

He said this in Parliament in December 1959. The date of discussion
of the frontier with his colleagues was not indicated in his statement.
The western sector had come into the limelight only by about
1957/1958 after China had completed the construction of the Aksai
Chin road. Prior to this, the entire discourse was focused on the
McMahon Line and China had given enough indications that it was
willing to concede it to India. Be that as it may, the people consulted
were either his colleagues in the cabinet or officers who had been
endorsing his line of thinking all along.

Nehru had occupied such a venerable position in Indian politics since the days of the freedom movement, and even in the early years after Independence, that his word was accepted without much questioning. Besides, all the facts about relations with China were kept under a tight lid of secrecy and people were unaware of what exactly was happening in India's relations with China. It was still in the bhai-bhai phase.

It was not until the Kongka Pass incident in October 1959 in which nine Indian police personnel on patrol duty were killed by the Chinese that his judgements started coming under scrutiny.

As discussed in Chapter 7, in negotiating the agreement on Tibet the question of frontiers specifically was not raised by either side. China emphasized that *questions ripe for settlement were settled* and India that *all outstanding issues had been settled.*[68] With that Nehru took it that everything, even if not discussed, was deemed settled.

The discussions and agreement remained confined broadly to the seven outstanding issues listed in the MEA's note of 2 August 1952 and Nehru's emphasis remained on them in his various communications.[69]

Later when asked at his press conference, 'How far does this disappearance of agreement over Tibet (of 1954) with China affect our position on Tibet?', Nehru said the agreement had referred to three things: (i) *withdrawal of military escort,* (ii) *pilgrimage, trade and trade routes and* (iii) *to certain passes over which these trade routes should pass.*[70] He did not refer to borders being settled in that agreement. Since Nehru had publicly declared that Indian frontiers were not negotiable, China now felt free to make territorial claims, presumably to make India ask for negotiations, just as it had successfully compelled India to ask for negotiations on Tibet by harassing the Indian mission and trade agencies there.

A mention had been made earlier about Burma's borders with China and the interest shown by Nehru. The Sino-Burmese frontier came up for discussion again in 1954. Zhou had visited Delhi and Rangoon in that year. After he had left, both Nehru and U Nu

exchanged notes on their discussions with Zhou. While briefing
Nehru, U Nu told him of his discussions on Burma's frontier with
Zhou. Nehru, however, said he did not discuss the frontier question
with Zhou since:

> We have, on our part, no matter to raise with him. Our border is
> quite clear. Since we were clear about this ourselves and have stated
> so quite openly, there was no point in my raising this question
> with him. In your case, however, there is a difference and so it is as
> well that you raise this matter clearly.[71]

In 1956, there was a fresh problem on the Burma–China border.
Since the Burmese government had earlier shared its concerns with
Nehru who had offered to speak to Zhou, Nu decided to consult
Nehru and sent his foreign minister to Delhi, ostensibly to discuss
trade but essentially to discuss the border problem with China. Before
the Burmese foreign minister arrived in Delhi, Nehru in a note to
the foreign secretary said that an aide-mémoire must be prepared for
presentation to the Chinese Government on the Burmese frontier
problem in which 'we should not raise directly the question of the
Indian frontiers with Tibet or China'. Among other things, Nehru
also said, 'In any event, no change can be made unilaterally' in the
borders, and added, 'Apart from international usage and convention,
any such unilateral action would be against both the spirit and the
letter of the Panchsheel doctrine to which China, Burma and India
and other countries have adhered.'[72] Apparently, Nehru lost sight of
the fact that only a couple of years ago, he himself had unilaterally
altered the western border with China.

Following the Burmese foreign minister's discussions in Delhi,
Nehru in a letter promised U Nu help from India in a friendly
way and advised him to go to China and settle the matter. He,
however, cautioned him if the dispute between Burma and China
is not approached in a friendly way, and satisfactorily settled
'the whole edifice of Five Principles and coexistence may crack'.

'That would be,' he said, 'most unfortunate and would have far reaching consequences.' He also cautioned him against adopting a rigid attitude because:

> Once this rigidity comes in, it becomes very difficult to deal with the matter, and the prestige of the countries concerned is involved.[73]

Nehru, conveying concerns of the Burmese to the Chinese Premier, told him that 'in these sparsely inhabited frontiers mountainous area frontiers and positions which are based on previous agreements and have also been accepted by usage, custom and tradition for appreciable periods *should not be disturbed or altered except by friendly agreements*'. 'Our general view and earnest hope is that these matters should not be allowed to lead to a deterioration in the relations between the two countries, as this is bound to have adverse effects,' added Nehru.[74]

His advice to Zhou now was in line with his own ideas which he wanted China to adopt with regard to the Indian frontier. Zhou's response was quite positive generally but he remained silent on the matter of the settlement of borders. He said that the peaceful coexistence 'we advocate is not only for a passive avoidance of mutual conflict, but also for the active establishment of peaceful and friendly relations between nations'. He described the boundary question as inherited from the past and mentioned that he would endeavour to settle it through peaceful negotiations.[75]

Following Nehru's advice, U Nu (also known as Thakin Nu) entered into negotiations with China. A portion of the Burmese border was also covered by the McMahon Line. Zhou told U Nu that though he believed the McMahon Line to be 'immoral' and based on an 'inequal treaty' which China had never accepted, for the sake of agreement he was '*prepared to accept this as a "de facto" northern frontier*'. This was conveyed by the Burmese ambassador in Beijing to Indian ambassador, R.K. Nehru, under instructions from U Nu and was, therefore, meant for the specific information of

the prime minister.[76] Zhou offered some interesting information to
U Nu regarding India. According to the Burmese ambassador, Zhou
told Nu that he intended to discuss the frontier question with Nehru
when he visited China in 1954 (but) in view of his (Nehru's) strong
attitude and since he had said that there was nothing to discuss, he
(Zhou) decided not to raise this question'.[77] It was a clear message for
Nehru that he should follow the advice which he himself had given
to the Burmese prime minister and negotiate India's borders directly
with Zhou.

Nehru, however, said:

> So far as we are concerned, the frontier (known previously as the
> McMahon Line) is not a matter of dispute at all and Zhou Enlai
> has accepted it. It is true that this acceptance was oral, but it was
> quite clear and precise.[78]

China in its efforts to sort out its border problems with Nepal and
Burma was sending a message to India of its reasonable attitude and
tried to sell the idea of a negotiated settlement to Nehru. Nehru,
however, remained impervious to any such idea applying to India's
own borders with China.

Nehru swore by Chinese friendship, while harbouring doubts
about China's acceptance of their borders. Stressing the need for the
settlement of borders, he had even in 1953 said, 'We cannot just do
something which will leave trails behind and which will pursue us
for generations to come.'[79] Yet again, while considering the question
of Indian trade agencies in Tibet and deciding to write to Zhou to
negotiate a settlement of their problems, he said, 'For the present we
need not raise the question of frontiers but this will have to be brought
in larger settlement.'[80]

For the most part, the focus remained on the north-eastern
frontier, that is, the McMahon Line. The western sector did not
draw any attention from Nehru until after the Tibet Agreement with
China had been signed in 1954. It did not draw attention even when

the maps published by the Survey of India depicted that frontier as 'UNDEFINED'. He lost sight of the fact that in the brief for talks on Tibet prepared in December 1953, Aksai Chin was mentioned as a disputed territory.[81] Similarly, as discussed in Chapter 7, while negotiating the Tibet agreement, India did not propose inclusion of some passes in the agreement since these were located in the disputed Aksai Chin area.[82] While going through the report of Dr Gopalachari, one of the officers who had negotiated the Tibet agreement in Beijing, Nehru had issued instructions to demarcate the western border, which was undefined:

> All our maps dealing with *this frontier* should be carefully examined and where necessary withdrawn. New maps should be printed showing our *northern* and north-eastern frontiers without any reference to any line. *These new maps should also* not *state that there is any un-demarcated territory.* The new maps should be sent to our embassies abroad and should be introduced to the public generally and be used in our schools and colleges etc.[83]

Having issued these instructions, the prime minister said, 'Both flowing from our policy and as a consequence of our Agreement with China this frontier should be considered a firm and definite one which is not open to discussion with anybody.'

He added that if China's maps continued to show it in its territory, then 'we shall have to point this out to the Chinese Government'. He further instructed, 'We need not do this immediately but we should not put up with this for long and the matter will have to be taken up.' Adding further, he said, 'Our frontier has been finalised not only by implication in this agreement, but the specific passes mentioned are direct recognition of our frontier.' He directed to set up check-posts which were necessary 'not only to control traffic, prevent unauthorised infiltration but as symbols of India's frontier'.[84]

In a separate note, he repeated these instructions to the secretary general and foreign secretary for compliance.[85]

Nehru did not realize that international borders are not settled unilaterally but in consultation with the other stakeholder. With his instructions, both the eastern and the western frontiers had become controversial. However, in Nehru's perception it was settled.

The western frontier, containing the contentious Aksai Chin area, was surveyed twice in the nineteenth century. Two lines had come under consideration. One was the Johnson–Ardagh Line which advocated inclusion of the whole of uninhabited Aksai Chin in India. This was part of the 'forward policy', which would take Indian frontier to the borders of China and give India control of the northern approaches. The viceroy, Lord Elgin (1861–63), termed this policy as 'impractical and unnecessary', and recommended acceptance of the other line, the McCartney–MacDonald Line which would give China 'the whole of Karakash Valley, a trade route, and almost all of Aksai Chin proper except the Lingzi Thang salt plains and the whole of Chang Chenmo Valley'. Neither this nor the earlier Jhonson–Ardagh line had received formal recognition and acceptance from the Chinese and, 'on account of another bout of Russo-phobia', the British frontier policy reverted to the inclusion of Aksai Chin within the British territories during the term of Lord Hardinge (1910–16). Since no formal agreement with China was worked out, the boundary in this region remained undefined when India became independent in 1947.[86] It may be noted that the pre-Independence Survey of India's maps with the western boundary marked as undefined were subsequently reissued in 1952 and 1953 by the Survey of India and continued to show it as such, until Nehru's instructions mentioned earlier were issued. Later, Nehru approved T.N. Kaul's suggestion, which had also been endorsed by the foreign secretary and secretary general, that while preparing the new maps 'the most favourable line as our frontier' be shown and without waiting for 'detailed surveys', since that would take a long time.[87]

Accordingly, in demarcating the western frontier in the new maps, the Survey of India chose the Johnson–Ardagh Line which included the Aksai Chin in India. Foreign Secretary R.K. Nehru had later recalled that

Our experts had advised us that our claim to Aksai Chin was not too strong. The Prime Minister was 'agreeable' to adjustment in Aksai Chin and one or two other places being made as part of a satisfactory overall settlement.[88]

Even a former foreign secretary, Shyam Saran, said:

> But it must be acknowledged that the Survey of India maps inherited from the British show much of the area in the western sector as 'undefined'. It was only in 1954 that a decision was taken to replace these maps with new one showing the boundaries as fixed, with an alignment that incorporated Aksai China in Indian territory. In retrospect, this may *not* have been a wise decision since it deprived the Indian side of flexibility in negotiating a compromise with the Chinese.[89]

In June 1954 during Zhou's visit to India, both prime ministers had extensive discussions on international affairs but little time was spent on bilateral matters. Nehru raised the frontier question with Zhou but only in the context of Burma's border problem and added that while Chinese maps, too, were showing some Indian areas, 'I am sure these were old maps and you did not mean it.'[90] This was what Nehru had also told a press conference earlier on 3 November 1951.[91]

At the Bandung Conference, Zhou accepted that China's borders with neighbours were unsettled and assured that these would be settled by 'peaceful means'.[92] China at no time claimed that its borders with neighbours were settled and fixed.

Soon after the agreement on Tibet had been signed in 1954, China began nibbling on the border areas, beginning with Bara Hoti along the Uttar Pradesh border. On 6 May 1956, Nehru had yet again, referring to his talks with Zhou, admitted that 'in fact, China never clearly accepted our frontier as it is'. Regarding the border incidents which were now reported, he satisfied himself that such minor incidents used to occur 'long before the Chinese came to Tibet' and conceded that the 'frontier is not clearly demarcated and some doubts may arise about some points along it'. He was not worried about the roads and airports being constructed in Tibet, which he described as normal activity to improve communications. Ambassador R.K. Nehru advised, 'We should bide our time and not take any active step.'[93] Soon there were reports of an airstrip being built in Tibet and again it was accepted as normal activity for improvement of infrastructure. Nehru said that there was 'no danger of physical or aerial attack' and recommended similar development of communications in the border areas of India, too, which remained unimplemented.[94] However, he once again accepted that the border question would have to be taken up 'some time or the other'. While not taking up the question of borders with China, he also vetoed any suggestion to strengthen India's defence potential, describing it 'against our basic approach to the problem of defence'. He said if India was to buy the expensive bomber as suggested, 'we do not equip ourselves with more useful aircraft and delay, to some extent, our industrial development'.[95]

At the end of December 1956, Zhou Enlai again came to India. The Dalai Lama was also in India in connection with the 2,500th birthday celebrations of Lord Buddha. While Nehru was discussing the global situation, Zhou cut him short to discuss Tibet, not its border but the simmering revolt there. After providing details of the actions taken by China in Tibet since 1950, Zhou referred to the troubles there and held Kalimpong to be the epicentre of Tibet's troubles. He particularly pointed to the speeches of the mayors of Bombay and Madras who had referred to Tibet as a separate country. Nehru described Kalimpong as the 'nest of spies', giving credence to Zhou's charge. Perceiving Nehru to be anxious for China's acceptance of the McMahon Line, Zhou assured him that he had recently come to know about it while studying the China–Burma border. Nehru gave him the background of the Line and, clarifying India's position on Tibet, assuring Zhou that India did not regard Tibet an independent country since it had no foreign relations. On the status of Bhutan and Sikkim, Zhou reassured Nehru that

China had no claim on either of them, as, even under the imperial power, these were never under China. Having said all that, Zhou did tell Nehru that irrespective of the past, the McMahon Line was an *accomplished fact* and China would recognize it despite Tibetan Government's reluctance'. Zhou agreed that 'the question can be resolved and we think it should be settled early'.[96]

Zhou was also anxious that the Dalai Lama should not seek asylum in India, as was being suspected, and did not want him to visit Kalimpong also, which the Dalai Lama was otherwise planning to visit since, he said, plans for Tibet's independence were being made there. Zhou further suspected that US agents were active in Kalimpong and were trying to create trouble for China.[97] India's position all along was that while sovereignty rested with China, Tibet should be autonomous.[98]

As the revolt in Tibet gathered momentum, to India's chagrin, China continued to blame Kalimpong as the hotbed of rebellion and the source of China's problems in Tibet. India's denial had no impact on Beijing.

Delhi did feel exasperated as a series of border-related incidents in places as far apart as Bara Hoti, Shipki La, Wu je (Longju) and Nilang had taken place. Despite feeling uncomfortable with these violations, Delhi took them in its stride and did not see any particular pattern or design in them.

It was also at this time that the Cold War had crept at India's doorstep, with Pakistan joining defence pacts with the United States and receiving sophisticated defence equipment from them. As pointed out earlier, Nehru's answer to this development was to establish friendlier relations with China, to prevent the two neighbours on its two flanks from being united in a common cause against India. His perceived friendship with China was seen as vindication of his policy both towards Pakistan and nonalignment. Nevertheless, he was worried that the balance of power was disturbed in the subcontinent. He wanted to counter Pakistan's alliance politics by further policy initiatives than challenging it upfront. The Indian ambassadors in African and West Asian countries were asked to bring to the attention of their host governments 'the evil' and dangerous consequences of Pakistan's actions in the hope that their pressure would make Pakistan reconsider its decision.[99] This was a naïve move that yielded disappointing results. Other countries may sympathize with you but to expect them to take up the cudgels on your behalf, whatever be your standing with them, is hardly the way countries fashion their foreign policies and international relations.

He believed in his soft power, which relied only on goodwill as the key to security. He was happy to anchor India's security on the combination and permutation of factors that were external to India. He consciously ruled out any shift in India's security paradigm built on military strength. He said a competitive military build-up would be an exceedingly wrong policy and would lead us in the wrong direction.[100] For Nehru, a bilateral approach to normalization of relations with China was the more optimal way to mute the security dilemma. But he shied away from discussing the borders with China since he remained trapped in his own position, having publicly committed himself to a stance of 'no discussion' on borders.

He believed that the peace area concept was viable because through deft diplomacy both blocs could be assured that neither would gain relative advantage by absorbing non-aligned areas into their orbits. Nehru rejected a narrow balance-of-power approach to security in favour of an ambitious quest to stabilize the geopolitical status quo by promoting an area of agreement in contesting zones around India's neighbourhood.[101]

Responding to public demand for expansion of the army, he said it was 'far more important to expedite the execution of the existing defence schemes and to lay greater stress on the development of the National Cadet Corps (NCC) and its auxiliary and expanding the Territorial Army (TA)'.[102] It was a different matter that the nature of existing defence schemes remained obscure, and if defence schemes were anchored on the NCC or the TA, it was strategically not a prudent choice since neither the NCC nor the TA was trained for warfare. These were not even paramilitary outfits.

Internationally, Nehru at this time was at the crest of his popularity. The non-aligned movement had started taking shape. Besides himself, the Egyptian President Gamal Abdel Nasser, Ghanian President Kwame Nkrumah and Yugoslavian President Marshal Tito were the leading lights of that movement. He was particularly sought after by world leaders and received in many countries. The leaders of several countries also visited India, which resulted in Nehru enjoying a high profile in international politics. The 27 November 1958 letter of the US President Eisenhower stands testimony to his standing in world politics.

He wrote:

Universally you are recognised as one of the most powerful influences for peace and conciliation in the world. I believe that because you are a world leader for peace in your individual capacity . . . your influence is particularly valuable in stemming a global drift towards cynicism, mutual suspicion and finally disaster.[103]

Such handsome tributes would boost any one's ego. Nehru who was prone to adulation was mighty happy at these tributes that, too, coming from the head of the most powerful country in the world. It was not for nothing that Mountbatten later remarked, 'If Nehru had died in 1958, history would have remembered him as the greatest statesman of the twentieth century.'[104] Mountbatten was perhaps right since his policies had not yet been put to test and appreciated universally. With such high standing in the world, he found it unnecessary to divert India's scarce resources for defence.

In the process, he allowed a vacuum in India's defence and security architecture. He placed his trust in China's friendship and all-round goodwill, even as Pakistan turned hostile in Kashmir. As the relations with China 'seemed to flourish' in his perception, and the non-alignment gathered steam, Nehru rejoiced at the success of his policies, and so did the Indian public. For Nehru, this was India's answer to Pakistan's military alliances and a guarantee of India's security. The non-alignment movement finally inched closer to the Soviet Union, which extended support to its agenda and bared its anti-West fangs. This had the effect of India getting alienated from the West though it continued to receive developmental assistance.

Meanwhile, China continued to nibble at India's borders, without raising too much concern in Delhi. Bara Hoti, which was the first to be encroached despite talks with China to resolve the issue, remained stalemated. In the following months and years, China was seen raising many more such claims. There were several incidents, but in a scattered manner, at Shipki La, Nilang, Walong, Migyitun, Khinzemane, Longju, Spanggur, Khunrak and so on.

Responding to the border-related concerns of G.L. Mehta, the ambassador in Washington, reflected in the 'Foreign Report' (a confidential report circulated by the *Economist* of London) of 8 July 1957 on 'China's expansionist aims', Foreign Secretary Subimal Dutt assured him not to worry, as the ministry was aware of the Chinese maps and its claims, 'particularly a *part of Kashmir* and the whole of North East Frontier Agency (NEFA) within her borders'. He said there were also other areas which had been claimed by China. Trying to set Mehta's concerns at rest, Dutt said China had agreed to settle these matters through consultations. He also assured him that there were no signs of China subverting our minorities in the north-east.[105] The foreign secretary's mention of Kashmir (Ladakh) in this context was significant since apart from this there had been no mention of it in any other discussion so far.

Despite a series of claims made by China on Indian territory, Nehru, in his speech in the Rajya Sabha in March 1957, had referred to China as a country which 'counts in the world' and had lamented that it had not yet been represented in the UN. There was no mention of any of the incidents along the border or claims made by China on Indian territory.[106] Delhi, too, pooh poohed reports appearing in the *Times,* London, of Chinese intrusion in the Garhwal border areas.[107] Surprisingly, when all this was happening, the Indian public had no inkling of any of these unsavoury developments. These events were swept under the carpet to protect the 'bhai-bhai' relationship with China.

Nehru's public postures towards China and his real feelings were at conflict with each other, and he did not express them in public perhaps for tactical reasons. Nehru, sounding friendly in public and taking a benign attitude on the issues concerning China, did portend the dichotomy in India's policy towards an intensely nationalistic neighbour, which was fast turning from unfriendly to hostile.

Prior to Nehru's visit to China in October 1954, Ambassador Raghavan felt anguished at China's lack of appreciation for India and Indian policies.[108] However, six months down the line, following Nehru's tumultuous welcome in China in October 1954, he changed his views, in line with Nehru's own exuberance on his visit.[109] The notion that the Indian public was sufficiently hypnotized by the bhai-bhai (India and China are brothers) syndrome was not in doubt. That within a few years, India forgot the rebuffs repeatedly inflicted by China spoke volumes for GoI's audaciousness.

Nehru did not like the idea of a Maginot Line (the one France had built against Germany after the First World War) as a measure of security. He said, 'In particular, we have to have peace, quiet and contentment on our side of the border. I am more worried about the Naga trouble from this point of view than about anything that the Chinese may do.'[110] With this sort of attitude at the highest level, the neglect of the borders was not surprising.

The issue of maps came back to haunt Delhi once again. The reply Delhi received to the note it had shared with China regarding the publication of a small-scale map in the July 1958 issue of the *China Pictorial*[111] raised Indian hackles. While conceding that the maps were old, China said:

> The Chinese Government has not yet undertaken a survey of
> China's boundary nor consulted with the countries concerned,
> and that it will not make changes in the boundary on its own.[112]

Nehru was distressed with the reply even though it was rational.
He had expected China to accept the borders as delineated in the
Indian maps and replicate them in the Chinese ones. As pointed out
earlier, the Chinese maps had been showing Indian areas in China
since the thirties and this was not a new phenomenon. Any country
drawing new maps of its frontiers would conduct surveys and hold
consultations with the country sharing that border to come to an
agreed demarcation to avoid any future problems. Since Nehru had
unilaterally declared Indian borders and made them non-negotiable
and had even altered them, he expected the others to fall in line
and accept the alignment drawn on the Indian maps. This was an
unrealistic expectation, which was at the root of India's problem.

In the face of Indian disappointment, China sent another
memorandum clarifying its position. Recalling the discussions
between the two prime ministers when Nehru had visited China in
1954, it said:

> This was made clear to His Excellency Prime Minister Nehru by
> Prime Minister Chou Enlai when the former visited China in
> 1954. Premier Chou Enlai explained then to His Excellency Prime
> Minister Nehru that the reason why the boundary in Chinese maps
> is drawn according to old maps is that the Chinese Government has
> not yet undertaken a survey of China's boundary, nor consulted
> with the countries concerned and that it will not make changes in
> the boundary on its own. The Chinese Government notes with
> satisfaction that the Indian Government recognise the force of
> Premier Chou Enlai's statement on this matter.[112a]

Realizing that the exchange of notes was not bringing the two
countries anywhere nearer to a solution, and that it was gradually

getting acrimonious, Nehru decided to take up the matter with Zhou at a personal level to inject some much-needed potency and urgency into the issue. In his letter of 14 December 1958 to Zhou, he said that the areas shown in Chinese maps were undoubtedly Indian and there was no dispute about them and wondered what would be achieved by surveys which China wanted to conduct.[113]

But Nehru, sworn to Chinese friendship, perhaps found it embarrassing to share differences on the borders with the public. Even when discussing the question of maps in the Lok Sabha on 22 April 1959, he played down the Chinese reply, saying the Chinese had conceded that the 'maps may be incorrect largely but what exactly should be correct is the thing we want to go into before changing them'.[114] His reply did not seem to show the umbrage that he had taken in his letter to Zhou.

Nehru's desire to visit Tibet came a cropper since China kept postponing it repeatedly on one pretext or the other, essentially on account of the simmering revolt in Tibet. He, instead, visited Bhutan. In Bhutan he tried to allay their fear of China suggesting that one should not give too much importance to the factor of communism, since all powerful states tend to be expansionist and, in this category, Nehru had included the United States and the Soviet Union too.[115]

By 1956/1957, the Chinese had completed construction of the Sinkiang–Tibet Highway through Aksai Chin and had even announced it. India, after confirming the existence of the road through a survey party, 'protested' its construction which, in Indian perception, violated Indian territory. Perhaps to underline the 'seriousness' of the matter, the foreign secretary himself chose to hand over the note to the Chinese ambassador. But much of the gravity was diluted since, for inexplicable reasons, the note was described as 'Informal' instead of a 'protest'. The note also lost much of its significance due to the way it was worded, exposing India's naiveté. It said that neither had the Chinese government sought India's permission to construct the road nor had the men deployed on its construction obtained Indian visa to enter the area.[116]

What was bizarre was that in the same note India requested China to help in locating some Indian personnel, who had gone missing on patrol duty, in the area which it claimed to be Indian.[117] On 3 November, China confirmed that it had located and arrested a group of armed Indians on the Sinkiang–Tibet road 'in Chinese territory conducting unlawful surveys'. China also mentioned that they were taking steps to deport them back to India.[118] India's reply hurt Indian interests further by suggesting that 'the question whether this particular area is in Indian or Chinese territory is a matter in dispute which is to be dealt with separately'.[119] The reply confirmed that India itself had doubts about the ownership of Aksai Chin where the road had been constructed. It was not a small road. It was 1200 kilometres long, out of which 120 kilometres fell in Aksai Chin and employed over 3000 civilian workers during its construction.[120] Aksai Chin itself is a vast swathe of territory, about 5180 square kilometres in area. It was an area of great importance to China since it provided a link to Tibet through Sinkiang. China claimed that in 1950 the Chinese army had entered the Ari area of Tibet via this route. It was claimed that 'in the nine years since then, they have been making regular and busy use of this route to bring supplies' to Tibet and it was through this same route that the road in question was constructed, cutting across high mountains. China claimed that it had conducted several activities in this area in the last nine years and yet India remained unaware of them. The Chinese asserted that 'this is eloquent proof that this area has indeed always been under Chinese jurisdiction and not under Indian jurisdiction'.[121] Another six-man armed Indian patrol was apprehended while going in the direction of west of Digra and south of Pangong Tso 'as Chinese claimed it was unlawful intrusion'. They were detained and disarmed by Chinese frontier guards and later returned to India 'in view of friendly relations' as the Chinese claimed. The Chinese note of 6 August 1959 repudiated Indian claim to the Pangong Tso along with claims to 'Spanggur and Khurnak Fort to its east'.[122] However, the Indian note of 13 August 1959 reiterated its claim and accused China of establishing a camp at Spanggur in Indian territory, and asked for it to be vacated.[123] The Prime Minister, replying to a question raised in the Lok Sabha on the incident, said that

> It would hardly be correct to say that our area is under occupation of the Chinese, that is, under any kind of a fixed occupation. But their patrols have come within our territory two or three miles or thereabout. That is our knowledge so far as we know.[124]

Replying to another question, he said, 'In all this area there is no actual demarcation. So far as we are concerned our maps are clear that this is within the territory of the Union of India. But it is a fact that part of Ladakh is broadly covered by the wide sweep of their maps.'[125]

As far as the road was concerned, India was not completely unaware of some construction activity in the area for some time. Nehru's official biographer, Dr Gopal noted:

> [B]y May 1956 GOI had reports that the Chinese were using caravan route from western Tibet to Sinkiang that runs through Aksai Chin. Chinese patrols were also regularly visiting southern Demchok, a village in Kashmir near the Tibetan boundary . . .[126]

Later in 1963, Nehru, replying to the debate on the President's address in the Lok Sabha, had said:

> In 1955, we did not know this date, we found out later—the Chinese started levelling the caravan route for the purpose of using as a motor-able tract, it took them a couple of years. It was not clear to us then whether this proposed motor-way crossed our territory . . . [127]

The road was completed in 1957 and, as Nehru had said, it took them a couple of years to build it. Obviously, it was under construction in 1954/1955, if not earlier, and given Dr Gopal's assertion that the Chinese were using it even in May 1956, India should have been worried.[128]

The Indian *Charge d'affaires,* Purnendu Kumar Banerjee, speaking to Zhou, had to cut a sorry figure when Zhou asked him, 'Where were the Indians when the road was under construction?' Banerjee had no answer.[129] Another observation of Dr Gopal is significant. He said:

> He (Nehru) was insufficiently alert to possible Chinese encroachments on a major scale. Curiously, the reported presence of Chinese personnel in Aksai Chin, and the defiance of Indian sovereignty that this implied, roused no marked reaction in Delhi. Infiltration elsewhere was thought to be of greater danger and it was planned to deal with this by methods other than confrontation.[130]

Dr Gopal raised another pertinent question: Was he smitten with love for China that he took a benign view of it? He answered this himself, saying:

> In September (1957) the Chinese announced the completion of road which seemed to run across the eastern extremity of Aksai Chin. But Nehru was determined to strive to work with China rather than to regard her as a potential foe, for he was convinced that this was more worthwhile and perhaps only feasible policy.[131]

General (Retd) J.J. Singh in his book *The McMahon Line* claimed that the Chinese had a fair idea that Nehru was likely to be aware of the road being constructed in the Aksai Chin area but chose not to acknowledge its significance and decided to play it down. Even the military attaché in the Indian embassy in Beijing, Brigadier Mallick, had sent a special report on this project to the Ministry of External Affairs in 1956.[132] Since the Military Attaché had sent the report to the MEA, it can be safely assumed that the ambassador was in the know of it and it should also be presumed with a certain amount of certainty that he, too, would have reported the road to Delhi.

In her recently published book *When Nehru Looked East,* Professor Emerita Francine R. Frankel refers to the adventures of an American spy Sydney Wignall in Tibet, who had reported about the road, when it was under construction in 1955, and had estimated it would be completed by 1957. According to her, Wignall had intended to pass on the information to India through his contacts in the Indian Army. Nehru, however, instructed the military intelligence 'not to gather information on the Chinese presence across the Tibetan border'. Interestingly, Wignall, who was arrested by the Chinese when he was on his mission, was later released by them and Nehru was one of the persons who was said to have intervened with the Chinese on his behalf. After his release, Wignall came to Delhi and visited the Ministry of External Affairs to thank Nehru for his help in his release. Wignall's contacts in the Indian Army blamed 'that vindictive man Krishna Menon' for directing the army to concentrate on Pakistan while dismissing any threat from China.[133]

It was with the same mindset that Nehru assured Parliament that there was not the 'remotest chance of a remote chance' of India having any kind of military conflict with Russia or China.[134]

It was indeed realized, but too late, that neglecting the borders had cost India dearly and it was then decided that the Indian-claimed areas would be aggressively patrolled as part of the new forward policy. As pointed out earlier, the patrol party which went to confirm the existence of the road had returned safely. The second that went was apprehended by the Chinese and yet another was involved in an armed clash at Kongka Pass and suffered heavy casualties, which created a political storm within the country. China was accused of being the villain of the piece which had acted perfidiously.

Apparently, Nehru did not attach much importance to the road since in his letter of 14 December 1958 to Zhou he made no mention of the road. He restricted himself to the eastern sector alone, ignoring the western sector altogether.[135] It was not until October

1959, after the Kongka Pass incident, that the western border got the needed traction in the India–China discourse. As pointed out earlier, Nehru was more worried about the Naga problem than China's encroachments into Indian territory.

Several points that stand out in the narration so far are:

(i)   Nehru had doubts about the boundary between the two countries;

(ii)   China not signing the Simla Convention offered enough hints that it would not accept the McMahon Line;

(iii)   In the MEA's own assessment, legally, the McMahon Line was untenable;

(iv)   Nehru did repeatedly feel the need for taking up the issue of borders with China, but made no particular attempt and instead declared them non-negotiable;

(v)   G.S. Bajpai's recommendation for a detailed note to be sent to China giving facts on Indian frontiers, as claimed by India, was ignored;

(vi)   India had unilaterally altered the international frontier in the western sector and declared it, like the eastern frontier, not open for discussion;

(vii)   It was well known to Nehru that Aksai Chin was a disputed area, but no effort was made to resolve this dispute;

(viii) It was only in 1956 that clear instructions were issued that checkposts be set up along the entire frontier more especially in such places as might be considered disputed areas . . . and in *uninhabited areas like Aksai Chin; but no checkposts were set up as later admitted by Nehru despite the fact that Aksai Chin was a disputed area;*

(ix)   The Chinese had completed the road in the Aksai Chin but India remained unaware of it. The patrol parties which went to the area earlier apparently did not go deep enough into Aksai Chin otherwise it would have been possible to detect the road much before its completion;

(x)   Nehru himself remained immune to the advice he gave
       liberally to U Nu, that is, to negotiate a border agreement
       with China by give and take and not follow a rigid line;

(xi) It was an erroneous understanding of Nehru that in 1954 the
       matter of the borders was settled despite his own instructions
       to not discuss them.

Until the incidents mentioned earlier took place, India had not raised
the issue of the western sector. It was left to Zhou to question the
boundary in both the sectors insisting that 'historically no treaty or
agreement on the Sino-Indian boundary has ever been concluded
between the Chinese Central Government and the Indian Government'
and that the boundary between them was yet to be delimited. While
Nehru asserted that even if the border was not delimited it was well
known by usage and custom, Zhou was of the opinion that since the
maps were old and not rationally drawn there was a need to define
the borders in terms of latitude and longitude, which had not been
done. China did not recognize the McMahon Line, however, it was
willing to take a realistic view of it as in the case of Burma, since
it was a common factor between both. He also conceded that since
India was already in occupation of the McMahon boundary, China
would accept it as an accomplished fact. To that extent, most of the
discussions on the eastern sector were academic. China, of course, was
keeping India guessing all the time since it wanted to use McMahon
Line as chip to get the western border settled.

   China continued to insist that the McMahon Line was the
product of the 'British policy of aggression' and 'juridically too it
cannot be considered legal'. Zhou reiterated:

*[A] friendly settlement can eventually be found for this section of the
boundary* (McMahon Line).[136]

It was Zhou who for the first time raised the question of boundary
in the western sector as depicted in the Indian maps, which he

said in his letter of 23 January 1959 needed to be delineated. The recent 'minor' border incidents were inevitable 'pending formal delimitation of the boundary'. He suggested maintenance of status quo until then.[137]

Replying to Zhou's letter, Nehru referred to past agreements such as the Simla Convention, the agreement between the governments of Kashmir and Tibet in 1842, and the Anglo-Chinese Convention of 1895 having settled the boundary in both the sectors. Nehru's letter, however, went on to add that 'the remaining sector from the tri-junction of the Nepal–India and Tibet boundary up to Ladakh is traditional and follows well-defined geographical features'.[138] But the question that remained unanswered, if the borers indeed were defined as claimed, why was the western border left 'UNDEFINED' in the Survey of India maps until 1954?

Alongside the differences between the two countries regarding the borders, differences also started showing up at the political level. These were regarding the question of leadership of the third world countries. India favoured a non-aligned approach which excluded China. China, however, favoured the second Bandung of Afro-Asian countries. It may be recalled that the first such conference was held in 1955 at Bandung (Indonesia). The visit of Chinese foreign minister Chen Yi to Jakarta in April 1961 called for the convening of the second Bandung at the earliest. Nehru continued to canvass in favour of the first conference of non-aligned countries which was eventually held in Belgrade in September 1961 to the chagrin of China. This, too, became a bone of contention between them. After the Belgrade conference, there was no enthusiasm left for a second Bandung, which upset China.

Progressively, the exchanges regarding the border became sharper with the corresponding increase in the tempo of revolt in Tibet. The Dalai Lama's escape and his asylum in India added to China's indignation. As pointed out in the previous chapter, admiration and reverence for the Dalai Lama as a religious leader attracted the attention of the Indian people. Demonstrations and conferences organized by private institutions in his favour and against China evoked Chinese propaganda that spewed venom against India. In Tibet, the life of the Indian traders who had settled there long before the Chinese occupation became unbearable. Exchange and currency regulations, along with citizenship regulations, were made increasingly stringent which adversely affected them. As already mentioned, an anti-Chinese demonstration in Bombay where the portrait of Mao was 'insulted' took further toll on the relations between the two countries despite Delhi's attempts to smoothen the rough wrinkles on Chinese faces.[139]

These developments added to Nehru's disillusionment with China and its leadership. He told Ambassador Parthasarathi that it seemed to him that the Chinese authorities had developed a habit of trying to bully and use offensive language in the hope that it would yield the desired results.[140] The ambassador, however, pointed out that the issues raised went beyond Tibet and concerned the frontiers and, of course, the presence of the Dalai Lama in India had become 'an affront to them'. The Indian position in Chinese media was distorted to make it look as though India was dependent on imperialist support.[141] Gradually, the tirade against India in China, and against Nehru specifically, became more vituperative. The Chinese appreciated an article written by the Indian communist leader B.T. Ranadive in the *New Age*, which asked, 'Why does Nehru arrogantly try to advise great China?'[142] While making these charges, China, for cosmetic reasons and public consumption, continued to insist that 'through the joint efforts of both sides, great and long-standing friendly relations between China and India will be further consolidated and developed', China appeared to be following a two-pronged policy of being difficult officially while showing a friendly face to the people of India.[143]

Under the shadow of developments in Tibet, the prime minister came under sharp attack from the opposition benches in the Rajya Sabha. Nehru in his statement on 4 May 1959 tried to impress on the members the need for restraint in their statements since such statements only created misunderstandings. He said these unsavoury developments had created 'cracks in people's mind' but he hoped that it would be gradually overcome. He strongly defended his non-alignment policy which had attracted censure from the members. Speaking on Pakistan, Nehru said that while he was ready to settle with Pakistan, he questioned the need for a 'joint defence' between India and Pakistan, for which Pakistan was keen. Nehru, however, said it was not possible since Pakistan followed different foreign and defence policies.

Giving details of the Dalai Lama's flight from Lhasa, he said India was in no way responsible for the events in Tibet and his escape.[144] Interestingly, though a lot was happening on the borders he refrained from making any reference to the hostile attitude of the Chinese there.[145] Nehru's conciliatory approaches did not prevent China indulging in anti-Nehru propaganda. On 6 May 1959, the *People's Daily* in an editorial under the heading: 'The Revolution in Tibet and Nehru's Philosophy' indicted Nehru, calling him a 'self-styled sympathiser of the Tibetan people'.[146]

The editorial was greatly appreciated by the Soviet ambassador in Beijing who said that 'the historical facts and political logic as mentioned in the article was irrefutable'.[147] Following this, Parthasarathi had a long talk with the Russian ambassador in Tibet. Reporting to Delhi on his talks, he said while he was friendly, he had a doctrinaire mind. His approach to Tibet was similar to that of the *People's Daily,* and he had 'some fantastic notions about Kalimpong and about the India–China frontier being a British creation'.[148]

There was yet another debate, this time in the Lok Sabha, which was entirely confined to the events in Tibet and Sino-Tibet relations. Nehru strongly defended the 1954 Tibet Agreement with China, which had come under criticism from members for giving up Indian facilities there without any quid pro quo. He continued to believe that both from the short- and long-term perspective India and China 'should be friends and should be cooperative'. Significantly, in his extremely lengthy statement there was no mention of the differences on the borders which were bothering him otherwise. About the Chinese maps claiming Indian territory, he merely said that though they were old maps, they were irritating. He avoided any reference to China's territorial claims in the Aksai Chin and the road that had been constructed by China. He described China as a great country and said that India, too, was a great country but 'not so much about military power, although from the point of view of defence or offence, no doubt, China's potentials are considerable'. Conceding that China was strong and growing stronger, he said, 'But even from the Chinese point of view it is not a good thing to have a hostile India.'[149]

A couple of days later, the prime minister told Parthasarathi that the silence of the Soviet Union and other socialist countries would work in India's favour. He felt relieved that Parliament had adjourned for three months and there would be no more speeches and expected the press to tone down its rhetoric somewhat. Suggesting that China had the tendency to act as a bully, he said that 'India for all her moderation and restraint has also a good deal of pride and self-respect'. [150]

To Nehru's disappointment, the Chinese ambassador on 16 May 1959:

Made a long and highly contentious verbal statement to the foreign secretary, blaming India for 'deplorable abnormalities' in their relations and refused to accept any part of the blame. Blowing hot and cold, he said though India was a friend of China and would continue to be for thousands of years to come, China's enemy was the United States and China's attentions were directed towards them only. He further said, '*China would not be so foolish as to antagonise the United States in the East and antagonise India in the West.*' He warned that unless India gave up its rhetoric against China the current differences between them would not be resolved.[151] The foreign secretary was indeed irritated and, as he described his meeting to Ambassador Parthasarathi, he said, '[the]two of us spoke two different languages'.[152] In Beijing, the vice foreign minister, giving a copy of the above statement to Parthasarathi, made the usual affirmation of Sino-Indian friendship and maintained that the disagreement over Tibet was a small matter in the context of their historic friendship. Having said that and without yielding any ground, he affirmed that 'current blows' would be continued so long as India interfered in Tibetan affairs 'by words and deeds'. G. Parthasarathi pointed out to Foreign Secretary Subimal Dutt that China's reference to the 'two fronts' was intended to remind India of its weakness and compulsions, and that it had no ground to manoeuvre and was immobilized in its policy of non-alignment.[153] Upset at the Chinese ambassador's statement, the prime minister took upon himself to draft a reply for the foreign secretary to make to the Chinese ambassador.[154] The foreign secretary, batting on Nehru's draft, made a strong pitch, described the ambassador's behaviour 'discourteous' and his actions 'not in consonance with facts'. The Chinese ambassador denied this. He told Foreign Secretary Dutt that while the Chinese were keen on maintaining their friendship with India, they thought it necessary 'to clear the boundaries between right and wrong and that freedom should not be made a pretext for departing from the Five Principles'.[155]

Nehru remained reluctant to admit in public that there were any major differences with China on the frontiers. The Indian public still remained ignorant of the discontent that was brewing. The prime minister seemed keen to ensure that his policy of friendship with China should not be questioned. He perhaps hoped some acceptable solution would emerge in due course and all would be well.

To Nehru's disappointment, the border question continued to return rather frequently. Answering a question in the Lok Sabha on Chinese occupation of Ladakh, Nehru confirmed that there had been violations but the matter was under correspondence and a reconnaissance party had gone missing but had been eventually found by the Chinese who, while returning it, had claimed the territory to be Chinese. About the road in Aksai Chin, he said, 'it passed through a corner of our north-eastern Ladakh territory' and that there is no physical demarcation of the frontier in these mountainous passes, although our maps are clear on the subject.

Answering a supplementary question, he said:

This was the boundary of the old Kashmir State with Tibet and Chinese Turkestan. Nobody had marked it. But after some kind of broad surveys, the then Government laid down that border which we have been accepting and acknowledging.

Answering yet another one, he said:

There were other areas as well which had 'no demarcation in the past'.[156]

Nehru added the following about certain parts of the borders:

[It] is rather difficult to say where the immediate border is, although broadly it may be known. But it is very difficult in a map to indicate it; if a big line is drawn, the line itself covers three or four miles . . . there are other parts still where there has been no demarcation in the past.

Referring to 'the two or three miles', he said, '(These) are not visible in those maps. But it is a fact that part of Ladakh is broadly covered by wide sweep of their maps.'[157] A part of his reply was used by Zhou in his letter of 8 September 1959 to buttress his argument that the borders were neither delineated nor demarcated and India's action was unilateral.[158] Speaking on an adjournment motion in the Lok Sabha, he again played down Chinese intrusions, calling them 'petty' and ascribed them to there being *no demarcation at all and parties sometimes may cross*. When members remained dissatisfied with his response, Atal Behari Vajpayee suggested a White Paper dealing with border questions. The prime minister offered to consider that.[159]

And that was the trigger for the White Papers, containing the official correspondence exchanged between the two governments, which were eventually published by the Ministry of External Affairs. Altogether thirteen of them were published.

The White Papers, welcome as they were, turned out to be a major miscalculation for the government. Not only did they fail to tone down criticism but they also inflamed parliamentary and public opinion and brought the government under intense, unremitting pressure. Pushed against the wall, the space for diplomatic manoeuvrability shrank. Subsequently, it seemed that the prime minister had to constantly assess what the political marketplace would bear, and he was compelled to adopt only those policies which could conceivably be sold to the public.[160] The wisdom of quiet diplomacy away from public glare was sacrificed at the altar of expediency to ward off public criticism of his policies. But it did not happen that way either.

Indian missions abroad were given a detailed briefing of the latest situation and were asked to brief their host governments, since the Chinese had launched a propaganda drive against India.[161] Separately, Nehru told the British prime minister, Harold Macmillan, of the 'progressive Chinese unfriendliness towards India' causing concern, but he said he did not 'expect any major crisis arising in the near future' or that China would 'take any extreme step'. He did add that they 'feared a break with China, which India would like to avoid'.[162] Ambassador Parthasarathi cautioned Delhi that the Chinese 'would try their best to sharpen the space between India and Pakistan' taking advantage of the present situation.[163]

Zhou in his letter of 8 September 1959 offered a historical background to various sections of the frontier and ascribed the differences on the boundary as 'complicated' and 'fundamental'. To substantiate his point, he referred to Nehru's own statement in the Lok Sabha on 28 August 1959 (mentioned earlier). Regarding the western sector, he said, 'As a matter of fact, it was not Chinese maps but the British and Indian maps that were unilaterally altered. Nevertheless, since China–India had not delimited the mutual boundary through friendly negotiations and joint surveys, China had not asked India to revise the maps in 1954.' He said despite the border incidents 'caused wholly by the trespassing of Indian troops, until the beginning of this year, the atmosphere along the Sino-Indian border had, on the whole, been fairly good', and he suggested that in order to maintain this amity and to rule out tension on the borders, the delimitation of the boundary between the two countries had become necessary.[164]

On September 9, Zhou had a long talk on the border question with Ambassador Parthasarathi that lasted over two hours. Zhou said while China was prepared to accept the status quo inherited by India, it was not prepared to accept (what he called) the legacy of 'the British imperialism'. He reminded the ambassador that India had on Independence promised to Tibet 'the maintenance of *status quo* till [a] new agreement was reached' between them.[165] Since India was prepared to have a new agreement at that time, why was India avoiding it now? He also showed several maps to Parthasarathi to prove that India had cut into Chinese territories beyond the McMahon Line. Summing up his discussions, Zhou made three points: (i) the border question existed and China sought a friendly solution, (ii) pending formal delimitation of the boundary, status quo was to be maintained and (iii) the border question could be settled through diplomatic channels and negotiations when both sides were animated by the spirit of traditional friendship.[166]

Interestingly, just a day earlier Zhou had briefed the visiting foreign minister from Afghanistan at length on the Sino-Indian border question. When Parthasarathi called on the Afghan minister later, he told him:

(a) Zhou was very irritated with Indian criticism of the situation in Tibet;

(b) China had a good case on the borders;

(c) China was anxious to resolve the border question through negotiations; and

    (d)   China was most anxious to maintain Sino-Indian friendship.[167]

The Chinese press propaganda continued unabated. The Praja Socialist Party (PSP), the Jan Sangh and Indian 'rightist' newspapers were criticized by China for 'stirring up hatred against China'. The statement issued by A.K. Gopalan of the Communist Party of India advocating settlement through negotiations was given prominence to convey their approval of it.[168]

Moscow, for the first time, broke its silence on the clash at Longju, where the Chinese had fired on Indian security personnel, causing casualties. Moscow issued a statement through its official news agency *Tass,* and deplored the efforts of certain political circles 'to drive a wedge' between India and China whose friendship was considered vital for peace and international cooperation. It affirmed Moscow's friendly relations with both and expressed the hope that they would resolve all 'misunderstandings in the spirit of their traditional friendship'. China, of course, was critical of Soviet's neutral position.[169] The sudden Soviet interest was perhaps due to Foreign Secretary S. Dutt speaking to the Soviet ambassador on 2 September on the issue regarding the borders, canvassing Soviet support. This prompted Ambassador K.P.S. Menon in Moscow to speak to Nikita Khrushchev, the then secretary general of the Soviet Communist Party, on the borders, who drew Menon's attention to the statement issued by *Tass.* While doing so, he, too, gave Menon a piece of advice which was similar to what Nehru had said to the Burmese prime minister in 1956, that is, to sort out the problem by give and take. What Moscow wished to convey to India was to give up its claim on Aksai Chin and settle the matter as the Soviets had done with Iran by ceding the territory under dispute to Iran. He said the Soviet and the Chinese people were 'linked by unbreakable ties of fraternal friendship based on socialist internationalism' and added that the dispute involved an area which had little economic value and 'what higher prestige could a country have than a good friend and a tranquil frontier?' He stressed that a friendly frontier was more important than mere prestige and added he would convey similar sentiments to the Chinese.[170] Obviously, this was directed at Nehru to give up his claim on the Aksai Chin in the western sector, since Nehru himself had described the area as worthless where not a blade of grass grew.

After the Kongka Pass incident where nine Indian policemen on patrol duty were killed in an ambush by the Chinese, which was more serious than the Longju incident, Khrushchev addressing the Supreme Soviet, the Soviet Parliament, on 31 October 1959 deplored the incident and expressed the hope that the disputed border would be resolved by friendly consultations between the two neighbours. He described it 'sad' and 'stupid' to the correspondent of the CPI mouthpiece, the *New Age*, and again cited the settlement of the Soviet Union's border with Iran as an example. Nehru, however, did not take the hint.[171] There were visible signs of deterioration in relations between the two fraternal allies Soviet Union and China. Nehru, too, remained discreet thereafter in asking Soviet support to resolve the dispute,[172] so as not to embarrass Moscow. China, however, resented Soviet neutrality and continuation of their economic aid to India.

The Soviet leaders did not take a firm stance in public yet in private did not fight shy of deriding the Chinese leadership for creating a chasm in their relations with India, a non-aligned country, which was otherwise friendly towards China. Khrushchev had gone to Beijing on the occasion of the tenth anniversary celebrations of the founding of the People's Republic of China and had a stormy meeting with the top brass of the Chinese leadership which included Mao. Khrushchev spoke rather frankly and took the Chinese to task for their failures along the borders and in Tibet. He said that despite Nehru blaming the Soviet Union regarding the Hungarian revolt Moscow did not break its relations with India. Khrushchev added:

Differences are to be managed and not allowed to widen.[173]

He put the responsibility for loss of life in the Longju incident on China and did not believe the Chinese version of the events which said that India attacked first. To put the Chinese on the defensive, he said, no one was killed on the Chinese side, the casualties were among the Indians. As such the *Tass* statement was justified. Finally, Mao said that 'the border issue with India will be decided through negotiations'.[174]

Zhou justified the Chinese actions. Khrushchev told him, 'You have been Minister for Foreign Affairs of [the] PRC for many years and should know better than me, how one can resolve disputed issues without (spilling) blood.' About this particular case, he said, 'If the Chinese and the Hindus (Indians) do not know where the border goes between them, it is not for me, a Russian, to meddle. I am only against the methods that have been used.' When Chen Yi said that he was outraged that he blamed China for aggravation of relations with India, Khrushchev retorted that he, too, was 'outraged by your (Chen Yi's) declaration that we are time servers. We should support Nehru for him to stay in power'. Khrushchev, too, blamed China for its failure to manage things in Tibet. He said:

> The events in Tibet are your fault. You ruled in Tibet, you should have had your intelligence there and should have known about the plans and intentions of Dalai Lama.[175]

The tension on the border was escalating without any possibility of an amicable solution in sight. To minimize the incidents along the border, Nehru gave instructions to the security forces to reduce the possibility of any conflict with China, which, he said, 'would also help us to clear our own minds and guide us in the future'. His instructions were:

(i)   To avoid actual conflict unless thrust upon us;

(ii) On no account our forces to fire unless they were actually fired upon;

(iii) Our forces must keep on our side of the border; and

(iv) If Chinese armed detachment come to our side, it should be told to go back and only if they fired on our men, they could return fire.[176]

He wanted the Aksai Chin to be 'left as it is'. He conceded that India had neither any checkpost there nor any means of access to the area. For the present, he said, '*We have to put up with the Chinese occupation of this North-east (western) sector and their road across it.*' He insisted that any question relating to major changes in the border such as 'envisaged in the Chinese maps cannot be considered by us in this way'. Clarifying, he also said that the 'status quo that has existed for some time, should be maintained'.[177]

India later, in a note to China, explained the absence of any Indian border outpost in the Aksai Chin due to it being sparsely populated. India mentioned that it had 'no reason to anticipate any aggressive intention on the part of the Chinese government'. Border outposts are a sign of sovereignty and announce the ownership of the country concerned. It may be recalled that in 1956 the prime minister had approved instructions for the setting up of checkposts 'in all the disputed areas without delay, especially at the suitable points . . . and with regard to other inaccessible and uninhabited areas like Aksai Chin, we might send reconnaissance and survey parties'.[178] Aksai Chin by all accounts was a disputed area and the absence of any checkpost was a major lapse on the part of India.

In other words, India, after drawing the line to convert the 'undefined' border into a marked boundary in the western sector in 1954, took no steps to announce its sovereignty in the area by establishing either checkposts or planting even a flag to indicate its sovereignty in any form. India was content to send patrol parties to these areas occasionally. About the survey parties, it was said:

Indian survey and reconnaissance parties which went from Leh to Lanak La in 1954 and 1956 did not come across any evidence of

Chinese occupation. For the first time in 1957 signs of intrusion by the outsiders were noticed at Shinglung and some places further north. Obviously such intrusions must have occurred in these places for the first time in 1957.[179]

Later in Parliament, the prime minister said:

> It is a fact, which we may deplore, that in Aksai Chin area there is no representative of the Indian Government; neither is one there now nor has one been there for some time . . . we can go there only, more or less, at the present moment after some kind of conflict and after exhibiting high mountaineering skills . . .[180]

Though until 1958 Indian patrols had been going to places like Qaratag Pass, Haji Langar, a place close to Lanak La, and another place across the road on the Aksai Chin-China border,[181] it remained a mystery that they failed to notice the 120-kilometre road which was then under construction across Aksai Chin. If, however, they failed to meet any Chinese individual, it was nothing unusual, as Nehru said: 'These territories are so high up that they are hardly inhabited, there is no communication, there are hardly any trees or any blade of grass.'[182]

The adoption of forward policy and regular patrolling of the border areas began on both sides, leading to an increase in the number of clashes. With that happening, particularly after the Kongka Pass incident, the border question received greater attention both inside and outside of Parliament. Strangely, the All-India Congress Committee in its meeting in Chandigarh noted with 'grave concern the recent developments on 'the north-east frontier of India and the claim of Chinese Government to large area of India',[183] but there was no mention of the western sector where the problem had become serious.

Nehru's letter of 26 September, replying to Zhou's on 8 September, which he said had 'greatly surprised and distressed' him, signalled the end of the bhai-bhai phase in their relations. In the letter, he lamented his failure to inform the Indian public of the various Chinese incursions since 1954 as well as the construction of the road across the Indian territory and the arrest of Indian personnel, in order to find a solution without public excitement, which 'now resulted in sharp but legitimate criticism of the Government both in parliament and in the press'.[184]

It was a long letter in which Nehru yet again conceded that the Sino-Indian boundary had not been formally delimited in its entire region, but the mountainous nature of the boundary in many places made such an exercise impossible to even undertake. He repeated his original stand that the boundary was either defined by treaty or recognized by custom or both. He rejected Zhou's claim that the boundaries of Sikkim and Bhutan did not fall within the scope of their discussions.[185]

Referring to reports that the Chinese officials had been proclaiming that China before long would take possession of Sikkim, Bhutan, Ladakh and the North East Frontier Agency, Nehru questioned their authority to make such claims, particularly when he had already on 28 August declared that any aggression against them would be considered aggression against India.[186] Clarifying the position, he told the Lok Sabha that while India was indeed responsible for the defence of Bhutan, 'we keep no forces in Bhutan and there is no intention of sending any forces (to Bhutan) and it is for the Bhutan Government to decide and when and what kind of help they require from us'. About Sikkim, he said, 'It is included definitely in our immediate liabilities—protection I mean.'[187]

India had regretted the Chinese invitation to an Indian delegation for the tenth anniversary of Chinese National Day celebrations only a few days before the event, both on account of short notice and also because of prevailing climate of distrust in relations.[188]

Regarding the invitation for the vice president, which was pending with Delhi for some time, it was regretted too. The ambassador had advised that it was not the appropriate time for a visit since (i) Indian public opinion would resent it, (ii) world opinion might consider it a sign of weakness, (iii) China did not hint on limiting the frontier issues to be discussed and (iv) the visit should take place when India felt strong enough diplomatically to negotiate and only when India's defence preparedness, presently underway, had been achieved.[189]

As a consequence of Khrushchev's indictment of Mao, there appeared some softening of China's stand on the borders. Mao apparently did order cessation of all polemics against India in the official press. This indication came at the meeting Mao and Liu Shaoqui had with Ajoy Ghosh, a leading member of the Communist Party of India who was on a visit to Beijing. They reportedly told Ghosh that China planned to hold negotiations with India. Foreshadowing Zhou's package deal, Ghosh said:

[China] was prepared to trade the eastern sector for the western sector.[190]

It was not until the Kongka Pass incident that Zhou took the initiative to propose talks with Nehru.[191]

As pointed out earlier, the foreign secretary's statement to the governors of the states that 'the Sikkim-Tibet boundary delimited in 1896 was the only boundary along the entire frontier which was properly delimited' was enough of an admission which put a question mark to the Indian stand on the frontiers.[192]

Nehru, realizing the gravity of the situation on the borders, asked Krishna Menon, holding the defence portfolio and busy in New York, to return to Delhi since his absence would be difficult to explain under the prevailing circumstances.[193]

As the tension increased, it was found that the state police forces that were manning these borders were not adequately equipped to handle the new situation. It was, therefore, decided to hand over the entire border to the army.[194] The NEFA border came under the command of the Calcutta-based Eastern Command of the Indian Army.

It would be pertinent to point out here that before the above-mentioned rearrangement was ordered, the general commanding officer of the Eastern Command, Lt Gen. S.P.P. Thorat, worried at the state of affairs in the vicinity of his Command, had suggested to the Army Chief to entrust the responsibility for the defence of the NEFA to his Command. The Army Chief approved it and recommended this to the Ministry of Defence for acceptance. Defence Minister Krishna Menon 'brusquely rejected it'. According to Lt Gen. Thorat, when he wanted to discuss the subject later with Menon in Delhi, he, in his usual 'sarcastic style', said:

> There would be no war between India and China and in the most unlikely event of there being one, he was quite capable of fighting himself on the diplomatic level.[195]

After Menon had rejected the proposal, he and the Army Chief, Gen. Thimayya, 'broached the subject with the Prime Minister and Defence Minister on a number of occasions but they did not take serious note of our views'. They would not believe that China could attack India and feared the move suggested by the army might, on the contrary, annoy China.[196]

As the lid over the developments started lifting, particularly after the Kongka Pass incident, public anger against the Chinese took a sharp turn for the worse. Since the public had been kept unaware of the unsavoury developments for too long, and fed on the staple of India–China friendship, a sense of betrayal on the part of China was allowed to be built in the public mind, which it was thought would save the government a lot of criticism. The feeling of betrayal created a wave of patriotism in the country and a gullible public accepted the government's position that perfidious China had stabbed India in the back. This had a long-term deleterious impact on the Indian psyche that China was perfidious and could not be trusted, and this feeling has lingered on ever since. This made any rational solution of the border problem difficult then and since.

The prime minister, too, did not escape the collateral loss of image for being too naive. He came under incessant attack for keeping the nation in the dark. He held a special briefing for about a hundred Congress members of parliament and explained to them the issues.[197] Warding off pressure to give up the policy of non-alignment, he told Krishna Menon that non-alignment was his fundamental policy which *he would never give up, as otherwise world peace would get threatened.* While suggesting the need for effective measures, he insisted that his preference for peaceful settlement always remained according to our firm policy. Yet he told Menon that 'we cannot have any negotiations on the basis laid down by the Chinese who claim as right large areas of our territory'. He mentioned that the Chinese claim included 31,000 square miles of the NEFA, 300 square miles in Bhutan, 100 square miles in Uttar Pradesh and 11,500 square miles in Ladakh, which included 25,000 square miles in Pakistan-occupied areas.[198] His worry for world peace overwhelmed him and he vehemently stuck to it. The government of India in its note of 4 November once again went into the history of the border dispute and, in rejecting the Chinese version of Kongka Pass incident, reiterated its endeavour to settle all disputes by peaceful methods, but it warned, 'Where aggression takes place, the people of India inevitably have to resist by all means available to them.'[199]

On 7 November 1959, Zhou described the Kongka Pass incident as 'unfortunate' but claimed that it happened in the Chinese territory. As in the past, he repeated that the boundary was not delimited. Referring to Nehru's letter of 26 September, he said that it contained many 'viewpoints which the Chinese Government cannot agree [to]' but their elaboration he left to another time. He suggested a 20-kilometre withdrawal at once from the 'so-called McMahon Line' in the east and similar withdrawal in the western sector from the 'line up to which each side exercises actual control', while retaining the civil administration. In conclusion, he said:

[B]efore and after delimitation of the boundary between our two countries through negotiations, the Chinese Government is willing to do its utmost to create the most peaceful and most secure border zones between our two countries so that our two countries will never again have apprehensions or come to a clash on account of border issues.[200]

Zhou, in pursuance of his decision already indicated to Communist leader Ajay Ghosh, took this opportunity to suggest a meeting between the prime ministers of the two countries in the immediate future 'to resolve the border issues'.[201]

Nehru in his first reaction to Krishna Menon described the proposal for withdrawal of armed forces 'reasonable' but added he could not accept it, since it was 'very disadvantageous' to India and suggested making counter proposals for avoidance of clashes.[202]

Foreign Secretary Subimal Dutt shared tentative views of the ministry on Zhou's offer of talks with the Indian missions in Moscow, Washington, Cairo and London, and expressed reservations on the 20-kilometre withdrawal, as it would mean India withdrawing from a forward post in the eastern sector and moving back to areas which would be less defensible. In the western sector, he showed an inclination to make 'a concession' on the Aksai Chin area where 'the Chinese have constructed a road and *where in the past we have not sought to exercise any active occupation*'. The concession was that 'China could keep civilian personnel in occupation of this road and a stretch west of the road on our side'. The prime minister feared that without a general appreciation of each other's point of view it could lead to subsequent bitterness. India also doubted the sincerity of the Chinese offer since they had been dragging their feet on the return of the dead bodies and release of captured police personnel in the Kongka Pass incident.[203]

Parthasarathi, analysing the Chinese offer, among other reasons, suggested that their friends (socialist countries) had perhaps made the Chinese realize that they (the Chinese) had overreached themselves, and a confident India after President Eisenhower's visit raised China's expectation that India would agree to China's claim over the western sector in lieu of China's acceptance of India's claim to the McMahon Line. Regarding India's response to China's proposal, he suggested that 'the two questions of the definition of the frontier and demilitarisation should be taken up together for discussion. In the ambassador's view, the Chinese might have wanted to stabilize the frontier at the level they had reached. He, however, added that China might be working on the assumption that they wish to settle the problem once and for all by a 'compromise' and added in parenthesis that some communist diplomats and even some Indian communist leaders had similar ideas. The ambassador was also of the opinion that the Chinese proposal had a 'strong propagandist flavour' and as such our response 'has to be constructive, perhaps cooperative'.[204]

At this critical stage, when serious developments were taking place on the borders, there was an unfortunate controversy between the chief of army staff and the defence minister, who was known for his toxic tongue and arrogant behaviour towards his officers, irrespective of their seniority and rank. General Thimayya had submitted his resignation as the army chief because his military appreciation of the dangers looming on the borders was not acceptable to his defence minister. Even though the spat between them was sorted out by the intervention of the prime minister, not much changed in their relations at a critical juncture in post-independent India's short history. Thimayya as the chief of the army was well aware of the weakness of the army to take on the Chinese in any open conflict. Later in retirement and much before the war, in July 1962, he had said: 'I cannot even as a soldier envisage India taking on China in an open conflict on its own . . . It must be left to our politicians and diplomats to ensure our security.'[205]

Nehru's letter of 16 November 1959 regretted that China did not accept the Indian position and facts on the frontiers. He now proposed if the patrolling was stopped in forward areas any chance of clash would be eliminated. Nehru reiterated the Indian claim on McMahon Line as in the past. He remained anguished at the Chinese maps being small-scale and the delay in China providing the large-scale maps of their claim line in Ladakh. While he welcomed Zhou's proposal for the two prime ministers to meet, he suggested that, for the talks to be meaningful, it would be preferable that some 'preliminary steps' be taken to prepare for the meeting as otherwise there was the danger of it being unproductive.[206]

In his statement to the Lok Sabha on 19 November 1959, the prime minister was unable to confirm the construction of an airfield in the Aksai Chin area since, as he said, 'None of our people have been there', but he confirmed that there was no Chinese airfield near Chusul in Ladakh.[207] Replying to a question in the Rajya Sabha on the Aksai Chin road, he said it came to India's attention for the first time in 1957 through the Chinese announcement, and further said:

[S]urely a road in our territory can be used by people walking up and down. I do not see any conflict. This road is, as many roads there have been, a kind of caravan route for a long time past and we do not wish to come in the way of its use as a caravan route but we object to its military use.[208]

The question was not of the use of the road but the construction of it in the Indian-claimed territory and its defence potential. It had ceased to be a caravan route once the road was constructed and was used particularly for defence.

Nehru, replying to the criticism in the Lok Sabha on 27 November 1959, exuded confidence that he could meet the Chinese challenge and said that 'a strong China is normally an expansionist and this had been the case throughout history'. Describing the issues involved as grave, he mentioned, 'We have to think how will we go and kick them out' (since) China was not a small country nor was India. He described it absurd for anyone to think that China could 'sit on India or crush India', as India also could not do that. He dismissed the idea of China being a strong military power, but said, 'when two giant countries come into conflict, a life and death struggle may happen here and there on the borders'. He expressed confidence that India could deal with it.[209] There was yet another occasion when the prime minister had to defend himself against the charge of defence negligence. Speaking this time in the Rajya Sabha, he said, 'I confess today that I did not expect that there would be aggression on the part of China.' He again referred to the building of industrial strength as a prelude to defence build-up and that his stress had been on peace and would continue to be on peace. While speaking of defence, he said India's responsibility also extended to Sikkim, Bhutan and Nepal.[210] This time Nepal objected to being bracketed with Sikkim and Bhutan, and India taking over the responsibility for its defence. Nehru explained this with reference to the Indo-Nepal Treaty of 1950 and the letters exchanged therewith.[211]

Speaking about the visit of President Eisenhower to India, which was then taking place, Nehru tried to delink it from the troubles with China and said that he did not consider his problems in the context of these larger developments.[212]

Zhou's reply to Nehru's letter of 16 November was conciliatory in tone and accepted the Indian proposal of both sides not patrolling the contentious areas to avoid clashes. Regarding the Indian proposal for withdrawal by both the countries in the western sector, Zhou pointed out that while India had no presence in the area and, therefore, there was no need for withdrawal by India, if China were to withdraw from east of the boundary, as suggested by India, they would have to withdraw from 30,000 square kilometres, both the military personnel guarding its frontiers and also its civil personnel. He insisted that in 1950 Chinese had used this route (in their attack at Chamdo). Claiming that, unlike India, China had made no demand on India withdrawing south of the McMahon Line, Zhou reminded Nehru that the Indian maps had even in the 1950, 1951 and 1952 editions showed the boundary in the western sector 'UN-DELIMITED'. He repeated his proposal for the two prime ministers to meet and even suggested a date, 26 December 1959, and the venue as Beijing or even Rangoon.[213]

Nehru, in his comparatively brief response, regretted that Zhou had not agreed to Indian frontiers and also to the facts relating to the Kongka Pass incident. He had no objection to their meeting in principle but reminded him of the complete disagreement about the facts that needed straightening and conveyed his inability to meet in Rangoon or elsewhere on 26 December, as proposed.[214]

Ambassador Parthasarathi was asked to come to Delhi for consultations. Zhou, who knew about this, met the ambassador and reiterated the desirability of the two prime ministers meeting to break the logjam since the exchange of notes was not taking them anywhere and was merely adding to the tension. Zhou was willing to wait until Nehru was able to spare time.[215]

Nehru's statement in Parliament was full of remorse that Zhou had not responded favourably to his suggestion to lessen the border tensions. Differences on borders continued to be on basic facts. He particularly regretted the 'deplorable treatment' meted out to the Indian police personnel whom the Chinese had captured in the Kongka Pass incident. He did not agree with Zhou's claim that the police personnel who were apprehended were treated in a 'friendly manner'. Regarding Zhou's proposal for a meeting between them, while he showed readiness to meet, he wondered whether in view of the complete disagreement in their perceptions an agreement would be possible at all.[216]

The Chinese response was long and repetitive of old arguments, and now it accused the British for having left behind a 'heritage of certain disputes'. Zhou insisted their meeting had become essential since the Indian charges against China were unacceptable. In China's perception, the basic fact that the entire boundary had 'never been delimited and therefore yet to be settled through negotiations' should be accepted. Appearing conciliatory, the note concluded:

> The Chinese Government wishes to reiterate here its ardent
> desire that the two countries stop quarrelling, quickly bring about
> a reasonable settlement of the boundary question, on this basis
> consolidate and develop the great friendship of the two peoples in
> their common cause.[217]

The year 1959 remained the most hectic year in India–China
relations, but a great disappointment for India. At no point in time
in the last ten years had India found China to be accommodative of
its concerns or found it solicitous of friendship. In fact, India was
rebuffed many a time by China, yet Nehru plodded along in the hope
that China's friendship would be a great asset for a peaceful world
order. But Nehru's terms for friendship were the ones dictated by
him and not accommodative of another point of view. The escalation
of revolt in Tibet impacted developments on the frontiers. The Dalai
Lama leaving Tibet and taking refuge in India was taken as a slight
by Beijing, which blamed it on India.

The Kongka Pass incident was too serious to be swept under the
carpet. The reaction in public and in Parliament became much too
serious for Nehru to cope with. It made him defensive for the first
time. The Indian newspapers had described the incident as 'the brutal
massacre of an Indian police party'. *The Hindu* on 29 October 1959
described Nehru as 'giving [the] impression of standing alone against
the rising tide of national resentment against China. The resentment
against China was suddenly seen to have become synonymous with
Nehru'.[218] Even when the border conflict had come to the blistering
point and his policies needed a fresh look, he continued to insist that
'non-alignment was the best guarantee for peace' and he held on to
it. His fear of losing a friend and appeasing China only whetted the
Chinese appetite. India was in consequence left to learn the hard way
that fanaticizing about strength on false premises was a sure recipe
for disaster. Nehru's audacity was the outcome of his conviction that
China would not attack India and his statements would not be put
to test.

Despite all these unsavoury developments, the wisdom that strong nations alone get secure borders failed to impress him. The wisdom of agreed borders was not realized either. He did not care to build a consensus on the borders with the other stakeholder and create an agreeable frontier, which is the recipe for peaceful coexistence. In modern times, borders between nations are precise and well delineated. India knew its northern border was not delineated and there was a need for it. He also showed little faith in the advice he himself gave to others of not being rigid, since it hardened positions and defied solutions. Even after exchange of copious notes and his personal correspondence with Zhou during 1959, his rigidity stood in his way of finding a workable solution through negotiations and discussions by sitting around a table.

In the end, he found it difficult to reject a summit with Zhou. It was settled that the two prime ministers would meet in Delhi on 20 April 1960. However, neither the basis for the discussion nor the agenda for the summit was fixed. Finally, open-ended discussions were slated to take place which did not portend well for a consensus.

10

Nehru–Zhou Summit, April 1960

Zhou Enlai's proposal for talks between the two prime ministers initially met with Nehru's unenthusiastic response; however, he finally agreed to it since the alternative was war. Zhou intended to discuss the entire boundary question face to face and remained optimistic that it would be entirely possible to settle the boundary issue in a friendly manner.[1] A fortnight later, Nehru, while briefing the chief ministers of the states, drew an optimistic picture of the economy and assured them that full attention was being paid to defence, but qualified it to the industrial and economic strength of the country.[2] His claim to defence preparedness stood challenged at the Bangalore session of the Congress party, in January 1960, when it was suggested that India seek foreign military assistance from abroad—'it was euphemistically termed Cooperative defence'. Nehru, as always, remained against any foreign aid for defence. He said, 'If [the] Indian army could not defend India, then freedom was lost and whatever the consequences there would be no foreign armies on India's soil.'[3] This spirited response would have earned him a big thumbs up from the party. For him, seeking military aid was a manifestation of weakness. He continued to believe that the policy of non-alignment was a sufficient guarantee of its security and any compromise with it was profane and a display of irreverence against the very philosophy on which the entire Indian foreign policy had been worked out since Independence. However, there was never a forensic audit of India's defence capabilities or preparedness in relation to any possible challenge that India then faced on the borders.

The president's address to the parliament on 8 February 1960 reflected the government's hallucinations:

> My Government particularly deplores the unilateral use of force by our neighbour on our common frontier, where no military units of the Union were functioning. This is a breach of faith, but we may not lose faith in the principles which we regard as basic in relation between nations . . . My Government therefore pursues a policy, both of peaceful approach, by negotiations *under appropriate conditions*, and of being determined and ready to defend our country . . . This and the weight of public opinion which is adverse to her (China's) actions, we should hope, China, sooner than later come to agreement in regard to common frontiers, which for long have been well established by treaties, customs and usage.[4]

The tension on the borders had been building for quite some time and yet the president's address claimed that 'no military units of the Union were functioning' on the borders. That created doubts in the government's claim that it was 'determined and ready to defend' the country. It was rather naive of the government to expect that under the weight of public opinion China would come to an agreement 'sooner or later'. The absence of any mention of the projected summit talks in the President's address once again underlined lack of his enthusiasm for talks. That the prime minister was going into the talks without any expectations was evident from what Nehru had told the Nepalese prime minister, B.P. Koirala, a week before the talks began. He told him, 'As far as I can see, there will be no real approach to any kind of agreement between India and China in the course of my meeting with Premier Chou Enlai next week.'

About the Chinese, he said they were 'difficult people' because 'of their being communist' and added, 'I am inclined to think that the former has been more obvious in these border problems in recent months.'[5]

The Chinese, however, remained optimistic that the talks would lead to a solution of the border problem. Ambassador Parthasarathi, reflecting on the optimism of the Chinese, said they were offering friendly vibes and hoped that the forthcoming negotiations would resolve the border problem and that the people would be surprised by the results. A month before the talks began, on 21 March the Chinese Foreign Office had conveyed their optimism to one of our embassy officials, who had called on the director of the Asia Department. The latter was reported to have said that since the two sides had different conceptions of the boundary which had remained 'vague and undefined for centuries', there was 'genuine misunderstanding on both sides' which could be 'corrected by agreeing in a friendly way to delimit the boundary'.[6]

On the Indian side, there were hesitations and reservations which were reflected in Nehru's letter of 5 February 1960 to Zhou. The letter mentioned that the 'respective view points of our two governments, in regard to the matters under discussion, were so wide apart and opposed to each other that there was little ground left for useful talks'. He also challenged the Chinese claim that the Sino-Indian boundary had never been delimited. Nevertheless, he assured him:

> I have endeavoured and shall continue to endeavour to find a way
> to a peaceful settlement and for restoration of friendly relations.[7]

Zhou in his reply avoided any contentious issue. He thanked Nehru for his invitation to Delhi and expressed confidence that the border question would be settled.[8]

Parthasarathi, having read Nehru's mood, also turned unenthusiastic. In his comments, he highlighted the past differences and insisted that unless the Chinese met Indian expectations there should be no agreement. He stressed that 'by no account we are going to agree to a bargain if a deal was suggested on the basis of mutual concessions'. His advice was not conducive to any settlement.[9] The longest serving foreign secretary, Subimal Dutt, also remained equally despondent and echoed Nehru's mood while conveying to Parthasarathi the strategy that India had planned to adopt for the talks. According to him, the frontier was traditional, well-recognized and beyond any doubt, and as such India could only 'consider minor rectification, and we would refuse to base any discussion on the assumption that the frontier is un-delimited'.[10] China, however, continued to express confidence in 'finding a solution in the forthcoming meeting'. Ambassador Parthasarathi and the foreign secretary continued to advocate that India should clearly say 'no' to any attempt to delimit the entire boundary or sections thereof.[11] The ambassador yet again in another telegram emphasized that India should not agree to any concession involving a deal 'on the basis of mutual concessions' and agreement should be 'on the basis of a broad but clear acceptance by the Chinese of the Indian alignment of the boundary'. He said, 'Diplomatically our position is strong which means we need not give much ground'. The ministry asked Parthasarathi whether there was something to our advantage in the Chinese border agreements with Nepal, which had only been signed in March 1960, or with Burma, which was scheduled to be signed in October, and could be quoted in our favour. Ambassador Parthasarathi advised that the terms of settlement reached by China with both the counties 'are not such that we can quote them to our advantage except in regard to the points relating to the principle of watershed'.[12] Evidently, there was a hardening of Indian views which was least conducive for a settlement.

Instead of looking positively towards finding a solution, the ambassador recounted China's compulsions which had driven it towards proposing talks with India. Among these were its international isolation, the remilitarization of Japan, the Tibetan revolt, food problems and the need for it to seek support of

Afro-Asian nations. The Chinese were not hiding their problems either. The Chinese foreign minister, Chen Yi, during the course of his talks with railway minister Swaran Singh on 23 April 1960, had volunteered these concerns to him.[13] The failure of the 'Great Leap Forward' which otherwise was designed for rapid industrialization of their country but had even damaged the economy generally sharpened differences within the Chinese Communist Party.[14] China, with its back to the wall, had apparently become accommodative in their approach to neighbours. It was now for India to take advantage of their compulsions and drive a smooth bargain by having a flexible approach to clinch the border agreement, particularly when India itself had been expressing doubts about China's acceptance of its borders historically.

A fortnight before the scheduled talks, China sent a longish note detailing the Chinese position on various sections of the frontier. Tucked in that note was a small paragraph which was a reminder to Nehru that he had unilaterally altered the border in the western sector. It said:

> Since the boundary between two neighbouring countries according to internationally recognised principles has to be jointly defined by the two sides, any unilateral announcement by either side of its boundary line or change in the delineation of the boundary on maps in any manner obviously has no legal validity and it is not binding on the neighbouring country concerned. Naturally, violation of the traditional customary line and expansion of extent of occupation by unilateral action all the more cannot constitute a legal basis for acquiring territory.[15]

This was not for the first time that China had reminded India of its unilateral action. Zhou himself, in his letter of 17 December 1959, had reminded India that in 'the official maps compiled by the Survey of India in [the] past, up to [the] 1938 edition, the delineation of the eastern section of the Sino-Indian boundary still corresponded to that on [the] Chinese maps, while the western section of the Sino-Indian boundary was not drawn at all; even in [the] 1950, 1951 and 1952 editions, published after the founding of the People's Republic of China . . . [it] was clearly indicated as un-delimited' boundary. He added that he failed to find any satisfactory answer to this when he made a detailed study of the 'heap of data' supplied by India.[16]

China had, yet again, on 26 December1959 alluded to India's altering the boundary unilaterally by pointing out:

[I]t is only in 1954 that this un-delimited sector of the boundary has suddenly become a delimited boundary.[17]

These were telling reminders that India had taken liberty with the international frontier in the western sector. Ambassador Parthasarathi's comments did not refer to the basic point made by the Chinese. On the contrary, he said that the Chinese 'will propose a compromise on the basis of give and take, in short, a deal as [the] only possible way of reaching [a] settlement which they will urge is necessary in [the] larger interest of the two countries'. He said that the note was meant to make India 'prepare for [a] compromise settlement'.[18] This indeed was the purpose of China in reminding India repeatedly of its indiscretion in unilaterally altering the international border in 1954. Ambassador Parthasarathi, instead of advising in the direction of a settlement, was seen nursing Nehru's doubts further. His approach was unlike what is expected from a senior diplomat charged with the responsibility of giving advice to highest political executive.

India's defence establishment under Krishna Menon at this time appeared to be in disarray. Nehru's confidence in his defence minister did not inspire a corresponding confidence in the armed forces. Defence Minister Menon, known to spend more time at the UN than at the defence ministry, was known for his talent at delivering speeches than building organizations and was famous for creating a coterie than providing leadership to men under his charge,

He was known for his acerbic tongue that made more enemies than friends. All these 'qualities' took a heavy toll on both the discipline of the armed forces and on India's defence preparedness. Menon even antagonized the Western countries by taking noxious swipes at their policies and programmes at the UN and outside. Even Dr Sarvepalli Gopal had pointed out to Menon's devious ways of functioning. Though his propensity to create coteries was known to Nehru, he perhaps thought them to be minor drawbacks, which were more than balanced by his energy and his commitment to national self-reliance and his experience of world affairs.[19] Since the talks between Nehru and Zhou were taking place in the background of the Kongka Pass incident, and the public outcry against China, it did shrink Nehru's space for any compromise.

Before we continue with this discussion, readers are reminded of the statement made by the foreign secretary the previous year which mentioned that the Sikkim–Tibet boundary was the only part of the long border between the two countries which was properly delimited.[20] This was the true state of the borders between the two countries. There was, as such, a need for a scientifically surveyed, delineated and demarcated boundary between the two countries. The talks provided that opportunity.

Chinese Premier Zhou Enlai accompanied by Foreign Minister Chen Yi landed in Delhi on 19 April 1960, with an entourage of twenty-nine officials and seven journalists. There were customary speeches at the airport. Prime Minister Nehru in his welcome did not leave Zhou in any doubt about India's hurt feelings and said the unfortunate events had 'shocked' the Indian people and 'imperilled' relations between them for the present and the future. Zhou, appearing reasonable and avoiding any controversial remarks, replied, 'This time I have come with the sincere desire to settle questions (and) seek avenues to a reasonable settlement of the boundary question.'[21]

At the banquet the next evening, Nehru again referred to the unfortunate differences but assured his guest that India would endeavour to do its best to lead the discussions towards success, while 'ensuring maintenance of peace with dignity and self-respect for both our great nations'. Zhou in his reply described the differences as temporary and as ones left over by history and colonialism.[22]

The Chinese Premier spent six days in Delhi from 20 to 25 April 1960 and had almost twenty hours of one-to-one talks with Prime Minister Nehru, spread across seven sessions. At Nehru's suggestion, Zhou also held talks separately with Vice President Dr Radhakrishnan,[23] Home Minister Govind Ballabh Pant,[24] Finance Minister Morarji Desai,[25] besides R.K. Nehru, secretary general in the MEA[26] and a former ambassador in Beijing. Swaran Singh held separate talks with Chen Yi, and both had travelled together to Agra as well.[27] Defence Minister Krishna Menon also met Zhou, but informally, since his conversations were not officially recorded. He himself kept a record of his talks with the Chinese, which was in the form of a note and not verbatim like other conversations and was found in 2019 when his private papers were released for research by the Nehru Memorial Museum and Library.

It was unfortunate that instead of the finance and home ministers calling on Zhou, it was he who had to call on them, in a breach of protocol, which was certain to have hurt Zhou. Swaran Singh, however, called on Foreign Minister Chen Yi at the Rashtrapati Bhavan.

Since a mass of notes and memoranda had already been exchanged between the two governments, both Nehru and Zhou were fully aware of each other's position on the various aspects of the frontiers. As it happened, neither of them tried to rise above their known positions. To that extent, they did not have much to add to the information already dished out by one to the other. Nevertheless, the ritual of talks for which they had assembled had to be gone through, and they did go through it religiously. There was no plenary session since the talks were between the two prime ministers only.

The Talks

Zhou began with a frank statement, '[L]ast year we might have hurt each other and there might have been some misunderstandings between us. But let bygone be bygone.' He said he had now come to clear the misunderstanding and find a common ground.[28]

At the very beginning, Zhou told Nehru that he had nothing to add to what China had already said in its notes and correspondence and left it to Nehru to state the Indian position.[29]

Eastern Sector

The Indian Case

Nehru, remaining loyal to his position, reiterated in some detail his views that were already known, deviating a little. Nehru did not agree with the Chinese position that the entire frontier was neither defined nor delimited. If delimitation could take place according to the definition of high mountain areas and watersheds, as per the formally accepted principle of demarcation, then it was precisely defined in the past, maintained Nehru. He added that physical marking in the mountainous areas is also difficult.[30] On the first day, the first session was held by Nehru in dilating on the Indian case. His opening salvo was that the controversies about borders were of recent origin, and otherwise it was a peaceful border. He held China responsible for the recent problems, disputing China's contentions regarding the delineation of the border.[31]

Rejecting China's argument that there were territorial claims of Tibet in India, Nehru said, 'We have shown these areas in maps in precise latitude and longitude and this description was before China and the world for a considerable time and no objection was taken to these by the Chinese Government since 1949.' He further mentioned that even in the past neither China nor Tibet had raised any objection to Indian frontiers. Indian minds were associated with the Himalayas, he averred. The prime minister said that be it the eastern sector or the western sector, there was a complete 'difference of opinion on facts between them', and added categorically that 'in no time of recorded history was this area ever a part of China or Tibet, of course leaving

out a few minor dents'.[32] Answering the concerns raised by China of
it not having signed the Simla Convention, Nehru insisted that the
Chinese representative was indeed present at Simla and had initialled
the Convention. He said, 'It may not be binding on China, but the
Chinese representative was present, was all along in the picture and
he certainly knew about it.' All records that we have indicate that
the Chinese representative was chiefly interested in the boundary
between Inner and Outer Tibet. Nehru also mentioned that since
Tibet was represented separately and was functioning 'practically as
an independent entity and functioning with full authority, it was
legally competent to do what it did'.

Nehru pointed out that in the past the British policy towards
Tibet was directed at Tsarist Russia and had nothing to do with
China. It was India that gave up its rights inherited from the British
in Tibet. India's interest in Tibet was only cultural. India, too, had
security apprehensions because these areas, which were almost the
heart of India, had a greater effect on India than on China, since
they were distant areas in a vast Chinese territory.[33] Nehru did not
elaborate on the security aspect implied in his statement. It was left to
Secretary General R.K. Nehru to elaborate on this separately during
his meeting with Zhou and Chen Yi. Elaborating, R.K. Nehru said:

> The border from Peking was 3000 miles away, but from Delhi
> it was only a few hundred miles and that made a tremendous
> difference and affected our security.[34]

Later, when Swaran Singh made a similar point while talking
to Chen Yi, the latter felt disturbed since it was a challenge to
China's peaceful approach in relations to India. To meet Indian
apprehensions on security, Chen Yi offered a treaty of friendship
for either ten, twenty or forty years, as desired by India.[35] After
explaining his position, the prime minister added that 'the one
distressing feature of recent events has been the shock it has given to
our basic policy of friendship and cooperation'.[36]

Answering Zhou's criticism about the Dalai Lama, Nehru said when he came, he was advised to go back to Tibet but he stayed on. He was advised from the very beginning that he and other Tibetans 'must not function in a political sense and broadly speaking he accepted our advice'. Nehru, however, conceded that 'occasionally they [Tibetans] did say something which we did not approve and we told them so'. Zhou, however, pointed out that there were occasions when the Dalai Lama exceeded the limits of political asylum and there were objective facts to prove it. Nehru also pointed out that Indian public organizations did hold meetings in his favour in which the Government of India could not interfere even if it did not approve of them. He also rejected the Chinese charge that the Tibetan rebellion was inspired by India and denied the claim that India had ever interfered in Tibet.[37]

Regarding recent troubles in Tibet, Nehru said they were internal and had nothing to do with Kalimpong, as alleged by China. Since China in 1957 and even later went on insisting that the problems in Tibet were made-in-Kalimpong, Nehru mentioned that it was possible that 'some refugees there and elsewhere who sympathised with the rebels . . . [had] occasionally exchanged letters but they were not allowed to function as such'. It may be recalled Nehru had conceded earlier that Kalimpong was a 'nest of spies', which perhaps encouraged Zhou to put Kalimpong in the dock.[38]

Reacting to Zhou's suggestion of setting up a joint committee to sift through the historical evidence to establish claims of either party, Nehru said that it would 'necessarily consist of officials and the like and in such vital matters it cannot go far. If we two of us ourselves disagree how a joint committee composed of officials would agree?'[39]

Nehru finally said that the Indian maps were in the public domain and the attention of the Chinese was drawn to them when India had protested against the Chinese maps. He claimed he did not remember China ever raising any objection to the Indian maps and added:

I do not say that you have formally accepted our maps but you had raised no objections either and this was in spite of the fact that these maps told precisely what our position with respect to the western and the eastern sectors, was.[40]

He rejected the Chinese contention that the borders between China and Bhutan and Sikkim did not fall within the scope of these discussions.

Eastern Sector

The Chinese Case

Zhou in his response pointed out that as modern nations the boundaries between the two countries have to be defined in terms of latitude and longitude and that India–China borders had not been delineated in that manner. While China did not recognize the McMahon Line, it had taken a realistic view of the China–Burma border falling along with McMahon Line. Likewise, since McMahon Line was a common factor between both Burma and India, he would also accept it in the case of India. He also added since India is already in occupation of the McMahon Line boundary, China would accept it as an accomplished fact. He insisted that while not recognizing it they would yet 'not cross it', and asserted:

[W]e did not put forward any territorial claim. We only advocated maintenance of the status quo.[41]

Regarding the maps, he conceded that there were differences between China's maps and the maps of neighbouring countries, and China would revise its maps after proper surveys and consulting the countries concerned. China could not revise its maps according to Indian maps.[42] It may be pointed out that whenever Nehru had referred to the Chinese maps in the past, the Chinese had maintained that those were old maps of the Kuomintang period, which were being reprinted now and would be revised in due course. China never committed itself to any particular position. Zhou further told Nehru that Indian forces occupied Tawang (NEFA) 'in the last few years *i.e.*, after independence and China never made it an issue'. He clarified that when he said China respected the status quo, he meant the 'status quo generally prevailing after independence'. He touted it as a sign of China's friendliness towards India.[43] To prove the subservient status of Tibet, Zhou mentioned that treaties signed by Tibet in the past had to be approved by the Chinese government and that the British government had recognized that fact. As such, he said, the Simla Convention could not be the legal basis of the Indian claim.[44]

Zhou initially dismissed the McMahon Line as a result of imperial aggression and the outcome of a convention which China had never signed. However, his final position that he committed to Prime Minister Nehru, the vice President, home and finance ministers and also to R.K. Nehru was that China intended to follow the same course in the case of India, which was being contemplated in the case of Burma. He assured that the new border which China was proposing to Burma would be coterminous with the McMahon Line and would follow the customary and traditional line. Both Zhou and Chen Yi repeated several times that in a renegotiated agreement in the eastern sector, China would accept the present border and claim no territory to the south of the McMahon Line.[45] Separately, when Swaran Singh had asked Chen Yi that since China was willing to accept the McMahon boundary in a fresh agreement,[46] why was China insisting on another agreement at all? Chen Yi replied that the existing arrangement had been imposed by imperialists and was an outcome of aggression and China could not accept it.[47] The McMahon Line had become a curse to the Chinese, a scar which Zhou had also mentioned to Panikkar in 1952.[48] What essentially the Chinese were driving at was that in a freshly minted agreement, China would concede the McMahon Line border in the eastern sector, and that would remove the stigma of the unequal treaty and India would not stand to lose any territory south of the Line.

Zhou, of course, for argument's sake, continued to emphasize that the area to the south of the McMahon Line had belonged to Tibet and the customary line had been changed subsequently. He further pointed out that this was done only after 1947, which was a fact since India extended its control in Tawang only in 1951 and that, too, under protest from the Tibetans.[49]

China's foreign minister, Chen Yi, insisted that 'liberated China and independent India must shake off the influences left over by imperialists' and accept a friendly attitude to settle the question. At the end, Chen Yi regretted Indian reluctance and said:

[A]fter five days of our talks, my personal view is that the Indian friends and the Government still do not have a profound understanding of the point of the Chinese Government absolutely does not recognise the Simla Convention and the McMahon Line. This has made us very unhappy.[50]

Zhou opined that the new agreement would give this border a legal footing as well. He reminded Nehru, yet again that Indian forces 'moved up to the line only in the last few years, that is, after independence. But we never made this point as a pre-requisite. When we say, *status quo, we mean status quo prevailing generally after independence and this would also show the*[51] *friendliness of our attitude'.* Since India continued to bat on the Simla Convention and the McMahon Line emerging from it, Zhou spelt out his position more precisely:

(i)   We cannot recognize McMahon Line;

(ii) We will not cross that line since Indian troops have already reached it; and

(iii) As regards two or three points where Indians have exceeded the McMahon Line, we are willing to maintain the status quo pending negotiations.

He clarified that the three points he mentioned at the end pertained to Tamadem, Longju and Kinzamane. However, these were termed as 'minor points' by Zhou.[52]

Western Sector

Nehru said China's claim in the western sector was not clear when that area had come under its control. Remembering his visits to Ladakh some forty-four years ago (c.1916) for trekking and again 'five or six years ago' (c.1954–55), this time by air, he said that he did not find Chinese presence there and, therefore, in his opinion *'this occupation has taken place in the last year or two and is of recent origin'*.[53] If, however, he did not find the presence of any Chinese, it should not have been surprising. Nehru later in his budget speech in the Lok Sabha had said, 'These territories are so high up that they are hardly inhabited, there is no communication, there are hardly any trees or any blade of grass'.[53A]

Nehru mentioned that India was greatly surprised and distressed when China laid claim to vast areas and said that the frontier was not delimited. Regarding Aksai Chin, Nehru mentioned that it was a large area, and did not span the whole area along which the road had been constructed. He said that their facts differed so much that there was confusion. He believed the place where the Chinese had built the road was a caravan road through which China used to send supplies. While China built its road in the eastern part of the area but long after the Sinkiang–Tibet highway was built, there were no Chinese or Tibetans in other parts of Aksai Chin according to the Indian patrol parties. It was only later that China set up posts and built roads in other areas of Aksai Chin.[54]

Nehru believed that the area was defined. The first argument about this area arose when India asked China about the Indian patrol party that had been arrested by the Chinese. That was also the time when India had protested against the road. Conceding that India had changed the boundary line in 1953–54, Nehru said it had been done after careful consideration and that the boundary might have been un-demarcated on the ground but he could not agree that it was 'not defined in the sense that it was known precisely although there may be some doubts here and there'. Throughout the discussions, Nehru's stress remained on the fact of the boundary being 'traditional and customary', since there was no actual line in the western sector like the McMahon Line that existed in the eastern sector.[55]

Referring to the history of Ladakh, Nehru referred to the war between Tibet and Ladakh in 1841 concluding with the Treaty of 1842 which set the boundary between them. Nehru, in support of the Indian case, quoted revenue records and travellers' account and offered details of the topography of the area.

Nehru had, in his note on 'Border Dispute with China', said that 'India had neither any check-post there nor any means of access to the area'.[56] It was an admission of neglect by India of its own territory. As pointed out in the previous chapter, when the Indian *Charge d'affaires* protested to Zhou about the road, he had shot back: '[I]t took seven years for China to construct the road, where were the Indians if that were their territory?'[57]

Zhou, while arguing his point of view, once again raised the question of demarcation of the boundary, which he said in modern times was done scientifically. He did not agree with Nehru that the 1842 agreement laid down the boundary between Tibet and Ladakh.[58] Referring to the maps, he said that unlike the Chinese maps, the Indian maps changed several times. He pointed out it was only in 1954 that 'an ordinary boundary line was drawn and the word "undefined" was removed'. He quoted Nehru who had said in Parliament that 'this part of the boundary was somewhat vague' and he also referred to Nehru's statement of 28 August 1959 when, in answering a question in the Lok Sabha, he had conceded that:

[This boundary] was the boundary of the old Kashmir State with Tibet and Chinese Turkestan. Nobody had marked it. But, after some kind of broad surveys, the then Government had laid down that border which we have been accepting and acknowledging.[59]

Zhou charged that India had changed its maps without consulting China. The status of the area had been changed from 'undefined' to 'defined'. Regarding this, he also reminded India that it had occupied some part of Tibet only after 1947. That it was a reference to Tawang, mentioned in the earlier section, was clear.

He said that since liberation the Chinese troops had been going to Ari in Tibet via this route and it had since then been used for sending supplies. He claimed that in 1891–92, the Manchu government sent people to Karakoram and Chang Chenmo valley in order to carry out surveys, and these people had confirmed that the Chinese boundary lay there.[60] Zhou claimed that to the south of the Kongka Pass, the area to the west belonged to Ladakh and the areas to the east belonged to Tibet. He claimed that the northern border of the Aksai Chin had always been under Sinkiang and had been under China for the last 200 years.[61] Zhou reiterated that the area to the north and east of the Karakoram watershed belonged to Sinkiang and that the boundary line started from that point continued through the Kongka Pass and continued down to the south from the Chang Cenmo valley, Pangong lake and the Indus valley. Areas to the east of this belonged to Tibet and China patrolled that area.[62]

Zhou summed up the points, which he said should form the common ground:

i.   The boundaries were not delimited and therefore there was a dispute;

ii.   There is a line of actual control in all the three sectors;

iii.   Geographical features like watersheds, rivers, valleys, mountains and passes should be applicable in all the sectors;

iv.   Each side should keep to its line and make no territorial claims while admitting individual adjustments along the border later

v.   National sentiments tied to Himalayas and Karakoram must
be respected.[63]

Zhou appealed to Nehru to come to the negotiating table and settle
all disputes in an amicable manner. Zhou stated that China had
already reached an agreement with Burma on the entire boundary
question and that the same should be applicable to the Sino-Indian
boundary, particularly when it was a continuous boundary on both
sides (this specifically referred to the McMahon Line).

Nehru hesitated to negotiate the Aksai Chin area, when in
India's own perception it was a disputed territory, a status accepted
as early as 1953 or even in 1949, when the Kuomintang government
had asked for its delineation.[64]

The talks ended in a stalemate with little progress towards either
easing the tension along the borders or in mutual understanding of
each other's point of view. As Dr Gopal noted, in the talks between
the two prime ministers, there was not even a distant approach
towards a solution.[65]

Since no agreement between the two prime ministers appeared
possible, Nehru reluctantly agreed to Zhou's suggestion for formation
of a joint committee of officials to go into the historical records and
other relevant data that each side possessed and determine the merits
of each other's case. This proposal was like putting the cart before the
horse. In any dispute, it is a normal practice for officials to flag the
contentious points first and the political leaders to subsequently take
a call and work out a consensus between them, keeping in view the
overall interests of both the parties and in the interest of maintaining
cooperative and friendly relations.[66]

In this case, the reverse was happening. The discussion on merits
which should have taken place before the talks between the two leaders
were now scheduled after their talks. Nehru was right to suggest this
route at the very beginning when the summit was proposed. However,
since Zhou had insisted on talks at their level, Nehru agreed so as not
to appear to be blocking the negotiations. At the summit, the two

prime ministers had taken certain positions and it fell to the lot of their officials to find enough evidence not necessarily on merit of their case but to bolster the stand of their respective prime ministers, sacrificing the actual merit in the process. No set of officials could afford to put their prime minister in the wrong. The result was that neither at the political nor at the official level did the discussions lead to any workable solution. A stalemate surprised no one.

Despite the failure of the talks, Zhou remained positive at the end and insisted that since it had not been possible to find a solution now:

> I would still very much like to see that favourable conditions are created for future talks.[67]

Giving a statement on the talks in Parliament, Nehru conceded there was no meeting ground between the two sides. He said that according to us, 'their forces came into this area, within quite recent times; naturally, they did not enter a broad area on one date, but in the main, they had come to this area in the course of the last year and a half or so'. Having said that, he agreed 'there exists disputes on the boundary between the two sides', and added that there was also 'a line of actual control up to which each side exercises administrative jurisdiction'. Each side should adhere to the line of actual control and should not put forward territorial claims. To maintain tranquillity on the borders both sides must refrain from patrolling the border. He did not think that given the vast differences in their facts it was useful to carry on the discussion.[68]

Two pieces of conversation between Zhou and Defence Minister Krishna Menon, and between Swaran Singh and Chen Yi, need to be noted. Menon's meeting, even when informal, had special significance since he was also the defence minister and had some acquaintance with the Chinese leaders, having met them in Geneva and because he had also travelled to Beijing earlier at Zhou's invitation to discuss the issues connected with Indo-China. His talks, which were spread over three sessions, too, turned out to be of a routine nature. Much of the emphasis continued to be on the McMahon Line, which China had conceded in favour of India. His note on the conversations, which he recorded himself, was not a detailed one and was undated. According to Menon, Zhou easily conveyed the impression that 'he (Zhou) will leave the McMahon Line alone'. He, however, conveyed to Zhou the 'deep sense of shock that India had suffered, making it clear it was not a shock of fear but of friendship outraged'. Reminded of Indian efforts on China's behalf at the UN, Zhou conveyed his appreciation. Later, Menon confided in the British High Commissioner Malcolm MacDonald, which the latter reported to London, '[T]here was the possibility of compromise between the two prime Ministers and [the] Vice-President too was agreeable but his colleagues in the Cabinet were opposed to it.'[69]

Swaran Singh in his talks with Chen Yi generally followed the Nehru line and Chen Yi the line taken by Zhou. Chen Yi told Swaran Singh that he felt disturbed by the remarks of R.K. Nehru about security, as already stated earlier. Swaran Singh, seizing the opportunity, said that the recent incidents had 'definitely shaken the confidence of the people' of India and appreciated his efforts to 'repair the damage'. Chen Yi, in trying to meet India's security concerns, had offered a long-term treaty of friendship, as stated earlier.[70]

Chen Yi, in his own way, tried to allay India's concerns and said that the renegotiation of the Simla Convention would 'not mean that we want to take chunks of Indian territory south of the (McMahon) Line'. Answering Swaran Singh's point that certain obligations following from previous agreements had to be honoured, Chen Yi, while repeating that China had not signed the Convention and that it was illegal, assured Swaran Singh that renegotiation would not lead to any Chinese claim over any territory south of the McMahon Line. He regretted that China had failed to make India appreciate its point of view. There was no discussion between them on the western sector.[71]

Chen Yi candidly informed Swaran Singh about China's anxiety to negotiate an agreement soon and also referred to China's various problems, both internal and external, including the food problem and confessed that in such a situation 'it would be stupid if we created tension with India'. This explains China's attempts to reach out to Burma, Nepal and Afghanistan in India's neighbourhood.[72]

Since there were differences between the two sides on almost all matters, it was no wonder that there were also differences on framing the joint communiqué. The communiqué that finally emerged said practically little of substance as far as the negotiations were concerned. It simply noted that each side had reiterated its stand, which had led to a greater understanding of each other's point of view.[73] At the end, the two countries stood as apart as they were at the beginning of the talks.

Shorn of verbiage, China conceded India's claim to the McMahon Line but in a renegotiated agreement. The problem remained centred on the western sector, since Nehru continued to insist on his point of view, forgetting that in India's own official records the area had been accepted as 'disputed' and its maps had until 1954 shown the border as 'UNDEFINED', and the fact that he had ordered the alteration of the international border unilaterally and, therefore, there was a need for discussion and settlement. Khrushchev's advice that a friendly frontier was more important than mere prestige had not impressed Nehru. He, too, did not practise the advice he gave to U Nu in 1956, which the latter had actually put to good use, and settled his border problem with China.

In negotiating an agreement, both parties make sacrifices to come to a settlement. One country cannot dictate terms to the other. China showed wiliness to accommodate India on the McMahon Line, which had economic value and was a populated area. India, however, failed to show any accommodation in the western sector, which was barren and had little economic value and no population and had also been accepted as disputed by India. China asked for negotiations and delineation of the borders as a normal exercise because they had hitherto not been scientifically delineated at any time, but India refused. An opportunity to settle the dispute by applying the principle of give and take was allowed to slip away. As Foreign Secretary Dutt recalled:

> The talks between the two prime ministers failed to resolve even a single point of dispute. Hours were spent on discussing the position of the international frontier in the western sector, but Nehru refused to accept the Chinese contention that they were in control of the entire area up to their map line.[74]

The official team appointed by the two prime ministers to sift through the past records also failed to achieve even a joint report. Each side submitted its own report to its government separately and no meeting between them took place thereafter.

[*The above narration of discussions between the two prime ministers is based on the verbatim records of their discussions which are available in Document No: 1633 to 1655 in the Five-Volume study of India–China Relations; 1947–2000 edited by the author, and in the Haksar Papers available in the Nehru Memorial Museum and Library, New Delhi.*]

The talks ended in a stalemate, essentially due to India's domestic political compulsions. The Kongka Pass incident had taken its toll. As it happened, the Indian people, who had been fed on the staple of Hindi–China Bhai Bhai, found that all was not well in the bilateral relations between the two countries. China was now presented as a villain that had deceptively usurped Indian territory and had also killed Indian policemen. It was a rude shock to the people of India that a country which, until the other day, was presented the closest friend of India had acted 'treacherously'. Public opinion hardened against showing any accommodation to China. In the face of public outcry, Nehru, too, suffered loss of face. The cabinet, too, suffered the same and was not prepared to let Nehru compromise on the position he had taken until then. Nehru found his back against the wall and his options restricted. Any accommodation with China now was like committing political hara-kiri. There was divide in the Congress Party, which came to light in the meeting of the Congress Parliamentary Party held on 28 April 1960.[75]

That India even after having altered the border in 1954 had taken no steps to establish its military, political or administrative presence in the area proved fatal. No checkpost had been set up; no flag was unfurled to announce its sovereignty. India thought that merely drawing a line on the maps was enough to announce its ownership. The vacuum was allowed to be created. Nature hates vacuum and it has the tendency to fill it up and it was indeed filled up.

There were senior ICS officers involved in the top hierarchy of the ministry of external affairs and, in the absence of a foreign minister, it was their duty to advise the prime minister. However, apparently they found the prime minister's persona too daunting to offer any contrary advice. They suffered from the 'Pandit-jee-knows-best' syndrome. Jagat Mehta who was involved before, during and after the 1960 talks on the Chinese border issue in the MEA and who finally became the foreign secretary described Nehru as:

> The greatest democratic dictator in history, but twelve years (*sic*) of his prime minister-ship were largely wasted . . . We shall never again have the likes of Nehru and we the professionals, lacked the courage to offer him timely corrective counsel. Panditjee could call one a 'damn fool' but if one stood one's ground, he was willing to change his own opinion in pursuit of the national interest. His bark was frightening.[76]

Maulana Abdul Kalam Azad, former education minister in the first cabinet of independent India, had something similar to say about him. After his press conference in May 1946 on the Cabinet Mission Plan, Maulana Azad had said:

His nature is however such that he often acts on impulse. As a rule he is open to persuasion but sometimes he makes up his mind without taking all the facts into consideration. Once he has done so he tends to go ahead regardless of what the consequences may be.[76a]

The border problem was the natural outcome of Nehru's policies to keep under wrap all the facts governing India–China relations generally, and those relating to the borders particularly. This resulted in an uninformed public falling prey to what was dished out by the official media. Krishna Menon recalling Zhou's visit later had a different take and said:

> 1960 was spoiled by the fact that we had too many people involved in it. It was not known to what extent the Chinese came here to sort out our differences. I believe Chen Yi was bad influence that there were great changes taking place inside China at that time. On our side the Congress and the country, public opinion had become aroused so that it was no longer possible to talk in terms of negotiations. And the Home Minister, who had by then acquired a powerful influence over the Prime Minister, was not in favour of negotiations.[77]

On the last day of the talks, 25 April, just before leaving for Kathmandu, Zhou Enlai addressed a press conference in New Delhi, from 22.45 hrs to 01.00 hrs the next morning. At the beginning of the press conference, Zhou cautioned Indian journalists that apart from what had been reported in the Indian press, his press conference would also be reported by the New China News Agency (*Hsinhua*) and later published in the *Peking Review* for record. By this announcement, he sought to caution the Indian press not to take liberties with his statement or his replies to their questions.

Zhou prefaced his press conference with a statement which said that though there was no agreement, there was a desire on both sides to 'find common points of proximity'. He did not apportion any blame for the stalemate in the talks. He said he had come with the conviction that a fair and reasonable settlement was possible between them. Hinting that China had accepted the McMahon Line in a renegotiated agreement, he said:

> We have requested the Indian Government to take an attitude towards this sector (western sector) of boundary similar to the attitude which the Chinese Government has taken towards the eastern sector of the boundary.

In simple words, he proposed India should accept the Chinese position in the western sector as China had accepted India's in the eastern sector. Since India had not accepted China's position in the western sector, Zhou said that 'there is a bigger problem with regard to the western sector of the boundary'.

While he had no objection to India giving asylum to the Dalai Lama, he insisted that he had exceeded the limits that the Indian government had promised the Chinese government by being involved in political activities against China while in India.

Though the press conference appeared to be too long, at two hours and fifteen minutes, considering the interpretation involved both from English to Chinese and vice versa, it could not have effectively been for more than forty-five minutes or so. Zhou ended his press conference on a hopeful note, suggesting that things would move in the direction to the advantage of friendship even if it might take some time. He further said that if he did not have that hope he would not have come to Delhi. He expressed his confidence that if necessary, 'he himself or his colleagues may come again for the sake of enhancing the friendship between two great nations'.[78]

Nehru's reaction not only to the press conference but to the very idea of the summit was not positive. Attributing motives to Zhou for his visit, he said in the Lok Sabha:

Because something important had happened, the important thing being that according to us, they had entered our territory, over a large area of our territory, which we considered aggression. That was the whole basis of his coming here.[79]

It was an unfortunate remark. Zhou, regretting Nehru's unkindly comments from Kathmandu, said he did not say so at their face but only after they had left Delhi. Zhou's reaction still remained friendly and he said 'we understand that the Prime Minister Nehru might have difficulties, but the unity of one thousand million people of China and India is extremely important'.[80]

Nehru told the Rajya Sabha that 'I am not sure in my mind whether I used the word (aggression) or not and it is quite possible that I did not use the word . . .' But the words are recorded in the proceedings of the Lok Sabha.[81]

The *People's Daily* editorial while blaming India for the failure of talks, was not unfriendly, and suggested that the result would have a 'positive (impact) on the maintenance of tranquillity on the borders'. It insisted there was 'no conflict of fundamental interests between us' and these differences 'would eventually be solved reasonably'.[82] As stated earlier, in the face of Nehru's predetermined attitude towards the talks, as conveyed to the Nepalese prime minister,[83] the outcome was not too surprising. His being so categorical in advance meant in his scheme of things there was no scope for adjustment. Ananth Krishnan, a journalist associated with *The Hindu* and the weekly *India Today*, was someone who spent ten years in China. In his recent book, *India's China Challenge*, referring to the failure of the talks, said, 'The exchanges between Zhou and Nehru leave you with the impression that only one side was serious about making concessions in the talks. And that side wasn't India.' He went on to add that 'his approach to discussing the boundary doomed any chance of settling question from the start . . . No government in Beijing could accept his maximalist position'.[83a]

Nehru, in his statement in the Lok Sabha, apart from giving the reasons which prompted Zhou to come to India, disputed the facts of Chinese claims on various parts of the borders in both the sectors, and said that 'an attempt was made frequently to equate the eastern sector with the western sector' but insisted the 'conditions are quite different'. He said 'if facts differ, inferences differ, arguments differ'. He had doubts that the process of officials going through the past records would 'make it easy of solution' and it did not.[84]

At the Congress Parliamentary Party meeting a few days after the end of the talks (28 April), Krishna Menon had come under intense attack. Nehru knew the attack was actually directed at him which upset him and he said:

> Let us be frank about it. I have had enough of this. I don't want to be the leader of this party or any other party because I am slack, advantage is taken of that. Because I am slack, everybody attacks the Government, my colleagues are attacked. Congressmen are attacked. Defence Minister is attacked. Is this how a party should behave, I want to know.[85]

Nehru's biographer, Dr Gopal, however, said at no time during these talks did Zhou offer explicitly to recognize the McMahon Line in the east, in return for the secession by India of Aksai Chin in the west.[86] The telegram that the foreign secretary sent to heads of Indian Mission contradicted Gopal's claim. The foreign secretary had said that:

> [It appeared] to be the Chinese aim to make us accept their claim in Ladakh as a price for their recognition of our position in NEFA . . . It was also obvious if we accepted the line claimed by China in Ladakh they would accept the McMahon Line.[87]

If that was the instant assessment of the foreign secretary, one cannot quarrel with Zhou telling the media at the press conference that it was India's failure to accept the Chinese position in the west that resulted in the failure of talks. Dr Gopal's understanding was flawed.

In his internal discussions on the swapping, Nehru remained firm and said 'if I give them [Aksai Chin] I shall no longer be Prime Minister of India—I will not do it'.[88] 'Settlement of boundary dispute [between the two stakeholders after due discussions] cannot be held to be a cession of territory,' as the Supreme Court had later ruled, in the case of *Union of India Vs Maganbhai* in 1969.[89] The court was adjudicating whether cession of territory to a foreign state needed constitutional amendment or could be done by an ordinary law. It ruled that it does require constitutional amendment but it was not cession of territory.

There was a full but acrimonious discussion in both houses of Parliament on 29 April when charges and countercharges were freely exchanged between the PM and the Opposition. The fact of the matter was, as Nehru told Rajya Sabha, 'these talks have not helped in the least in the solution of the problems' or helped him in understanding Zhou better. It might have helped Zhou in better understanding the Indian point of view. About the Aksai Chin road, he said it was a caravan route which was used by the Chinese in 1950–51 and which they later converted into a road, probably in 1957 or 1958 and even occupied more areas. Members held Nehru personally responsible for present situation since 'no other person (was) concerned with foreign policy'. Nehru resented the Opposition's criticism that 'China was increasing its military strength and this might prove unfavourable to India'. Defending the Panchsheel, he said that if 'countries misbehave or invade or commit aggression' that cannot be blamed on the Panchsheel since it was only a code of conduct among nations. He agreed with the need to have a strong border which, he insisted, was dependent on the strength of the industrial development since 'nothing else can make it stronger'. Not wanting to be strong like China, he belittled the concept of strong defence involving deployment of armed men in remote border areas.[90]

Prime Minister Nehru had a comparatively a tougher time in the Lok Sabha where he encountered a hostile House. He charged that the members' intervention comprised 'petty disputes, petty references, insinuations, and some brave words'. He chided them for use of strong language and said 'we may be small people and individuals, but somehow we are conditioned and placed at a moment of tremendous historical significance for our country, for Asia and the world'. Replying to the suggestion to give up the policy of non-alignment, he said it would amount to 'taking shelter under somebody else's umbrella, seek help of others to defend yourself, to protect you because you are weak'. Deprecating use of strong language by members, he said the brave words had little meaning and this kind of 'things may well be said at the *Ramlila* Ground, Gandhi Grounds in Delhi'. An upset Atal Behari Vajpayee said that it was likely that the Opposition had failed to understand the situation, but 'the Hon'ble Prime Minister too has failed to meet the situation'. Another member charged that the prime minister was wasting time since he had nothing to say. Nehru also took exception to the criticism of the defence minister in the newspapers and described them as 'irresponsible' and their stories as 'untrue'. He feared:

[The recent policies spread the] feeling of despondency or lack of self-reliance, and asking others to help. There is nothing more fatal. What will happen in future I don't know? I hope that whatever happens we shall never have the feeling of despondency and want others to pull us out of our difficulties in a matter of this kind.

At the end, he said:

It is admitted that we have to face this tremendous problems and tremendous menace that has come to us, an event of the most vital importance to our country and to our nation.[91]

The National Council of the Communist Party of India in its resolution adopted on 12 May 1960 noted that the talks had led to 'lessening of tension' between the two countries, and warned the government that 'there were powerful forces both within the country and outside, who are interested in keeping the dispute between India and China alive and in causing discord and tension between the two countries'. However, the Working Committee of the Jan Sangh, the forerunner of the Bharatiya Janata Party, on 27 August expressing 'deep concern' over the 'cartographic and military aggression of China and the talks had confirmed its fear that Chinese assurances could not be relied upon'.[92]

Most of the criticism in Parliament and the press remained focused on the western sector. Had the border in that sector been discussed with China in 1954, before declaring it 'DEMARCATED', perhaps all the trouble could have been avoided. By unilaterally doing so, India opened itself to the avoidable charge of unilateralism and, therefore, created a dispute. Even at the risk of repeating, one has to recall the remarks of former Foreign Secretary Shyam Saran that 'in retrospect, this may not have been a wise decision since it deprived the Indian side of flexibility in negotiating a compromise with the Chinese'.[93]

The Chinese optimism before the talks was anchored on their willingness to accept the McMahon Line which was a live and populated area and had been the subject of much discussion both internally and externally. Even in the case of the western sector, China beseeched India to enter into negotiations to work out a solution of the disputed area acceptable to both but the prime minister remained in denial.

After the summit, the issue became more political and ceased to be merely a border question. The Chinese expressing their disappointment to the Soviet ambassador in Beijing said on 17 May 1960 that they were confirmed in their opinion that Nehru was responsible for anti-Chinese feelings in India since he was under pressure from the 'right and other reactionary' forces. The Chinese, too, believed that Nehru did not want to resolve the border issue since it was profitable for India, in that it ensured American aid.[94] Zhou, from his experience at the talks, referred to him as 'discourteous', while talking to US President Nixon during his visit to Beijing in 1971, and as someone 'who would not allow us the courtesy of replying'.[95]

China now decided to strengthen its position militarily in the western sector. A proposal made by Zhou was approved by Mao and Deng Xiaoping and it supported the implementation of the scheme to strengthen Chinese hold in the western sector.[96] That the Chinese had indeed followed Mao's instructions was confirmed by Nehru in his speech in Lok Sabha on 28 November 1961. He said:

> [The Chinese had] spread even beyond the 1956 Chinese claim line in Ladakh to establish new posts, and that they have constructed roads to link these posts with rear bases . . . These fresh instances of violation of Indian territory by the Chinese establish conclusively that the Chinese are guilty of further aggression against India and their protestations to the contrary are only a cloak to cover up these renewed incursions and aggressive activities.[97]

Nehru's biographer Dr Gopal in making an appraisal of Chinese policies towards India was constrained to point out that since 1957 China's attitude towards India was cooling off and pointed to various strands in their policies to confirm it. He said that China even tried to minimize India's role in world affairs.[98]

The year 1960 ended on a troublesome note for India–China relations. The coming months did not portend better times in their relations either. The stage was set for confrontation in the times ahead.

11

Towards 1962

The summit talks between Zhou and Nehru had ended in vain. Zhou showed no remorse or regrets or even apportioned any blame for the failure of the talks and remained hopeful for the future. He expressed his confidence that, if necessary, he would come again 'to resolve the issue and enhance friendship between the two great nations'.[1] Nehru remained somewhat diffident and even attributed motives to Zhou's initiative to visit India, which was that they had committed aggression.[2]

The officials who were asked to study the relevant material on both sides, as expected, and as pointed out in the previous chapter, were unable to agree between them and submitted separate reports to their respective governments. That they failed to produce even a joint report was no surprise.

Zhou was unhappy at Nehru attributing motives to him and said that Nehru had not said it 'face to face' but only after they had left, and that this was 'not an attitude to take towards guests'. Yet, giving Nehru the benefit of doubt, he said he might have faced difficulties and also added that 'the unity of one thousand million people of China and India is extremely important'.[3]

The New China News Agency, or *Hsinhua*, in a commentary repeated the official line that the boundary had never been formally delimited. It further claimed that the customary line claimed by India had 'no treaty, historical or factual basis' and that there existed between it and the traditional customary line a difference of about 120,000 square kilometres.[4]

In early 1962, the former Burmese prime minister U Nu happened to be on a pilgrimage tour of India. Nehru met him in Varanasi on 13 January. He told Nehru that during his talks with Zhou and Chen Yi, he had found them to be earnest regarding their desire to settle their border dispute through negotiations. U Nu added that they found it difficult to make a move because of his (Nehru's) insistence that 'China should vacate large areas of territory before any negotiations could take place'. He had found the Chinese government friendly and Burma had reached a 'good settlement with them'. Convinced about China's sincerity, Nu pointed out, 'China, which had been occupying some Burmese territory, had even vacated it when this was suggested to them.' Nehru in his note on the conversation said that Nu had told him that China would be 'more reasonable if he took the lead'. Since Zhou had been to India twice [Zhou visited thrice actually], the Chinese expected Nehru to visit Beijing. Nehru remained hesitant. Nehru told him that he was interested in negotiations since the alternative was war, but added he could not go to Beijing, since there was no firm basis for talks and 'talking vaguely about negotiations was not helpful'. He also added that the secretary general's visit to Beijing on his way back from Mongolia, the previous year, had 'not produced any hopeful result'. He mentioned the anti-India propaganda by the Chinese and their approaches to Pakistan were not helpful factors.[5]

The stalemate in political relations created difficulties for the Indian consulate, the trade agencies and the Indian traders in Tibet.[6] Gradually, the officials of the Indian embassy in Beijing, too, became a target of Chinese pomposity and disdain.[7] India, deciding to give China the taste of its own pudding, had in the previous year placed some restrictions on the Chinese consulate in Kalimpong.[8] Feeling the pinch, the Chinese had complained but had been ignored.[9]

There were disturbing reports from Gangtok regarding the Chinese encouraging chauvinistic tendencies among the Tibetans in border areas. Similar reports had come in the previous year as well, and Nehru had pointed it out to Zhou. What disturbed India was what Baleshwar Prasad, the dewan of Sikkim, conveyed to Apa Pant, the political officer. He mentioned that the *maharajkumar* of Sikkim would try to 'play off India against China' and increase his stakes since India was afraid of China.[10]

China continued to dominate the narrative in the Indian press and Parliament. Nehru, in his speech in the Lok Sabha on the budget of the MEA, acknowledged the wide gulf in relations with China. Nehru agreed that enough steps had not been taken in the western sector as compared to the eastern frontier. About Longju, located on the Tibet–NEFA border where a clash had taken place in August 1959 with two Indian casualties, he said, it 'has no importance . . . except for its psychological and sentimental value', and it was a matter of 'I think two square kilometre. In the 'larger scheme of things it has no importance to them or to us' and 'it can be settled in no time'. About Ladakh, he said it had 'vast importance, both in regard to the extent of its area and other consequences that may come from the Chinese occupation'. He further added that 'these territories are so high up that they are hardly inhabited, there is no communication, there are hardly any trees, or any blade of grass'. He admitted the lack of roads beyond Srinagar, but said 'we did think of building that road to Leh for the last few years. May be we could have done it quicker and sooner'.[11]

Simplifying the issue, and to put China in the wrong, he said:

We are taking certain action . . . in the eyes of the world, of other countries in Asia, Europe, America etc., a certain momentum of feeing in regard to this matter. It is no small matter that the

Chinese Government has to face a certain criticism from these
other countries . . . (and) their prestige suffers.[12]

Once again, he seemed to rely on uncertain factors which were
external to India's own defence abilities.

R. K. Nehru, secretary general in the MEA, had, a year ago, made
a transit halt in Beijing on the way home from his visit to Mongolia,
and had had some discussions with the Chinese on the borders. It
had been agreed that Ambassador Parathasarathi and Zhang Wenji,
the director in Asia Department in Weichiaopu, would carry forward
the discussions on the borders. Subsequently, they had three rounds
of talks—two in Shanghai on 17 July 1961 (in two sessions) and
one in Beijing.[13] These did not result in much. Parthasarathi,
concentrating on Sikkim and Bhutan, asked his interlocutor about
China's attitude to India's relations with them in the diplomatic
sense. Puzzled, Zhang wondered why India's attention had been
diverted from the borders towards Sikkim and Bhutan. Zhang, not
wishing to be drawn into discussion on the two Himalayan states,
said 'this goes beyond the scope of border issues . . .' and added 'we
do not wish to damage China's relations with Bhutan and Sikkim,
nor do we wish to damage China's relations with India'. This was yet
again a hint that China would deal with the two Himalayan states
independently and not through India. He deprecated India's stance
of treating Sikkim as its protectorate, and said 'this kind of practice is
rare in Asian and African countries'. Regarding the McMahon Line,
Zhang said 'except for a small area south of the McMahon Line *there
was not much disagreement*' and repeated that since '*China did not
cross the McMahon Line—the problem is in fact, nonexistent*'.[14] Not
much was expected and not much was gained from these discussions.

Meanwhile, both sides continued to hurl accusations at each
other of land border and air space violations. Under these antagonistic
circumstances, India did not react positively to China's suggestion
for extension/renewal of the 1954 Agreement on Tibet, which was
due to expire at the end of April 1962 after it had survived its life of

eight years. India regretted that soon after the agreement had been signed, China had started progressively curtailing Indian facilities in Tibet and harassing Indian traders and pilgrims. India found it 'reprehensible' that China started 'to encroach, at first insidiously and later openly, on territories which had clearly been accepted as Indian, and by 1958, began to make open claims followed by aggressive military activity, on several thousand square miles of Indian territory'.[15] In view of Indian reservations, the agreement was allowed to lapse without any regrets on the part of anyone.

In December 1961, India had liberated Goa from Portuguese colonial rule and faced criticism from the Western countries, but China had come out in India's support and had said that 'the action of the Indian Government to recover Goa reflects the just demand of the India people'.[16]

India had by 1959 established new military posts in Ladakh in pursuit of its forward policy. As pointed out in Chapter 9, both countries were now patrolling the area aggressively. This led each to accuse the other of trespassing into its territory. The language of the notes became sharper. China now blamed the previous British government for its aggressive policies in the past, which 'took advantage of the unfortunate situation in which the Indian people were powerless, and used India as its base, expanded into China's Tibet and Sinkiang regions'. China again suggested fresh negotiations for a peaceful settlement of the border dispute.[17] India, on the contrary, said that 'the British policies actually helped China to consolidate its authority in these regions'.[18]

Zhou Enlai, while reporting his discussion in Delhi to the Second National People's Congress in April 1962, accused India of claiming Chinese territory and laying down unacceptable conditions for discussions.[19] The *Hsinhua* commentary of 28 April 1962 repeated what Zhou had told the NPC.[20]

Elsewhere in the book it has been mentioned how Sino-Pakistan relations flourished despite Pakistan's military alliances with the West against communism. Pakistan's dexterity and China's adroitness enabled the two to manage their contradictions. The acerbic Indian relations with both Pakistan and China afforded these two nations an opportunity to craft a new relationship between them to give India a new headache. As early as 1959 Ambassador Parthasarathi had cautioned Delhi that China would try its best to sharpen the relations between India and Pakistan. This was viewed by Delhi as another example of China taking undue advantage of India's adversarial relationship with Pakistan. To queer the pitch for India, Pakistan told India in December 1962 that it had decided to negotiate an agreement with China on their boundary involving the area of the state of Jammu and Kashmir under its illegal occupation. India had, however, announced that it would not recognize any such agreement.[21] India followed it up with an official note protesting the proposed agreement.[22]

India was embarrassed when China denied the Indian claim that Zhou in his discussion with the then Ambassador R.K. Nehru on 16 March 1956 had given an impression that 'Kashmir people had already expressed their will'.[23] China asked India to produce documentary evidence in support of their claim.[24] There was none. A reading of the above-mentioned note would give the impression that it was Ambassador Nehru's delusion at work and his remarks were self-promotional.[25] R.K. Nehru did something similar once again in 1961, making use of his transit halt at Beijing on his way back from Mongolia. Beijing again said it was India's 'unilateral misrepresentation of facts and a delusion imposed on others, to which the Chinese Government categorically object'.[26] India was embarrassed since there was no documentary evidence to pin China down. Even the prime minister, after going through R.K. Nehru's note on his talks with Zhou, remarked 'what they said about Kashmir is, to a small extent and rather negatively in our favour'.[27] The Chinese Government protested to P.K. Banerjee, India's *charge d'affaires* in Beijing, at the misrepresentations of Ambassador Nehru and Delhi was duly informed.[28] R.K. Nehru's assertion in 1956 claiming China's support on Kashmir and again now in 1961 was self-promotional, which led to national embarrassment. But he got away unscathed despite the fact that his action was unbecoming of an officer of his rank. He being the cousin of the prime minister perhaps helped him to escape the censor.

China, rejecting India's objection to its settling its boundary with Pakistan in Pakistan-occupied Kashmir, said that India while refusing to a settlement of its border would not even permit China in negotiating a boundary settlement with Pakistan. It also pointed out the fact that China had successfully settled its borders with Nepal and Burma. In typical Chinese style, it warned India that 'whipping up anti-Chinese sentiments will only be lifting a rock to crush its own toes in the end'.[29]

Intensive patrolling by both countries in both sectors led to an increase in the exchange of notes and memoranda in which they accused each other of border violations. The Indian note of 14 May 1962[30] drew the attention of the Chinese to the prime minister's announcement of 2 May in Parliament that 'India does not want war', and reminded China of the prime minister's offer of 16 November 1959 for reciprocal withdrawals in the western sector. The Indian note suggested continued civilian use of Aksai Chin road by China pending negotiations.[31]

Gradually, the notes had become controversial in tone. The Chinese note of 19 May 1962 described the Indian charge of China's violation of Longju as 'slanderous', and 'demanded' India's withdrawal, otherwise the Chinese Government would 'not stand idly by seeing its territory once again unlawfully invaded and occupied by India and that the Indian Government must bear the responsibility for all the grave consequences arising there from'.[32] Strangely enough, as stated earlier, the prime minister in April 1961 had described Longju a minor issue involving merely a 2 square kilometre area, which could be 'settled in no time'. In yet another similar strongly worded note, China accused India of encroaching into Chinese territory and remaining indifferent to its repeated protests.[33] The sharpening of the language of correspondence was accompanied with the heightened tension on the borders. China described the Indian proposal of allowing China use of Aksai Chin road for civilian traffic as an 'absurdity' and said why should China ask India for the use of its road in its own territory.[34]

China now accused India of changing the status quo of the boundary and setting up military strong points in Chinese territory. It also accused India of 'carrying on provocations, so that the border clash may touch off any moment'. China, claiming to stand for peaceful settlement of the dispute, blamed India for creating a tense situation on the borders. Claiming that the doors for negotiations were still open, China asked India to stop its military provocations. Such warnings were becoming worrying to Delhi.[35] India repeated its unfortunate understanding that in 1954 'there was no difference of opinion between the two countries regarding the boundary alignment and that the present tension on the borders was the result of subsequent Chinese aggressive activities'.[36] (For a detailed discussion of this, please see Chapter 7.)

On 13 June 1962, members in the Lok Sabha expressed concern at the reported movement of Chinese tanks and armoured vehicles in the Indian territory occupied by China. Defence Minister Menon denied any knowledge of such a development. Even when the members persisted with the question, Menon insisted, 'We know nothing about these tanks or anything.' Despite Menon's denial, members would not be satisfied. The prime minister intervened and said, 'We have no information about . . . MIG fighters or tanks in western Tibet.' He dismissed the whole thing saying that 'I think much of this information that sometimes appear in the press, we have found, has little justification or basis'. When the members still persisted, a desperate Nehru said, 'I do maintain, Sir, that the kind of questions that have been asked are not helpful in building up the morale of the country . . .'[37]

From July 1962, the relations between the two countries entered the crucial stage which finally triggered the conflict. On 8 July 1962, China accused Indian troops for violations in the Galwan Valley area in the western sector and warned that while it was trying to avoid a clash, it would 'never yield before an ever deeper armed advance by India, nor will give up its right to self-defence when unwarrantedly attacked'.[38]

On 10 July, China in yet another note accused Indian troops of further violations at several places and of establishing a new military strong point west of the Spanggur Lake in Chinese territory.[39] The Indian note of 12 July 1962 confirmed seven Chinese posts in the Chip Chap River region, and one each in Chang Chenmo Valley and Spanggur region. It said six of the nine posts were 'not only well inside Indian territory but well beyond even the boundary alignment claimed by the Govt. of China' in their 1956 map.[40] The Chinese note of 13 July yet again demanded Indian withdrawal from the Galwan Valley to avoid any untoward incident and accused India of reinforcing its armed strength and isolating the Chinese from their post along the Galwan River. The Chinese claimed that 'as part of the whole Aksai Chin area, the lower reaches of the Galwan Valley have always been Chinese territory'.[41] In the following weeks, both sides continued to make claims and counterclaims to the Galwan Valley, Pangong Tso and other places in their vicinity. Both continued to charge each other of committing border violations.

On 6 August 1962, the prime minister, making a statement in the Lok Sabha on the situation in the areas of Galwan and Chip Chap Valleys, said that the recent increase in tension in the Ladakh region 'has been the direct result of intensified Chinese military activities which is inconsistent with the Chinese professions of their desire to settle the question by peaceful negotiations'. He said, '[I]n recent weeks troops in superior strength have sometimes come up close to our posts with a view to harassing and intimidating them.' An undaunted Nehru said, '[W]e will not hesitate to meet any threat to our territorial integrity with firmness and where necessary, by force.' He, however, added that for any further discussions on the report of the officials to take place, 'the climate has to be created first'.[42] On 17 August, there was a firing incident at the Galwan Valley for which China accused the Indian troops.[43] On 22 August, India said that China had set up 'no less than 18 new aggressive military posts deep inside Indian territory, 10 in Chip Chap region, 2 in Galwan Valley region, 3 in Pangong-Spanggur region and 2 in Qara Qash region'.[44] A week later, India reported another four posts (two each in Pongong-Spanggur and Qara Qash regions) which the Chinese had set up in Ladakh.[45] On 7 September, India yet again reported that China had set up two additional posts, one each in Chang Chanmo Valley and Pongong-Spanggur region.[46] China claimed that India had set up six strong points in Chinese territory in the regions of Sinkiang, Chip Chap Valley and Pangong-Spanggur areas.[47]

Such accusatory notes always ended with warnings such as the one given on 21 July by the Chinese:

> [A]t this critical moment, the Chinese Government demands that the Indian Government immediately order the Indian troops to stop attacking the aforesaid Chinese posts and withdraw from the area lest the situation should further aggravate. If the Indian Government should ignore the warning of the Chinese Government and continues to persist in its own way, India must bear the full responsibility for all the consequences that may arise there from.[48]

Two days later, on 23 July, Defence Minister Krishna Menon, meeting Chen Yi over breakfast in Geneva, discussed ways and means to cool the situation. Chen Yi rejected any proposal coming from Menon out of hand. Their discussions did not contribute to any relaxation of tension either.[49] Nehru speaking in the Lok Sabha on 14 August said that he had told Menon 'to meet him [Chen Yi] and talk to him, he could not negotiate. There is no question of any negotiations'.[50] But a week later, the deputy external affairs minister, Dinesh Singh, in an answer to a question raised in the Rajya Sabha, said that Menon in his talks with Chen Yi 'had expressly referred to the serious situation created in Ladakh by the unlawful infiltration of Chinese forces.

The Chinese foreign minister had however, refused to accept this and tried to place the onus on India. There was no specific outcome of these discussions'.[51]

On 29 July 1962, while addressing the meeting of the Uttar Pradesh Congress Legislature Party, Nehru said that though he did not want a war with China, the situation along the northern border had worsened of late, and he thereby did not rule out 'some chance' of an armed conflict breaking out. He assured the members that India was not weak; however, it was the terrain which had made it weak since, apart from other problems, it was even 'difficult for an ordinary man to breathe'.[52]

On 13 August 1962, the prime minister informed the Lok Sabha about incidents of Chinese firing in the Pangong Tso area and to the north-east of the Daulat Beg Oldi, but said that no damage was done. He reiterated India's precondition for talks, which was withdrawal of Chinese troops from areas in Ladakh which it had occupied since 1957. He would not accept the Chinese position, which claimed the area to be Chinese and it could not be expected to withdraw from its own areas.[53]

A week earlier, on 6 August, the prime minister had charged China with 'intimidating and harassing' Indian troops in the Chip Chap Valley and Pangong areas by intensified military activity. He had also claimed that the establishment of India's advance posts in various places had made it very difficult for Chinese troops to advance. He repeated his suggestion for talks, subject to an appropriate condition being created. Refusing to be intimidated by China's warnings, Nehru said:

> We will not hesitate to meet any threat to our territorial integrity
> with firmness and where necessary, by force.[54]

On 16 August, the prime minister told the Rajya Sabha that while it was difficult to give a precise estimate of the area seized by China, about 10,000 to 12,000 square miles were under Chinese occupation.

While measures had been taken to prevent further encroachments, the Chinese had not withdrawn from the already occupied area.[55]

On 22 August, Nehru informed the Rajya Sabha that, in the military sense, 'we are much stronger than we were a year or two ago'. He, however, continued to put his faith in India's clout in the non-aligned world which he thought would inhibit China in its aggressive approach.[56]

As far as armed strength was concerned, India remained diffident to meet the Chinese challenge. Already in August the Western Command of the army, which looked after the western sector, worried by its weakness of men, materials and logistics, had warned Delhi that 'political direction was not being based on military means'.[57]

The chief of general staff, Lt Gen. L.P. Sen, given the strength of the Western Command, cautioned the army headquarters that in view of its deficient resources 'forward patrolling as called for by the Government would invite a sharp Chinese reaction with the possibility of the international border, which is dormant at the moment, being active'. He further added that, with the limited strength available, the army would not be in a position to counter effectively any large-scale incursion by the Chinese. The defence ministry passed on this information to the Ministry of External Affairs and the latter was livid at the sluggishness of the army to implement decisions.[58]

Later when the army headquarters asked the Western Command to project its force demand in pursuit of forward policy in Ladakh, it again was found diffident to take on additional task without increase in logistical resources.[59]

The situation on the eastern front was hardly better. Lt Gen. Umrao Singh had informed the Eastern Command that 'an attempt to clear the Chinese south of the Thag La ridge would amount to rashness' and adequate resources in ration and ammunition were not available.[60]

In a surprise move, on 26 July 1962, Delhi asked its *charge d' affaires* in Beijing, P.K. Banerjee, to convey to Premier Zhou the following oral message:

India would be prepared to send a ministerial level delegation to Beijing to discuss without preconditions all bilateral problems and disputes.

Zhou being occupied, Chen Yi received Banerjee, and he found:

[The proposal] unacceptable unless the GOI unequivocally and publically withdrew all fictitious and false claims on Chinese territory. The present proposal was loaded with ammunition for Indian propaganda against the Chinese and it was a trap and therefore not acceptable.[61]

Banerjee informed Delhi of the above and received no further instructions.[62] The whole episode remained a mystery. The Chinese rejection of the above proposal perhaps also stemmed from the fact that a note received by them on the same day (26 July) through official channels had repeated the preconditions for talks, insisting on an 'appropriate climate' being created for negotiations.[63] China, therefore, considered the verbal offer of unconditional negotiations a trap. The prime minister's statement in Parliament on 6 August 1962 did not refer to any such offer having been made. Instead, his statement and subsequent notes repeated the precondition of China vacating the territory it was occupying in Ladakh since 1957.[64] The prime minister's statement of 6 August held China responsible for increase in the tension in the Galwan and Chip Chap Valleys, which was not in keeping with the Chinese assurances that they intend to settle the boundary question by peaceful negotiations.[65] On 13 August, there was a firing incident in the Galwan Valley. China accused the Indian troops for firing on Chinese frontier guards.[66]

Earlier, a note sent on 26 July by India had suggested talks between the two countries, based on the officials' report, but only after the current tension had eased. The precondition of an 'appropriate climate' being created proved a hard nut to crack.[67] The GoI had defined the 'appropriate climate' in its note of 6 July, when it said that while China could continue to use the road in Aksai Chin for civilian traffic, it must vacate the area it had occupied, particularly since 1957.[68]

Following the firing incident in the Chip Chap Valley, tension escalated. The facts, however, remained in dispute. In the notes exchanged on the incident, both blamed each other. India suggested talks and China showed willingness on the basis of the officials' report but repeated that 'there need not and should not be any preconditions for such discussions'. The Chinese note said since neither side wanted war and both wanted to settle the boundary through discussions, there should not be any further delay.[69]

Nehru, while presenting the White Paper No. 5 in Parliament on 6 August, had said that in view of the various steps taken by India it had become 'very difficult for Chinese forces to make any further advance now'. He referred to the Indian note of 14 May where the suggestion for mutual withdrawal in the western sector had been made to create the necessary atmosphere for talks. He regretted the fact that China had not given a concrete response.[70] In the meantime, there was a further spurt in incidents in the western sector, and both accused each other for intrusions and firing. The Indian note of 22 August 1962 accused China of progressively encroaching into Indian territory and at the same time using the Italian-Swiss Radio TV network for wider coverage of its point of view.[71] China continued to insist that asking it to withdraw from its own territory was 'impossible' and India was delaying negotiations on the pretext of restoring the status quo of the boundary which had been altered since 1957.[72] India believed that initiating negotiations without Chinese withdrawal would 'leave the aggressor who altered the status quo, 'in possession of the fruits of aggression'.[73]

It was a complete stalemate. India in its note of 19 September had proposed two-stage discussions—(1) to define measures to restore the status quo in the western sector and (2) implementation of (1) would create a climate of confidence 'which alone can make possible constructive discussions to resolve the differences between their Governments . . .'[74] In the meantime, clashes which for sometime were confined to western sector began taking place in the eastern sector too. An attack on Indian patrol, three miles to the south of the Thagla Ridge in the eastern sector, had resulted in three casualties.[75] In yet another incident, one Chinese was killed and one injured. The Chinese not only demanded compensation for the killed and injured, but also an apology.[76] This was a new situation. The attention now appeared to be shifting from the western sector to the eastern one. Che Dong in the eastern sector became the new hotspot. It was the place where the incident had taken place and China claimed it to be north of the Thagla Ridge in Chinese territory. On 20 September, China had already lodged a protest against the Indian troops crossing the McMahon Line and establishing an aggressive strongpoint at Che Dong, Le Village.[77] India rejected China's accusation of crossing the Thagla Ridge, which was the boundary defined by the McMahon line in that region, and instead accused China of intruding south of the line into Che Dong of Le village in the Indian territory. India described the Chinese demand for apology as 'misconceived' and insisted that no Indian forces or defence works of any kind existed to the north of the Thagla Ridge.[78] Along with these fresh cases of intrusion in the eastern region, the incidents of border violations in the western sector, too, continued unabated.

Che Dong in the NEFA area had become active since 8 September. It was under dispute, as China claimed that it lay north of the McMahon Line and India insisted it was south of it. In its note of 13 October, China accused India of air-dropping its soldiers north of the McMahon Line 'in preparation for war' and warned that the Chinese frontier guards would continue to strike back resolutely.[79] India had rejected the Chinese accusation and accused China of adopting a 'dual' policy of professing a desire for peaceful settlement, while pursuing the 'path of flagrant aggression'. India strongly asserted that 'no threat of force or use of force (would) deter the GoI from their firm determination to defend the territorial integrity of India'.[80]

The escalation in border incidents and casualties bode ill for peace between the two neighbours. A worried Government of India had for some time been thinking of measures to retrieve some of its freshly occupied territory by China in the eastern sector. It thought that this would convey a strong message to China—that India would not take Chinese intrusions lying down any more. At a review meeting in the chamber of the minister of defence on 22 September, the chief of army staff had asked specifically 'whether action to evict the Chinese can be taken as soon as the *Brigade has concentrated*'. It was pointed out that 'the decision throughout has been, as discussed in the previous meeting, that the army should prepare and *throw the Chinese out as soon as possible*. The Chief of the Army Staff was accordingly directed to take action for the *eviction of the Chinese in Kameng division of NEFA* as soon as he was ready'.[81]

It was clearly meant to be a limited action by a *brigade* in the specific area of Kemong Division where the Thagla Ridge was located. A brigade could not launch attacks all along the border, stretching for thousands of kilometres. Nehru on 12 October, while he was leaving for Colombo, said to journalists at the airport that he had issued instructions to the army to clear the Indian territory of Chinese intrusions, and the date for it had been left to the army to decide.[82] This impromptu remark proved most unfortunate. Coming from the highest political authority, it sounded like a war bugle. Nehru's was an unqualified statement giving the impression that India was about to undertake some action against China. It provided China an *alibi* to act on its aggressive agenda all along the borders in both the sectors in full force. Some confusion had already been created by a press report in the *Times of India* that said:

> [A] task force was being sent to NEFA charged with pushing the Chinese out.[83]

It was probably a leak, but a garbled version of the above-mentioned decision had appeared in the *Times of India*. Nehru objected to the report and asked the army chief, Gen. Thapar, on 5 October 1962 about it and yet, a week later, he himself made that provocative statement. Though the *Times of India* report was denied, the real damage was done by Nehru's casual but provocative warning to China. Two days after Nehru's warning, on 14 October, Defence Minister Krishna Menon poured more fuel to the fire with his thundering speech in Bangalore where he reiterated: 'India's determination to push the invading Chinese out of NEFA areas ...'[84] His remarks following the prime minister's did give the impression that something indeed was cooking. These remarks were exploited by the Chinese to pin the responsibility for the war on India's shoulders.

Nehru's biographer, Dr Gopal, making light of Nehru's remarks described it as a 'wholly unobjectionable statement'. He said that the policy of evicting the Chinese was not a new one, and he quoted another statement of Nehru in Colombo, 'I do not think they have the slightest claim, historically, politically, or anything'.[85] Whatever the justification, to announce publically and casually a decision with wide implications, when the tension on the borders was already running high, could hardly be described as prudent.

Gopal felt there was no complacency in Nehru's approach. Nehru had seen that the situation in the eastern sector was deteriorating fast and, at long last, he had realized that trouble on a big scale was in the offing.[86]

Was India actually prepared or was preparing for the action that happened on 20 October? If one were to analyse the above-mentioned decision of the meeting held at the defence ministry, it was meant to be a localized affair in the Kemong Division of the NEFA in the area where border violations were taking place in recent days. A brigade can take action in a limited area specifically assigned to it. Even otherwise, the ground situation and the circumstances did not justify a large-scale action. Defence Minister Krishna Menon was in New York from 17 to 30 September to attend the UNGA session.

On 8 September, the prime minister had left for London to attend the Commonwealth Prime Ministers' Conference and returned only on 2 October after visiting Paris, Lagos and Accra and was again away to Colombo for a pre-scheduled engagement from 12 to 16 October. The chief of general staff, Lt Gen. Kaul, was holidaying in Kashmir until 2 October. It is inconceivable that a country preparing for a war would allow its top political leaders and military brass, responsible for crucial war-related decisions, to be away from the capital.

As against this, if one were to look at the massive attack China launched all along the frontier in both the eastern and western sectors, it would convince anybody that China indeed was in any case ready for an all-out war, as otherwise, logistically speaking, it was not possible to gather such a massive force scattered along the most challenging borders in a week's time after Nehru's impromptu remarks of 12 October.

That China had actually decided to go to war with India on the border question has been admitted by a Chinese scholar Chaowu Dai, distinguished professor at the Yunnan University and the director of YNU Institute for India Studies in Kunming, who in his lengthy paper said:

> [From 1960 to October 1962] judging that India was unwilling to negotiate a solution, China made preparations for deployment of its military and adopted a policy of "never yield while striving to avoid bloodshed, create interlocking positions for long-term armed coexistence" on the border issue ultimately proceeding to the border conflict.[87]

It appeared that by this time Mao had concluded that to bring India round to the Chinese position on the borders needed a different kind of treatment; it needed to strike hard. Beijing had come to believe that India's forward policy stemmed from its design on Tibet. As late as 16 October 1962, an internal Chinese report claimed that India's aggressive posture reflected its desire to make Tibet an Indian 'colony or protectorate'.[88]

Even the Chinese note of 3 October was ominous and full of forebodings. It accused India of answering Chinese peace proposals with 'rifles and guns'. Declaring the McMahon Line as 'utterly illegal' and accusing India of crossing it and firing at Chinese frontier guards, it warned that 'China is sure to strike back'. It charged India with 'downright hypocrisy' insisting on preconditions for talks, while China put no such preconditions.[89] Apparently, Mao had directed the central military committee to launch a 'fierce and painful' attack by a coordinated assault in both the sectors.[90]

Be that as it may, Nehru's impromptu remarks provided an *alibi* to China.

The *People's Daily* in its 14 October editorial said:

So it seems that Mr. Nehru has made up his mind to attack China on an even bigger scale.[91]

China, too, made use of Nehru's remarks to justify its attack on India to the Soviets. The Chinese Ambassador in Delhi told the Soviet counterpart that India was precipitating the conflict to receive American money and also that Defence Minister Krishna Menon, when confronted with the facts of the latest clash, had acknowledged that the clash had taken place in an area north of the McMahon Line, but would not admit it.[92]

China, to queer the pitch for India, once again on 11 October accused it of intruding into Che Dong in the eastern sector and attacking the Chinese frontier guards, killing and wounding twenty-two of them. China further claimed that when China counter-attacked, six Indians were killed and their bodies were left behind by the Indians, whom the Chinese had buried.[93]

Internationally, China found the situation perfectly conducive to its plans. President Kennedy had announced a naval blockade to prevent the Soviet nuclear missiles being ferried to Cuba, where, if they were placed, they would threaten United States' security. The world faced the possibility of a nuclear war between the two superpowers. China was convinced that Moscow would fall in line with its plans and would not dare to oppose its actions, since it would need China's support in its confrontation with the US.

The Chinese calculations proved right. Caught in the Cuban conundrum, the Soviet Union chose to propitiate Beijing and appreciated its efforts to end and settle the dispute with India peacefully. Swearing by the 'unbreakable fraternal friendship', Moscow agreed with Beijing that 'McMahon Line is not an established boundary' but an imperialist legacy.[94] In a separate communication on the same day, Moscow assured Beijing that the aircraft and helicopters that it had sold to India had 'no military significance' and would 'not affect the balance of power'.[95]

India, not appearing to be intimidated after China's attack on the Thagla Ridge, prior to its all-out attack, warned China that 'it cannot and will not permit intrusions and aggressive activities against the Indian defence forces in Indian territory to go unchallenged'. The note added that it was the Chinese who had to accept the 'guilt' for intruding into the Indian territory and mounting concerted attacks. Blaming China for refusing to create 'the appropriate climate for purposeful talks and discussions', India held it responsible for creating further tension and conflict in the eastern sector.[96] In yet another note on 19 October, India challenged Chinese allegations of firing by the Indian side as 'absolutely baseless' and said 'no threat of force or use of force by the Chinese will deter the GoI from their firm determination to defend the territorial integrity of India'.[97] Nehru, whether actually prepared or not, did not want to lose the battle of nerves.

Already in his letter of 12 October to the chief ministers of the states, Nehru had conveyed the impending danger of escalation of tension in the north-east which might 'lead to major conflict'. He mentioned the developing dangerous situation where 'petty conflicts were going on in the NEFA border and [there was] an ever-present possibility of a large conflict', which had made it all the more difficult 'for us to sit down at the table to discuss our controversies'.[98] A day after China's attack, Nehru in yet another letter of 21 October to the chief ministers expressed his confidence that India was prepared for any eventuality, and as a proof he claimed that in a recent clash only eleven Indians were killed but on the Chinese side the casualties were 'probably 100'. He considered the attack to be only a border incident, as he said 'petty conflicts' could turn into a 'larger conflict.' Sounding confident, he said:

> We shall build our strength, both military and economic, to win this battle of Indian freedom. We shall always be willing to negotiate peace, but that can only be on conditions that aggression is vacated. We can never submit or surrender to aggression. That has not been our way and that will not be our way in the future.[99]

These were ominous developments. He found to his regret that his earlier perceptions of the Himalayas providing security to the northeast were erroneous. The confidence that he repeatedly exuded in the Himalayas, its terrain and the climate was proving deceptive.

In the meantime, China in its statement (which was also repeated in Zhou's letter to Nehru), while recalling the history of the dispute, suggested disengagement along 20 kilometres and talks between the two prime ministers once again.[100] Nehru described his proposal as old, something which India had already rejected, and likened it to 'demand for surrender' to which India could not agree. He did not feel it was merely a question of territorial dispute, which could have been settled by talks, but was the following:

> [One of] peaceful coexistence between States with different social systems. The Chinese Government seems to have decided against peaceful coexistence between the Chinese social system and the Indian way of life.[101]

To allay Soviet concerns on the deteriorating situation between India and China, Nehru took the Soviet leader Khrushchev into confidence and in his letter of 22 October recalled for his benefit the long history of border dispute and also mentioned his efforts in the past to get China its rightful place in the UN and the world. He insisted that any effort at peace must be preceded by restoration of 'status quo as it was prior to 8 September (1962)'. The reference to 8 September was actually a reference to the Chinese intrusion in the Thagla Ridge area in the eastern sector. Nehru, not concentrating on the Thagla Ridge alone, said when it was vacated, '[W]e could then consider what further agreed steps should be taken to correct the situation created by the earlier unilateral alteration of the status quo of the boundary . . .' to start the negotiations. Now his terms for negotiations had become even more rigid than before.[102]

The Soviet leader Khrushchev, however, advised Nehru not to look back but ahead and work for a ceasefire by 'accepting Zhou's proposals', which he said were 'reasonable because they contain the main basis for the settlement of the dispute—to ceasefire immediately without any preconditions . . . and sit down on the table of negotiations'. He also in his letter referred to China as 'a neighbour and brother' and India a 'neighbour' with whom Moscow had friendly relations.[103] It may be recalled that in 1959 Khrushchev had advised India in favour of tranquil borders by settling the borders by give and take. The present advice was also in line with the earlier advice.

Stunned by initial reverses on the borders, Nehru in his address to the nation on 22 October wrote off north-east India when he said *my heart goes to the people of Assam* which then included apart from Assam, Nagaland, Meghalaya, Mizoram and NEFA (now Arunachal Pradesh).[104] It, too, would have been a loss of the states of Manipur and Tripura. [The official version of his speech omits the line in italics but the author vouches for its authenticity, since he himself had heard the speech.] Later, however, Nehru tried to explain it away to the speaker of Assam's legislative assembly by saying that he was greatly pained at what had happened.[105]

Nehru, in his briefings to the heads of foreign government, gave a summary of the dispute and accused China of occupying 112,000 square miles of Indian territory. He appealed to them for their sympathy and support, 'not because of their friendly relations with us but also because our struggle is in the interest of world peace and is directed to the elimination of deceit, dissimulation and force in international relations'.[106] Separately, he also addressed personal letters to some select heads of government—such as those of Pakistan, Ceylon, Yugoslavia, Egypt, Ghana and Nepal. The responses, particularly from Ceylon and Yugoslavia, were extremely positive while others showed mere concern and sympathy. Pakistan's response was unfortunate. President Ayub Khan, taking a jibe at Nehru, said:

I agree with you when you say that no effort should be spared to eliminate deceit and force from relations. In this respect I am constrained to point out that various outstanding disputes between India and Pakistan can also be settled amicably should the GOI decide to apply these principles with sincerity and conviction.[107]

Nehru, replying to Zhou's letter, expressed his deep anguish and said:

Nothing in my long political career has hurt and grieved me more than the fact that the hopes and aspirations for peaceful and friendly neighbourly relations which we entertained, and to promote which my colleagues in the Government of India and myself worked so hard, ever since the establishment of the People's Republic of China, should have been shattered by the hostile and unfriendly twist given in India–China relations during the past few years. The current clashes on the India–China border arising out of what is in effect a Chinese invasion of India, which you have described as 'most distressing', are the final culmination of the deterioration in relations between India and China.[108]

Showing no apparent signs of being overawed by Chinese invasion, and the reverses at the front, he minced no words to tell Zhou that 'an attack on this scale could only have been made after careful preparations' and expressed deep regrets that China had 'paid back India with evil for good', and blamed China acting with 'sheer hypocrisy'. Accepting Zhou's offer for talks either at Beijing or Delhi, Nehru preferred the later city as the venue but only after his original precondition of China's return to the pre-8 September 1962 position had been met.[109]

Since both could not agree on the basic facts, the Chinese attack gathered momentum and Indian forces had to repeatedly fall back. Zhou continued to repeat that the Aksai Chin area had always been in China's possession. He challenged the argument that China came to this area only in 1957. Ironically, China regarded the present conflict only as 'border incidents' where its 'frontier guards' were involved. The fact that China did not mention the involvement of the People's Liberation Army was significant.[110]

Even in the midst of military reverses, Nehru remained firm on the necessity of 'minimum corrective action'. He insisted that until 8 September 'no Chinese forces had crossed the frontier between India and China in the eastern sector as defined by India, that is, along the highest watershed in the region, in accordance with the Agreement of 1914'. He insisted the restoration of the status quo ante 8 September 1962 for starting any dialogue on the borders.[111]

India, to make up its shortage of war material and other supplies, had requested the United States and the United Kingdom for urgent airlifting of war material and they responded with speed. The situation was not retrieved and the Indian Army continued to suffer reverses. At midnight of 19 November, Zhou summoned *Charge d'affaires* Banerjee and told him that 'Nehru was being misled with wrong advice' and he who had followed the policy of non-alignment was now accepting military aid while 'there was still time to stop the war and negotiate'. That was also the day when Nehru had written two letters to President Kennedy and perhaps Zhou had got a wind of them and that had made him summon Banerjee the very next day again. He had no clue why he was being summoned within twenty-four hours of the last meeting. This time, he was asked to come half an hour past midnight, and on arrival was told of China's decision to call a ceasefire. Zhou wanted Banerjee to convey to Nehru 'to turn a new page of peace, friendship and cooperation between China and India'. As Banerjee came out of the meeting, he found that before him a Reuters correspondent had already been briefed about the ceasefire.[112] Reuters made sure that the news was flashed all over the world instantly.

India's stand on its preconditions proved a villain of a piece. In a rancorous situation, it is normal practice for the two parties to the dispute to enter into negotiations and discuss without preconditions to find a solution acceptable to both. If China were to vacate the areas, as demanded by Nehru, extensive areas which China claimed to be its own, it would put itself in the wrong even before the negotiations began.

A few days after the border conflict had begun, the *People's Daily* carried an indictment of India and its prime minister under the title, 'More on Nehru's Philosophy in the Light of Sino-Indian Boundary Question'. It was a very long article which traced the history of India–China relations, and said India wished China not to become a strong country; not to develop industry; not to develop military strength; not to have a large population; and not to be India's neighbour and to change its geographical location. Repudiating the past history of China's conquests it insisted that now the socialist China would fight for peace and against aggression and as proof mentioned the friendship treaties it had signed with other countries. He used Nehru's book *Discovery of India* to show Nehru's chauvinistic tendencies and his feudal mindset. It examined the Indian class structure of big bourgeoisie and big landlords who were 'represented by Nehru' and analysed their relations with the British bourgeoisie.[113]

In short, it found everything wrong with Indian society and its history before and since Independence, including its leadership.

By the time of the ceasefire, the Indian Army had suffered all round reverses, exposing Nehru's claim of being prepared for any eventuality as hollow. His policy of non-alignment, too, suffered a severe jolt when he had to request the United States and the United Kingdom for all manner of military equipment, though in the past they were at the receiving end of his stick for their policies on issues of war, peace and security. In his letter of 19 November, Nehru had practically outsourced the defence of India to the United States, since he feared that China would capture the whole of eastern India and much more. India had heaved a sigh of relief when China announced ceasefire.

Though there was no immediate need for American military assistance, it nevertheless appeared imperative to shore up India's defences against any future eventuality. Nehru's past policies were in tatters and its policy of non-alignment, too, stood discredited. Much against his past thinking, a major drive was launched to build a strong defence force. And also much against his wishes, he had to part company with his protégé Krishan Menon who was made to resign from the post of defence minister. The president of India on 26 October issued a proclamation under Clause (1) Article 352 of the Constitution of India to declare a state of emergency because of China's 'betrayal' of India.[114] Persons of Chinese origin, settled in India for long time, were rounded up and put in camps, since they were considered a security risk.[115] Eventually, China repatriated most of them to China. China, declaring the ceasefire on 21 November effective from the midnight of 22 November, had reiterated its earlier three proposals of 24 October for a settlement and had also announced its decision to withdraw from 1 December 1962, 20 kilometres 'behind the line of actual control which existed between China and India on 7 November, 1959', thereby 'the Chinese frontier guards will be far behind their positions prior to September 8, 1962'. While doing so it warned India:

> [That should the] Indian troops cross the line of actual control and recover their positions prior to September 8, that is to say, cross the illegal McMahon Line and reoccupy the Kechilang river area north of the line in the eastern sector, reoccupy Wuje (Longju) in the

middle sector, and restore their 43 strong points for aggression in
the Chip Chap River Valley, the Galwan River Valley, the Pangong
Lake area, and the Demchok area or set up more strong points for
aggression on Chinese territory in the western sector the Chinese
Government solemnly declares that should the above eventualities
occur, the Indian Government will be held completely responsible
for all the grave consequences arising there from.[116]

In the statement earlier, Zhou again suggested talks between the two
prime ministers and invited Nehru to Beijing, and added should it
be inconvenient for him to come to Beijing, he himself would be
prepared to come to Delhi.

Zhou, in another letter of 28 November to the prime minister,
said that in taking this decision the Chinese Government had given
'full consideration to the decency, dignity and self-respect of both
sides' and suggested that while the measures China had decided to
take were 'not conditional on simultaneous corresponding measure
to be taken by the Indian side', he stressed that unless India, too,
took similar measures it would not prevent the recurrence of border
clashes. He added if India agreed to his above proposal, then officials
of both the countries could meet in various places on the border 'to
discuss matters relating the 20-km withdrawal of the armed forces of
each party to form demilitarized zone, the establishment of checkposts of each party on its own side of the line of actual control and the
return of captured personnel'. Remaining hopeful, Zhou said China
had taken the first step of declaring the ceasefire and 'is going to take
the second step i.e., withdrawal. I hope the Indian Government will
give positive response and make efforts in the same direction'.[117]

Nehru, however, confirmed the ceasefire in his statement in the
Lok Sabha on 10 December. He also agreed to the disengagement
but added a rider that it could be on the basis of agreed arrangement,
that is, China vacating the aggression committed as on 8 September
1962. Regarding the meeting of officials to create a demilitarized
zone, he said that it was subject to clear and precise instructions as to

the ceasefire and withdrawal arrangements which the officials were supposed to implement.[118] Zhou, in yet another letter, persisted on disengagement since without that stability of the border could not be ensured and clashes could occur. In the absence of Indian disengagement, Zhou suggested that when the Chinese forces were withdrawing, 'Indian troops should stay in their present positions along the entire Sino-Indian border'. He suggested that in the meantime the officials of the two countries should meet 'to discuss such matters of withdrawal arrangements for the disengagement of the armed forces of the two sides, establishment of check-posts and return of captured personnel.'[119]

Nehru, replying to Zhou, again went over past history and said he had not seen any Chinese in Ladakh during his visits in the last seven or eight years. Nehru, in stating this, contradicted himself when he repeatedly stressed that it was an area where no habitation was possible and there was no vegetation and not a blade of grass grew.

Regarding any future course of action, he insisted on China fulfilling his earlier laid down precondition of China returning to the position of 8 September 1962.[120] The exchange of correspondence led them to no concrete position and a stalemate was created which has continued to this day. China did vacate the areas south of the McMahon Line and India reoccupied them. In the western sector, China remained entrenched in all those areas which it had claimed to be its territory. Since Nehru had not agreed to an agreed disengagement and creation of a demilitarized zone, no official line exists either on the ground or on any map showing the position of the two armies on the 21 November 1962, when the Chinese had called a unilateral ceasefire.

There are various views why China launched such a major offensive if it had to withdraw from occupied areas eventually. Nehru himself remained puzzled and thought that the Chinese invasion was more than a territorial dispute, as he told the chief ministers of the state:

Countries do not take such action involving dangerous consequences without a much deeper reason.[121]

In his interview to a Japanese newspaper *Mainichi*, he said, 'I suppose they do not like India's social structure to be advancing. They wanted to know their strength and superiority and influence (over) other countries in Asia.' He also said 'it is Chinese expansionism supported, if you like, by Communist ideas'.[122]

As speculated earlier, the Chinese attack was not related to territory or boundary question. In the words of Liu Shaoqi, it was 'to demolish India's arrogance and illusion of grandeur'. He said, 'China had taught India a lesson and would do so again and again.'[123]

Later in 1972, Zhou had told President Nixon:

He (Nehru) was so discourteous; he wouldn't even do us the courtesy of replying, so we had no choice but to drive him out. So we had gone to war, justifiably in 1962 to teach India a lesson.[124]

One reason why Zhou spoke of the discourtesy could be that he was made to call on the home and finance ministers when he came in April 1960, which was breach of even elementary protocol. It must have rankled in his mind all this time.

Nehru had believed it was a sort of competition between the Chinese way of socialism and India's way of peaceful development. China wanted to prove India's policies a failure and not worthy of being emulated by other countries.

One other reason, and probably the most important one, was perhaps China's fear of getting bogged down in the wintry conditions that had already set in and sustaining a large force with its lines of communication and supplies stretching across the high icy Himalayas across long distances, which would expose its army into an untold misery.

Yet another reason which could be speculated was that the campaign had achieved its objective. China had repeatedly shown readiness to accept the McMahon Line and by withdrawing from the area south of that line showed its seriousness to its commitment. Their main objective was India's acceptance of its strategic claim to the western sector forever as a *quid pro quo*. Even though China did not get India's acceptance by declaring the ceasefire, it had achieved it practically and India was no longer capable of challenging it.

The maxim of 'strong nations secure borders' asserted itself. A weak nation having disproportionate confidence in its strength had to suffer the ignominy at the hands of the strong. The wisdom of agreed borders asserted itself. Nehru cared for neither of the two. The 1962 conflict and Nehru's second letter of 19 November to President Kennedy stand testimony to the truth of both.

India's was a self-imposed double whammy—unilaterally declaring its borders, making them sacrosanct and not developing muscles in their defence nor negotiating them to create an agreed border. Delhi would not even negotiate unless its impossible precondition was met. As the narrative bears out, Nehru himself had doubts on China's acceptance of Indian borders. Similarly, India unilaterally altering the international border in the western sector from 'undefined' to 'defined' was a miscalculation. Being an international border, India needed to consult the other stakeholder before drawing a line to make the border defined or demarcated. If the British had left the border in the Ladakh region undefined, it was because no consensus had been built with China. Nehru's insistence that India's borders were what they were, maps or no maps, was unsustainable and proved disastrous for him and the nation which felt humiliated and demoralized.

12

1962 and After

By the time China declared ceasefire, India had been sufficiently demoralized. Its army was in retreat all along in both the eastern and the western sectors. A day before China declared ceasefire, Nehru, facing a desperate situation, had sent two letters to President Kennedy. It was evident from the second letter dated 19 November 1962 that the situation had gone beyond India's ability to face the Chinese. He feared:

Unless something is not done immediately to stem the tide the whole of Assam, Tripura, Manipur and Nagaland would pass into Chinese hands. The Chinese have poised massive force in the Chumbi Valley between Sikkim and Bhutan and another invasion from that direction appears imminent.

Other areas threatened, as mentioned by Nehru were, Uttar Pradesh, Punjab and Himachal Pradesh, as also Ladakh.[1]

He thanked him for the assistance already provided and mentioned that now 'more comprehensive assistance' was required if eastern India was to be saved from the Chinese. He not only asked for war material but also requested for full air cover, including fighter and transport aircraft, radar cover, and so on, all *manned by the U.S. Air Force personnel*, since India had neither facilities nor trained manpower to handle them. He also asked for two squadrons of B-47 bombers.[2] It was a tall order. He virtually asked the United States to join the war against China. This was surprising for a country which until the other day had been deriding the United States. The ceasefire saved much of the humiliation by obviating the need for 'American military boots' on the Indian soil.

One can get an idea of the desperate situation that prevailed from the fact that the Ministry of Defence had initiated studies of resistance stories from other countries, how they, in similar desperate situations, had organized their resistance against foreign invaders. The author, who was then working in the Joint Intelligence Organisation of the Ministry of Defence had conducted one such study of the Cypriot resistance movement. Similarly, other officers were asked to conduct studies of other resistance movements in some other countries.

Now that the ceasefire had been declared, Nehru, too, started thinking of how best to resolve the issue. Arbitration or reference to the International Court of Justice was one of the alternatives he thought about, but he remained sceptical of China accepting either of them.[2] As a larger policy issue, he told the Maharaja of Bhutan that India would not negotiate with China 'unless they agree to our proposal, namely the restoration of at least the status quo prior to 8th September 1962, when the Chinese aggression started'.[3] Ironically, a couple of days after the Chinese attack, Nehru decided to support the Soviet resolution on China's admission to the UN since India supported the principle of 'universality of membership of the UN, the only effective way to check the Chinese military adventure is to make her accept her responsibility as member of the world organisation and be subject to the views and discipline of this world organisation'.[4]

Delhi in a note to China on 4 December 1962 had said that Chen Yi's stand 'that no force in the world could oblige Chinese troops to withdraw from their own territory' had made a mockery of the Chinese desire for discussion on the border question. It once again reiterated its willingness to enter into discussions provided the latest aggression of the Chinese government was vacated.[5]

China yet again described the Indian claim that Che Dong was situated on the Indian side as 'wholly groundless'. As regards Longju, it said, 'Longju is a village in the Migyitun area, and India itself has admitted Migyitun is situated on the north of the illegal McMahon Line.' China added that it was invaded and occupied by Indian troops in June 1959 but recovered by China in August 1959 when China had restored its administrative control and since maintained a post there. China described the Indian claim of a mutual agreement between them that neither side would occupy it was a 'pure fabrication'.[6]

There remained a major gap in the understanding of the two countries regarding negotiations, as Nehru told the editor of the *New Statesman* (of London), Kingsley Martin. He said the disputed area 'included strategic points of great importance to India'. Replying to his question 'whether it was physically possible to drive the Chinese from this area', Nehru said, 'he was not thinking of a military attack but of bringing such pressure on the Chinese to induce them to be reasonable'. Regarding the absence of support from the non-aligned countries, he said, 'He would have liked the nonaligned powers to refer to China's recent aggression, but he understood and did not resent their reticence.'[7]

For the future, Nehru decided to focus on building a strong defence mechanism, and embarked on a major expansion of the defence forces and arms procurement from the Western countries, principally the United States and the United Kingdom, and sent their heads of government personal letters.[8]

He justified foreign arms assistance, in the context of his policy of non-alignment, which he now believed was a result of the war experience and had its own dynamics. He said:

War has its own momentum . . . sometime we have to do such things as obtaining arms aid from various countries, especially the

west, which normally we would not have done. But when one has
to struggle for existence one has to do this kind of thing.[9]

He, however, remained firm that in accepting foreign military aid he
did not propose to accept terms 'which are humiliating'.[10]
Lest Bhutan should have doubts about India's commitment
to its defence in the new circumstances, on 6 December the prime
minister conveyed to the Maharaja of Bhutan that 'the destines of
Bhutan and India are inextricably linked together (and) I would like
to assure Your Highness that the defence and other needs of Bhutan
are foremost in our mind'.[11]
    Fearing another Chinese attack if India did not accept the
Chinese terms for negotiations, Nehru assured President Kennedy
that India would do nothing to provoke China.[12]
    Deferring to the suggestions which, under the circumstances,
amounted to pressure from the United States and the United Kingdom,
India reluctantly entered into talks with Pakistan to resolve the Kashmir
imbroglio. After six unsuccessful rounds, the talks were abandoned.
Pakistan, however, continued to dub the India–China conflict as nothing
more than a border clash 'brought upon by India's own impetuosity'
for using it 'to re-arm itself not necessarily against China but against
. . . her No.1 enemy, that is, Pakistan'.[13] Soviet Ambassador Vladimir
Benediktov, on his return from Moscow, conveyed Khrushchev's
greetings and in trying to reassure Nehru said Moscow was looking
for some way to settle the India–China conflict by negotiations.[14] The
real thinking of Moscow on the dispute came from Soviet Defence
Minister Marshal Rodion Malinovsky, who had a lengthy meeting with
Ambassador T.N. Kaul on 15 December 1962. It was Kaul's assessment
that Khrushchev was largely advised by the Marshal about the Sino-
Indian borders. The suggestions he made to Kaul to resolve the issue
were in line with what Khrushchev had advised the Indian ambassador
in 1959. The Marshal lamented that given the inhospitable climate and
barrenness of Aksai Chin, it was not of any particular importance or
value to either of the two countries and both were standing on prestige,
otherwise the problem could be settled easily if they sat together and

negotiated.[15] Kaul said in the Marshal's opinion neither was China capable of defeating India nor India of defeating China. Kaul doubted if the Soviet Union and the socialist countries would remain neutral if 'we were driven willy-nilly into an open war with China'.[16]

War left China in occupation of the Aksai Chin in the western sector. In the east, China had vacated areas south of the McMahon Line which India reoccupied. The line of actual control between them remained nebulous and indefinable since Nehru had not agreed to China's proposal to create a non-militarized zone between the two armies.[16a]

At the initiative of Sri Lankan Prime Minister Sirimavo Bandaranaike, six nonaligned countries—Sri Lanka, UAR (Egypt), Burma, Indonesia, Cambodia and Ghana—met in Colombo and agreed on a set of proposals which could possibly bring both India and China to the negotiating table. She attached the proposals emerging from the conference, with her letter to Nehru, and suggested that as per the Conference decision she would visit Delhi and Beijing personally and explain the proposals to the prime ministers of the two countries. She sought Nehru's convenience for her visit to Delhi.[17]

A three-nation delegation composed of Ceylon, UAR and Ghana were in Delhi from 10 to 14 January 1963. The members of the delegation explained the proposals at some length to Nehru and, similarly, they visited Beijing and explained the same to the Chinese Premier. Essentially, Nehru found them acceptable and worthy of further consideration taking into account the clarifications personally provided by the visiting delegation. The proposal for a demilitarized zone in the western sector was considered a substantive part of the proposals.[18]

The principles that the conference followed in devising its proposals were unexceptional:

(i)   To create an atmosphere for peaceful resolution of the dispute;

(ii) The proposals intended to create such an atmosphere;

(iii) The Conference welcomed the unilateral declaration of ceasefire and withdrawal made by China;

(iv) Neither side should benefit from military operations;
stable ceasefire was to precede any attempt to negotiations,
and the ceasefire should be without prejudice to the claims
of either side.[19]

Before the arrival of Bandaranaike, Nehru had described the proposals
'vague'. He gave a 'lukewarm endorsement' to the proposals in his
interview to W.B. Friedenberg, which was published in the *Washington
Daily News* on 14 January 1963.[20] However, once Bandaranaike had
amplified them, he felt inclined to look at them favourably. Even before
the Chinese reaction was received, he told Dinesh Singh, his deputy
minister, that 'it is to our advantage to approve them generally . . .'[21]

The proposals boiled down to the following points:

Western sector: Recognizing the status quo that existed before the
start of the war, China to carry out their 20-kilometre withdrawal
from their posts as proposed by Zhou in his letters of 21 and 28
November 1962. India was asked to remain where it was and the area
so vacated by China to be demilitarized with no army deployment,
and to be administered by civilian posts of both sides without
prejudice to their existing positions.

Eastern sector: The line of control recognized by both could serve
as the ceasefire line. It meant India could move up to south of the
McMahon Line and China would withdraw north of the line. Longju
and Che Dong were considered disputed areas for which immediate
negotiation was suggested. It was felt that these proposals would
consolidate the ceasefire and pave the way for discussions between
them for a final settlement.

Middle sector: Status quo to be observed.[22]

Prime Minister Bandaranaike was informed of Indian acceptance
after they were discussed and accepted in toto in Parliament, while

China accepted them in principle. Pointing to the reservations of China, India said that both the governments 'must accept' them before the stage for a discussion on the remaining issues was set.[23]

A day before India's acceptance, the *People's Daily* said they contained 'ambiguities and inconsistencies'.[24] On 17 February 1963, Chen Yi had in an interview with the Swedish Broadcasting Corporation said that China accepted them in principle as a 'preliminary basis' for talks since there was a great 'discrepancy' between the clarifications as given to India and China, and China was not obliged to accept them in toto.[25] Now 'in toto' became the stencil while referring to the proposals. Sri Lanka, however, cleared the air by denying in an official statement made in its parliament that 'there were two sets of clarifications or there was any discrepancy' in them.[26] Nehru, too, explained his position to the heads of the government of the Colombo Conference countries, pointing out that non-acceptance by China was an act of discourtesy to them.[27]

Zhou asked Nehru to open negotiations since China had vacated the area under dispute and accepted the Colombo proposals in principle. He maintained that 'the 20-Km withdrawal by them from the line of actual control has put them far behind their position as of 8th September 1962'.[28] Nehru stressed the need for acceptance of the proposals in toto, since acceptance 'in principle' did not create the necessary basis for talks. He also suggested reference to the International Court of Justice or arbitration if they fail to resolve the issue between themselves.[29]

Zhou pointed to the complicated nature of the border dispute and said the Colombo proposals were mediatory in nature and not an arbitration award. Since the borders involved the question of sovereignty, it could not be subjected to arbitration and India's insistence on their acceptance was like 'an ultimatum', which was unacceptable and sounded as 'oblique warning'. He warned that India's failure to start negotiations would make it appear that Nehru was under some sort of 'internal or external pressure' and China would patiently wait, but he cautioned Nehru:

[I]f under outside influences the Indian Government should put blind faith in force and provoke fresh conflict on the Sino-Indian border that will be something which the Chinese Government does not want to see, and which will not be excused by the Chinese and Indian peoples and the people of the whole world.[30]

Zhou now told Indian *Charge d'affaires* P.K. Banerjee in Beijing that Nehru had 'lost his sense of reality . . . and was practicing distortion and displaying contradictions'.[31]

Nehru remained equally firm in denouncing China's technique of surprise attack and occupation of Indian territory and attempts to force India to negotiate on Chinese terms.[32]

The Chinese stand on Colombo proposals was not too unreasonable. The conference countries had taken up the mediation on their own to facilitate negotiations and were not asked either by China or India separately or together to undertake any 'facilitation' or arbitration on their behalf. They did not even talk to the two countries before giving their suggestions. Theirs was not an arbitration award, which both had to accept, as it is understood in cases of arbitration. It was yet another rigid stand of Nehru, similar to such stands which he had taken in the past. Another opportunity was allowed to pass. The Colombo conference countries did not think it prudent to involve themselves any further and lost interest, without blaming either country for obstructing the negotiations. It was not until Zhou's visit to Colombo in 1964 that the Ceylonese prime minister informally discussed the issue with her guest.

She proposed a resumption of talks, particularly when the ceasefire had held for over a year. She pointed out that the only obstacle to the resumption of talks appeared to be 'the presence of 7 Chinese posts in the demilitarised portion of Ladakh sector' and asked him 'whether he would be willing to withdraw those posts as a means of bringing about immediate and direct negotiations'. Zhou offered to consider the withdrawal of the seven posts if the two countries could sit together and work out certain principles on which the boundary line could be demarcated. Prime Minister Nehru in replying to Bandaranaike insisted that China must accept the Colombo proposals which would create the necessary atmosphere for discussing the issues involved. It was, therefore, he said 'not for the GOI to make any suggestions to vary the Colombo proposals in any way'. The vacation of the seven posts, he said, was also considered with the emissaries of Earl Russell (British activist for peace and Nobel laureate, trying for peace between India and China) when they had visited India in 1963. Nehru said that if China were ready to withdraw the posts in question, then he would discuss the proposals with his colleagues. He insisted it was 'for China to create such a new situation meriting consideration by the GoI'. The initiative of the Ceylonese prime minister to revive the proposals did not help in breaking the ice.[33]

The initiative taken by Earl Russell the previous year by the despatch of his two emissaries was ineptly handled by them and had little chance of success. His two emissaries, R.B. Schoenmen and P.B. Pottle, came to India ostensibly to talk to the Gandhi Peace Foundation but actually to resolve the issue between India and China. They met Nehru in Kashmir and then went to Beijing where they conveyed to Zhou a suggestion that had presumably come from Nehru:

[That the strip formed by the Chinese in the 20-kilometre withdrawal in the western sector could] become a no-man's land and be vacated of all civilian posts. If this was done Nehru was agreeable to join negotiations and not allow the talks to fail. He would discuss the whole question of the boundary and in the talks there would be give and take.

But later, in another meeting, Schoenmen said the idea of a 'no-man's land' did not originate with Nehru but they had put it to Nehru who had said if that happened he would negotiate. China found the interlocutors unreliable and asked them to suggest to Nehru to make such a proposal himself directly to China.[34]

India suddenly taken by surprise lost no time in disowning the initiative. It said that these gentlemen did make a courtesy call on Nehru and had merely suggested that China might be amenable to accept the proposal that no country had posts in the demilitarized area. Nehru had mentioned that it would be a new situation and if such a proposal indeed was made, 'it might merit consideration (and) would have to be discussed by him with his colleagues'. India made it clear that 'no message of any kind was given by the Indian Prime Minister to the representatives of Earl Russell' for being conveyed to China on his behalf.[35] Later, on 13 April 1964, Nehru told the Lok Sabha that he would have considered the proposal made by Russell's emissaries and also as suggested by Zhou to Bandaranaike, if China had made this proposal to India.[36]

Referring to a news item in the *New York Times* of 7 April 1964, Lord Russell conveyed his concern to Nehru at the report that 'India was preparing to regain territory along the northern border now occupied by Chinese Communist troops' and that 'Indian defence preparations not only were aimed at meeting any future Chinese threat, but also sought to regain the territory lost to China, including Aksai Chin'.[37] Nehru in reply assured him he was anxious for a peaceful settlement with China and the report was 'not quite accurate'.[38]

Nehru once again narrated in Parliament the long history of the India–China dispute from the 1950s and his desire to maintain friendly relations with China. Taking a historical perspective, he said that a border which was dead had now become alive.[39]

The trouble with the Indian understanding was the lack of historical perspective as Shyam Saran, a former Foreign Secretary, observed:

India found itself in an unexpected clash of arms mainly as a result of its unfamiliarity with Chinese culture and ways of thinking. Indian leaders failed to pick up cues and oblique hints which if understood accurately may have led to a different outcome than humiliating defeat.[40]

Contrary to Nehru's presumption, the India–China border was never dead. Ever since 1914 no Chinese government had accepted it despite the British making several attempts to get China to accept the Simla Convention, nor did Tibet, as the history of the dispute discussed in detail in Chapter 9 would show. It was Nehru taking liberty with the western border that had invited trouble. India became a victim of its wrong presumptions. Despite being aware of all these uncertainties and challenges, if India still considered the borders were dead, it must accept its failure to grasp the reality of the prevailing situation. Instead of meeting the situation head-on, Nehru had allowed his doubts to simmer and hoped that time would resolve the problems, as he said in Parliament in December 1959.[41]

In trying to resolve the impasse on the borders, Zhou made yet another attempt. He sent a personal message to Nehru via *Charge d'affaires* Banerjee, cautioning him that it should be delivered to the prime minister only and in person and alone since it was 'strictly for Nehru'. Banerjee flew to Delhi, avoiding all possibilities of a leak, and made sure it was conveyed to Nehru alone and in private. The message was:

(i) Both countries make no controversial remarks against each other for the next three months; and

(ii) Two prime ministers to meet quietly at some place without any fanfare and exchange ideas for settlement of the borders. This meeting should not last more than two days.

Zhou's idea was that at this meeting they could discuss, besides the borders, cooperation in areas of trade, culture and science and technology and so on, to create a much-needed climate of trust.[42]

Nehru, after giving some thought, did not feel like responding and told Banerjee 'matters had gone too far'. After confirming with Banerjee that he had neither shared nor discussed the 'message' with anyone else, gave his response which Banerjee described thus:

He (Nehru) struck a match, held the paper to the flame and burnt
it over a large ashtray . . .[43]

The flames not only burnt the paper but also extinguished, in no
time, yet another possibility for settlement. The proposals coming
straight from Zhou and, confidentially, did deserve better treatment,
at least a wider consultation or some response at least.

Banerjee had found Nehru in a pensive mood when he met him
again before returning to Beijing. Nehru told him about the defence
preparations, reorganization of the defence establishment, a new
wave of enthusiasm, and so on, but expressed his anguish, too, at the
possibility of 'the corrupting spirit of vengeance and hate'.[44]

On the prime minister's asking about Zhou's game plan,
Banerjee's assessment was that Zhou had no initiative in these
matters. It was Mao who framed the policy and Zhou only executed
it. He was essentially Mao's spokesman in international affairs 'to
which he might have given a touch of class and sophistication'.[45]

Zhou questioned Banerjee on his return about Nehru's
response. He had no answer, since his proposal had been put to
flames. An embarrassed Banerjee could only tell him about the
'current atmosphere in India' and that Nehru wanted him to first
accept the Colombo proposals in toto. Zhou understood and was
disappointed but not angry. He added, 'He had done everything in
his power and India would be responsible for the future stalemate
and complications.'[46]

On 6 September 1963, India suggested a Five-Point proposal
to break the logjam, which included the following points: (i)
China accept the Colombo proposals in toto; (ii) followed by
meeting of officials of both sides; (iii) the proposal arrived at
must be implemented by the officials of the two countries; (iv)
in a better atmosphere officials can take up border questions for
settlement; and (v) if they still fail, further consideration of ways
and means to settle the border problem, failing which both sides
could consider reference to ICJ or international arbitration.[47]

China, wasting little time, described them 'hotchpotch of the unreasonable prepositions which China had already rejected and could not accept them'.[48]

In August 1963, Zhou had proposed a conference of the heads of government of all the countries to consider a universal nuclear disarmament, including a ban on nuclear tests, and had sought Nehru's support.[49] Nehru, in disagreeing with the proposal, pointed out to the various deficiencies in Zhou's proposal and the efforts already being made in the same direction at the United Nations.[50]

Meanwhile, a new development, which had been brewing for some time under the surface, suddenly erupted in the open and took the world by surprise. It was the Sino-Soviet ideological conflict. Nehru took note of it in his letter of 11 November to President Kennedy, which was a couple of weeks before he was shot dead, and expressed his fears that it might lead to China threatening Indian security again. Appreciating the defence equipment which the United States had supplied to India in the last one year, Nehru mentioned that he was nevertheless concerned at the lack of supply of machinery for manufacture of defence equipment in India indigenously. He also drew his attention to the west-European countries supplying all types of machinery and equipment for China's all-round industrial development in the lure for short-term political gains. He described that this would lead to a long-term threat to peace not only in Asia but across the world. He felt that the Chinese threat to India and Asia essentially was a long-term one. 'The only way of meeting and containing this threat,' he said, 'is to go about with plans of economic development as a battle between the Indian way of life and the Chinese way of life (which) will be won or lost ultimately by the speed and the extent of progress on the development front.'[51]

All initiatives having failed one by one, a stalemate became inevitable. The language of notes became more truculent and undiplomatic. China did not give up its policy of needling India on one count or another. Zhou had categorically said in 1960 that 'China respects India's proper relations with Sikkim and Bhutan', but in December 1963 on the accession of the Chogyal of Sikkim, President Liu Shaoqi greeted him directly which was objected to by India, and China was asked to send such messages only through India, which was responsible for Sikkim's foreign relations.[52]

Though Nehru had justified arms assistance as necessary, he remained worried about his policy of non-alignment. He did not want to negate it altogether. As the India–United States talks on arms assistance at the experts' level ended and a concrete plan emerged, it became clear to Delhi that the United States, while extending arms aid, was keen to wean India away from its past to a new direction in which it would defer to United States' concerns. After the assassination of President Kennedy on 23 November, Lyndon Johnson had assumed the Presidency. A worried Delhi, not sure how the new administration would look at its relations with India, was warned by its ambassador in Washington, B.K. Nehru, that the new administration under Johnson expected India to help it 'psychologically and militarily in Southeast Asia'; India–Pakistan '*rapprochement* to be arrived at through an alteration of our stand on Kashmir' and the abandonment of non-alignment or the modification of it to an extent as to make it meaningless. The ambassador, however, added:

> These prices are not to be extracted all at once but this is the direction in which American policies over the years will be directed . . . pressure will be brought on us, requests will be made, sometimes bluntly and harshly; sometimes gently and diplomatically, with one individual contradicting the other, but all working in the same direction. It is for us to settle on our responses.[53]

Soon enough, the US ambassador presented an aide memoire to Secretary General M.J. Desai, promising short- and long-term arms assistance, both as grant-in-aid and credit. In the text of this aide memoire a caveat was embedded at the end, which read:

The long term program of military assistance assumed that India would continue her efforts to improve her relations with Pakistan and would also have a common understanding with the U.S.A. in regard to extent of Chinese Communist threat to Southeast Asia and the steps required to meet it.[54]

This is what Ambassador Nehru had warned earlier and an alert Secretary General M.J. Desai now strongly objected to it and expressed reluctance at accepting any assistance under these conditions. The Americans quietly withdrew their condition and paved the way for India's acceptance of American military assistance.[55] On 25 April 1964, Nehru shared with President Johnson the security situation around India and said that while India was making efforts towards forging better relations with Pakistan, the differences continued. About China, he said that it continued to be in a truculent and aggressive mood and India continued to face a threat from that country. While India's defence plans were now ready, he hoped that US help would continue to be available.[56]

The exchange of notes and the acrimony between India and China in the following days and months only increased and their respective positions hardened. The Chinese did not desist from the use of vituperative language in its notes, which Delhi found 'offensive and unbecoming and against normal international practices and usage'.

Until Nehru's death in May 1964, or even thereafter, no new ideas acceptable to both the countries had emerged from either side. Other countries had given up and left them to settle their dispute between themselves.

As pointed out in the previous chapter, India had occupied the area vacated by China in the eastern sector, and in February 1987 India converted it into a state of the Union, Arunachal Pradesh. China which had repeatedly declared and accepted India's claim on the McMahon Line, in the interregnum somewhere in 1985 staged a volte face and went back on its long-held position in the eastern sector. It now claimed the eastern sector which effectively meant the state of Arunachal Pradesh, leaving little space for India to manoeuvre. It has since remained a complicated issue, which if it was difficult to resolve in the past had since become much more difficult.

Nehru was a moralist and an idealist statesman of his time, but he was also self-opinionated and self-righteous. His foreign policy was based on the ancient Indian classical treatise on statecraft. He followed Ashoka's world view, which was extremely limited by today's standards—following the path of ahimsa and peace, abhorring war of any kind and appealing to higher principles to establish its superiority. The policy of nonalignment fitted into these characteristics and gave him a higher profile internationally than India's resources commanded at that time. Countries subscribed to it since it was a fit-all-size policy and carried no obligations. Unfortunately, he did not take into account the realities of national self-interest. His policy towards China was too romanticized. At the end as he felt disillusioned and became aggrieved, he felt cheated by China. However, it was too late; the public and the Parliament had become alienated and hostile towards China and not amenable to any meaningful compromise with it.

It is now more than half a century since 1962. The border question had receded to the backburner. The two countries have since made substantial progress in other areas of cooperation that helped thaw their relations. The representatives of the two countries continue to meet now and then, ostensibly to find a solution to the intractable problem of the borders, but end up each time shaking hands and having tea and cookies, even as the situation on the borders continues to remain combustible. Despite long periods of tranquillity that generally had prevailed on the borders, there have been confrontations between them. The Line of Actual Control (LAC) is neither demarcated on the ground nor on any map. Both work on the basis of perceptions that lead to border stand-offs sometimes of a serious nature. It may be recalled that in 1962 Nehru did not accept China's proposal to establish a demilitarized zone between the two armies, leaving the situation fluid.

To end this narrative, it is only appropriate to recall what Nehru said in 1953 while stressing the need for better understanding with China. He had said: '[W]e cannot just do something which will leave trails behind and which will pursue us for generations to come.'[57] Years later it had become a distant memory. His words to Banerjee, while burning Zhou's proposals, had left him remorseful in suggesting that 'it would take more than a quarter of a century for any fresh proposal to emerge'. It is now more than half a century, the albatross round India's neck has found itself in a cosy place and refuses to leave. India, too, seems to have become used to it and does not appear to be in any hurry to get rid of it. We continue to be prisoners of our past.

The events of 1962 remain a traumatic experience for the people of India and at the end, a tragic part of Nehru's life. Banerjee who had met Nehru on his return from Beijing while he was headed to Washington to take up his new assignment found him a broken man and not in a healthy state. He had suffered in health, a stroke had paralysed him partially. Six months later, on 28 May 1964, he suffered yet another stroke, which took him away, leaving behind a tragic chapter in the short history of independent India.

Epilogue

Borders are lines on maps that separate the geographical and political jurisdiction of countries that lie on either side of those lines. They reflect the vagaries and irrationalities of history. They are symbols of sovereignty and imply the limits up to which a government may exercise its political and economic jurisdiction. Nations take borders seriously and often conflicts arise when a country transgresses the established and agreed line separating it from another. Border agreements are, therefore, the main instruments that nations enter into to avoid future conflicts. Today the borders have become more precise than at any time in the past. They are not only delineated on the maps but also marked on the ground with the help of markers of agreed shape and size and separated at agreed distances. These are even periodically checked and repaired if damaged.

The two World Wars and the disintegration of colonial empires gave birth to many new countries, at times with borders that were undefined and controversial. Diplomatic negotiations leading to agreements helped in averting conflicts among them. Well-defined borders that have been mutually agreed on are, therefore, important for maintaining good relations between nations. They come into being as a result of agreement between the stakeholders by adjustments of rival claims, interests and ambitions at points where they adjoin.

India inherited its borders as bequeathed to it by the British when demitting power in 1947. Since India's northern border with Tibet was fixed by Henry McMahon on a map without surveys and was not delineated, as admitted by him later, it needed to be surveyed, delineated and demarcated. The border in the western part of the country, between Sinkiang and Ladakh, was actually undefined at the time of India's Independence in 1947. The need for scientific delineation and demarcation of the borders both in the eastern and western sectors had become necessary, particularly when the prime minister himself had doubts about the McMahon Line in the eastern sector. Even Kuomintang China had not accepted this line. Not only that, the Tibetans had even asked for retrocession of vast swathes of territories in India, which they claimed to be theirs and which the British had gradually included in India in the past.

Prime Minister Nehru was a great statesman and had a vision of India as a great country even before Independence. He was educated in England and was much impressed by the Western contemporary liberal thinkers; however, even while imbibing their liberal ideas, he remained imbued with the Asian spirit. He looked at Asia as a great continent and India and China as ancient lands and civilizations, embodying the Asian spirit. He remained proud of Indian culture and its ancient inheritance. He had been greatly influenced by the Himalayas and the rivers which flow across the plains of India and sustain life. He found that while the traces of the Indus Valley Civilization had been lost, the Vedic civilization continued to rule Indian thoughts, cultural moorings, ethos, religious and social values.

Though both India and China were connected with each other in some ways for centuries, they did have multiple differences in their perspectives. Their contacts were individual initiatives and not planned in any organized manner. Buddhism did provide some glue, but the formidable geographic factors and distances between them did not allow for the frequent contacts to flourish.

In the new world order that had emerged after the Second World War, Nehru tried to build relations with China on the strength of the contacts he had established with the country since 1927 while attending the 'Conference against Imperialism' at Brussels. In the post-war world, he saw India and China, standing side by side, as symbols of Asian solidarity. He believed that the two Asian countries would help create a vibrant Asia. He seemed to have conceded China to be the senior partner, since he repeatedly referred to China as a great country. His approach to China was determined by his desire to approach the world problems from an Asian perspective and to arrive at an Asian solution to, at least, the Asian problems.

In his larger policy perspective, he had convinced himself that the future of Asia depended on the goodwill and good neighbourly relations among Asian countries, and of these China and India, the two largest, would obviously play a dominant role. His convening the Asian Relations Conference in March 1947, even before India gained independence, was a proof of his desire that Asia should get its lost primacy and glory back.

He wished the friendship of the two counties 'to endure and grow'. It was not that this realization about China came to him suddenly as he saw the rise of communist China; in fact, it predated the communist revolution as he reflected in his book the *Discovery of India* and in his earlier speeches on free India's foreign policy after the British had withdrawn from India.

The Himalayas fascinated him more than anything else. For him they were not merely mountains but the life breath of India and Indian culture. He also saw in them a shield against any possible danger to India's physical security from the north. He repeatedly made this point and said its terrain, its climate and its ruggedness provided the greatest protection to India from any invasion from the north. On the flip side, this sense of security had a deleterious impact on him, since he did not feel it necessary to take any defensive measures against any possible danger to Indian security from that direction and, therefore, looked upon China's occupation of Tibet benignly in the beginning. He expected communist China to be somewhat deferential towards India for his past sympathies when it was being oppressed by the Europeans, who had nibbled at its coastal areas and monopolized its geological wealth.

After the British, who were the most powerful entity in this part of the world, had left Asia, communist China emerged as a force to reckon with. For China, regaining its old glory and position of leadership had become a priority. It saw in India a challenger and competitor who needed to be dislodged from its inherited position. The moral leadership of Nehru was being rated high among the countries of Asia and Africa as they became de-colonized. Nehru remained unaware that China in its new avatar would challenge his leadership, when even the Kuomintang had challenged his leadership at the Asian Relations Conference. The communists, not giving up the legacies of its ancient civilization and not wailing at the lost glory of China during the past century, swore to regain it, unmindful of the immense challenges that it faced.

Nehru's attitude towards communist China suffered from contradictions. He was willing to share the eminence and glory of Asia with China but was not willing to abdicate in its favour. Unfortunately, his judgement of the characteristics of the Chinese communist leaders remained dyed in the Kuomintang colours. He did not know the new Chinese leaders since he had neither met them nor interacted with them. Moreover, he failed to understand the signals emanating from them that they were no friends of his or India's where China's interests were concerned. Unlike Nehru, who had an emotional attachment to China, the communists were matter-of-fact people who drove a hard bargain in their favour on any issue. If one takes a look at the history of the decade of fifties when Nehru had to deal with the Chinese communists, the lack of their friendship for him and India stands out in bold relief. To start with, Nehru was viewed by the Chinese as the lackey of the United Kingdom and the United States; he was seen as someone representing their imperial interests. In 1950, while occupying Tibet,

China bluntly asked India to keep its hands off Tibet since it was an internal affair. As China invaded Lhasa, Tibet's request to India for the Dalai Lama's asylum was accepted, but later in the face of China's warning against it, he was hinted to stay away. In 1952–53, India got the wrong end of Chinese stick for its resolution in the UN General Assembly on the repatriation of the Korean prisoners of war. In Tibet, as China nibbled at the facilities of the Indian Mission and trade agencies and made their functioning impossible and the life of Indian traders difficult, Nehru thought that entering into a new arrangement with China would ensure that it allows Indian establishments to breathe easy. On the contrary, their harassment only increased. While negotiating the agreement on Tibet in 1954, China was found to be more sensitive to Pakistan's interests than India's. Not only that, China dragged its feet on every single issue until India yielded to its diktats to clinch the agreement after four long months of negotiations. Ambassador Raghavan was peeved at China's lack of appreciation for Indian efforts on its behalf and had lamented to Nehru (before Nehru's visit to China). However, after Nehru's visit to Beijing, where he received a tumultuous welcome, he and the entire country seemed to have been mesmerized by the adulation and exaltation he received. As China's position in Tibet came under challenge, it saw in India a villain in everything that went wrong for it there. The asylum given to the Dalai Lama in 1959 was another affront which China found difficult to accept.

Nehru, still in pursuit of an elusive friendship, committed himself to China and challenged those who looked at its emergence differently. Nehru was warned not once but several times by the political officer and the mission-in-charge at Lhasa about the long-term implications of China's occupation of Tibet on the north-eastern region of India, and on the security of the bordering states of India. Nehru not only ignored these warnings but also snubbed both of them. He did not give the impression of being worried about China's shenanigans but seemed unperturbed by the fact that in supporting China he invited the odium of the Western countries, the United States particularly.

For fear of antagonizing China, he would not respond positively to hints of India getting a seat on the UN Security Council in place of China. He tenaciously pleaded at the UN for China's admission and its recognition by the international community, even when China neither acknowledged nor appreciated his efforts. Ironically, it is the same China that today opposes a seat for India in an enlarged and reformed Security Council.

In a world divided by the Cold War, free from all the prevailing prejudices, Nehru sought to devise his own path not only to live in peace but to enlarge the area of peace. He held out his hand of friendship to the countries newly emerging from colonialism to independence to join in the quest for peace. His idea of non-alignment gave him the option to stay out of the Cold War politics of the superpowers. He insisted that the success of Indian foreign policy should not be judged in the narrow sense of 'our own petty success or failure' but whether it 'involves the success or failure of the whole world'. These parameters influenced him to look towards China as a partner in his campaign for peace and to achieve Asian solidarity. He was willing to sacrifice India's core interests even when China was not reciprocating.

Peace, by itself, is an elusive commodity. It can be defended by the strength and the muscle that a country builds in its support, otherwise it remains an instrument of the weak. Nehru ignored this basic truth. For India, ignoring this simple truism and relying disproportionately on factors which were foreign to it for security became the blight on Nehru's foreign and defence policies.

The emergence of China in communist colours was a new phenomenon. Though the old China was dead, somehow Nehru insisted on building his relations with the new China on the foundations of the past. It took some time, to his regret, to find that the new China was different from the old one. It was no longer a meek country but a self-possessed, assertive China. Nehru, in finding a modus vivendi, chose not to challenge it. The more assertive China became, the more yielding he became in search of an elusive peace. Quite often China's behaviour was not only aggressive but demeaning, yet it was not challenged. In the process, he neither achieved peace nor Asian solidarity.

When all is said, it also needs to be said that there were certain constraints which did not give him enough elbow room to opt for a tougher position. India had emerged from colonialism to independence only a couple of years before the communist revolution in China. Its defence forces and assets had been split. Within a couple of months of Independence, its army had to face an aggressive Pakistan in Kashmir. After more than a year of war with Pakistan, and with limited resources, the Indian Army was not in a position to take on a strong and revolutionary People's Liberation Army in the rugged mountains of the Himalayas. There were millions of Partition refugees who needed to be settled. There were food shortages. Food had to be imported with the limited resources that were available. The economy had been hit hard due to Partition. These constraints were indeed daunting. But it is or was anybody's case then or later that India needed an aggressive approach to China by taking up arms. It only required policy calibration to meet the new challenges. Unfortunately, Nehru did not see any of the Chinese actions as a challenge. He did calibrate his policies but they looked more like acquiescence in China's aggressive approaches than adjustment.

On the crucial subject of the frontiers, which proved the Achilles' heel, he did not think it necessary to even calibrate and negotiate with China, which had become its contiguous neighbour for the first time in history. As stated in the beginning, frontier agreements are the foundations of *entente cordial* between neighbours. Peaceful frontiers could be obtained by adjustments of rival claims, interests and ambitions. Nehru was fully aware that neither Kuomintang China nor Tibet, before the emergence of the communists, had accepted India's northern frontiers as bequeathed by the British. There was full consciousness that the communists would challenge them, but Nehru remained hesitant, nay unrelenting, to discuss them to reach an amicable settlement. In the western sector, his unilateral demarcation of the border by his fiat and then his adamant refusal to discuss it proved to be the nemesis which was entirely avoidable. The need of the time was to properly survey the un-demarcated frontiers, for which Zhou had pleaded repeatedly. Nehru remained in denial of the facts on the ground. Only if he had followed the advice that he liberally gave to the Burmese prime minister to negotiate his country's borders with China and not adopt a rigid line, India would have saved itself the ignominy of 1962. He did not even heed the advice of Khrushchev who, by his country's example, tried to bring home to him the virtues of a tranquil border. Flexibility was a virtue he did not display while dealing with China on the frontier question.

The adjustment of borders between neighbours is a normal exercise which does not involve cession of territory, as the Supreme Court had later ruled in the case of *Union of India vs Maganbhai* in 1969. India, too, adjusted its borders with Pakistan and Bangladesh, after surveys, even when they had been marked with a line drawn by Radcliffe in 1947.

Nehru was aware that India had to build up its strength. That strength to Nehru meant not so much the frontier outposts or the defence forces but internal strength—political and economic. He was quite conscious that one of the significant factors in Asia was the rate of progress of India and China for which peace among the nations was a prerequisite. He worked for it. But his dogged pursuit of it, without caring for other competing interests, was like missing the woods for the trees.

What is the way out of the current impasse on border question?

Both India and China need to introspect. China had offered in 1960 to accept the McMahon Line in the north-east provided India accepted China's position in the western sector or at least negotiated the border which it had unilaterally altered. China, since the middle of eighties of the last century, has withdrawn that offer and now claims Tawang (Arunachal Pradesh), too, while retaining the Aksai Chin in the west. China's new stand makes any settlement today more difficult than ever before. Its claim in the eastern sector rests on two pillars, as Dai Bingguo, who was China's Special Representative for talks with the Indian counterparts on border settlement and who had represented China at thirteen such meetings between 2003 and 2013, said: (i) India now controls majority of the disputed territory and (ii) it was 'inalienable from China's Tibet in terms of cultural background and administrative jurisdiction'. China believes that it would 'correct the wrong done by the colonialists and restore fairness and justice'. Asking India to sacrifice Tawang, now Arunachal Pradesh, a state of the Union, has put a stiffer price on peace than at any time before and which no Indian government can accept.

No settlement is ever possible on conditions imposed by one party. If any meaningful settlement is to be arrived at, it has to be on the basis of recognizing the existing realities and the security interest of both the countries, which the status quo of the present position serves. The Chinese in 1960 had offered the quid pro quo solution and repeated it in 1979 to Atal Bihari Vajpayee (then foreign minister) and in 1980 to an Indian journalist in an interview. Even then India would find it a very difficult job on its hands to agree. Given the fractious nature of Indian politics, any government which accepts the 1960 formula, fair as it is, would be accused of gifting away Indian territory which Nehru had refused to buy peace, no matter how faulty his position was. Unfortunately, we have become prisoners of the past. The writing of history has been impeded by successive governments for fear of exposing the weakness of the Indian case on the borders. Locking the archives is like depriving the nation of its history. A nation that does not know its history or ignores its history is condemned by history is an accepted axiom.

To begin with, it requires convincing the Indian public that the position taken by India in the past was not a rational one and that China was not altogether perfidious as it was made out to be. It would be necessary to open the MEA archives in their entirety and let the public convince itself of the correct position by studying the archives, which, even after decades, are still inaccessible in violation of the archival rules of 1997. Some trickle has found its way in the public domain only recently, which enabled the writing of this book, and does give some idea of the problem, but the complete availability of archives is a must if a meaningful exercise is to be conducted and the people convinced beyond an iota of doubt that it was India that should have been a little more flexible; China indeed was interested in resolving the border problem. Without this minimum exercise of opening the archives, the people will remain prisoners of the past and remain wary of any adjustment made now by give and take. The whole exercise would result in controversial debate and the facts would get lost in the din that is generated. There have been stand-offs along the border at times because of the ignorance of the facts and the debate that is unleashed in the media on the basis of half-baked facts leaves the TV-driven public more confused than wiser. What has been the result of past policies? For almost six decades since 1962, thousands of square kilometres of India's claimed territory remains outside its reach. The sword of Damocles hangs on one state of the Union, Arunachal Pradesh with a population of 1.75 million and it is a constant irritant in the relations between India and China.

The challenge for any government is tough but it is within the realm of possibility. It needs will and determination. If a resolution of this problem that is more than half a century old has to be found, the bull has to be taken by its horns. Educating the public opinion of the correct position is a must and is the only feasible way to resolve the issue. Half-hearted measures like opening selected archives would leave the people suspicious that something vital is being held back on the pretext of security. Nothing would be lost than has already been lost by the opening of the archives. Truth must prevail. Can the government accept the challenge and bite the bullet?

Notes

A Note on Sources

The book is mainly based on archival material contained in the Nehru collection and housed in the Nehru Memorial Museum and Library, New Delhi. This collection throws light on a variety of subjects. Among those, the ones dealing with India's relations with China were published in a five-volume series in 2018 by the author, together with documents gathered from the Foreign Department/MEA files in the National Archives of India, New Delhi. Some secondary sources have also been used in this book, wherever considered necessary, to supplement the text. This book, however, primarily remains based on the above-mentioned five-volume publication of the author.

In giving references both sources—the Nehru Papers and the author's five-volume study have been catalogued. For instance, a reference would read:

Note by Secretary General G.S. Bajpai, 21 Nov 1949; Foreign Dept, file no. 7/13/nec/49-secret; NAI (0108).

In the reference, the number within brackets is the document number from the five-volume series where all the documents have been numbered seriatim.

Here is another example:
Indian embassy in Beijing to MEA, 22 Mar. 1951. Nehru Papers, folio. 78-i p. 8; (0300). Here (0300) refers to the document number in the five-volume series.

It is hoped readers who want to access the text have the choice to access it from either of the two sources convenient to them.

*

Introduction

1.   Jawaharlal Nehru, *The Discovery of India* (New Delhi: Oxford University Press [OUP], 1985), p. 116.
2.   Sarvepalli Gopal (ed.), *Selected Works of Jawaharlal Nehru (SWJN)*, vol. I, p. 102.
3.   Nehru, *The Discovery of India*, p. 85.
4.   Tansen Sen, *India, China and the World* (New Delhi: OUP, 2018), p. 337.
5.   Gopal (ed.), *SWJN,* vol. 9, p. 406.
6.   Ibid.
7.   Gopal (ed.), *SWJN,* vol. I, p. 249.
8.   Ibid., p. 293
9.   Interview with the Radio Pravo in Paris on 31 July 1938; *SWJN,* vol. 10, First Series, p. 91.
10.   *SWJN,* First Series, vol. 10, p. 102.
11.   Ibid., p. 91.
12.   SWJN, vol. 10., p. 102.
13.   PM's Note to Foreign Secretary on Situation in Asia, 14 Dec. 1948 (0056).
14.   Foreign Dept, file no. 202 (15), p. 46 (pt-I), pp. 12–14 (NAI).

Chapter 1: India, Tibet and China—A Historical Perspective

1.   Tansen Sen, *India, China and the World: A Connected History* (New Delhi: OUP, 2018), p. 247.
2.   Alastair Lamb, *The McMahon Line: A Study in the Relations between India, China, and Tibet* (Routledge & Kegan Paul/University of Toronto Press, 1966), p. 6.

3. Ibid., p. 49.
4. Ibid., p. 93.
5. Ibid., p. 110.
6. Ibid., p. 108.
7. Ibid., p. 27.
8. Ibid., p. 149
9. Text of 1908 Trade Regulations, P. Mehra, *The North-Eastern Frontier*, vol. 1 (OUP, 1979), pp. 8–14.
10. Warren Smith, *A History of Tibetan Nationalism and Sino-Tibetan Relations* (New Delhi: HarperCollins, 1977), pp. 166–67.
11. Lamb, *The McMahon Line*, p. 199.
12. Ibid., p. 206.
13. Ibid.
14. Ibid., p. 209.
15. Ibid., p. 210.
16. Ibid., p. 213.
17. Ibid., p. 216.
18. Ibid., p. 217.
19. Ibid., p. 224.
20. Lamb, *The McMahon Line*, vol. 2, p. 348.
21. Smith, *A History of Tibetan Nationalism and Sino-Tibetan Relations*, p. 182.
22. Memorandum from the British Minister in Peking, John Jordan, to the Chinese Foreign Office, 12 August 1912, in Parshotam Mehra, *The North-Eastern Frontier*, vol. I (OUP, 1979), pp. 66–67.
23. Ibid., p. xxxi.
24. Parshotam Mehra, *The McMahon Line and After* (Madras: Macmillan, 1974), p. 140.
25. Ibid., p. 145.
26. Ibid., pp. 145–46.
27. Smith, *A History of Tibetan Nationalism and Sino-Tibetan Relations*, p. 183.
28. Neville Maxwell, *India's China War* (Bombay: Jaico Publishing House, 1970), p. 46.
29. Lamb, *The McMahon Line*, p. 465.
30. Ibid., p. 468.
31. Mehra, *The North-Eastern Frontier*, vol. 1, p. 79.
32. Mehra, *The McMahon Line and After*, p. 165.

33. Ibid., p. 168
34. Mehra, *The North-Eastern Frontier*, vol. 1, p. 71.
35. Ibid., p. 72.
36. Ibid., p. 79.
37. Ibid., p. 86.
38. Document no. 1, vol. 1; Text of Notes in Bhasin, *India–China Relations, 1947–2000: A Documentary Study*, five volumes (New Delhi: Geetika Publishers, 2018), p.1.
39. Mehra, *The North-Eastern Frontier*, vol. 1, p. 84.
40. For the text of the convention, please see Bhasin, *India–China Relations*, doc. no. 2 pp. 2–6.
41. Mehra, *The McMahon Line and After*, p. 275.
42. Dorothy Woodman, *Himalayan Frontiers: A Political Review of British, Chinese, Indian and Russian Rivalries* (Barrie & Jenkins, 1969), p. 183.
43. Mehra, *The North-Eastern Frontier*, vol. 1, pp. 107–08.
44. Ibid., pp. 127–28.
45. Ibid., p. 133.
46. Lamb, *The McMahon Line*, p. 524.
47. Woodman, *Himalayan Frontiers*, p. 176.
48. Ibid., 176
49. Mehra, *The McMahon Line and After*, p. 286.
50. Ibid., p. 288.
51. Woodman, *Himalayan Frontiers*, p. 176.
52. Mehra, *The McMahon Line and After*, p. 288.
53. Mehra, *The North-Eastern Frontier*, vol. 1, p. 116.
54. Smith, *A History of Tibetan Nationalism and Sino-Tibetan Relations*, p. 201.
55. Ibid., p. 212.
56. Maxwell, *India's China War*, p. 49.

Chapter 2: The Fall of Kuomintang China

1. Viceroy to Secretary of State for India, 3 Apr. 1944, Foreign Dept, file no. 234-CA/44 Secret, NAI, New Delhi; (0005).
2. A.S. Bhasin, *India–China Relations, 1947–2000*, vol. I, pp. xxxiv–xxxv.

3. *SWJN*, First Series, vol. 14, p. 463.
4. Ibid., 466.
5. *SWJN*, First Series, vol. 15, p. 566.
6. *SWJN*, First Series, vol. 1, p. 446.
7. *SWJN*, Second Series, vol. 1, p. 440.
8. Sen, *India China and the World*, p. 339.
9. Foreign Dept. to Political Officer (PO), 8 Apr. 1947 in Nicholas Mansergh and Penderel Moon (eds), *Transfer of Power*, HMSO, vol. x, p. 156, 1981; (0019).
10. Ibid.
11. PO to MEA, 23 July 1947, Foreign Dept, file no. 12(4)NEF/47, NAI, New Delhi; (0023).
12. Ibid.
13. Ibid.
14. Tibetan Govt to British High Commissioner, 16 October 1947, Foreign Dept, file no. 12(4), NEF/47-Secret, NAI, New Delhi; (0026).
15. 16 Oct. 1947, Foreign Dept, file no. 12(4)NEF/47-Secret (0027).
16. Nehru's letter to Zhou Enlai; 26 Sep. 1959, para 14: White Paper-II, pp. 35–46; (1498).
17. Sen, *India China and the World*, pp. 363–64, quoting West Bengal State Archives file. no. 923/44, serial no. 302:381.
18. 24 Mar. 1948, Foreign Dept, file no. 7/2/NEF/48-Secret, NAI, New Delhi; (0044).
19. Foreign Dept, file no. 7/2/NEF/48-Secret; NAI, New Delhi; (0045).
20. Note from MEA to Chinese Embassy, 9 Feb. 1948; (0043).
21. *SWJN*, Second Series, vol. 7, p. 610.
22. *SWJN*, Second Series, vol. 1, p. 473.
23. K.M. Panikkar, *In Two Chinas: Memoirs of a Diplomat* (London: George Allen and Unwin Ltd, 1955), pp. 26–27.
24. Sen, *India China and the World*, p. 340.
24a. Website of Asian Relations Conference, New Delhi, Mar. 1947.
24b. Sen, *India China and the World*, p. 295.
25. Ibid., p. 346.
26. Foreign Dept, file no. 12(4)NEF/47-Secret; NAI (0029).
27. Foreign Dept, file no. 12(4)NEF/47-Secret; NAI (0035).

28. Smith, *A History of Tibetan Nationalism and Sino-Tibetan Relations*, pp. 259–61.
29. Ibid., p. 260.
30. *SWJN*, Second Series, vol. 9, p. 69.
31. PM's talks with Tibetan Delegation, 8 Jan 1949; (0061).
32. Foreign Dept, file no. 12(4)NEF/47-Secret; NAI (0031).
33. Mission Lhasa to PO Sikkim, 4 Jan 1948, Foreign Dept, file no. 12(4)NEF/47-Secret NAI (0039).
34. Mission Lhasa to PO 4 Jan 1948, Foreign Dept, file no. 12(4) NEF/47-Secret; NAI; (0038).
35. Governor General to Secretary of State, HMG, 29 Aug 1947, Foreign Dept, file no. 12(4)NEF/47-Secret; NAI; (0025).
36. Mission Lhasa to MEA, 17 Oct 1947; Foreign Dept, file no. 112(4) NEF/47 Secret (0028).
37. Mission Lhasa to PO 14 Jan 1948; Foreign Dept, file no. 112(4) NEF/47-Secret (0042).
38. Richardson to PO, 14 Jan 1948; Foreign Dept, file no. 12(4) NEF/47 Secret (0042).
39. MEA to Mission Lhasa and PO 30 July 1948 For. Dept, file no. 7/2/ NEF/48 Secret; (0047).
40. H.E. Richardson, *Tibet and Its History* (OUP: 1962), p. 174.
41. Foreign Dept, file no. 7/13/NEF/49-Pt.II, Secret, NAI; (0036 and 0040).
42. Indian Embassy, Nanking to MEA, 12 Jan 1949, Foreign Dept, file no. 7/2/NEF/48-Secret, NAI; (0062).
43. MEA to Indian Embassy, Nanking, 15 Jan 1949, Foreign Dept, file no. 7/2/NEF/48-Secret, NAI; (0063).
44. MEA to Indian Embassy, Nanking, 15 Jan 1949, Foreign Dept, file no. 7/2/NEF/48-Secret (0063).
45. MEA to Indian Embassy, Nanking, 13 Mar 1949, Foreign Dept, file no. 7/2/NEF/48-Secret (0068).
46. Ibid.
47. Note by PM to Foreign Secretary, 5 June 1949; (0077).
48. Ibid.
49. Footnote on p. 114 to doc no. 0077, Foreign Dept, file no. 611-CA/49-Secret.
50. Ibid.

51. Footnote on p. 114, Foreign Dept, file no. 611-CA/49-Secret; (0078 fn).

52. Extracts from PM's letter to Premiers of Provincial Govts, 4 June 1949; (0076).

53. Woodman, *Himalayan Frontiers*, pp. 215–16.

Chapter 3: India and Communist China: The Beginnings

1. Margareta MacMillan, *Nixon and Mao: The Week That Changed the World* (New York: Random House, 2006), p. 100.

2. PM's note on situation in Asia, 14 Dec.1948; (0056).

3. 3 June, 1949, Foreign Dept, file no. 611-CA/49-Secreta; (0074).

4. Extract from the PM's letter to the Premiers of Provincial Govts, 4 June 1949; (0076).

5. Note from the PM to Foreign Secy, 5 June 1949; (0077).

6. PM's note on Policy towards Tibet, 9 July 1949; (0083).

7. MEA to Indian Embassy, Nanking, 16 Aug. 1949; Foreign Dept, file no. 611-CA/49-Secret; (0090).

8. Note by PM, 17 Nov. 1949; (0115).

9. Foreign Relations of the United States (FRUS), 1949, The Far East, vol. ix, telegram no. 693.

10. FRUS, 1949, The Far East, vol. ix, telegram no. 1221.

10a. FRUS, 13 Oct 1949, The Far East, vol. ix, doc. no. 142.

11. FRUS,4 Nov.1949, The Far East, vol. ix, doc. no. 182

12. FRUS, 7 Nov. 1949, The Far East, vol. ix, telegram no. 1375, doc. no. 190.

13. FRUS, 6 Dec. 1949, The Far East, vol. no. ix, telegram no. 1518.

14. *SWJN*, vol. 14-I, p. 366.

15. FRUS, 19 Dec. 1949, The Far East—China, vol. ix, doc. no. 253.

16. Message from Indian Embassy, Nanking to MEA, 6 Jan. 1950; (0142).

17. MEA to Indian Embassy, Nanking; 6 Jan. 1950, Nehru Papers, folio no. 34, p. 84; (0143).

18. Indian Embassy, Beijing, Letter to MEA, 15 Mar. 1950; (0162).

19. Indian Embassy, Peking, to MEA, 20 May 1950, Nehru Papers, folio no. 44-II, p. 282; (0172).

20. Panikkar, *In Two Chinas*, p. 177.

21.   Sen, *India China and the World*, p. 386.
22.   *SWJN*, vol. 7, p. 610.
23.   Sen, *India China and the World*, p. 387.
24.   PM's note to F.S. on the situation in China, 5 Dec., 1948; (0055).
25.   FRUS, Near-East, South Asia and Africa, vol. V, pt.-I, tel. no. 1108 of 22 Dec. 1948.
26.   *SWJN*, vol. 9, p. 175; 2 Jan. 1949.
27.   *SWJN*, vol. 9, p. 285. PM's fortnightly letter to the Premiers of the Provincial Governments, 23 December 1948.
28.   *SWJN*, vol. 8, p. 335, 17 Dec. 1948.
29.   PM's fortnightly letter to the Premiers of the Provincial Governments, 17 January 1949; *SWJN*, vol. 9, pp. 290–91.
30.   *SWJN*, vol. 10, p. 303, 1 Apr. 1949.
31.   *SWJN*, vol. 11 p. 389, 5 June 1949.
31a. Nehru's note to Secretary General and Foreign Secretary, 15 June 1949, *SWJN*, vol. 11, p. 389.
32.   Ranjit Singh Kalha, *India–China Boundary Issues: Quest for Settlement* (New Delhi: ICWA, 2014), p. 13.
32a. Nehru's address to the nation on Independence Day, 15 August 1949; *SWJN*, vol. 12, p. 34.
33.   Nehru's speech at the Colombo Conference, 10 Jan.1950; *SWJN*: vol. 14-I, p. 527.
34.   Letter from PM to Finance Minister John Mathai, 10 Sept. 1949; (0095).
35.   Note by PM on policy towards Tibet, 9 July 1949; (0083).
36.   Note by PM on policy towards Tibet, 9 July 1949; (0083).
37.   Panikkar to Foreign Secretary K.P.S. Menon; 7 Sept. 1949; Foreign Dept, file no. 611-CA/49-Secret; (0094).
38.   Summary of World Broadcasts, part V, 1949, no. 24, p. 22; quoted in Tsering Shakya, *The Dragon in the Land of Snow: A History of Modern Tibet since 1947* (Great Britain: Penguin, 1999), p. 3.
39.   MEA to PO Sikkim; 04 Sept. 1949; Foreign Dept, file no. 7/13/NEF/49-Secret; (0091).
40.   Extract from the Monthly Report of Mission Lhasa, 15 Sep. 1949; (0101).
41.   Article by a Chinese Jurist in *People's Daily*, 13 Sept. 1949; (0098).
42.   Foreign Secretary's note, 19 Nov. 1949, Foreign Dept, file no. 7/13/NEC/49-Secret; (0108).

43. Panikkar, *In Two Chinas*, p. 220.

44. Note by Panikkar on Tibet Policy, 21 Nov. 1949, Foreign Dept, file no. 7/13/NEC/49-Secret, NAI, New Delhi; (0108).

45. Note by F.S., 12 Nov. 1949, on Panikkar's note on Tibet Policy of 4 Nov. 1949, MEA, file no. 7/13/NEC/49-Secret, NAI; (0108).

46. Note by Secretary General G.S. Bajpai, 21 Nov. 1949, Foreign. Dept, file no. 7/13/NEC/49-Secret, NAI; (0108).

46a. Nehru's remarks at the Standing Committee of Legislature for MEA, 7 Dec. 1949; (0126).

47. Smith, *A History of Tibetan Nationalism and Sino-Tibetan Relations*, p. 247.

48. Ibid., p. 249.

49. Michael Brecher, *Nehru: A Political Biography* (London: Oxford University Press, 1959), p. 76.

49a. Zhou's conversation with Panikkar, 28 Sept. 1951; (0354).

50. PM to Panikkar, 2 Oct. 1951; (0354).

51. Panikkar's conversation with Zhou at a dinner, 2 Oct. 1951; (0354: fn).

52. PO to MEA, 20 Oct. 1949, Foreign Dept, file no. 7/13/NEF/49, pt II, Secret, NAI; (0105).

53. Ibid.

54. Ibid.

55. Ibid.

56. Nehru's note to Secretary General in MEA, 9 July 1949, *SWJN*, vol. 12, pp. 410–11.

57. Nehru's letter to the Premiers of the Indian Provincial Governments, 1 Dec. 1949, *SWJN*, vol. 14, pt I, p. 367.

58. Ibid.

58a. Note by PM to Secretary General and Foreign Secretary, 17 Nov. 1949; (0115).

59. Extract from the proceedings of the Standing Committee of Legislature, 17 Dec. 1949; (0126).

60. PM's meeting with senior officials, 30 Dec. 1949, Foreign Dept, file no. 7/13/NEF/49-Pt.II, Secret, NAI, New Delhi; (0140).

61. FRUS, April 1959, vol. ix, pp. 1065–068.

62. Shakya, *The Dragon in the Land of Snow*, p. 60, quoting US Foreign Policy Documents, vol. VI, (1950), p. 611.

63.   Bruce Riedel, *JFK's Forgotten Crisis* (India: HarperCollins, 2016), p. 119.

63a. PM's letter to the Chief Ministers of Indian States, 17 Nov. 1950; (0268).

64.   Nehru's letter to the Chief Minister of West Bengal, *SWJN*, vol. 11, p. 184.

65.   Nehru's letter to the Chief Ministers of the Indian States, *SWJN*, vol. 14-I, p. 393 (fn).

66.   MEA to Indian Delegation at UN, 21 Nov. 1949; (0117).

67.   Secretary of State for Commonwealth Relations, HMG to MEA; 28 Nov. 1949, Foreign Dept, file no. 7/13/NEF/49-Pt.Io, Secret, NAI, New Delhi; (0118).

68.   Note by F.S. on his talks with Frank Roberts of the UK High Commission, 1 Dec. 1949; (0121).

69.   PO to MEA, 2 Dec. 1949, Foreign Dept, file no. 71/3/NEF/49-Pt. II, Secret, NAI, New Delhi; (0122).

70.   Melvyn Goldstein, *A History of Modern Tibet, 1913–51* (Berkeley: University of California Press), p. 624; and PO to MEA, 9 Nov. 1949; (0110).

71.   Panikkar to Nehru, 10 Aug. 1949, Foreign Dept, file no. 611-CA/49 -Secret; (0088).

72.   MEA to Indian Embassy, Nanking, Foreign Dept, file no. 611-CA/49-secret; (0090).

73.   MEA to PO, 4 Sep. 1949, Foreign Dept, file no. 7/13/MEF/49 Pt. II, Secret; (0091).

74.   Indian Embassy, Nanking, to MEA, 5 Sep. 1949, Foreign Dept, file no. 7/13/NEF/$9-Pt.II; (0092).

75.   Indian Embassy, Nanking, to MEA, 5 Sep. 1949; Foreign Dept, file no. 7/13/NEF/$9-Pt.II; (0092).

76.   Article by a Chinese Jurist, 13, Sep. 1949; (0098).

77.   Indian Embassy, Nanking, to MEA, 4 Nov. 1949; (0107).

78.   Indian Embassy, Nanking, to MEA, 4 Nov. 1949; (0107).

Chapter 4: The Tibet Conundrum

1.   Letter from Burmese PM to PM, 5 Jan, 1950; (0141); Letter from PM to Burmese PM, 7 Jan.1950; (0144).

2.   Note by Panikkar on Tibet Policy; 21 Nov. 1949; Foreign Dept, file no. 7/13/NEC/49-Secret; (0108).

2a. *SWJN*, vol. ix, p. 290; PM's fortnightly letter to the Premiers of Provincial Governments, 17 Jan. 1949.

3.   Aide Memoire from PO to Tibetan Government, 7 Dec. 1944; Foreign Dept, file no. 157-CA/44-Secret; (0017).

4.   Note by the British FS to Chinese Ambassador in London on the status of Tibet; 5 Aug. 1943, Foreign Dept, file no. 13(4)NEF/47-Secret; (0004).

5.   Minutes of the Meeting taken by Chief of Staff with MEA, 29 Dec. 1949, Foreign MEA. File no. 7/13/NEF/49-Secret; (0137).

6.   Secretary of state for Commonwealth Relations, HMG to MEA, 28 Nov. 1949; MEA, file no. 7/13/NEF/49-Pt. II, Secret; (0118).

7.   Indian Embassy, Nanking, to MEA, 29 Nov. 1949; MEA, file no. 7/13/NEF/49-Pt-II, Secret (0120).

8.   Note of the meeting taken by PM with senior officials, 30 Dec. 1949, MEA, file no. 7/13/NEF/49-Pt. II, Secret; (0140).

9.   Ibid.

10. MEA to Mission, Lhasa, 9 Jan. 1950; MEA file no. 7/13/NEF/48-Pt-II, Secret; (0147).

11. Broadcast from All India Radio on 7 September 1946.

12. MEA to Embassy, Beijing, 24 May 1950, Nehru Papers, folio no. 45-II, p. 167; (0174).

13. *SWJN*, vol. 7, p. 610 and 12 September 1948.

14. *Jawaharlal Nehru's Letters to Chief Ministers*, edited by G. Parthasarathi, vol. iv, p. 237.

14a. Melvyn Goldstein, *A History of Modern Tibet, 1913–51*, vol. 2 (Berkeley: University of California Press, 1991), pp. 23, 28.

15. Statement by spokesman of the Chinese Foreign Office, 20 Jan. 1950; (0157).

16. Indian Embassy, Nanking, to MEA, 26 Jan.1950, MEA, file no. 7/13/NEF?49-Pt.II, Secret; (0159).

17. MEA to Mission, Lhasa, MEA, file no. 7/13/NEF/49-Pt.II, Secret; (0156); Message from American Ambassador to Secretary General, MEA, 1 Jan. 1950 (0161).

18. Note on PM's meeting with Senior Officials, 30 Dec. 1949, MEA, file no. 7/13/NEF/49 Pt-II, Secret; (0140).

19. FRUS, 10 Jan. 1950, East Asia and Pacific, vol. vi, tele. no. 793B.00/1-1050.
20. FRUS, 20 Jan. 1950, vol. vi, tele. no. 793B.02/1-2050.
21. Peking Radio Broadcast on 13 May 1950; (0169).
22. Shakya, *The Dragon in the Land of Snow*, p. 25, quoting British Foreign Office Consultation 371-76315.
23. Kalha, *India–China Boundary Issues*, p. 23, quoting British Foreign Office Consultation No. 371/35 755 of 7 May 1943.
24. Letter from Foreign Dept to PO, 8 Apr. 1947; (0019).
25. Note by Panikkar on Tibet Policy, 4 Nov. 1949, Foreign Dept, file no. 7/13/NEC/49-Secret; (0108).
26. Foreign Secretary, HMG to Secretary of State for India, 3 Apr. 1944; Foreign Dept, file no. 234-CA/44-Secret; (0005).
27. Letter from Secretary of State for India to Foreign Secretary (HMG) May 1944, Foreign Dept, file no. 157-CA/44-Secret; (0007).
28. Secretary of State for India to Governor General, 28 May 1944, Foreign Dept file no. 234-CA/44 Secret; (0008).
29. FRUS, 21 Nov. 1949, vol. ix, tel. no. 893.00/11-2149.
30. MEA to India Del., New York, 21 Nov. 1949; (0117).
31. FRUS, 21 Nov. 1949, vol. ix, tele. no. 1441.
32. FRUS, Far East: China, 12 Dec. 1949, vol. ix, Telegram from the American Embassy in London to State Department, Washington no. 893.00 Tibet-1249.
33. FRUS, East Asia and Pacific,1 Mar. 1950, vol. vi, telegram no. 793B.56/3-150.
34. FRUS, 1950, East Asia and Pacific, 8 Mar. 1950, vol. vi, tele. no. 793B.00/3-850.
35. FRUS, East Asia and Pacific, vol. vi, tele. no. 301 of 8-3-50
36. Meeting of the Standing Committee of Legislature, 17 Dec. 1949; (0126).
37. MEA to Mission Lhasa, 9 Jan. 1950, MEA, file no. 7/13/NEF/49-Pt-II, Secret (0147).
38. MEA to Mission Lhasa, 9 Jan. 1950, MEA, file no. 7/13/NEF/49-Pt. II, Secret; (0147).
39. Mission Lhasa to MEA, 13 Jan. 1950, MEA, file no. 7/13/NEF/49-Pt-II, Secret; (0152).
40. MEA Note to Min. of Def., 16 January 1950, MEA, file no. 7/13/NEF/49.Pt-II, Secret'; (0155).

41. Smith, *A History of Tibetan Nationalism and Sino-Tibetan Relations,* pp. 270–71, fn.

42. Ibid., p. 271.

43. Ibid., p. 272.

44. Ibid., p. 275.

45. Mission Lhasa to MEA, 24 Jan. 1950, MEA, file no. 7/13/NEF/49, Pt-II, Secret; (0158).

46. PO to MEA, 18 Apr. 1950, MEA, file no. 7/13/NEF/49-Pt.II; (0166).

47. Smith, *A History of Tibetan Nationalism and Sino-Tibetan Relations,* p. 272

48. Peking Radio Broadcast, 13 May 1950; (0169).

49. 20 May 1950, Nehru Papers, folio no. 44-II, p. 282; (0172).

50. Smith, *A History of Tibetan Nationalism and Sino-Tibetan Relations,* pp. 277–78.

51. PM's conversation with the Tibetan delegation, 5 Sep. 1950; (0212); Smith, *A History of Tibetan Nationalism and Sino-Tibetan Relations,* p. 271.

52. Smith, *A History of Tibetan Nationalism and Sino-Tibetan Relations,* p. 276, quoting FRUS, 1950, vol. vi, p. 377.

53. Ibid., p. 275, quoting US Foreign Policy Doc. 1950, vol. 361, 9 June 1950.

54. FRUS, East Asia and Pacific, vol. vi, tele. no. 611.93B/8-1450=14 Aug.

55. FRUS, East Asia and Pacific, 8 Aug. 1950, vol. vi, tele. no. 611-93B/8-1450.

56. FRUS, East Asia and Pacific, 10 Sept. 1950, vol. vi, tele. no. 609.

57. FRUS, East Asia and Pacific, 26 Oct. 1950, vol. vi, tele. no. 793B.00/10-2650.

58. Indian Embassy, Beijing, to MEA, 30 Oct.1950, Nehru Papers, folio no. 61-II, pp. 363–64; (0249).

59. FRUS, East Asia and Pacific, 14 Aug. 1950, vol.vi, tele. no. 611.93B-1450.

60. FRUS, East Asia & Pacific, 25 Aug. 1950, tele. no. 479.1.

60a. Ibid.

61. Shakya, *The Dragon in the Land of Snow,* p. 31.

Chapter 5: The Chinese Occupation of Tibet

1.   Indian Embassy, Beijing, to MEA, 26 May 1950, file no. 7/13/
     NEF/49-Pt.II, Secret; (0176).
2.   Min of Def. Note, file no. 7/13/NEF/49-Part. II; Secret; (0179).
3.   PO to MEA, 29 June 1950, MEA, file no. 7/14/NEF/49-Pt.II,
     Secret; (0182).
4.   Embassy of India, Beijing, to MEA, 6 June 1950, Nehru Papers, folio
     no. 46-I, p. 64, 64a and 65; (0178).
5.   MEA to PO, 18 July 1950, MEA, file no. 7/13/NEF/49-Pt.II,
     Secret; (0188).
6.   MEA to Embassy, Beijing, 20 July 1950, Nehru Papers, folio no.
     49-I, p. 33; (0190).
7.   Ibid.
8.   Indian Embassy, Beijing, to MEA, 22 July 1950, Nehru Papers, folio
     no. 49-I, pp. 70–71; (0191).
9.   Panikkar to Nehru, 2 Aug. 1950; Nehru Papers, folio. no. 53-II, pp.
     185–86; (0193).
10. Indian Embassy, Nanking, to MEA, 10 Aug. 1950, MEA, file no.
     729-CJK/49, Secret; (0195).
11. PO to MEA, 17 Aug. 1950, Nehru Papers, folio no. 52-I, p. 181;
     (0197).
12. Ibid.
13. PO to MEA, 19 Aug. 1950; Nehru Papers, folio no. 52-I, pp. 123–
     24; (0201).
14. Ibid.
15. Shakya, *The Dragon in the Land of Snow*, p. 31.
16. Indian Embassy to MEA, 21 Aug. 1950, Nehru Papers, folio no. 52-
     I, pp. 215–17; (0202).
17. 22 Aug. 1950, Nehru Papers, folio no. 52-II, pp. 314–16; (0203).
18. Ibid.
19. Extract from PM's telegram to Panikkar, 19 Aug. 1950; (0200).
20. Panikkar to PM, 22 Aug. 1950, Nehru Papers, folio no. 52-II, p.
     314–16; (0203).
21. Ibid.
22. MEA to Mission Lhasa, 24 Aug. 1950, Nehru Papers, folio no. 52-II,
     p. 276; (0205).

23. Shakya, *The Dragon in the Land of Snow*, p. 63.
24. MEA to Indian Embassy, Beijing, 24 Aug. 1950, Nehru Papers, folio no. 52-II, p. 275; (0206).
25. MEA to Indian Embassy, Beijing, 24 Aug.1950, Nehru Papers, folio no. 52-II, p. 275; (0206).
26. Chinese note to MEA, 16 Nov. 1950 (230[v]).
27. Chinese note to MEA, 17 Nov. 1950, *SWJN*, vol. 15-II, p. 343 fn.
28. Nehru to Panikkar, 20 Nov. 1950, *SWJN*: vol. 15-II, p. 350.
29. Panikkar to MEA, *SWJN*: vol. 15-II, p. 350 fn.
30. PM's Telegram to Panikkar, 20 Nov. 1950; (0271).
31. Nehru's Press Conference, 5 Apr.1959, Nehru Papers, folio no. 59-II, p. 299; (1224).
32. 1 Sep. 1950, Nehru Papers, folio no. 52-II, p. 275; (0206).
33. MEA to Indian Embassy, Nanking, 15 Jan. 1949 Foreign Dept. file no. 7/2/NEF/48-Secret; (0063).
34. MEA's telegram to Indian Embassy, Nanking, 21 Mar. 1949, tele. no. D.1445-NEF/49; (0069).
35. Note by PM on Policy towards Tibet, 9 July 1949; (0083).
36. 3 Sept. 1950, Nehru Papers, folio no. 54-I, pp. 125–26; (0209).
37. Conversation of PM with the Tibetan Delegation, 6 Sep. 1950; (0212).
38. PM's message to Chinese Premier, 27 September 1950; (0217).
39. Zhou's report to the National Committee, 2 Oct. 1950, Nehru Papers, folio no. 58-I, p. 65; (0220).
40. 2 October, and 12 Oct. 1950, Nehru Papers, folio no. 58-I, p. 65; folio no. 59-I, p. 204; (0220 and 0223).
41. PO to MEA, 17 Oct 1950, Nehru Papers, folio no. 60-I, p. 83; (0219).
42. 16 Oct 1950, Nehru Papers, folio no. 59-II, p. 394; (0226).
43. Note by FS on his talks with Chinese Ambassador, 17 Oct. 1950, Nehru Papers, folio no. 60-I, pp. 102–03; (0227).
44. Ibid.
45. FRUS, East Asia and Pacific, vol. vi, tele. no. 47 of 9-7-50.
46. FRUS. 1950, East Asia and Pacific, 13 Oc. 1950, vol. vi, tele. no. 918; (693.93B-1350).
46a. MEA to Panikkar, 17 Oct.1950, Nehru Papers, folio no. 60-I, pp. 102–03; (0228).

47. Ibid.

48. PM telegram to Panikkar, 19 Oct. 1950; (0229).

49. Note by Secretary General G.S. Bajpai, 24 Oct.1950, Nehru Papers, folio no. 61-I, pp. 11–12; (0232).

50. Indian Embassy, Peking, to MEA and notes by F.S. S.G. and PM, 25, Oct. 1950, Nehru Papers, folio no. 61-II, p. 76; (0233); Note by S.G., folio no. 61-I, pp. 11–12; (0232).

51. Indian Embassy, Peking, to MEA and notes by F.S. S.G. and PM. 25 Oct. 1950, Nehru Papers, folio no. 61-II, p. 76; (0233); Note by S.G. folio no. 61-I, pp. 11–12; (0232).

52. PM to Panikkar, 25 Oct. 1950, Nehru Papers, folio no. 61-I, p. 54; (0234).

53. PM to Panikkar, 25 Oct. 1950; (0235).

53a. PM to Panikkar, 25 Oct, 1950; (0235).

54. PM to Panikkar, 25 Oct. 1950; (0235).

55. MEA to Indian Embassy, Beijing, 17 Oct. 1950, Nehru Papers, folio no. 60-I, pp. 102–03 (0228); 26 Oct. 1950, Nehru Papers, folio no. 61-I, pp. 114–15; (0236).

56. 26 October, 1950, Nehru Papers, folio no. 61-I, p. 141 (0237).

57. FRUS, East Asia & Pacific, 25 October 1950, vol. vi, tele. no. 693.93B/10–2550.

58. 29 Oct. 1950, Nehru Papers, folio no. 61-II, p. 263; (0246).

59. 30 Oct. 1950, Nehru Papers, folio no. 61-II, p. 266; (0250).

60. FRUS, East Asia & Pacific, 31 Oct. 1950, vol. vi, tele. no. 693.93B/10–3050.

61. FRUS, East Asia & Pacific, 27 Oct. 1950, vol. vi, tele no. 693B.00/10-2750.

62. FRUS, East Asia & Pacific, 31 Oct. 1950, vol. vi, no. 1042.1.

62a. FRUS, East Asia & Pacific, 31 Oct. 1950, vol. vi, no.1030.

63. FRUS, East Asia and Pacific, 3 Nov. 1950, vol. vi, no. 1072.1.

64. 26 Oct. 1950, Nehru Papers, folio no. 61-I, pp. 114–15; (0238).

65. 27 Oct. 1950, Nehru Papers, folio no. 61-II, p. 224; (0240).

66. PM's Press Conference, 27 Oct. 1950; (0241).

67. A circular telegram from MEA to Indian Missions, 27 Oct. 1950, Nehru Papers, folio no. 61-II, p. 226; (0242).

68. Mission, Lhasa to MEA, 27 Oct. 1950, Nehru Papers, folio no. 61-II, pp. 220–21; (0239).

69. Ibid.
70. 28 Oct. 1950, Nehru Papers, folio no. 61-II, pp. 245–46; (0244).
71. 29 Oct. 1950, Nehru Papers, folio no. 61-II, pp. 263; (0246).
72. PO to MEA, 29 Oct. 1950, Nehru Papers, folio no. 61-II, p. 278; (0247).
73. 28 Oct. 1950 (0230 -iii), 30 Oct. 1950 (0249), Nehru Papers, folio no. 61-II, pp. 463–64; (0249).
74. Note by F.S on his meeting with the Chinese Ambassador, 2 Nov 1950, Nehru Papers, folio no. 62-I, p. 81; (0256).
75. Note by F.S., 26 Oct. 1950, Nehru Papers, folio no. 61-II, p. 76; (0233).
76. Note by Sec. Gen., 27 Oct. 1950, Nehru Papers, folio no. 61-I; (0233).
77. Ambassador to Bajpai; 26 Oct. 1950, Nehru Papers, folio no. 61-I, p. 141; (0237).
78. Nehru's telegram to Panikkar, 27 Oct. 1950, Nehru Papers, folio no. 61-II, p. 22; (0243).
79. Gopal (ed.), *SWJN*, vol. 2, p. 107.
79a. Panikkar to PM, 1 Nov. 1950, Nehru Papers, folio no. 62-I, pp. 84–88; (0252).
80. PM's letter to Chief Minister of States, 1 Nov.1950; (0254).
81. PM's letter to Chief Ministers, 1 Nov. 1950; (0254).
82. PM's interview with I.F. Scot, 1 Nov. 1950; (0253).
83. Indian Embassy, Beijing, to MEA, 30 Oct. 1950, Nehru Papers, folio no. 61-II, pp. 263–64; (0249).
84. Panikkar to Nehru, 1 Nov. 1950, Nehru Papers, folio no. 62-I, pp. 84–88; (0252).
85. Nehru to Rajagopalachari, 1 Nov. 1950, Nehru Papers, folio no. 62-I, pp. 58–59; (0251).
86. PM's letter to the Chief Ministers of States, 1 Nov. 1950; (0254).
87. PM's note on Policy towards East and South East Asia; 8 Nov. 1950 (0266).
88. PM's note on Policy towards South and South East Asia, 8 Nov. 1950 (0266).
89. PM to Panikkar, 20 Nov. 1950; (0271).
90. M's Note on Policy towards China and Tibet, 18 Nov. 1950; (0269).

91. PM's Telegram to Permanent Representative in UN, 19 Nov. 1950; (0270).
92. Kalha, *India–China Boundary Issues*, p. 39.
93. PM's Note on Policy towards China and Tibet, 18 Nov. 1950; (0269).
94. PM's speech in Parliament, 7 Dec.1950; (0273).
95. PO to MEA, 29 Oct 1950, Nehru Papers, folio no. 61-II, p. 278; (0247).
96. MEA to Mission Lhasa, 29 Oct. 1950, Nehru Papers, folio no. 61-II, p. 278; (0248).
96a. PM's letter to the Chief Minister of States, 17 Nov. 1950; (0268).
97. Ibid.
98. Ibid.
99. PM to Panikkar, 20 Nov. 1950; (0271).
100. PM's Note on Policy towards China and Tibet, 18 Nov. 1950; (0269).
101. PM to Panikkar, 23 Jan. 1951, Nehru Papers, folio no. 71-I, pp. 64–66; (0277).
102. Letter from Sardar Vallabhbhai Patel to PM, 7 Nov. 1950; (0264).
103. Letter from Deputy Prime Minister, Patel to Secretary General in MEA, Girija Shankar Bajpai, 4 Nov. 1950; (0263).
104. Note by PM setting policy towards China and Tibet, 18 Nov. 1950; (0269).
105. Ibid.
106. Ibid.

Chapter 6: The 17-Point Agreement

1. Circular Telegram from MEA to Indian Missions abroad regarding Tibetan appeal to the UNO, 29 Oct. 1950, Nehru Papers, folio no. 61-II, p. 263; (0246).
2. Mission Lhasa to MEA, 16 Oct. 1950, Nehru Papers, folio no. 58-II, p. 394; (0226).
3. Indian Embassy, Beijing, to MEA, 12 Nov. 1950; (0267).
4. Bhasin, *Nepal–India: Nepal China Relations*, vol. 1, p. xxvii.
5. PM letter to Chief Minister of States, 17 Nov. 1950; (0268).
6. Ibid.
7. Extract from PM's note on policy towards East and South Asia, 8 Nov.1950; (0266).

8. PM's letter to CMs of states, 17 Nov. 1950; (0268).

9. Ibid.

10. Note by Foreign Secretary on Tibet, 1 Nov. 1950, Nehru Papers, folio no. 62-I, pp. 70–72; (0255).

11. Note by Foreign Secretary on his meeting with the Chinese Ambassador; 2 Nov. 1950, Nehru Papers, folio no. 62-I, p. 81; (0256).

12. PO to MEA, 2 Nov. 1950, Nehru Papers, folio no. 62-I, p. 102; (0257).

13. Indian Embassy, Beijing, to MEA, 3 Nov.1950 Nehru; Paper: folio no. 62-I, p. 146; (0258).

14. Extract from PM's note on policy towards East and South Asia, 8 Nov. 1950; (0266).

15. Patel's letter to Nehru, 7 Nov. 1950; (0264).

16. Nehru's letter to Chief Minister of States, 17 Nov. 1950; (0268).

17. Note by PM on policy towards China and Tibet, 18 Nov.1950; (0269).

18. Nehru's Policy note, 18 Nov. 1950; (0268).

19. Goldstein, *A History of Modern Tibet*, pp. 750–51.

20. Ibid., p. 753

21. Ibid., pp. 755–56

22. Indian Embassy, Beijing, to MEA, 27 Jan. 1951, Nehru Papers, folio no. 71-II, p. 218; (0280).

23. Indian Embassy to MEA, 22 Mar. 1951, Nehru Papers, folio no. 78-I, pp. 6–7; (0300).

24. Indian Embassy to MEA, 22 Mar. 1951, Nehru Papers, folio no. 78-I, pp. 6–7; (0300).

25. Indian Embassy in Beijing to MEA, 22 Mar. 1951, Nehru Papers, folio no. 78-I, p. 8; (0300).

26. Indian Embassy, Beijing to MEA, 22 Mar. 1951; Nehru Papers, folio no. 78-I, pp. 7–9; (0300).

27. Ibid.

28. FRUS, Korea and China, 12 January 1951, vol. vi, p. II, no. 1691.

29. MEA to PO, 24 Mar. 1951, Nehru Papers, folio no. 78-I, p. 99; (0301).

30. MEA to PO; 25 Mar. 1951; Nehru Papers, folio no. 78-I, p. 115; (0302).

31. FRUS, Korea and China, vol. viii, pt. II, 29 Mar. 1951.

31a. Smith, *A History of Tibetan Nationalism and Sino-Tibetan Relations*, p. 294 fn.

31b. Bajpai's note, 23 Mar. 1951 on Ambassador's telegram of 22 Mar. 1951, Nehru Papers, folio no. 78-I, pp. 9–11; (0300).

32.   MEA to Embassy in Peking, 31 Mar. 1951; Nehru Papers, folio no. 78-I, p. 115; (0304).

33.   Shakya, *The Dragon in the Land of Snow*, p. 64.

34.   Goldstein, *A History of Modern Tibet, 1913–51*, p. 759.

35.   FRUS, Korea and China, 27 Mar.1951, vol. vii, pt. ii, no. 2586.

35a. Goldstein, *A History of Modern Tibet, 1913–51*, p. 759.

35b. Ibid., p. 760

35c. Shakya, *The Dragon in the Land of Snow*, p. 66.

36.   Ibid., p. 65

36a. Ibid.

36b. Ibid.

37.   Ibid., pp. 68–69.

37a   Goldstein, *A History of Modern Tibet*, p. 770.

37b. Howarth David (ed.), *My Land and My People; Autobiography of Dalai Lama* (Bombay: Asia Publishing House, 1962), p. 81.

37c. Shakya, *The Dragon in the Land of Snow*, p. 71.

37d. Ibid., p. 67.

38.   Ibid., p. 71.

39.   John W. Garver, *Protracted Contest; Sino-Indian Rivalry in the Twentieth Century* (New Delhi: OUP, 2002), p. 50

39a. Goldstein, *A History of Modern Tibet*, p. 771.

40.   Ibid., p. 772

41.   Ibid., p. 771

42.   Indian Embassy, Beijing, to MEA, 28 May 1951, Nehru Papers, folio no. 86-II, p. 302; (0310).

43.   Indian Embassy, Beijing, 28 May 1951, Nehru Papers, folio no. 86-II, pp. 331–32; (0312).

44.   Indian Embassy, Beijing, to MEA; 30 May 1951, Nehru Papers, folio no. 87-I, pp. 51–52; (0314).

45.   Mission Lhasa to MEA, 31 May 1951, Nehru Papers, folio no. 87-I, p. 122; (0315).

46.   Parliamentary Debates (Council of States), vol. V, 24 Dec 1953; cols 3590–99.

47. Woodman, Dorothy, *Himalayan Frontiers*, p. 223
48. Ibid.
49. Subimal Dutt, *With Nehru in the Foreign Office* (Calcutta: Minerva Associates, 1977), p. 87.
50. FRUS, Korea and China, 31 May 1951, vol. vii, pt ii, no. 3433.
51. FRUS, Korea and China, 3 June 1951, vol. vii, pt ii, no. 3433.
52. Mission Lhasa to MEA, 2 June 1951, Nehru Papers, folio no. 97-II, p. 238; (0316).
53. Indian Embassy, Beijing, to MEA, 02 June 1951, Nehru Papers, folio no. 87-II, p. 240; (0317).
54. PM's remarks at a press conference on Tibet, 11 June 1951; (0322).
55. Embassy in Beijing to MEA; 28 May 1951, Nehru Papers, folio no. 86-II, pp. 331–32; (0312).
56. Mission Lhasa to MEA, 7 Sep. 1951, Nehru Papers, folio no. 98-II, p. 193; (0348).
56a. Goldstein, *A History of Modern Tibet*, p. 784.
56b. Ibid.
56c. Shakya, *The Dragon in the Land of Snow*, p. 75
57. Note by Additional Secretary in MEA, S. Dutt, after his meeting with the American charge d'affaires, 27 June 1951, Nehru Papers, folio no. 90-I, p. 24; (0326).
57a. MEA to the PO, 11 July 1951, Nehru Papers, folio no. 91-I, p. 175; (0329).
58. MEA to PO, 18 July 1951, Nehru Papers, folio no. 91-II, p. 391; (0331).
59. Radio Beijing broadcast, 26 Oct. 1951, Nehru Papers, folio no. 104-II, p. 245; (0365).
60. Goldstein, *A History of Modern Tibet*, p. 801.

Chapter 7: The India–China Agreement on Tibet

1. Bhasin, A.S. *Nepal–India, Nepal–China Relations*, vol. v (New Delhi: Geetika Publishers, 2005), p. 3042.
2. Mission Lhasa to MEA; 24 Apr. 1952, Nehru Papers, folio no. 125-II, p. 387; (0415).
3. Embassy, Beijing to MEA, 15 June, 1952, Nehru Papers, folio no. 134-I, pp. 148–49; (0438).

4. Embassy, Beijing to MEA, 15 June, 1952, Nehru Papers, folio no. 134-I, p. 148; (0438).

5. PM to Panikkar, 16 June 1952, Nehru Papers, folio no. 134-II, p. 202; (0439).

6. Panikkar to PM, 23 June 1952, Nehru Papers, folio no. 136I, p.11; (0444).

7. Embassy, Beijing to MEA; 18 July1952, Nehru Papers, folio no. 139-I, p. 113 (0451); and MEA to Indian Embassy, Beijing, 31 July 1952; Nehru Papers, folio no. 140-II, pp. 328–29; (454).

8. PO to MEA, 20 Aug. 1953 (0573); and Consulate, Lhasa to MEA, 20 Aug.1953, Nehru Papers, folio no. 196-I, p. 15; (0574).

9. Consulate, Lhasa to MEA, 31 Aug.1953, Nehru Papers, folio no. 199-I, p. 1; (0579).

10. Extract of a letter from Governor of Bombay G.S. Bajpai to Secretary General in MEA, 14 July 1952, Nehru Papers, folio no. 138-II, pp. 273–74; (0449).

11. PM's Press Conf. 21 June 1952 (0443).

12. Note on the difficulties faced by the Indian Consulate in Lhasa, 28 Aug. 1953; (0578).

12a. Aide memoire from PM to Chinese premier. 1 Sep. 1953, Nehru Papers, folio no. 199-I, pp. 274–80 (0581).

13. Indian Embassy to MEA, 28 Aug. 1953, Nehru Papers, folio no. 141-I, p. 77; (0455); and note from MEA to Indian Embassy in Peking, 31 July 1952; Nehru Papers, folio no. 1140-II, pp. 328–29; (452).

14. MEA to Indian Embassy, Beijing, 31 July1952, Nehru Papers, folio no. 140-II, pp. 328–29, (0454); handed over to Weichiaopu on 2 Aug. Nehru Papers, folio no. 141-I, P77 (0455).

15. Nehru's aide memoire to Zhou Enlai, 1 Sep. 1953, Nehru Papers, folio no. 199-I, pp. 274–80; (0581).

16. Aide Memoire to Chinese Embassy, 5 Sep.1953 (0581).

17. Indian Embassy, Beijing to MEA, 18 July 1952, Nehru Papers, folio no. 139-I, p. 113 (0451).

18. MEA to Ambassador, 31 July 1952 (0453).

19. Bajpai to Panikkar, 7 Aug. 1952, Nehru Papers, folio no. 142-I, p. 108 (0460).

20. MEA to Indian Embassy, Beijing, 29 Sept. 1953, Nehru Papers, folio no. 203-II, pp. 218a–219; (0585).

21. PM's to Chinese Premier, 22 Oct. 1953; (0593).

22. Letter from Ambassador in Cairo, Panikkar to MEA, 31 Oct. 1953, Nehru Papers, folio no. 210-II, pp. 303–06; (0594).

23. Panikkar to F.S.; 31 Oct. 1953; Nehru Papers, folio no. 210-I, pp. 303–06 (0594).

24. Bajpai to Panikkar, 7 Aug. 1952; Nehru Papers, folio no. 142-I, p. 108 (0460); and Panikkar's letter to Bajpai, 4 Aug. 1952, Nehru Papers, folio no. 142-I, pp. 106–07 (0456).

25. Consulate, Lhasa, to MEA, 27 Nov. 1953, Nehru Papers, folio no. 217-I, p. 23; (0595).

26. Brief for Beijing Talks, 3 Dec. 1953, Nehru Papers, folio no. 218, pp. 200–08; (0596).

27. Ibid.

28. MEA to Indian Embassy, Beijing, 7 Dec. 1953, Nehru Papers, folio no. 219, p. 136; (0597).

29. Indian Embassy, Beijing to MEA, 23 Dec. 1953, Nehru Papers, folio no. 223-I, pp. 142–43; (0600).

30. Indian Embassy, Beijing, to MEA, 31 Dec. 1953, Nehru Papers, folio no. 226-I, pp. 14–15; (0602).

31. Ibid.

32. Ambassador to PM, 2 Jan. 1954, Nehru Papers, folio no. 226-I, p.42; (0603).

33. Ambassador to PM, 4 Jan. 1954, Nehru Papers, folio no. 226-I, p. 106; (0604).

34. Indian Embassy, Beijing to MEA, 8 Jan. 1954, Nehru Papers, folio no. 227-II, p.190 (0610).

35. Ambassador to PM, 8 Jan. 1954, Nehru Papers, folio no. 227-II, p. 190; (0610).

36. Indian Embassy, Beijing to MEA, 8 Jan. 1954, Nehru Papers, folio no. 227-II, p. 190 (0610).

37. MEA to Indian Embassy, Beijing, 16 Jan. 1954, Nehru Papers, folio no. 230-II, pp. 247–49; (0619).

38. Indian Embassy, Beijing to MEA, 9 Jan. 1954, Nehru Papers, folio no. 227-II, pp. 289–90; (0611).

39. Indian Embassy, Beijing to MEA, 12 Jan. 1954, Nehru Papers, folio no. 228, pp. 215–18; (0615).
40. Indian Embassy, Beijing, to MEA, 12 Jan.1954, Nehru Papers, folio no. 228 pp. 215–18 (0615).
41. Article V of the Agreement.
42. PM to Ambassador, 31 Dec. 1953, Nehru Papers, folio no. 225, p. 119; (0601).
43. Indian Embassy, Beijing, to MEA,`11, Jan.1954, Nehru Papers, folio no. 228, pp. 127–30; (0613).
44. Indian Embassy, Beijing to MEA, 20 Jan. 1954, Nehru Papers, folio no. 230-II, pp. 247–48; (0621).
45. Indian Embassy, Beijing to MEA, 18 Mar. 1954, Nehru Papers, folio no. 241-I, pp. 96–97(0638).
46. MEA to Indian Embassy, Beijing, 21 Mar.1954, Nehru Papers, folio no. 241-II, p. 272; (0641).
47. Indian Embassy, Beijing, to MEA, 23 Mar. 1954, Nehru Papers, folio no. 241-II, p. 418; (0643).
48. MEA to Indian Embassy, Beijing, 19 Mar. 1954, Nehru Papers, folio no. 241-I, p. 160; (0639).
49. MEA to Indian Embassy, Beijing, 21 Jan. 1954, Nehru Papers, folio no. 230-II, p. 269–70; (0623); MEA to Indian Embassy, Beijing, 19 Mar. 1954, Nehru Papers, folio no. 241-I, p. 160 (0639); 21 Mar. 1954, folio no. 241-II, p. 272; (0641).
50. Indian Embassy, Beijing, to MEA, 23 Jan. 1954, Nehru Papers, folio no. 23, p. 82; (0625).
51. MEA to Indian Embassy, Beijing, 25 Jan. 1954; Nehru Papers, folio no. 231, p. 216; (0628).
52. MEA to Indian Embassy, Beijing, 15 Jan. 1954, Nehru Papers, folio no. 229-II, p. 182; (0618).
53. MEA to Indian Embassy, Beijing, 23 Mar. 1954, Nehru Papers, folio no. 241-II, pp. 475–78; (0642).
54. Ibid.
55. MEA to Indian Embassy, Beijing, 2 Apr. 1954. Nehru Papers, folio no. 244-I, p. 120; (0647).
56. Indian Embassy, Beijing, to MEA, 3 Apr. 1954, Nehru Papers, folio no. 244-II, p. 202; (0648).
57. Indian Embassy, Beijing to MEA, 8 Apr. 1954; Nehru Papers; folio no. 254-II, p. 191; (651).

58. MEA to Indian Embassy, Beijing; 9 Apr. 1954; Nehru Papers, folio no. 245-II, p. 189; (0653).
59. Indian Embassy, Beijing; 10 Apr. 1954; Nehru Papers, folio no. 246-I, p. 70; (0655).
60. PM to Ambassador Raghavan, 16 Apr. 1954; Nehru Papers, folio no. 247, p. 19; (0657).
61. MEA to Indian Embassy, Beijing, 20 Apr. 1954; Nehru Papers, folio no. 247, p. 231; (0659).
62. Indian Embassy, Beijing to MEA, 23 Apr. 1954; Nehru Papers, folio no. 248-I, p. 185 (0662).
63. Agreement between India and China on Trade and Intercourse, 29 Apr. 1954 (0674).
64. PM's speech in Lok Sabha on the Agreement, 15 May 1954; (0677).
65. PM to Ambassador Chettur in Rangoon, 9 May 1954 (0686).
66. PM's note to Secretary General/ Foreign Sec. 18 June, 1954; (0699).
67. Woodman, *Himalayan Frontiers*, p. 226.
68. Woodman, *Himalayan Frontiers*, p. 226.
69. Woodman, *Himalayan Frontiers*, p. 226
70. PM's Note on Policy towards East and South Asia, 8 Nov. 1950; (0266).
71. Sen, *India, China and the World*, p. 405.
72. MEA to Indian Embassy, Beijing, 1 Sep. 1953, Nehru Papers, folio no. 199, pp. 274–80; (0580).
73. Brief for discussion for an agreement on Tibet, 3 Dec. 1953; (0596).
74. MEA to Consulate, Lhasa, 27 Jan. 1954, Nehru Papers, folio no. 232-I, p. 80; (0630).
75. T. N. Kaul's Report on negotiation in Beijing, Nehru Papers, folio no. 252-II, pp. 358–65; (0678).
76. Note by Secretary General in MEA on Kaul's letter, and PM's telegram to Ambassador Raghavan (Nehru Papers, folio no. 246-I, p. 131; folio no. 246-II, pp. 252, 255, 258.
77. Nehru's remarks on T.N. Kaul's report; 12 May 1954; Nehru Papers, folio no. 252-II, pp. 358–65; (0678).
78. Ibid.
79. Remarks by PM on Gopalachari's Report, 1 July 1954, Nehru Papers, folio no. 265-I, pp. 34–36; (0681).

Chapter 8: Revolt in Tibet

1. Report of Political Officer on his visit to Tibet, 28 Nov. 1957, Nehru Papers, folio no. 579-II, pp. 203–28; (1012).

1a. Ibid.

2. Ibid.

3. PM's Comments on the PO's Report, 26 Dec. 1957; Nehru Papers, folio no. 579-II, pp. 203–28; (1012).

4. Nehru's Comments on PO's Report. 26, Dec, 1957, Nehru Papers, folio no. 579-II, pp. 203–28; (1012).

5. Letter from Apa Pant to PM, 3 Jan. 1957; (0987).

6. Gopal (ed.), *SWJN*, vol. 3; p. 79:

7. Michel Peissel, *Cavaliers of Kham: The Secret War in Tibet* (London: Heinemann, 1972), p. 23.

8. M. Taylor Fravel, *Strong Borders Secure Nations* (Princeton University Press, 1971), p. 76

9. Riedel, *JFK's Forgotten Crisis*, p. 59.

10. Ibid., p. 49

10a. Ibid., p. 49

11. Note of Chinese Foreign Ministry, 10 July 1958, White Paper-1, pp. 60–62; (1040).

11a Record of Nehru–Zhou discussions, 31 Dec. 1956; (0981).

12. Chinese note of 10 July 1958 (1040).

12a. Note of MEA, 2 Aug 1958; White Paper-1, p. 23; (1047).

13. Congendia, Lhasa to MEA, 19 July 1958; Nehru Papers; folio no. 634, p. 202; (1044).

13a. MEA to Indian Embassy, Beijing and H.C. London. 2 Aug.1958; Nehru Papers, folio no. 639-I, p. 96; (1046).

14. Statement by Chinese Ambassador, 3 Aug.1958; White Paper-I, p. 66; (1048).

15. MEA to PO, 11 Aug. 1958; Nehru Papers, folio no. 641-I, pp. 98–99; (1050).

16. PO to MEA, 1 Nov. 1958, Nehru Papers, folio no. 659-I, p. 25; (1071).

17. PM to F.S. 26 Nov.1958, based on C.G's reports; (1079).

18. Note by PM's; entry of Khampas to Bhutan, 10 Dec.1958, Nehru Papers, folio no. 665-II, pp. 363–64; (1082).

19. Note by PM, 10 Dec. 1958, Nehru Papers, folio no. 665-II, pp. 363–64; (1082).
20. Dalai Lama, *The Dalai Lama of Tibet: My Land, My People*, ed. David Howarth (London: George Weidenfeld and Nicolson Ltd.), p. 149.
20a. Congendia, Lhasa to PO and MEA, 11 Mar. 1959; Nehru Papers, folio no. 676-II, p. 270; (1086).
21. Congendia, Lhasa, to MEA, 13 Mar. 1959, Nehru Papers, folio no. 676-II, p. 344; (1089).
22. Congendia, Lhasa to PO, 14 Mar. 1959, Nehru Papers, folio no. 676- II, p. 370; (1094).
22a. PO to MEA, 14 Mar. 1959. Nehru Papers, folio no. 676-II, pp. 374–75 (1096).
23. MEA to C.G. Lhasa, 15 Mar. 1959; Nehru Papers, folio no. 677-I, p. 18 (1100).
24. Kalha, *India–China Boundary Issues*, p. 97.
25. Ibid.
26. Nehru to President, 30 Mar. 1959(1191).
27. Congendia, Lhasa, 11 Mar. 1959, Nehru Papers, folio no. 676-II, p. 270; (1086).
28. Speech of PM in Lok Sabha, 17 Mar. 1959; (1117).
29. Statement by the Chinese Vice Minister for Foreign Affairs to the Indian Ambassador, 22 Mar. 1959; (1142); Indian Embassy, Beijing to MEA, 22 Mar. 1959; Nehru Papers, folio no. 677-II, p. 331 (1140).
30. Indian Embassy, Beijing to MEA, 20 Mar. 1959, Nehru Papers, folio no. 678-I, p. 223; (1128).
31. Indian Embassy, Beijing to MEA, 21 Mar.1959: Nehru Papers, folio no. 677-II, p. 298; (1133).
32. Congendia, Lhasa to MEA, 22 Mar. 1959; Nehru Papers, folio no. 677-II, p. 333; (1136).
33. Statement of Chinese Vice-Foreign to the Indian Ambassador, 22 Mar. 1959; (1142).
34. MEA to Indian Embassy, Beijing, 22 Mar.1959, Nehru Papers, folio no. 677-II, p. 328; (1141).
35. Adjournment Motion in the Lok Sabha, 23 Mar. 1959; (1152).
35a. Meeting of Soviet and Chinese leaders, 2 Oct. 1959; (1502).

36. Proclamation of the Tibet Military Area Command of PLA, 20 Mar. 1959; (1129); Telegram for Indian Embassy, Beijing, to MEA, 20 Mar. 1959, Nehru Papers, folio no. 678-I, p. 223; (1128).

36a. MEA to PO 15 Mar. 1959, Nehru Papers, folio no. 677-I, p. 14 (1098).

37. Congendia, Lhasa to MEA, 21 Mar. 1959, Nehru Papers; folio no. 677-II, pp. 295–96 (1132).

38. Indian Embassy to MEA, 23 Mar. 1959, Nehru Papers, folio no. 677-II, p. 394; (1146).

39. Congendia, Lhasa to MEA, 22 Mar. 1959, Nehru Papers; folio no. 677-II, pp. 295–96; (1132); PO to MEA, 22 Mar. 1959, folio no. 677-II, p. 332; (1135).

40. Indian Embassy, Beijing, 21 Mar.1959, Nehru Papers; folio no. 677-II, p. 298; (1133).

41. PO to MEA, 24 Mar. 1959, Nehru Papers, folio no. 677-II, p. 413; (1158).

42. Congendia, Lhasa to MEA 25 Mar. 1959, Nehru Papers, folio no. 678-II, pp. 41–42; (1161).

43. Indian Embassy, Moscow to MEA 30 Mar. 1959, Nehru Papers, folio no. 678-I, p. 226; (1192).

44. Report of the Central Committee of the CPSU on Tibet, 31 Mar. 1959; (1198).

45. Meeting among the Soviet and Chinese leaders, 2 Oct. 1959; (1502).

46. Indian Embassy, Beijing to MEA, 1 Apr. 1959, Nehru Papers, folio no. 679-II, p. 7; (1203).

47. Question in the Lok Sabha, 30 Mar. 1959; (1194).

48. MEA to High Commission, London, 2 Apr. 1959, Nehru Papers, folio no. 679-II, p. 28; (1345).

49. Dalai Lama's message to PM, 26 Mar. 1959; (1168).

50. MEA to Adviser, Governor Assam, 27 Mar.1959, Nehru Papers, folio no. 678-II, p. 122; (1170).

51. MEA to PO, 27 Mar. 1959, Nehru Papers, folio no. 678-II, p. 123; (1177).

51a. PO to MEA, 31 Mar. 1959, Nehru Papers, folio no. 678-I, p.295-96 (1197).

52. Record of PM's talks with Dalai Lama, 24 Apr. 1959; (1309).

53. Adviser, Governor Assam to MEA, 1 Apr. 1959, Nehru Papers, folio no. 679-II, p. 6; (1204).
54. MEA to Mehta, Adviser Governor Assam, 1 Apr. 1959; Nehru Papers, folio no. 679-II, p. 2; (1205).
55. Statement by PM in Lok Sabha, 3 Apr. 1959; (1211).
56. Indian Embassy, Beijing to MEA, 4 Apr. 1959, Nehru Papers, folio no. 679-II, p. 140; (1220).
57. MEA to ADGA, Shillong, 3 Apr. 1959, Nehru Papers, folio no. 679-II, p. 72; (1216).
58. PM to Governor of Assam, 3 Apr. 1959; (1217).
59. PM's Message to Dalai Lama, 3 Apr. 1959; (1218).
60. PM Message to Dalai Lama, 3 Apr. 1959 and instructions issued to the adviser to Governor K.L. Mehta; (1218).
61. MEA to PO, 4 Apr. 1959, Nehru Papers, folio no. 679-II, p. 134; (1221).
62. PM Advice to Dalai Lama, 13 Apr. 1959; (1258).
63. Press Conference of PM, 5 Apr. 1959; (1224).
64. PM message to British PM, 5 Apr. 1959; (1225).
65. Two reports of Pol. Officer, Kameng Frontier Division to Adviser, Governor, Assam, 5 Apr. 1959 and 6 Apr. 1959; (1226 and 1227).
66. PM's letter to Dalai Lama.6 Apr. 1959; (1228).
67. Pol. Officer, Kameng to Adviser, Governor Assam, 7 Apr. 1959; (1231).
68. Pol. Officer, Kameng to Adviser, Governor Assam, 7 Apr. 1959; (1231).
69. Note by Foreign Secretary, on the report of Pol. Officer, Kameng, 10 Apr. 1959; (1244).
70. PM's comments on Har Mander Singh's report, 12 Apr. 1959; (1244).
71. MEA to Adviser in Shillong for Menon, 10 Apr. 1959; Nehru Papers, folio no. 680-I, p. 31; (1248).
72. MEA to Adviser in Shillong for Menon, 10 Apr. 1959; Nehru Papers, folio no. 680-I, p. 30; (1247).
73. MEA to Adviser, 10 Apr. 1959, Nehru Papers, folio no. 680, p. 31; (1248).
74. Menon to MEA, 11 Apr. 1959; Nehru Papers, folio no. 680-I, p. 73; (1251).

75. PM to Dalai Lama, 13 Apr. 1959; (1258).
76. P. N. Menon, to MEA, 14 Apr. 1959; (1259); and Menon to MEA, 14 Apr. 1959; Nehru Papers, folio no. 680-I, pp. 182-83; (1261).
77. Foreign Secretary to PN Menon, 14 Apr. 1959; (1260).
78. P. N. Menon to MEA, 16 Apr. 1959, Nehru Papers, folio no. 680-I, pp. 182–83, p. 176, and folio no. 680-II, p. 206; (1261).
79. Indian Embassy, Beijing, to MEA, 8 Apr. 1959, Nehru Papers, folio no. 679-I, p. 327-28, 363, and folio no. 680-I, p. 38; (1236).
80. *People's Daily,* 15 Apr. 1959; (1263).
81. Circular Telegram from MEA, 16 Apr. 1959; (1267).
82. Indian Embassy, Beijing, to MEA, 20 Apr. 1959, Nehru Papers, folio no. 680-II, pp. 320–22; (1279).
83. Ibid.
84. PM to Ambassador in Beijing, 29 Apr. 1959, Nehru Papers, folio no. 681-II, p. 300; (1382).
85. PO to MEA, 20 Apr. 1959, Nehru Papers, folio no. No680-II, pp. 316–19; (1280).
86. PM talks with Dalai Lama; 24 Apr.1959; (1309).
87. Ambassador in Beijing to F.S., 26 Apr.1959, Nehru Papers, folio no. 681-II, pp. 183–84; (1318).
88. PM's Press Conference, 5 Apr. 1959; (1224).
89. MEA to Indian Embassy, Beijing, 26 Apr. 1959; Nehru Papers, folio no. 681-II, pp. 179–80; (1319); and Indian Embassy, Beijing to MEA, 26 Apr. 1959; Nehru Papers, folio no. 681-II, pp. 183–84; (1318).
90. Statement by PM in Lok Sabha, 27 Apr. 1959; (1321).
91. Congendia, Shanghai to Indian Embassy, Beijing and MEA, 27 Apr. 1959, Nehru Papers, folio no.681-II, p. 229; (1322); and PM statement in Rajya Sabha, 4 May 1959; (1393).
92. MEA to Indian Embassy, Beijing, 27 Apr. 1959; Nehru Papers, folio no. 681-II, p. 221; (1323).
93. PO to MEA, 2 May 1959, Nehru Papers, folio no.682-I, p. 39; (1325).
94. Dalai Lama to PM, 7 May 1959; (1327).
95. PM's oral Instructions to P. N. Menon, 9 May 1959; (1330).
96. PM's statement in Rajya Sabha, 4 May 1959; (1393).
97. Editorial in *Renmin Ribao,* 6 May 1959; (1394).

98.   Ambassador Parthasarathi to PM, 7 May 1959; (1399).

99.   Ambassador in Beijing to For. Sec. 8 May 1959, Nehru Papers, folio no. 682-II, p. 284; (1401).

100. PM to Ambassador in Beijing, 10 May 1959; (1403).

101. PM Speech in Lok Sabha, 8 May 1959; (1402).

102. Gopal (ed.), SWJN, p. 91.

103. Dalai Lama Statement, 20 June 1959; (1332).

104. MEA clarification on Dalai Lama's status, 30 June 1959; (1333).

105. Dalai Lama to PM, 25 July 1960, SWJN vol. 62, p. 567 (1668).

106. PM to Dalai Lama, 7 Aug.1960; SWJN, vol. 62, p. 507 (1670).

Chapter 9: The India–Tibet Frontier

1.   Indian Express, 27 Nov. 2019.

2.   A.S. Bhasin, India–Bangladesh Relations, 1971–2002, vol. v (New Delhi: Geetika Publishers, 2003, doc. no. 1107, p. 2689.

3.   Instructions from Foreign, New Delhi to the Political Officer, 29 Nov. 1944; (0016); Memorandum from PO to Tibetan Govt. 7 Dec. 1944, Foreign. Dept, file no. 157-CA/44-Secret; (0017).

4.   Tibetan Govt. to PM, 16 Oct. 1947, Foreign Dept, file no. 12(4) NEF/47-Secret; (0027).

5.   Foreign. Dep. To PO and Mission Lhasa 30 July 1948, Foreign. Dept. file no. 7/2/NEF/48-Secret; (0047).

5a.   Mission-in-Charge, Lhasa to Political Officer at Gangtok, 14 January, 1948, Foreign Dept, file no. 12(4)NEF/47-Secret; (0042).

6.   Mission Lhasa to PO, 14 Jan. 1948, For. Dept. file no. 12(4) NEF/47- Secret; (0042).

7.   MEA to PO and Mission Lhasa, 30 July 1948, F. No. 7/2/NEF/48-Secret; (0047).

8.   PO to MEA. 28 Oct. 1948, MEA, file no. 7-2/NEF/48 (Secret).

9.   Foreign Secretary meeting with Chinese Amb.2 Nov. 1950, Nehru Papers, folio no. No. 62-I, p. 81; (0256).

10.   Indian Embassy, Beijing to MEA, 22 Mar. 1951, Nehru Papers, folio no. 78-I, pp. 6–7; (0300).

11.   Mission Lhasa to MEA, 11 Mar. 1951, Nehru Papers, folio no. No. 76-II, p. 338; (0292).

12. Mission Lhasa to MEA, 16 Mar. 1951, Nehru Papers, folio no. 77-I, pp. 91–92; (0296).

13. Political Officer to MEA 13 Mar. 1951, Nehru Papers, folio no. 77-I, pp. 14–15.

14. MEA to PO, 19 Mar. 1951, Nehru Papers, folio no. 77-II, p. 192; (0298).

15. Trade, Yatung to MEA, 3 Apr. 1951, Nehru Papers. folio no. 79-I, p. 65; (0306).

16. Mission Lhasa to MEA, 20 Apr. 1951; Nehru Papers, folio no. 81-II, p. 323.

17. Mission Lhasa to MEA, 27 Apr. 1951, Nehru Papers, folio no. 82-II, p. 314.

18. Mission Lhasa to MEA, 15 Nov. 1951, Nehru Papers, folio no. 107-I, p. 2; (0370).

19. MEA to Mission Lhasa, 17 Nov. 1951, Nehru Papers, folio no. 107-I, p. 40; (0371).

20. S. Gopal (ed.) *SWJN*, vol. 2, p. 176.

21. MEA to Indian Embassy, Nanking, 13 Mar. 1949, MEA, file no. 7/2/NEF/48-Secret; (0068).

22. Indian Embassy, Beijing to MEA; 20 May 1950, Nehru Papers, folio no. 44-II, p. 282; (0172).

23. Note by PM, 8 Nov.1950; (0266).

24. Letter from PM to CMs of States, edited by G. Parthasarathi, vol. 2, pp. 262–72; 17 Nov. 1950; (0268).

25. Note by PM, 18 Nov. 1950 (0269).

26. Nehru's remarks to the Standing Committee of the legislature, 17 Dec.1949; (0126).

27. Note by PM on the situation on the north-eastern frontier, 5 Mar. 1953; (0561).

28. Ibid.

29. Note by PM on Ambassador Panikkar's note, 10 Oct. 1953, Nehru Papers, folio no. 209-I, p. 21–23; (0590).

30. PM meeting with Senior Officers, 30 Dec. 1949, MEA, file no. 7/13/NEF/49-Pt.II-Secret; (0140).

31. PM to Burmese PM, 7 Jan.1950 (0144).

32. Note by PM, 18 Nov. 1950 (0269).

33. Gopal (ed.) SWJN, vol. 2, p. 177

34. PM to Ambassador Panikkar, 2 Oct. 1949; (0104: fn).

35. PM to Ambassador Panikkar, 2 Oct. 1949; (0104).

36. Reply to debate on Foreign Affairs in Lok Sabha; 12 June 1952: India's Foreign Policy; Jawaharlal Nehru, Publication Division, GoI, 1961, p. 57.

37. Exchange of Note between India and China on Tibet, Oct.-Nov. 1950; (0230).

38. PM's Press Conference, 3, Nov. 1951; (0366).

39. Indian Embassy, Beijing to MEA, 24 Nov.1952; Nehru Papers, folio no. 152-II, p. 231-32, 241, 241A, 242 (0483).

40. MEA to Indian Embassy, Beijing, 25 Jan.1953, Nehru Papers, folio no. 161-II p. 315 (0552).

41. Note by PM, 23 Jan. 1953, Nehru Papers, folio no. 161-II. p.14; (0551).

42. PO to MEA, 18 Apr. 1952, Nehru Papers, folio no. 125-I, P .7 (0536); 18 Apr. 1952, Nehru Papers, folio no. 125-I, p. 134; (0537).

43. MEA Mission, Lhasa, 19 Apr. 1952, Nehru Papers, folio no. 125-I P 168, (0538).

44. 10 Mar. 1952; Nehru Papers, folio no. 120-I, p. 79; (0400).

45. Indian Embassy, Beijing to MEA, 11 Feb. 1952, Nehru Papers, folio no. No, 117-I, p. 183; (0395).

46. Indian Embassy, Beijing to MEA, 13 Feb.1952; (0396).

47. Ibid.

48. Ambassador in Beijing to Prime Minister, 15 June 1952, Nehru Papers, folio no. 134-I, pp. 148–49; (0438).

49. Prime Minister to Ambassador, 16 June, 1952, Nehru Papers, folio no. 134-II, p. 202; (0439).

50. Indian Embassy, Beijing to MEA, 17 June, 1952, Nehru Papers, folio no. 134-II, pp. 222–23; (0440).

51. Ambassador in Beijing to PM, 11 July 1952, Nehru Papers, folio no. 138-I, pp. 114 and 114a; (0448),

52. Letter from Governor of Bombay, 14 July 1952: Nehru Papers; folio no. 138-II, pp. 273–74; (0449).

53. MEA to Indian Embassy, Peking, 31 July 1952/2 Aug. 1952 Nehru Papers, folio no. 140-II, pp. 328–29 and folio no. 141-I, p. 77; (454 and 455).

54. Panikkar to Bajpai, 4 Aug. 1952, Nehru Papers, folio no. 142-I, pp. 106–07; (0456).

55. Bajpai to Panikkar; 7 Aug. 1952, Nehru Papers; folio no. 142-I, p. 108; (460).
56. Panikkar's observations on Bajpai's comments, 7 Aug. 1952, Nehru Papers, folio no. 142-I, p. 108; (0460).
57. Mission Lhasa to MEA, 14 May 1952, Nehru Papers, folio no. 141-II, pp. 404–05; (0429).
58. Note by Panikkar, 10 Oct. 1953, Nehru Papers, folio no. No, 209-I, pp. 21–23; (0590).
59. PM's Note to F.S., 26 Aug. 1956; (2482).
60. Journal of Royal Society of Arts, vol. 84, no. 4330; pp. 2–16 (JSTOR).
61. MEA note on problems faced by Indian agencies in Tibet, 30 Aug. 1953; (0578).
62. Nehru's Note for Zhou, 1 Sep. 1953; Nehru Papers, folio no. 199-I, p. 80; (0581).
63. MEA to Indian Embassy, Beijing, 31 July 1952, presented to Chinese Foreign Office on 2 Aug. 1952; Nehru Papers, folio no. 140-II, pp. 328–29; (0454).
64. PM to Chinese Premier, 22 Oct. 1953; (0593).
65. Panikkar to MEA, 31 Oct. 1953, Nehru Papers, folio no. 210-II, pp. 303–06; (0594).
66. Brief for Talks on Tibet, 3 Dec.1953, Nehru Papers, folio no. 218, pp. 200-08; (0596).
67. PM speech in Rajya Sabha, 9 Dec. 1959, India's Foreign Policy, Publication Division, 1961, p. 377.
68. Indian Embassy, Peking to MEA, 31 Dec. 1953, Nehru Papers, folio no. 226-I, pp. 14–15; (0603).
69. Nehru to Zhou 31 July 1952 and 1Sep. 1953, Nehru Papers, folio no. 140-II, pp. 328–29 and folio no. 199-I, pp. 274–80; (0454 and 0580).
70. PM's Press Conf. 5 Apr. 1959; (1224).
71. PM to Burmese PM, 9 July 1954; (2477).
72. PM to FS, 26 Aug. 1956; (2482).
73. PM to Burmese PM, 4 Sep. 1956; (2487).
74. PM to Chinese Premier, 12 Sep. 1956; (2491).
75. Chinese Premier to PM, 19 Oct. 1956, Nehru Papers, folio no. 481-I, pp. 20–21; (2498).
76. Ambassador in Beijing to PM, 28 Oct. 1956Nehru Papers, folio no. 482, pp. 176–77; (2500).

77. Ibid.
78. PM to Burmese PM, 27 Apr. 1957; (2506).
79. PM Remarks to HOMs in West Asia, 27 Mar. 1953, Nehru Papers, folio no. 172-II, pp. 145–47; (0565).
80. Note on problems faced by Indian Agencies in Tibet, 28 Aug. 1953; (0578).
81. Note for discussion on Tibet, 3 Dec. 1953, Nehru Papers, folio no. 218, pp. 200–08; (0596).
82. Indian Embassy, Beijing, to MEA, 23 Jan. 1954; (0625).
83. PM comments on Gopalachari' report; 1 July 1954, Nehru Papers, folio no. 265-I, pp. 34–36; (0681).
84. Ibid.
85. PM's Note Secretary General and Foreign Secretary, SWJN, vol. 26, p. 481.
85a. PM to F.S., 26 Aug. 1956; (2482).
86. Singh, The McMahon Line, p. 266.
87. Note on India–China Frontier, 15 May 1956, Nehru Papers, folio no. 443-I, p. 165; (0896).
88. Srinath Raghavan, contributory chapter in India and the Cold War, edited by Manu Bhagavan (India: Penguin, 2019), p. 104.
89. Shyam Saran, How India Sees the World (New Delhi: Juggernaut, 2017), p. 126.
90. Minutes of PM's meeting with Zhou in Beijing, 20 Oct. 1954; (0752).
91. PM's Remarks at his Press Conf., 3 Nov. 1951; (0366).
92. Woodman, Himalayan Frontiers, p. 227.
93. PM's Note, 6 May 1956, Nehru Papers, folio no. 443-I, pp. 163–64; (0895).
94. PM to FS, 12 May 1956; (0897).
95. PM's note to F.S. 12 May 1956; (0897).
96. Nehru–Zhou talks in Delhi, 31 Dec. 1956; (0981).
97. Nehru–Zhou talks in Delhi, 1 Jan. 1957; (0982).
98. Nehru–Zhou talks in Delhi, 1 Jan. 1957; (0983).
99. Bhasin, India Pakistan: Neighbours at Odds, p. 99.
100. Nehru Papers, folio no. 235-II, 19 Feb. 1954.
101. Zorawar Daulet Singh, Power and Diplomacy: India's Foreign Policy during the Cold War (New Delhi: OUP, 2019), p. 128.

102. *SWJN*, 28 Jan. 1954, vol. 24, pp. 454–55.

103. Kalha, *India–China Boundary Issues*, p. 117.

104. Gopal (ed.) SWJN, vol. 3, p. 75.

105. F.S. to Ambassador in Washington, 21 Sep. 1957, S. Dutt Papers; (1005).

106. PM's speech in Rajya Sabha, 27 Mar. 1957; (0986).

107. MEA to Indian Missions in Washington and London, 9 Nov. 1956, Nehru Papers, folio no. 398-II, p. 174; (0955).

108. Ambassador in Beijing to PM, 18 Mar. 1954, Nehru Papers, folio no. P-241, pp. 79–85; (0682).

109. Ambassador in Beijing to MEA, 26 Oct. 1954, Nehru Papers, folio no. 299-I, pp. 66–70; (0761).

110. Nehru's note to Defence Minister K.N. Katju of 28 July 1956, quoted in Gopal (ed.) *SWJN*, vol. 2, p. 34.

111. White Paper-1, p. 46.

112. Ibid., p. 47.

112a. Chinese memorandum, 3 Nov. 1958; (1522).

113. PM to Chinese Premier, 14 Dec. 1958, White Paper-I, pp. 48–51; (1084).

114. Question in the Lok Sabha, 22 Apr. 1959; (1350).

115. Note by PM on his visit to Bhutan, 26 Sep. 1958; (1064).

116. Informal Note by F.S. to Chinese Embassy; White Paper-I, p. 26, 18 Oct. 1958; (1068).

117. Informal Note by F.S. to Chinese Embassy; White Paper-I, pp. 26–27, 18 Oct. 1958; (1068).

118. Memorandum by China to Indian Embassy; White Paper-I; p. 28, 3 Nov. 1958; (1073).

119. Note by the Indian Ambassador to Chinese Vice Minister; White Paper-I, 8 Nov. 1958; (1074).

120. Woodman, *Himalayan* Frontiers, p. 254.

121. Zhou's letter to Nehru, 17 Dec. 1959, White Paper-III, pp. 52–57; (1542).

122. Chinese Note to Indian Embassy, 6 Aug. 1959, White Paper-I, pp. 39–40; (1441).

123. Indian note to Chinese Foreign Office, 13 Aug. 1959; White Paper-I, p. 42; (1450).

124. Question in the Lok Sabha, 28 Aug. 1959; (1461).

125. Question in the Lok Sabha, 28 Aug. 1959; (1461).
126. Gopal (ed.) *SWJN*, vol. 2, p. 33.
127. PM's Speech in Lok Sabha, 24 Feb. 1963; (2006).
128. PM in Rajya Sabha on 23 November 1959; (1537).
129. Purnendu Banerjee, *My Peking Memoirs of the Chinese Invasion of India* (New Delhi: Clarion Books, 1990), p. 65.
130. Gopal (ed.), *SWJN*, vol. 3, p. 34
131. Ibid., p. 38
132. Singh, *The McMahon Line*, p. 259.
133. Sydney Wignall, *Spy on the Roof of the World*, 1996; cited in Francine Frankel, *When Nehru Looked East* (New Delhi: OUP, 2020), p. 253.
134. Gopal (ed.), *SWJN*, vol. 3, p. 40.
135. Nehru's letter to Chinese Premier, 14 Dec. 1958: White Paper-I, pp. 48–51; (1084).
136. Zhou's letter to Nehru, 23 Jan. 1959: White Paper-I, pp. 52–54; (1342).
137. Ibid.
138. Nehru's Letter to Zhou, White Paper-I, pp. 55–57, 22 Mar. 1959; (1344).
139. F.S. to Ambassador in Beijing, 29 Apr.1959, Nehru Papers, folio no. 681-II, p. 296; (1370).
140. PM to Ambassador in Beijing, 29 Apr. 1959, Nehru Papers, folio no. 68-II, p. 300 (1382).
141. Ambassador in Beijing to PM, 3 May 1959, Nehru Papers, folio no. 682-I, pp. 68–69; (1389).
142. Ambassador in Beijing to FS, 4 May1959, Nehru Papers, folio no. 682-I, pp. 87–88 (1391).
143. Resolution of the Second National People's Congress, 28 Apr. 1959, Nehru Papers, folio no. 681-II, pp. 283–85; (1367).
144. PM's Statement in Rajya Sabha, 4 May 1959; (1393).
145. Ibid.
146. Editorial in *Renmin Ribao*, 6 May 1959; (1394).
147. Soviet Ambassador's letter of 7 May 1959; (1395).
148. Ambassador in Beijing to PM, 7May 1959; (1399).
149. PM's Statement in Lok Sabha, 8 May 1959; (1402).
150. PM to Ambassador in Beijing, 10 May 1959; (1403).

151. Statement by Chinese Ambassador to F.S. 16 May 1959, White Paper-I, pp. 73–76; (1409).
152. F.S. to Ambassador in Beijing, 17 May 1959, Nehru Papers, folio no. 683-I, p. 92; (1410).
153. Ambassador in Beijing to F.S.19 May 1959, Nehru Papers, folio no. 683-I, pp. 137–39; (1411).
154. PM's draft note for F.S., 22 May 1959; Nehru Papers, folio no. 683- I, pp. 209–10, 213, and folio no. 683-II, p. 265–66; (1412).
155. Statement by FS to Chinese Ambassador, 23 May 1959, White Paper-I, pp. 77–78; (1414).
156. Question in Lok Sabha, 28 Aug.1959; (1461).
157. Ibid.
158. Zhou to Nehru, 8 Sep. 1959; White Paper-II, pp. 27–33; (1469).
159. Lok Sabah Debates, 28 Aug. 1958, col. 4860-72.
160. Srinath Raghavan, War and Peace in Modern India (Ranikhet: Permanent Black, 2010), p. 253.
161. Telegram to Indian Missions abroad, 29 Aug. 1959, Nehru Papers, folio no. 689-II, pp. 286–88; (1462).
162. Nehru to Vijaya Laxmi Pandit, 29 Aug. 1959; (1463).
163. Ambassador Parthasarathi to F.S., 31 Aug. 1959; Nehru Papers, folio no. 689-II, p. 338; (1464).
164. Zhou's letter of 8 Sep. 1959 to Nehru, White Paper-II, pp. 27–33; (1469).
165. MEA to PO Sikkim and Mission Lhasa, 30 July 1948, file no. 7/2/NEF/48-Secret; (0047).
166. Parthasarathi to F.S., 9 Sep. 1959, Nehru Papers, folio no. 690-II, pp. 374–81; (1473).
167. Ibid.
168. Ambassador in Beijing to F.S., 11 Sep. 1959, Nehru Papers, folio no. 691-III, p. 131; (1475).
169. Ambassador in Moscow to F.S., 10 Sep. 1959, Nehru Papers, folio no. 691-III, p. 54; (1474).
170. Ambassador in Moscow to F.S. 12 Sep. 1959, Nehru Papers, folio no. 691-II, pp. 204–06; (1477).
171. Dutt, With Nehru in the Foreign Office, p. 137.
172. Ibid., p. 138
173. Meeting of Chinese and Soviet leader Khrushchev, Soviet Document, Woodrow Wilson Cold War Archives, 2 Oct. 1959; (1502).

174. Ibid,
175. Ibid.
176. PM's Note on Border dispute with China, 13 Sep. 1959; (1481).
177. Ibid.
178. Note dated 17 May 1956, Nehru Papers, folio no. 443-I, p. 165; (0896).
179. MEA Note to Chinese Embassy, 4 Nov. 1959, White Paper. II, p. 24; (1585).
180. Nehru's statement in Lok Sabha, 19 Nov. 1959; (1536).
181. Woodman, *Himalayan Frontiers*, map on page. 246.
182. Ibid., showing points to which Indian patrols had been going up to 1958.
183. AICC Resolution, 26 Sep. 1959; Nehru Papers, folio no. 691-I, p. 394; (1497).
184. Letter from PM to Zhou, 26 Sep. 1959; White Paper-II, pp. 34– 46; (1498).
185. Ibid.
186. Ibid.
187. PM in Lok Sabha, 16 Nov. 1959; (1534).
188. F.S. to Ambassador, 27 Sep. 1959; Nehru Papers, folio no. 691-I, p. 412; (1499).
189. Ambassador in Beijing to F.S, 27 Oct. 1959; Nehru Papers, folio no. 693-II, pp. 163–64; (1583).
190. Fravel, *Strong Nations, Secure Borders*, pp. 83–84
191. Zhou's letter to Nehru, 7 November 1959; White Paper-III, p. 46; (1527).
192. Foreign Secretary's Address to the *Governor's* Conference, 28 Oct. 1959; (1515).
193. PM to Krishna Menon, 2 Nov. 1959, Nehru Papers, folio no. 694-I P 32 (1520).
194. Letter from PM CMs of Uttar Pradesh, Punjab and Himachal Pradesh; 2 Nov. 1959, Nehru Papers, folio no. 694-I, p. 20; (1521).
195. S.P.P. Thorat, *From Reveille to Retreat* (Allied Publishers, 1986) p. 191.
196. Ibid., p. 196.
197. PM to Krishna Menon, 5 Nov. 1959; (1525).
198. PM to Krishna Menon, 5 Nov.1959, Nehru Papers, folio no. 694-I, pp. 169–70; (1525).

199. MEA note to Chinese Embassy, White Paper-II, 4 Nov. 1959; (1585).
200. Letter from Chinese Premier to PM 7 Nov. 1959, White Paper-III, pp. 45–46; (1527).
201. Ibid.
202. PM to Krishna Menon, 10 Nov. 1959, Nehru Papers, folio no. 694-II, p. 311; (1528).
203. MEA to Indian Embassy, Moscow, Washington, Cairo, London, 10 Nov. 1959; Nehru Papers, folio no. No, 694-II, pp. 313–14; (1529).
204. PM in Lok Sabha, 16 Nov. 1959; (1534).
205. Jairam Ramesh, *Krishna Menon: A Chequered Career* (New Delhi: Penguin, 2019), p. 506.
206. Letter from Indian PM to Chinese Premier, 16 Nov. 1959, White Paper-III, pp. 47–51; (1535).
207. PM statement in Lok Sabha, 19 Nov.1959; (1536).
208. PM's statement in Rajya Sabha, 23 Nov. 1959; (1537).
209. PM in Lok Sabha, 27 Nov.1959, India's Foreign Policy, Publication Div., pp. 364–71.
210. PM in Rajya Sabha. 8 Dec. 1959, India's Foreign Policy, Publication Div., pp. 371–79.
211. A. S. Bhasin, *Nepal's Relations with India and China, 1947–2005*, vol. I (New Delhi: Geetika Publishers, 2005), p. xxxix.
212. Rajya Sabha, 9 Dec. 1959, India's Foreign Policy, Publication Div., pp. 375–79.
213. Letter from Chinese Premier to PM, 17 Dec. 1959, White Paper-III, pp. 52–57; (1542).
214. Letter from PM to Chinese Premier, 21 Dec. 1959; White Paper-III, pp. 58–59; (1545).
215. Ambassador in Beijing to F. S., 21 Dec. 1959; (1547).
216. PM in Lok Sabha, 21 Dec. 1959; (1548).
217. Note of Chinese Foreign Ministry to Embassy of India, 26 Dec. 1959; White Paper-III, pp. 60–61; (1549).
218. Woodman, *Himalayan Frontiers*, p. 245.

CHAPTER 10: The Nehru–Zhou Enlai Summit

1. Zhou's letter to PM, 17 Dec. 1959, White Paper: III, pp. 52–57; (1542).

2. PM's letter to the CMs of the States, 1 Jan. 1960, *SWJN*, vol. 56, p. 5.
3. Gopal (ed.), *SWJN*, vol. 3, p. 128; pp. 15–16 Jan. 1960.
4. President's address to Parliament, 8 Feb. 1960; (1602).
5. Nehru to Nepalese PM; 13 Apr. 1960, *SWJN*, vol. 59, p. 357.
6. Ambassador in Beijing to F. S., 21 Mar. 1960; Nehru Papers, folio no. 701-I, p. 87; (1622).
7. PM to Chinese Premier, 5 Feb. 1960, White Paper-III, pp. 83–84; (1615).
8. Zhou to Nehru, 26 Feb. 1960; White Paper. III, p. 99; (1616).
9. Ambassador in Beijing to F.S., 31 Mar. 1960, Nehru Papers, folio no. 701-II, p. 355–63; (1623).
10. F.S. to Ambassador in Beijing, 27 Mar. 1960; (1611).
11. Ambassador in Beijing to F.S. 21 Mar. 1960; Nehru Papers, folio no. 70-I, p. 87; (1622).
12. Ambassador in Beijing to F.S., 31 Mar. 1960, Nehru Papers, folio no. 701-II, pp. 355–63; (1623).
13. Record of conversation between Swaran Singh and Chen Yi, 23 Apr. 1960, during their journey to Agra; (1645).
14. Order Mac Farquhar, ed., *The Politics of China* (Cambridge University Press, 1993), p. 112.
15. Chinese Note to Indian Embassy, 3 Apr. 1960, White Paper-IV, pp. 8–16; (1624).
16. Zhou to PM, 17 Dec. 1959, White Paper-III, pp. 52–57; (1542).
17. Chinese note to Indian Embassy, 26 Dec. 1959, White Paper-III, pp. 60–82; (1549).
18. Parthasarathi to F.S., 31 Mar. 1960, Nehru Papers; folio no. 701-II, pp. 355–63; (1623).
19. Gopal (ed.), *SWJN*, vol. 3, p. 129.
20. F.S address to Governors' Conference, 28 Oct. 1959; (1515).
21. PM's welcome remarks on arrival of Chinese Premier, 19 Apr. 1960 (1631).
22. PM's and Chinese Premier's Speeches at the Banquet, 20 Apr.1960 (1632).
23. Chou's talks with Vice President, 21 Apr. 1960; (1640).
24. Chou's talks with Home Minister, 21 Apr. 1960; (1642).
25. Chou's talks with Finance Minister, 22 Apr. 1960; (1643).

26. Chou's talks with Secretary General, 21 Apr. 1960; (1641).
27. Swaran Singh's talks with Chen Yi, 22 and 23 and 24 Apr. 1960; (1644 and 1645).
28. Second round of talks, 20 Apr. 1960; (1634).
29. Nehru–Zhou talks, 20 Apr. 1960; (1633).
30. Ibid.
31. Ibid.
32. Nehru–Zhou talks, 21 Apr. 1960; (1635).
33. Nehru–Zhou talks, 20 Apr. 1960; (1633).
34. Chou's talks with Secretary General, 21 Apr. 1960; (1641).
35. Swaran Singh-Chen Yi talks, 22 Apr. 1960; (1644).
36. Nehru–Zhou talks, 20 Apr. 1960; (1633).
37. Ibid.
38. Ibid.
39. Ibid.
40. Nehru–Zhou talks, 24 Apr. 1960; (1638).
41. Nehru–Zhou Talks, 20 Apr. 1960; (1634).
42. Ibid.
43. Nehru–Zhou talks, 20 Apr. 1960; (1634).
44. Nehru–Zhou talks, 22 Apr. 1960; (1636).
45. Nehru–Zhou talks, 21 Apr. 1960; (1635).
46. Swaran Singh–Chen Yi talks, 23 Apr. 1960; (1645).
47. Ibid.
48. Discussions between Swaran Singh and Chen Yi, 22–23 Apr. 1960 (1644 and 1645).
49. Nehru–Zhou talks, 24 Apr. 1960; (1638).
50. Swaran Singh–Chen Yi talks, 23 Apr. 1960; (1645).
51. Nehru–Zhou talks, 20 Apr. 1960; (1634).
52. Nehru–Zhou talks, 22 Apr. 1960; (1636).
53. 20 Apr. 1960; available in Haksar Papers, NMML; (1634).
53a. PM in Lok Sabha, 3 Apr. 1961; (1694).
54. Nehru–Zhou talks, 24 Apr. 1960; (1638).
55. Nehru–Zhou talks, 21 Apr. 1960; (1635).
56. PM's Note, 13 Sep. 1959; (1481).
57. Banerjee, *My Peking Memoirs of the Chinese Invasion of India*, p. 65.
58. Nehru–Zhou talks, 20 Apr. 1960; (1634).
59. Question in Lok Sabha, 28 Aug. 1959; (1461).

60. Nehru–Zhou Talks, 22 Apr. 1960; (1636).
61. Nehru–Zhou Talks, 23 Apr. 1960; (1637).
62. Nehru–Zhou Talks, 24 Apr. 1960; (1638).
63. Nehru–Zhou Talks, 23 Apr. 1960; (1637).
64. MEA to Indian Embassy in Nanking, 13 Mar. 1949, MEA file no. 7/2/NERF/48-Secret; (0068).
65. Gopal (ed.), *SWJN*; vol. 3, p. 134.
66. Nehru–Zhou Talks, 21 and 23 Apr. 1960; (1635 and 1637).
67. Press Conference of Zhou, New Delhi, 25/26 Apr. 1960; (1656).
68. PM's statement in Lok Sabha, 26 Apr. 1960; (1657).
69. Ramesh, *Krishna Menon*, p. 523.
70. Swaran Singh–Chen Yi talks; 22 Apr. 1960; (1644).
71. Ibid.
72. Swaran Singh–Chen Yi talks; 23 Apr. 1960; (1645).
73. Joint Communiqué, 25 Apr. 1960; (1655).
74. Dutt, *With Nehru in the Foreign Office*, p. 128.
75. Ramesh; *Krishna Menon* p. 521
76. Jagat Mehta, *The Trust Betrayed* (New Delhi: Penguin, 2010), p. 309.
76a. Maulana Abdul Kalam Azad, *India Wins Freedom* (Calcutta: Orient Longmans, 1959), p. 169.
77. Ramesh, *Krishna Menon*, p. 522.
78. Press Conference of Chinese Premier in Delhi, 25/26 Apr. 1960; (1656).
79. PM Statement in Lok Sabha, 26 Apr. 1960; (1657).
80. Chinese Premier Comments, 28 Apr. 1960, *Peking Review*, 3 May 1960; (1658).
81. PM in Rajya Sabha, 29 Apr. 1960; (1662).
82. *People's Daily*, Editorial, 27 Apr. 1960; (1661).
83. *SWJN*, vol. 59, p. 357.
83a. Ananth Krishnan, *India's China Challenge* (Noida, India: HarperCollins Publishers, 2020), p. 228.
84. PM in Lok Sabha, 26 Apr. 1960; (1657).
85. Ramesh, *Krishna Menon*, p. 523.
86. Gopal (ed.), *SWJN*, p. 136.
87. Circular Telegram, 27 Apr. 1960; (1660).
88. Singh, *The McMahon Line*, p. 281.

89. Durga Das Basu, *Shorter Constitution of India* (New Delhi: Prentice-Hall of India, 1994 [Eleventh Edition]), p. 11.
90. PM's Statement in Rajya Sabha, 29 Apr. 1960; (1662).
91. PM Statement in Rajya Sabha, 29 Apr. 1960; (1662).
92. Resolutions adopted by the Communist Party of India and Jana Sangh, 12 May 1960; (1664).
93. Saran, *How India Sees the World*, p. 126.
94. Kalha, *India–China Boundary Issues*, pp. 135–36.
95. Macmillan, *Nixon and Mao*, p. 238.
96. Fravel, *Strong Nations, Secure Borders*, p. 177.
97. Foreign Affairs Record, 1961, Ministry of External Affairs, p. 437.
98. Gopal (ed.), SWJN, p. 38.

Chapter 11: Towards 1962

1. Zhou at his press conference, 25/26 Apr. 1960; (1656).
2. Nehru's statement in Lok Sabha, 26 Apr. 1960; (1657).
3. Zhou's comments in Kathmandu, 28 Apr. 1960, *Peking Review*, 3(8); 3 May 1960; (1658).
4. *Hsinhua* commentary on the officials' report, 28 Apr. 1962; (1735).
5. Nehru–U Nu talks, 13 Jan. 1962, Nehru Papers, folio no. 729-I, p. 96; (2523).
6. Informal note handed over by F.S. to Chinese Assistant Minister Chiao Kuan Hua, 25 Apr. 1960; (1650).
7. Indian Note to the Chinese Ministry of Foreign Affairs, 26 Nov. 1960; (1679).
8. F.S. to Chief Sec. Maharashtra, 19 Jan. 1961; Subimal Dutt Papers, NMML; (1690).
9. Chinese note to Indian Embassy; 13 Mar. 1961, White Paper-V, p. 119; (1692).
10. PO to F.S. 28 Dec. 1962; Subimal Dutt Papers, NMML (1685); 20 Jan. 1962; (1721).
11. Statement by PM in Lok Sabha, 3 Apr. 1961; (1694).
12. Ibid.
13. Memorandum of Three Conversations, 17 and 19 July 1961; (1699).
14. Memorandum of Three Conversations, 17 July 1961; (1699).

15. MEA Note to Chinese Embassy, White Papers: VI, pp. 189–90; 15 Dec. 1961 (1718).

16. Chinese Government Statement on Goa, 19 Dec. 1961, *Peking Review*, vol. IV, no. 51, 22 Dec. 1961; (1719).

17. Chinese note to Indian Embassy, 22 Mar. 1962, White Papers: vol. VI, pp. 21–25; (1728).

18. MEA note to Chinese Embassy, 30 Apr. 1962, White Paper-VI, pp. 32–36; (1736).

19. Statement of the Chinese Government, 13 Apr. 1962; (1730).

20. *Hsinhua* commentary, 28 Apr. 1962; (1735).

21. PM Statement on China-Pakistan boundary agreement, 7 May 1962; (1738).

22. Chinese Note to Indian Embassy, 31 May 1962; White Paper-VI, pp. 99–102; (1750).

23. Ambassador R.K. Nehru's note on talks with Zhou, 16 Mar. 1956, Nehru Papers, folio no. 427-II, p. 264; (0884).

24. Chinese note to Indian Embassy in Beijing, 31 May 1962; (1750).

25. Nehru Papers, folio no. 427-II, p. 264; (0884).

26. Chinese note of 31 May 1962; White Paper-VI, pp. 99–102; (1750).

27. Note by PM, 29 July 1961, *JSW*, vol. 70, p. 555.

28. Banerjee; *My Peking Memoirs of the Chinese Invasion of India*, p. 23.

29. Chinese note of 31 May 1962, White Paper-VI, pp. 99–102(1750).

30. MEA note to Embassy of China, 14 May 1962, White Paper-VI, pp. 41–43; (1742).

31. Ibid.

32. Chinese Note to Embassy of India, 19 May 1962, White Paper-VI, p. 46; (1745).

33. Chinese Note to Embassy of India, 28 May 1962, White Paper-VI, pp. 54–55; (1748).

34. MEA note, 14 May 1962; (1742); 2 June, 1962; White Paper-VI, pp. 56–58; (1753).

35. Ibid.

36. Note of MEA to Chinese Embassy, 11 July 1962, White Paper-VI, p. 211; (1771).

37. Calling Attention; L.S. Debates, vol. 8 Cols. 10563-76: *SWJN*, vol. 77, p. 621.

38. Chinese Memorandum, 8 July 1962; White Paper VI, p. 78; (1769).
39. Chinese note to Embassy of India, 10 July 1962; White Paper-VI, p. 79; (1770).
40. MEA'S note Chinese Embassy, 12 July 1962; White Paper-VI, pp. 83–84; (1772).
41. Chinese note to Embassy of India; 13 July 1962; White Paper-VI, pp. 85–87; (1773).
42. PM's statement in Lok Sabha, 6 Aug. 1962; (1795).
43. Chinese note to Embassy of India; 17 Aug. 1962; White Paper-VII, p. 26; (801).
44. MEA note to Chinese Embassy; 22 Aug.1962, White Paper-VII, pp. 32–33; (1806).
45. MEA note to Chinese Embassy, 28, Aug. 1962, White Paper-VII, p. 47; (1816).
46. MEA note to Chinese Embassy, 7 Sep. 1962; White Paper-VII, p. 59; (1825).
47. Chinese Not to Indian Embassy, 10 Sep. 1962, White Paper VII, pp. 64–65; (1830).
48. Chinese Note to Indian Embassy, 21 July 1962; White Paper-VII, p. 1; (1777).
49. Ramesh, *Krishna Menon*, p. 570.
50. Nehru in Lok Sabha, 14 Aug. 1962, p. 619.
51. Question in the Rajya Sabha, 24 Aug. 1962, *SWJN*. vol. 78, p. 649.
52. PM's address to Congress members of UP Legislature, *SWJN*, vol. 78, p. 595, 29 July 1962.
53. Prime Minister in the Lok Sabah, 13 Aug. 1962, *SWJN*, vol. 78, p. 605.
54. PM Statement in Lok Sabha, 6 Aug. 1962 (1795); *SWJN*. vol. 78, p. 599.
55. Answering a question in Rajya Sabha; *SWJN*, vol. 78, p. 625.
56. Nehru in Rajya Sabha, *SWJN*, vol. 78, p. 629.
57. Gopal (ed.), *SWJN*, vol. 3, p. 218
58. D.K. Palat, *War in High Himalayas* (New Delhi: Lancer International, 1991), p. 155.
59. Maxwell, *India's China War* (Bombay: Jaico Publishing House, 1970), p. 202, quoting Mankekar, *Guilty Men of 1962*, p. 143.

60. Woodman, *Himalayan Frontiers*, p. 283, quoting B.M. Kaul, *The Untold Story*, p. 357.
61. Banerjee, *My Peking Memoirs of the Chinese Invasion of India*, p. 51.
62. Ibid.
63. MEA note to Chinese Embassy, 26 July 1962, White Paper-VII, pp. 3–4; (1783).
64. PM speech in Lok Sabha, 6 Aug. 1962; (1795).
65. PM Statement in Lok Sabha, 6 Aug. 1962, Nehru Papers, folio no. 736-I, pp. 52–55; (1795).
66. Chinese note to Indian Embassy, 17 Aug. 1962, White Paper-VII, p. 26; (1801).
67. MEA note to Chinese Embassy, 26 July 1962, White Paper-VII, p. 3; (1783).
68. MEA note to Chinese Embassy, 6 July 1962; White Paper VI, pp. 75–77; (1768).
69. Chinese note to Indian Embassy, 4 Aug. 1962; White Paper-VII, pp. 14–16; (1793).
70. PM's statement in Parliament, 6 Aug. 1962; (1795).
71. Indian note to Chinese Embassy, 22 Aug. 1962, White Paper-VII, pp. 36–37; (1808).
72. Chinese Note to Indian Embassy, 13 Sep. 1962, White Paper -VII, pp. 71–73; (1834).
73. Indian Note to Chinese Embassy, 19 Sep. 1962, White Paper-VII, pp. 77–78; (1838).
74. Ibid.
75. MEA note to Chinese Embassy, 21 Sep. 1962; White Paper-VII, p. 84; (1842).
76. Chinese note to Indian Embassy, 21 Sep. 1962; (1842).
77. Chinese note to Indian Embassy, 20 Sep. 1962, White Paper-VII, pp. 80–81; (1840).
78. MEA note to Chinese Embassy, 25 Sep. 1962; White Paper-VII, pp. 86–87; (1847).
79. Chinese Note to Indian Embassy, 13 Oct. 1962, White Paper-VII, p. 113; (1871).
80. MEA Note to Chinese Embassy, 19 Oct. 1962; White Paper-VII, pp. 121–22; (1875).

81. Note recorded by H.C. Sarin, Joint secretary, Ministry of Defence file no. 11987/JS(G) of 22-09-1962 (1845).
82. *SWJN*, vol. 79; p. 306. PM's remarks to the journalists while leaving for Colombo. 12 Oct. 1962.
83. Ramesh, *Krishna Menon*, p. 576.
84. Ibid.
85. Gopal (ed.), *SWJN*, vol. 3, p. 220.
86. Nehru to Morarji Desai, 11 October 1962, quoted in Gopal, *SWJN*, p. 221.
87. *Asian Perspective*, vol. 43, no. 3, Summer 2019; John Hopkins University Press (jhu.edu.article/732225).
88. Fravel, *Strong Nations, Secure Borders*, p. 194.
89. Chinese note to Indian Embassy, 3 Oct. 1962; (1856).
90. John Garver, *China's Decision for War*, p. 117–19 cited in Srinath Raghavan, p. 299.
91. Wikipedia, India–China War.
92. Conversation between Soviet and Chinese ambassadors in New Delhi, 10 Oct, 1962; (1864).
93. Chinese note to Indian Embassy, 11 Oct. 1962; White Paper-VII, p. 109; (1865).
94. Soviet Memorandum; 22 Oct. 1962 to China, *SWJN*, vol. 79, p. 749.
95. Soviet Memorandum for China; 22 Oct. 1962, *SWJN*, vol. 79, p. 755.
96. White Paper-VII, pp. 117–20, 16 Oct. 1962; (1874).
97. MEA Note to Chinese Embassy, 19 Oct. 1962; White Paper-VII, pp. 121–22; (1875).
98. Nehru letter to CMs, 12 Oct. 1962, Nehru Papers, folio no. 738-II, pp. 199–201; (1868).
99. PM to CMs of States, 21 Oct. 1962, Nehru Papers, folio no. 738-II, pp. 308–13; (1878).
100. Statement by the Chinese Govt., 24 Oct. 1962, White Paper-VIII, pp. 2–4, and White Paper-VIII, p. 1 (1881 and 1882).
101. PM to Zhou Enlai, 27 Oct. 1962; (1885).
102. Nehru to Khrushchev, 22 Oct. 1962, Nehru Papers, folio no. 738-III, pp. 328–33; (1879).
103. Khrushchev's letter to Nehru, 31 Oct. 1962, *SWJN*, vol. 79, p. 765.

104. PM's Radio broadcast to the Nation, 22 Oct. 1962; (1880).
105. Nehru's letter to the speaker of the Assam Legislative Assembly, 25 Nov. 1962.
106. PM to Heads of Government of foreign countries, 27 Oct. 1962; (1884).
107. Ayub Khan to Nehru, 6 Nov. 1962, *SWJN*, vol. 79, p. 775.
108. PM to Chinese Premier, 27 Oct. 1962; White Paper-VIII, pp. 4–5; (1885).
109. Ibid.
110. Chinese Premier to PM, 4 Nov. 1962; White Paper-VIII, pp. 7–10; (1894).
111. Nehru to Zhou, 14 Nov. 1962; (1909).
112. P.K. Banerjee, *My Peking Memoirs of the Chinese Invasion of India*, pp. 72–75.
113. *People's Daily*, editorial, 27 Oct. 1962; (1886).
114. PM to Secretary Lok Sabha, 4 Nov. 1962, Nehru Papers, folio no. 739-I, p. 84; (1893).
115. MEA Note to Chinese Embassy, 13 Dec. 1962; (1955).
116. Chinese statement of 21 Nov. 1962; (1922).
117. Zhou to PM., 28 Nov. 1962; (1932).
118. PM Statement in L.S. 10 Dec. 1962; (1949).
119. Zhou to PM, 30 Dec. 1962; (1974).
120. PM to Zhou, 1 January, 1963; (1978).
121. *Nehru's Letters' to the Chief Ministers*, edited by G. Parthasarathy, 22 Dec. 1962, vol. V, p. 540.
122. *SWJN*, vol. 80, p. 558.
123. Kalha, *India–China Boundary Issues*, p. 150.
124. Macmillan, *Nixon and Mao*, p. 238.

Chapter 12: 1962 and After

1. PM to President Kennedy, 19 Nov. 1962; (1916).
2. PM to Ambassador in Moscow, 3 Dec. 1962; (1936).
3. PM to Maharaja of Bhutan, 6 Dec. 1962; (1945).
4. Telegram from MEA to Indian delegation at the UN, 21 Oct. 1962: *SWJN*, vol. 79; p. 308.
5. MEA Note, 5 December 1962; (1944).

6. Chinese Note, 8 Dec. 1962; (1946).
7. *SWJN*, vol. 80, p. 344; PM's interview with Kingsley Martin for the *New Statesman*.
8. *SWJN*, vol. 80, p. 331, 339, 731.
9. PM to Ambassador in Moscow, 3 Dec. 1962; (1936).
10. Ibid.
11. Nehru to Maharaja of Bhutan, 6 Dec. 1962, *SWJN*, vol. 80, p. 318.
12. Nehru to President Kennedy, 10 Dec. 1962; *SWJN*, vol. 80. p. 337.
13. Bhasin, *India–Pakistan: Neighbours at Odds*, p. 136.
14. Conversation of Soviet Ambassador with PM, 12 Dec. 1962; Soviet Archives; (1952).
15. Ambassador in Moscow T.N. Kaul to PM, 17 Dec. 1962; (1961).
16. Ambassador in Moscow to PM, 17 Dec. 1962; (1961).
16a. Zhou's letter to Nehru, 28 Nov. 1962; (1932); Nehru's statement in Lok Sabha, 10 Dec. 1962; (1949).
17. PM, Sri Lanka, to PM, 15 Dec. 1962, White Paper no. 9, p. 184; (1958).
18. PM's statement on the visit of Colombo Conference delegation, 12 Jan. 1963 (1992).
19. Document underlying the principle of Colombo proposals; (1994).
20. *SWJN* vol. 80, pp. 363–65; PM's interview to *Washington Daily News*, 14 Jan. 1963.
21. *SWJN*, vol. 80, p. 419, 1 Jan. 1963; Nehru's note to Deputy Minister for External Affairs.
22. Colombo Conference proposals, 19 Jan. 1963 (1993).
23. PM to PM of Sri Lanka, 26 January, 1963, Appendix in White Paper No. 9, pp. 186–87; (2000).
24. Banerjee, *My Peking Memoirs of the Chinese Invasion of India*, p. 110.
25. Ibid.
26. Ibid.
27. PM to Heads of Govt. of Colombo power, 18 Feb. 1963; (2004).
28. Chinese Premier to PM, 3 Mar. 1963, White Paper no. 9, pp. 3–5; (2010).
29. PM to Chinese Premier, 5 Mar. 1963, White Paper no. 9, pp. 5–7; (2011).
30. Zhou's letter to Nehru, 20 Apr. 1963; White Paper no. 9, pp. 10–13; (2030).

31. Banerjee, *My Peking Memoirs of the Chinese Invasion of India*, p. 119.
32. Ibid., p. 120,
33. Nehru to Bandaranaike, 29 Mar. 1964, *SWJN*, vol. 85, p. 277.
34. Chinese Govt. Memorandum, 21 July 1963, White Paper no. x, pp. 3–5; (2057).
35. Note of MEA, 30 July 1963, White Paper no. x, p. 5.
36. Nehru's statement in Lok Sabha on demands for grants of the MEA, 13 Apr. 1964, Foreign Affairs Record, Apr. 1964, p. 112.
37. Earl Russell letter of 15 Apr. 1964, *SWJN*, vol. 85, p. 377.
38. *SWJN*, vol. 85, p. 292; Nehru's letter of 22 Apr. 1964.
39. PM speech in Lok Sabha, 24 Feb.1963 (2006).
40. Saran, Shyam, How India Sees the World; Juggernaut; New Delhi, 2017; p. 123
41. PM speech in Rajya Sabha, 9 Dec. 1959. India's Foreign Policy, Publication Division, 1961, p. 377
42. Banerjee, *My Peking Memoirs of the Chinese Invasion of India,* pp. 85–86.
43. Ibid., p. 101.
44. Ibid.
45. Ibid., p. 100.
46. Ibid., p. 110.
47. Indian Note, 6 Sep. 1963, White Paper. no. X, pp. 6–7; (2078).
48. Chinese Govt. Note, 6 Sep. 1963; White Paper. no. X, pp. 8–11; (2079).
49. Zhou's letter to Nehru 2 Aug. 1963; White Paper-X, pp. 115–16; (2062).
50. Nehru's letter to Zhou, 14 Aug. 1963, White Paper, pp. 116–20; (2067).
51. Nehru's letter to US President Kennedy, 11 Nov. 1963; (2095).
52. Indian Note to Embassy of China, 28 Dec. 1963, White Paper-X, p. 112; (2102).
53. Bhasin, *India–Pakistan: Neighbours at Odds*, p. 146.
54. Bhasin, *India–Pakistan Relations, 1947–2007* (New Delhi: Geetika Publishers), vol. VI, doc. no. 2168, p. 5088.
55. Note of Secretary General MEA on conversation with US Ambassador, 27 February 1964; (2109).
56. PM to US President, 14 Apr. 1964; (2114).

57.   PM to Heads of Mission in West Asia, 27 Mar. 1953, Nehru Papers, folio no. 172-II, pp. 145–47; (0565).

Acknowledgements

In writing this book, I have been guided by some very well-informed persons who had domain knowledge and had handled this area and the issues involved in their times in the Ministry of External Affairs. First of all, I would like to recall the help and guidance of Ambassador Shivshankar Menon, a former national security adviser, foreign secretary and ambassador in China, whom I consulted while planning the book. I am thankful to him for encouraging my academic endeavours. I take this opportunity to acknowledge his help not only for the present book but also in other academic works that I produced in my post-retirement career.

Going back to the people who helped me write the present book, I extend my sincere thanks to Ambassador Kishan Rana, former member of the governing council of the Institute of Chinese Studies (ICS) and currently professor emeritus at the same institute. I am grateful to him for taking time out from his busy schedule to go through some of the chapters and offer his valuable comments, which enabled me to remove some wrinkles that had developed while writing.

I would feel guilty if I fail to thank Ambassador Vijay K. Nambiar, a former ambassador to China, for reading the chapter on borders and offering his suggestions, which helped clarify my thoughts. I also wish to thank Ambassador C.V. Ranganathan who had been deeply involved in the issues discussed in the book and who has also authored a book on India–China borders and is presently enjoying his retired years in the salubrious climate of Bengaluru. For old time's sake, he responded to my request to go through the chapters on borders. Thank you, Sir.

Ambassador Chinmoy Garekhan has been kind enough to spare a lot of his time to go through the whole text and offer very valuable suggestions. I am grateful to him for encouraging me in this endeavour.

My granddaughter, Geetika, presently teaching in Vancouver, went through some of the chapters and improved the narrative. Thank you, little one. My friend, Shami Sharma, a former secretary to the Government of India, who has also taken to academic research after retirement and has already authored a book, has always been at hand for advice whenever I got stuck while writing. He is a constant companion and source of strength in my daily life as well. Many thanks, Shami. I also request Professor Neera Chandhoke to accept my thanks for her valuable suggestions in the course of writing of the book.

I would like to express my gratitude to T.C.A. Raghavan, director general of the Indian Council of World Affairs, for accepting my application to sponsor the present book under the ICWA umbrella, which carried a grant of Rs 3 lakh. However, on second thought, I decided not to accept this offer and decided go to a general publisher in the hope of wider circulation.

I have extensively used the Nehru Memorial Museum and Library at Teen Murti, New Delhi. As I said earlier, the bulk of the material came from that source alone which made the writing of my previous publication, the five-volume study of India–China Relations, and the present book possible. My sincere thanks to its former director, Mahesh Rangarajan, who is currently teaching at Ashoka University, and Shakti Sinha. The librarian Ajit Kumar at and his colleagues, too, offered their unstinted support during the days I was working on this book and earlier in accessing the documents which went into my five-volume study. Thanks to them all.

Other libraries I used were the library of the United Services Institution, the library of the Ministry of External Affairs and the library of the Institute of Defence Studies and Analysis. I am grateful to their librarians and officers for their wholehearted cooperation.

I would like to make a special mention of the library of the India International Centre, which I have been using for the last twenty years as a base. The library's rich collection of books on the subject of my study and the instinctive help I received at the library greatly facilitated the writing of the book. I wish to profusely thank its chief librarian, Usha Mujoo Munshi, for her cooperation, and providing a congenial atmosphere for serious academic research. It is also my pleasure to thank the other library officers, Shaffali, Rajiv, Kanchan and Hema, who instinctively had been helpful and, of course, Rakesh, Jagdish and Sunil.

I am highly appreciative of my daughter, Puneet, and son-in-law, Gurpreet, for their moral support and making me feel secure at my ripe age of eighty-five that they are always around whenever needed.

Finally, I remain fully responsible for the views expressed in the book and authenticity of the material used. Last but not the least, I express my appreciation for Shiny Das for diligently and intelligently undertaking the editing of the narration and Penguin Random House India for undertaking its publication.

Index

Scan QR code to access the
Penguin Random House India website